Aethereal Rumours

Aethereal Rumours

T. S. Eliot's Physics and Poetics

Benjamin G. Lockerd, Jr.

Lewisburg
Bucknell University Press
London: Associated University Presses

Associated University Presses
440 Forsgate Drive
Cranbury, NJ 08512

Associated University Presses
16 Barter Street
London WC1A 2AH, England

Associated University Presses
P.O. Box 338, Port Credit
Mississauga, Ontario
Canada L5G 4L8

The paper used in this publication meets the requirements of the American National Standard for Permanence of Paper for Printed Library Materials Z39.48-1984.

Library of Congress Cataloging-in-Publication Data

Lockerd, Benjamin G., 1950–
   Aethereal rumours : T.S. Eliot's physics and poetics / Benjamin G. Lockerd, Jr.
     p.   cm.
   Includes bibliographical references (p.   ) and index.
   ISBN 0-8387-5373-6 (alk. paper)
   1. Eliot, T. S. (Thomas Stearns), 1888–1965—Knowledge—Physics.
2. Literature and science—United States—History—20th century.
3. Literature and science—England—History—20th century.
4. Physics in literature. 5. Poetics. I. Title.
PS3509.L43Z6933   1998
821'.912—dc21   97-32662
                                            CIP

PRINTED IN THE UNITED STATES OF AMERICA

SECOND PRINTING 2000

For Micheline
dolce guida e cara!

Contents

Acknowledgments

My first reading of Eliot was prescribed by Phyllis Beauvais, who has guided me in the right direction in other matters as well. I still recall fondly early discussions of Eliot with my friend Rodney Mahaffey and with one of the finest teachers and scholars I have known, Margaret Demorest. The ideas expressed in this book began to form during discussions with Joel Westerholm as we commuted to the University of Connecticut for graduate seminars. Dr. Westerholm and another graduate school friend, Scott Kennedy, read a seminar paper in which I made a first, stumbling effort to discuss the elemental structure of *The Waste Land,* and they gave me very helpful comments. One of them summed up his response this way: "I think you are right, in spite of all that you say." This comment has stuck in my mind as I have gradually said more and more on the subject.

When I returned to the topic years later, I was materially assisted and encouraged by the administrative officers of Grand Valley State University, particularly by Dean Forrest Armstrong, Vice President John Gracki, and President Arend Lubbers. They provided me at various times with a sabbatical leave, a summer research stipend, a travel grant that allowed me to spend time in the Houghton Library at Harvard University, and funds to pay for permissions.

Additional financial support for my research was provided by the Marguerite Eyer Wilbur Foundation, whose trustees awarded me two different summer research grants. The Earhart Foundation later awarded me a summer research grant as well. Without the generous support of these foundations, I would have needed to spend my summers teaching and would probably have been incapable of completing the manuscript.

Several of my colleagues at Grand Valley State University have significantly assisted me on this project in a number of ways. I would like to thank, in particular, Laurel Balkema, Robert Franciosi, Michael Webster, Linda Chown, William Levitan, Kelly Parker, and Mark Pestana.

My colleague David Huisman, a more learned and judicious Eliot scholar than I, has had a major influence on this book in many ways. Conversations with him over the years have given me many insights, only a few of which I have been able to document in the text. Dr. Huisman has also given me a great deal of assistance with my bibliography, pointing me again and again to essential sources I had missed. He has generously

9

and meticulously read the manuscript at different stages, pressing me to rethink important issues, saving me from hundreds of errors, and helping me improve quite a number of phrases and sentences.

Many of the officers and members of the T. S. Eliot Society have listened to presentations of my ideas and given me helpful comments and various types of assistance, among them, Grover Smith, Jewel Spears Brooker, Linda Wyman, Anthony Fathman, Melanie Fathman, Lee Oser, Nancy Hargrove, Larry Melton, Lois Cuddy, Vinnie-Marie D'Ambrosio, Ronald Schuchard, and Virginia Phelan. Many thanks are due to these fine scholars and to the Eliot Society as an organization.

Several scholars have read one stage or another of the manuscript and offered suggestions and encouragement. William Charron read it and assisted me in clarifying Eliot's philosophical ideas. Ethan Lewis read several chapters and offered very helpful insights, especially with regard to phrasing and close readings.

William Blissett, who had earlier been my mentor when I was concentrating on Renaissance poetry, continued to guide me as I worked in the modern period. Professor Blissett's own work is extraordinarily wide ranging, and his editorial acumen is invaluable. It turned out that we had both been thinking about Eliot's use of Heraclitus, and Professor Blissett allowed me to read his essay on the subject before it was given to a publisher. At some point it became difficult to remember what I had worked out for myself and what I had learned from this work by the master, so I must here acknowledge a debt that is no doubt far greater than my few acknowledgments in the notes would indicate. Professor Blissett also read the entire manuscript and gave detailed corrections and suggestions for revision.

Another work that had an influence on my thinking greater than the notes can document is Sanford Schwartz's *The Matrix of Modernism*, the single most helpful work I read as I attempted to understand the philosophical background to Eliot's poetry. I later had the opportunity to meet Professor Schwartz, who graciously took a lively interest in my work and offered to read the manuscript. His responses to it helped me to see the contours of my argument, allowing me to shape them more consciously. He showed me which parts were stronger and which weaker, spending a great deal of time advising me on how to improve the latter. He gave me much-needed encouragement to persevere in revising the work and also gave me the opportunity to present parts of it on panels he organized for various conferences. I am much in his debt.

Richard Badenhausen read the manuscript for Bucknell University Press and made a number of extremely helpful suggestions concerning sources I had overlooked, as well as editorial suggestions. His careful attention to the manuscript gave excellent direction to the final revisions.

Mrs. Valerie Eliot was exceedingly gracious in allowing me to study a large number of her husband's unpublished manuscripts in the Houghton Library collection at Harvard University. She has further granted me permission to use rather extensive quotations from those manuscripts, without which this work would have been seriously weakened. I am very grateful for her kindness.

During my sabbatical leave I was invited by Russell and Annette Kirk to work at their Piety Hill library in Mecosta, Michigan. The extensive time I spent there turned out to be a formative scholarly experience for me. The library itself is highly concentrated in several areas important to Eliot studies. Dr. Kirk's book on Eliot is the best introduction to the man and his work that has been written, and over lunch at the local café I was privileged to hear further stories of Dr. Kirk's friendship with Eliot—while testing out some of my own ideas on Dr. Kirk. This book is only one of many that have germinated in the fertile soil of Piety Hill, tended with enduring generosity by the Kirks. The society gathered around them there bears comparison with the Ferrar community at Little Gidding. Dr. Kirk's passing was a great loss to our culture, but in the best passages of books like this one I hope the reader will hear a faint echo of the dead master's voice, for, in a passage from Eliot often quoted by Kirk (author of ghostly tales), "the communication / Of the dead is tongued with fire beyond the language of the living."

The reader will find that this book repeatedly emphasizes Eliot's Christian theology (and especially the Anglo-Catholic orthodoxy of his theology). This emphasis arises from my own convictions as a Roman Catholic. I would like to thank those who have helped me over the years to discern my calling and to deepen my understanding of the Christian faith, particularly the Franciscan Sisters of the Eucharist. I am grateful to the founders of that order, M. Rosemae Pender and M. Shaun Vergauwen; to the superiors of the Franciscan center here in Michigan, M. Mary Ann Schmitz and M. Rita Brunner; and to all the members of this order who have worked with my wife and me over the years. The Franciscan vision of the created world is central to my approach in this book. I would also like to thank M. Lucia Kuppens of the Benedictine Abbey of Regina Laudis in Bethlehem, Connecticut, who has held the contemplative dimension of scholarship in relation to my work since my days in graduate school. Mother Lucia is godmother to this book.

Finally, I wish to thank my family for their commitment and sacrifice during the long process of this book's composition. My mother, Julianne Marie (Clark) Lockerd, passed away before the work began, but she has no doubt exercised a good influence through her intercession within the communion of saints. My father, Benjamin G. Lockerd Sr., has steadfastly taken paternal pride in my work, which has been a great encouragement to me over the years. With my late father-in-law, Dr. Leslie McGraw, an outstanding research chemist, I had many fruitful discussions of the new physics, and my mother-in-law, Professor Marguerite Tousignant McGraw, has helped me with French translations and with unfailing support. My children have grown up with the difficulties and distractions of scholarly authorship, giving me their wholehearted love during times of frustration and disappointment, and celebrating with me just as wholeheartedly at each stage of completion. They have given much to this work, and I wish to name them and bless them here: Erika McGraw Lockerd, Anna Dawn Lockerd, Michael Benjamin Lockerd, Marie Sophia Jocelyn Lockerd, and Martin Benedict Lockerd.

When, in my first year of graduate studies, I asked Micheline McGraw to marry me and she accepted, I told her I assumed the wedding would have to wait a year and a half, until I had at least completed my M.A. degree and proven myself somewhat competent in my chosen field. She firmly rejected this expression of insecurity and held for our marrying as soon as possible. From the beginning, then, she has had greater faith in my work as a scholar than I have. Without her unwavering confidence and abiding love, I might never have had the courage to persist in this career, and the present work would certainly never have been written. The themes of the book have inevitably been a leitmotif in our conversations, and she has collaborated with me in forming the ideas expressed here. I dedicate this book to her.

*　*　*

The author gratefully acknowledges permission to quote from the following works:

Excerpts from *The Complete Poems and Plays* by T. S. Eliot reprinted by permission of Faber and Faber Ltd and Harcourt Brace and Company.

Excerpts from *Selected Essays* by T. S. Eliot, copyright 1950 by Harcourt Brace and Company and renewed 1978 by Esme Valerie Eliot, reprinted by permission of Harcourt Brace and Company and Faber and Faber Ltd.

Excerpts from *Four Quartets,* copyright 1943 by T. S. Eliot and renewed 1971 by Esme Valerie Eliot, reprinted by permission of Harcourt Brace and Company and Faber and Faber Ltd.

Excerpts from *Collected Poems 1909–1962* by T. S. Eliot, copyright 1936 by Harcourt Brace and Company, copyright 1964, 1963 by T. S. Eliot, reprinted by permission of the publisher.

Excerpts from *Knowledge and Experience* by T. S. Eliot. Copyright 1964 by T. S. Eliot. Copyright renewed 1992 by Mrs. Valerie Eliot. Reprinted by permission of Farrar, Straus and Giroux, Inc. and Faber and Faber Ltd.

Aethereal Rumours

1

Abstract Materialism and Incarnational Symbolism

If space and time, as sages say,
Are things that cannot be,
The fly that lives a single day
Has lived as long as we.

So begins a little poem by Harvard undergraduate T. S. Eliot, published in the *Harvard Advocate* of 3 June 1907.[1] Apparently, the novice poet is already alluding, in the first line, to Marvell's plaint "If there were world enough and time," but without giving it the ironic twist he will apply fifteen years later in *The Waste Land*. His aim here is just the same as Marvell's, to create a witty and specious argument for seduction, albeit for an imaginary one. The second pair of lines may conceivably allude to metaphysical seduction verse as well: perhaps Eliot's fly recalls Donne's flea, though Eliot's argument takes a slightly different turn, reducing man and woman to creatures of a day so as to convince the woman to seize that one day. The young poet who penned these lines certainly promises to be learned, metrically competent, and nearly as fully endowed with wit as the seventeenth-century masters he acknowledges. But where is the sign that he will be a poet of his own time, one who will be able to address the perennial questions in a modern idiom?

Returning to the opening, we find in place of Marvell's "world and time" a distinctively modern formulation, "space and time." Checking dates, we find that Eliot first wrote the opening lines for a version of the poem published at Smith Academy in 1905, the very year Einstein announced his Special Theory of Relativity. The poem's identification of the fly's life span with our own is compatible with Einstein's discovery that time is relative to the frame of reference of the observer; its connection of space and time echoes a keynote of Einstein's theory, which speaks of these two as one space-time continuum. This concept was, of course, a radical departure from Newtonian physics, which assumed that space was a regular three-dimensional volume and time was a separate fourth dimension determined by motion of objects in space. With this phrase, then, Eliot announces as a theme a fundamental question about the nature of physical reality and its relation to our own consciousness and knowledge.

This question, posed at the shifting border between physics and metaphysics, was also central to the thinking of the philosophical sages to whom Eliot was drawn in his early years. Henri Bergson's whole philosophy turned on the issue of how to conceptualize time. He claimed that Newtonian science chopped time into little pieces, while true time was an unbroken flow or "real duration." Bergson eventually wrote a treatise on Einstein's theories, *Duration and Simultaneity,* in which he concludes that "a philosophy in which duration is considered real and even active can quite readily admit Minkowski's and Einstein's space-time."[2] F. H. Bradley's metaphysics was also based on a confrontation with these fundamental issues of physics. Bradley's *Appearance and Reality* had been published when Eliot was a child (1893), though he probably did not read it before he entered graduate school. In his dissertation on Bradley, Eliot quotes a statement that could well serve as a gloss on the opening lines of this poem: "And time so far, like space, has turned out to be appearance."[3] Of course, the idea that space and time are in some sense illusory goes back to ancient philosophy and theology, but it was being raised anew and discussed in the terminology of modern physics by the thinkers Eliot found most compelling. It is unlikely that the young student from St. Louis had directly encountered the ideas of these men when he wrote this lyric, but the ideas were in the air. At the turn of the century, just as Eliot was coming to maturity, philosophers like Bergson and Bradley were mounting a frontal assault on the standing scientific definition of space and time, while scientists like Einstein were educing mathematical proofs that attacked the same definition from within its own domain. Growing up in this milieu, Eliot was bound to take such questions seriously, and he did. His poetic meditation on space and time begins with this early poem and continues through *Four Quartets:* in his beginning is his end.

This book is an examination of Eliot's thinking about changing concepts of space and time, primarily as this thinking was manifested in his poetry. The "physics" of my title refers broadly to knowledge of the physical world, including all the natural sciences and what used to be called "natural philosophy." Nor can physics be limited even to that broad definition, for its study always involves, for a thinker with Eliot's philosophical background, the question of how the material world is related to the psychic world—a question which is the province of psychology or theology. That point of connection between matter and spirit, object and subject, body and mind, was what Eliot ultimately sought. We can better understand the way he went about seeking it by examining his poetry in the context of the debate between science and philosophy.

The attitude toward the physical world which pervaded the culture into which Thomas Stearns Eliot was born was scientific positivism, the notion that science had very nearly figured out what the world was made of. As Sanford Schwartz puts it, "During the third quarter of the nineteenth century, scientists believed that they would soon possess an exhaustive description of the physical universe."[4] Eliot satirizes this world view in another early poem (untitled), which begins,

> He said: this universe is very clever
> The scientists have laid it out on paper. . . .
> Each atom goes on working out its law, and never
> Can cut an unintentioned caper.[5]

In this short poem, the confident rationalist is eventually confronted by the Absolute, lying in wait "like a syphilitic spider." There are things in heaven and earth "not dreamt of" by those who suppose the universe can be laid out on paper.[6] What science at the turn of the century had laid out on paper seemed to prove the ancient atomists right: matter was composed of indivisible particles moving in a void. Darwin had further proved, as it was widely thought, that human beings were the result of random combinations of these atoms, obedient to simple chemical laws and not to some Aristotelian guiding entelechy, much less (as Eliot, with growing conviction, would insist) to a creative Word.

Since science had found it could solve all mysteries, the world had become one in which the intellect was supreme, and yet the intellect itself was only a long string of accidental mutations, a chance recombination (or, to use the language of Epicurus, a "swerving") of the atoms.[7] People found themselves thinking in a new and often self-contradictory kind of dualism: mind was ultimately capable, yet everything, including the mind, was strictly material. On the other hand, matter itself was not substantial but rather mathematical: elements differed according to the *number* of electrons, protons, neutrons—so their qualities were all reducible to quantities the intellect could easily grasp, lay out on paper, and manipulate without benefit of common physical experience, traditional wisdom, judgment, or revelation.

At the turn of the century and beyond, however, a number of voices were heard crying out in the positivistic wilderness that natural science, no matter how accurate and effective, could not give total knowledge, precisely because its very method was to ignore certain questions concerning ultimate reality. When one takes scientific knowledge to be a full description of reality—that is, when one takes a scientific discovery to be a metaphysical statement—science becomes scientism, a system of belief. Moreover, just as Eliot went off to Harvard, the biggest revolution in physics since Newton was taking place, discrediting scientific positivism with mathematical proofs and eventually with empirical evidence.

One of the most famous books of the early twentieth century contesting the positivist assertion was Alfred North Whitehead's *Science and the Modern World* (1925). Because it elegantly summarizes much of what was said on the subject in the first quarter of the century, this book gives a good starting place for the present investigation. Whitehead captures the dualistic nature of scientism in the phrase "abstract materialism," meaning that science sees the world as entirely and simply material but deals with the world in the most abstract way possible, mathematically. He also uses the term "scientific materialism" to designate this highly effective yet narrow way of describing the physical world. In the scientific era, he writes,

> There persists . . . the fixed scientific cosmology which presupposes the ultimate fact of an irreducible brute matter, or material, spread throughout space in a flux of configurations. In itself such a material is senseless, valueless, purposeless. It just does what it does do, following a fixed routine imposed by external relations which do not spring from the nature of its being. It is this assumption which I call "scientific materialism." Also it is an assumption which I shall challenge as being entirely unsuited to the scientific situation at which we have now arrived.[8]

Thus, Whitehead criticizes the way scientific thought rejects qualitative distinctions and hence rejects any ontological way of thinking about matter that tries to consider "the nature of its being." At the same time, he asserts that the new physics has exploded the complacent certainties of positivism.

It must be said that Eliot did not follow Whitehead when the latter went beyond the limits of his own discipline and made religious pronouncements. In an unpublished review of Whitehead's books *Science and the Modern World* and *Religion in the Making* (1926), Eliot finds it "remarkable that so eminent a mathematician and physicist should have an historical mind" but finds that he does not have a theological mind. Whitehead's vague concept of religion is likened to the religious ideas of William James, Henri Bergson, and Matthew Arnold. Whitehead's God is "the Principle of Order" who, like the deities of these other thinkers, is "Wholly incapable of starting a religion."[9] Thus, Eliot finds inadequate the alternative Whitehead offers, and his review focuses almost entirely on this inadequacy. However, his briefly expressed admiration of Whitehead's "historical mind" points toward a fundamental agreement with the physicist-philosopher's critique of nineteenth-century scientific materialism.

As it happens, Eliot had already used the phrase "scientific material-ism." In a 1917 essay on William James, Eliot says that "He hated oppres-sion in any form; the oppression of dogmatic theology was remote from him, who lived in the atmosphere of Unitarian Harvard; but the oppres-sion of idealistic philosophy and the oppression of scientific materialism were very real to him."[10] This statement outlines Eliot's basic analysis of modern philosophy, which he found divided by the Cartesian split into two extreme camps, idealist and materialist. It was precisely in dogmatic theology, informed by Aristotelian philosophy, that he would eventually discover the balanced, integrative view he sought.

Whitehead, like Eliot, was influenced in his critique of scientific materi-alism by Bergson, with whom he agrees that the scientific method omits our corporeal, sensory experience of the world, even while assuming that the sensory world is all there is. The Romantic poets, Whitehead argues, effected a necessary readjustment when they opposed their organic view of nature, which arises from their direct sensory experience, to the mechanistic one.[11] Bergson points out that the scientific reliance on quan-titative analysis of physical reality misses precisely its concreteness. Speaking of the laws of physics, he says,

> . . . a law, in general, expresses only a relation, and physical laws in particular express only *quantitative* relations between concrete things. So that if a mod-ern philosopher works with the laws of the new science as the Greek philoso-pher did with the concepts of the ancient science, if he makes all the conclusions of a physics supposed omniscient converge on a single point, he neglects what is concrete in the phenomena—the qualities perceived, the per-ceptions themselves.[12]

Now, a keen student of pre-Socratic philosophy would see that the quali-tative, perceptual apprehension of the physical world spoken of by Berg-son is just the direct experience that told the ancient philosophers that the world was composed of four essential elements—earth, water, air, and fire. It was a world in which each thing had certain qualities (hot or cold; wet or dry) which were not reducible to quantities of something else. In this cosmos, too, the whole was greater than the sum of the parts—an Aristotelian dictum that precludes a strictly mathematical de-scription of reality.

At the same time, Eliot the poet saw the importance of these ideas for art. The abstraction of scientific materialism missed a concreteness that is essential to the poet. In their concreteness and symbolic richness, the four elements of ancient physics continue to make up the world of the modern poets, who, even when renouncing Romanticism, share the Romantics' reaction to science's denaturing of the world. In *The Heel of Elohim: Science and Values in Modern American Poetry* (1950), Hyatt Howe Waggoner effectively demonstrated the reaction of several modern American poets against the scientific conception of the world. More recently, Thomas Jackson has analyzed the varied ways in which Yeats, Mallarmé, and Williams rejected scientific positivism.[13] Michael Webster has shown that E. E. Cummings took a thoroughly antagonistic attitude toward science.[14] Waggoner, in his chapter on Eliot, argues "that both Mr. Eliot's poetry and his prose convey a complete condemnation of scientism and on occasion of science, and that this poetry achieves some of its effects by the poet's use of ideas about the world and man drawn from science."[15] The present study is, in part, a detailed elaboration of this assertion.

Eliot's response to science differs from that of other modern poets in that he increasingly places his poetry quite consciously and deliberately within the cosmos described by the ancient philosophical physics. When considering a material element, this physics did indeed attempt to determine "the nature of its being," each element being an "essence." Eliot had studied ancient philosophy intensively, first under George Herbert Palmer at Harvard, and he brought this awareness to his poetry throughout his life.[16] The greatest influence of all on Eliot's poetic physics, with the possible exception of Aristotle, was Heraclitus, whose importance to the poet has long been recognized but never studied in a concentrated way—at least not until William Blissett's recent essay on the subject.[17] In both *The Waste Land* and *Four Quartets,* Eliot identifies each section with one of the elements (including, in the former poem, the fifth element, the aether), and this arrangement is more significant than critics have acknowledged: the elements are major structural symbols in these works. Eliot responded to the way the old elemental cosmology presupposes meaning—that is, pattern and purpose—in matter itself, and he responded eventually to the way it, therefore, tends to imply a Creator. Scientific materialism, on the other hand, discovers "laws of nature" (what Whitehead describes as the "fixed routine imposed by external relations"), but it does not inquire into the "nature" of things, and it does not expect to find any underlying pattern that would give purpose and meaning to life. The elemental physics of his major poems, therefore, constitutes Eliot's response to scientific materialism.

Eliot created quizzical antagonists for this debate in his contribution to the *Little Review* entitled "Eeldrop and Appleplex" (1917). He explains that ". . . Eeldrop was a sceptic, with a taste for mysticism, and Appleplex a materialist with a leaning toward scepticism; that Eeldrop was learned in theology, and that Appleplex studied the physical and biological sciences."[18] Eeldrop the mystic resembles Eliot, who had read and taken notes on Evelyn Underhill's *Mysticism*. Underhill challenges the basic scientistic assumption: "We must come to this encounter with minds cleared of prejudice and convention, must deliberately break with our inveterate habit of taking the 'visible world' for granted; our lazy assumption that somehow science is 'real' and metaphysics is not."[19] In the somewhat farcical dialogue between Eeldrop and Appleplex, the mystic and the scientist confront each other, but in a rather ecumenical spirit, for they are united by their skepticism and their friendship. Eliot's treatment of the subject continued to have this eclectic spirit, accepting scientific truth, but only as part of the ever-mysterious wholeness of truth.

The critics of scientific materialism in the early twentieth century acknowledged the success of the scientific method for its own purposes, but they excoriated its philosophical naiveté and its narrow field of vision. One such critic who influenced Eliot at an early stage was Irving Babbitt. Waggoner concludes that "Deeper than Babbitt's cult of refinement, deeper than his aristocratic distaste for democracy, lay his reaction against scientism."[20] This critique was not merely an irrational reaction to rapid change or to the ascendancy of science in the academy. What Babbitt and others insisted upon was that science, by its own definition, limits its study to a part of reality, so its results should not be taken as total and ultimate truths. As Whitehead puts it, "If we confine ourselves to certain types of facts, abstracted from the complete circumstances in which they occur, the materialistic assumption expresses these facts to perfection. But when we pass beyond the abstraction, either by more subtle employment of our senses or by the request for meanings and for coherence of thoughts, the scheme breaks down at once."[21] The more subtle employment of the senses was being accomplished, beginning at the turn of the century, through the invention of extremely fine instruments, which helped Einstein and his colleagues find evidence for their antimechanistic mathematical theories. The request for meaning was being made by such philosophers as Whitehead, Bergson, and Bradley.

The last of these—and the most important to Eliot—makes exactly the same criticism of scientific narrowness and abstraction when he writes in *Appearance and Reality,* "It is doubtless scientific to disregard certain aspects when we work; but to urge that therefore such aspects are not fact, and that what we use without regard to them is an independent real thing—this is barbarous metaphysics."[22] Bradley placed this statement prominently at the end of his first chapter. Thus, we find that *Appearance and Reality,* the prime text for Eliot's dissertation, is to a large extent framed in terms of the epistemological problem created when scientific findings are extrapolated into the metaphysical realm. The scientist, Bradley insists, is always studying secondary qualities and has no reason to think them direct results of primary qualities: "Extension cannot be presented, or thought of, except as one with quality that is secondary. It is by itself a mere abstraction, for some purposes necessary, but ridiculous when taken as an existing thing. Yet the materialist, from defect of nature or of education, or probably both, worships without justification this thin product of his untutored fantasy."[23] Bradley thus scornfully attacks any attempt to make physics into metaphysics.

A similar statement about the narrow scope of science is to be found in an essay on "Religion and the Scientific Mind" written by Joseph Needham and published in *The Criterion*. Needham writes that in scientific analysis

> Natural objects and natural processes have to be torn first of all from the matrix of simple sense experience, and the facts so obtained have to be sorted into boxes according to what we are interested in at the moment, all their properties being subordinated to the one property which we are focusing our attention upon. . . . After this, science emerges with a collection of round hard balls, capable of functioning as units in mathematical calculation, and differing fundamentally from the unique events which they represent.[24]

This passage explains admirably how science abstracts from physical reality and reduces it more or less arbitrarily to quantifiable units so it can analyze it mathematically. The result is a description of the physical world that has little or nothing in common with our direct experience of it. This difference is what tends to put science at odds with both religion and poetry, which deal with direct experience.

At one point in his dissertation, Eliot teasingly adopts the materialist premise of scientific inquiry, only to show that the resultant truths are valid only in a very restricted way:

> [I]f you wish to say that only those truths which can be demonstrated can be called true, I will acquiesce, for I am as good a materialist as anybody; but though materialist, I would point out what a little way such truths bring us. For materialism itself is only an interpretation, and we cannot assert that all the types of object which we meet are reducible to this one type of thing. Any assertion about the *world*, or any *ultimate* statement about any *object* in the world, will inevitably be an interpretation. (*K&E*, 164–65)

Though Eliot is not serious about being a materialist, he is genuinely willing to accept scientific truths, so long as they are recognized as being interpretations of data from a limited range of experience. Any ultimate statement about an object would be a metaphysical statement, and since the scientific investigation has limited its scope to the physical level (and even to certain aspects of the physical level), the results cannot be extended into truths about ultimate reality—even the ultimate reality of physical objects.

Eliot consequently followed Bradley in questioning the putative objectivity of the scientific method. He explicitly rejects Theodor Lipps'

> assumption that in the sciences other than psychology we abstract from the psychical aspect. The psychical aspect he has shown himself is always present: wherever there is the *Ich,* there is a continuity between the *Ich* and its object; not only in the case of perception, but in every case of knowledge. (*K&E,* 74)

This is a challenge to the fundamental claim of science ever since Bacon's *Novum Organum*—the claim that through the scientific method one can know the object without any interference from the *Ich,* from one's subjectivity. Because Bradley believes that subject and object can never be entirely separated in any act of knowing, he denies the possibility of pure objectivity. "In science," Eliot goes on to say, "we have only abstracted from *one or several spheres of mental reality*—and from physical reality at the same time" (*K&E,* 74). Science narrows the field of knowledge by dealing with only a limited sphere and by abstracting from that. The abstraction from physical reality spoken of here is just the abstraction Whitehead addresses. Though science deals only with matter, it deals in abstractions (generally mathematical abstractions) and, consequently, ends up with an ideal interpretation of a slice of the real.

Like Bergson and Whitehead, Bradley insisted on a direct experience by which we intuitively know some aspects of reality unavailable to scientific experiment and calculation. Hence, Eliot describes Bradley's thought as "fundamentally a philosophy of common sense," and he goes on to contrast this commonsense system with narrowly scientific systems that lack it, for example, "unbalanced philosophies, such as Behaviourism." He concludes, as does Bradley, that when science is taken as the whole truth one misses essential elements of truth: "A purely 'scientific' philosophy ends by denying what we know to be true. . . ."[25]

SCIENCE AND SCIENTISM

It is important to emphasize that Eliot held scientific inquiry and those who practice it in high regard. In criticizing William Blake for partially squandering his great gifts, Eliot says that these gifts needed to be controlled, not only by a more orthodox theology but by a greater respect "for the objectivity of science."[26] He criticizes George Bernard Shaw in similar terms, predicting that ". . .we shall demand from our next leaders a purer intellect, more scientific, more logical, more rigorous. Shaw's mind is a free and easy mind: every idea, no matter how irrelevant, is welcome."[27] In his introduction to Paul Valéry's *Art of Poetry,* he notes that Valéry's ideal poet aims "to carry out the role of scientist as studiously as Sherlock Holmes did."[28] Statements such as these discredit the early analysis of Eliot's attitude toward science by Herbert J. Muller. Muller, in his *Science and Criticism: The Humanistic Tradition in Contemporary Thought* (1943), attacks Eliot for desiring a purely spiritual and narrowly orthodox world and for ignoring all scientific evidence so as to live in that fantasy world. Ironically, Muller presents not a shred of evidence to support this caricature.[29] An infinitely more just assessment is to be had from Russell Kirk, who writes that

> T. S. Eliot was very well aware that the natural sciences had worked a new Reformation. He is not defending medieval superstitions, or the pietism of the nineteenth century; still less the twentieth-century chaos of cults or the pseudo-religious "ethos of sociability." Instead, Eliot is doing this: he is endeavoring honestly, and with a high talent for penetration, to renew a type of perception from which the natural sciences, by their nature, are barred.[30]

The type of perception which must be renewed is the common sense or immediate experience of Bradley; or it is the undissociated sensibility Eliot attributed to Donne. It is a perception lost when science provides the only legitimate evidence, but one need not denounce science to achieve it. To be sure, the line between science and scientism is sometimes thin, and Eliot may at times straddle it, but he always endeavors to maintain this distinction.

Although he resisted the encroachments of science upon humanistic disciplines, Eliot frequently made use of scientific concepts. The best-known passage in which he employs a scientific analogy is the one in "Tradition and the Individual Talent" where he likens the poet's mind to a platinum filament used as a catalyst for a reaction between two gases. Eliot develops this comparison into an extended metaphor, going on for four pages (*SW*, 53–56). Gail McDonald places this analogy in the context of a fairly concerted effort by both Pound and Eliot to argue that poetry is an activity as rigorous and intellectually demanding as science.[31] McDonald rightly points out that Eliot particularly emphasized the poet's need for training and specialized knowledge. She further maintains that these poets were echoing the approach of many academics who were adapting the more scientific mode of the German universities to humanistic studies, and that this movement was an attempt to borrow some of the authority of science: "All this rather desperate talk of system and rigour indicates the degree to which poets and humanists felt embattled. Uncertain what language to speak, they appropriated a vocabulary that garnered respect."[32] This analysis is evidently true of the university leaders at the turn of the century, but it is not so true of the poets. Eliot was in fact appalled by the pseudoscientific progressivism of his relative Charles W. Eliot, who was president of Harvard from 1870 to 1909. If Eliot's use of the platinum filament metaphor were motivated as McDonald suggests, then he would fall under his own censure. McDonald does see the appropriation of scientific authority as Eliot's prime motive, and she further identifies this rhetorical ploy with another one by which he supposedly attempted to make poetry a virile act outside the realm of women. "Both codes are exclusionary," McDonald writes, "'science' because it emphasizes rigorous standards and training and misogynistic rhetoric because it excludes not just a gender but its unprofessional connotations."[33] I do not accept this interpretation: Eliot's use of scientific terms does not seem to me to be merely, or even largely, an attempt to ride on the manly coattails of science. He claims that the poet's mind is, indeed, as fine and exacting as the scientist's, but he also claims that they use different faculties to consider different matters. Unlike many educators and humanists of the time, he emphasizes, as we will see, the differences as much as the similarities and insists on the appropriate separation of science and criticism.

In an essay on Eliot's rhetorical strategies in his *Athenaeum* reviews of 1919 and 1920, Mark Jeffreys reaches a conclusion similar to McDonald's. He points out that these reviews "are peppered with terminology suggesting natural and empirical science," and he judges that "The point of view of the *Athenaeum* reviews is empiricist, often stridently so, although their author was almost certainly more of an epistemological skeptic than he allows himself to appear."[34] It is possible that in these early writings Eliot was using scientific terms in a way he would later reject, but it seems to me that he was at least attempting to make a distinction, even at this time, between legitimate and illegitimate uses of scientific thinking in nonscientific fields.

In contrast to the interpretations of Jeffreys and McDonald, I propose that Eliot's joining of science and poetry is best seen as part of his effort to combine subjective and objective ways of knowing. The scientist is supposed to be objective and impersonal; the poet, subjective and personal. This is a nineteenth-century supposition that Eliot rejects. In "Tradition and the Individual Talent" he emphasizes the possibility of an objective and impersonal type of poetry. In an essay published shortly afterward, "Modern Tendencies in Poetry," he makes the complementary point that the work of a great scientist has "a cachet of the man all over it."[35] What Eliot seeks is not to appropriate scientific authority but to discover ways of knowing that transcend the dualism of objectivity and subjectivity.

In his introduction to the *Pensées* of Pascal, Eliot speaks admiringly of Pascal's scientific mind, likening it to that of the great nineteenth-century physicist, James Clerk Maxwell. Pascal, he writes, "showed from his earliest years that disposition to find things out for himself, which has characterized the infancy of Clerk Maxwell and other scientists."[36] Here we find expressed again an ungrudging admiration for true scientific genius. Note, however, that Eliot praises a general quality of mind here. The kind of scientific thinking he admires involves an intellectual curiosity and an independence of mind that can be useful in other departments of life and learning.

One of the great scientists Eliot points to is Aristotle, and one contention of this study will be that Aristotle had a greater influence on Eliot than is acknowledged by most recent studies. In "The Perfect Critic" (1920), Eliot declares, "Aristotle had what is called the scientific mind—a mind which, as it is rarely found among scientists except in fragments, might better be called the intelligent mind."[37] This statement obviously cuts both ways: the scientific mind is to be highly regarded, but few scientists really have it. It is synonymous with intelligence, not with scientific method; and when Eliot goes on to say that "There is no method except to be very intelligent" (*SW*, 11), he may be disparaging the contemporary conception of the scientific method as much as certain pseudoscientific methods of literary criticism. In light of these disclaimers from the same period as the *Athenaeum* review, I would question Jeffreys's thesis that "A great deal of the severity and rigor of Eliot's early criticism was conjured by strategic deployment of scientific and pseudoscientific terms rather than by any trace of scientific method."[38] Eliot consciously rejects the application of scientific method, at least in the humanities and possibly even as the exclusive method of science, even as he accepts a certain type of scientific, objective thinking.

The true scientific mind does not (paradoxically) reduce everything to method—as has been the tendency in both science and philosophy ever since Descartes wrote the *Discourse on Method*. Nor does the careful thinker reduce everything to fomulae, as Eliot says in his dissertation: "The true critic is a scrupulous avoider of formulae; he refrains from statements which pretend to be literally true; he finds facts nowhere and approximation always. His truths are truths of experience rather than of calculation" (*K&E*, 164). To use a formula or to calculate would be to apply the scientific method in another field, and that is clearly what Eliot deplores. Critical taste is instead a "refined and subtilized common sense" (*K&E*, 164), which seems to be just what Eliot means by the genuine scientific mind. Scientific intelligence, in his sense, is applicable just as well to other areas of thought, as Pascal's intelligence is. Aristotle's scientific mind makes him the perfect critic, and another critic Eliot admires, Rémy de Gourmont, is said to have been "an excessively able amateur" in physiology (*SW*, 14). However, these true scientists do not apply the scientific method to other topics. What they do accomplish is an integration of two approaches to criticism defined much later by Eliot in "The Frontiers of Criticism" (1956). Criticism should aim at both understanding and enjoyment, he says, and it should avoid becoming unbalanced in either direction: "If in literary criticism, we place all the emphasis upon *understanding,* we are in danger of slipping from understanding to mere explanation. We are in danger of pursuing criticism as if it was a science, which it never can be" (*OPP,* 117). Thus, the perfect critic must have a scientific mind but must not attempt to make literary criticism into a science.

No doubt Eliot was aware that "science" meant originally "knowing" in general and was applied to all fields of knowledge until quite recent times. His "science" appears to mean an ability to stick to what one knows, to avoid flights of fancy. Thus, Aristotle "looked solely and steadfastly at the object" (*SW,* 11), and Gourmont had "a sense of fact" (*SW,* 14). In his analysis of this passage, Richard Shusterman is on the right track, though he confuses his point with exaggerated remarks about Eliot's ignorance of science, when he says that ". . .we soon see quite clearly what science ultimately meant here for Eliot (who indeed had no real grasp of it)—a magical, modern-day philosopher's stone whose invocation could conjure up objectivity in any field. . . ."[39] As Shusterman points out, science almost comes to mean something mystical, "that stage of vision *amor intellectualis Dei*" (*SW,* 15).

This is, indeed, quite a transformation of Aristotle's interest in biology and physics, but it is not, as Shusterman seems to imply, mere sleight of hand. For Eliot, as I will maintain, looking "steadfastly at the object" can lead quite naturally to the vision of God if the object is (in Aristotelian terms) set in motion by the desire of all things for the unmoved mover. "The Perfect Critic" is one expression of a growing conviction that the smallest facts are connected with the ultimate reality by threads one may at times discern. Pascal, too, attracts Eliot by his combination of scientific and mystic knowing. His is "the just combination of the scientist, the *honnête homme,* and the religious nature with a passionate craving for God" (*SE,* 367).

Even the skeptical idealist F. H. Bradley may seem scientific in Eliot's sense of the word. At least the former disciple identifies his old master with Aristotle, finding in the writing of both a "scrupulous respect for words" (*SE,* 404). This care for precision with words becomes part of the definition of science. Eliot tells us that Bertrand Russell's genuine scientific knowledge helped form his exemplary style of writing. Russell triumphed over German philosophy (meaning Kant and Hegel), and "His victory has been largely due to the possession of a science which most admirers of German philosophy in this country but imperfectly understood, but in the end will be due to his style, a style which this science has trained."[40] Of course, Eliot was later critical of Russell's *A Free Man's Worship*, which, in his view, abandons this scientific clarity and modesty of thought.[41] We may conclude that Eliot respected a science that was a general intelligence, an impulse and ability to find out for oneself by focusing on objects or facts and describing them in precise words—and that he thought science in this sense to be compatible with all other intellectual pursuits, even including mystical vision.

On the other hand, Eliot frequently attacks another kind of scientific thinking that, far from considering facts and objects steadfastly, fits all experience to a variety of related doctrinaire assumptions. Positivism, progressivism, mechanism, determinism, materialism, secularism—all of these myopic modern doctrines are closely related to the dogma of "scientism," which may be defined as metaphysical claims made solely on the basis of scientific findings. While the best scientific thinking aids one's apprehension and expression in other fields, this reductive scientific thinking adulterates thought in those fields. In his introduction to Josef Pieper's *Leisure: The Basis of Culture* (1952), Eliot recalls the infiltration of the philosophic camp by an imperialistic variety of science in his early days:

> At the time when I myself was a student of philosophy—I speak of a period some thirty-five to forty years ago—the philosopher was beginning to suffer from a feeling of inferiority to the exact scientist. It was felt that the mathematician was the man best qualified to philosophize. . . . Beyond this, some familiarity with contemporary physics and with contemporary biology was also prized: a philosophical argument supported by illustrations from one of these sciences was more respectable than one which lacked them—even if the supporting evidence was sometimes irrelevant.[42]

It is this importation of scientific terms for their cachet or authority that Eliot found damaging to philosophy.

In his essay on Lancelot Andrewes (1926), Eliot contrasts the Jacobean preacher's clear style with the jargon of much modern writing, in which "a word half-understood, torn from its place in some alien or half-formed science, as of psychology, conceals from both writer and reader the meaninglessness of a statement, when all dogma is in doubt except the dogmas of sciences of which we have read in the newspapers."[43] Rather than bringing scientific standards of clarity, precision, and objectivity to the study of the mind, the psychologists Eliot is thinking of (who could be either Freudians or behaviorists, as far as he is concerned—though more likely the latter) are trying to mold what they know of the mind to fit certain scientific dogmas. The problem is not so much their use of scientific terminology as their acceptance of scientific materialism as a first principle. They are assuming *a priori* that the mind is reducible to biological impulses of one type or another. As we have seen, Eliot gives behaviorism as an example of the sort of "purely 'scientific' philosophy" that "ends by denying what we know to be true" (*SE*, 403). In contrast to Bradley's or Aristotle's care with words, these pseudoscientists use ill-defined terms and repeat them until they acquire the illusion of meaning something.

Part of the problem, Eliot says, is that these ideas are popularized before they have had a chance to be tested and challenged in a truly scientific manner. He elsewhere criticizes the rapid dissemination of half-formed ideas by the press: "new discoveries are made known to the whole world at once; and everyone knows that the universe is expanding or else it is contracting."[44] The imperfect critic is one who imports popular scientific terminology and the attendant assumptions rather than applying true scientific intellect:

> When a distinguished critic observed recently, in a newspaper article, that "poetry is the most highly organized form of intellectual activity," we were conscious that we were reading neither Coleridge nor Arnold. Not only have the words "organized" and "activity," occurring together in this phrase, that familiar vague suggestion of the scientific vocabulary which is characteristic of modern writing, but one asked questions which Coleridge and Arnold would not have permitted one to ask. (*SW*, 1–2)

These questions are unacceptable in good criticism because they call forth answers (like the one quoted) which are too "abstract," in the sense that they have a "meaning which cannot be grasped by any of the senses" (*SW*, 8). In the phrase Eliot will later introduce, this abstraction is a mark of the "dissociation of sensibility." In contrast, if we follow real scientists like Pascal and Russell, "we believe that the mathematician deals with objects—if he will permit us to call them objects—which directly affect his sensibility" (*SW*, 9). Thus, Eliot delineates the problem much the way Whitehead will a few years later, but he suggests optimistically that even the most truly abstract science, mathematics, may stay in touch with the objects it describes and their effects on the person of the scientist. It is hard to imagine how this could be true of the mathematician, but Eliot is asserting the principle that the whole person must always be involved: the abstractions of science must not become a substitute for intelligent awareness of direct experience. In other words, even while being an objective observer, the scientific thinker must maintain subjective engagement and awareness, just as the critic must maintain objectivity while exploring the subjective expressions of a poem.

In "Second Thoughts about Humanism" (1928), Eliot gives another example of the way scientific terminology can pull the writer away from description of the material under consideration and toward introduction of scientistic dogma. He quotes a passage from a book by Norman Foerster, a disciple of Irving Babbitt's—a passage that begins with this sentence: "This centre to which humanism refers everything, this centripetal energy which counteracts the multifarious centrifugal impulses, this magnetic will which draws the flux of our sensations toward it while remaining at rest, is the reality which gives rise to religion." Eliot objects strongly to Foerster's use of scientific terminology for a basic definition of religion:

> His first sentence, for the meaning of which I am at a loss, is a cloudy pseudo-scientific metaphor; and his remark that "pure humanism is content to describe it thus in physical terms" seems to give his hand away completely to what he calls "naturalism." Either his first sentence is, as I think, merely a metaphor drawn from nineteenth-century physics—in which case it is not a "description" and no one can be content with it—or else the author is surrendering to the mechanistic ethics based upon old-fashioned physics. (*SE*, 431)

In other words, if Foerster borrows these terms simply as metaphors with a certain aura, then he is abstracting from the object under consideration rather than describing it with true scientific attention—much as the imperfect critic did. If Eliot stands accused of doing just the same thing in his early essays, we might answer in his defense that the analogy drawn between the poet's mind and the platinum catalyst in "Tradition and the Individual Talent" is precise and concrete where Foerster's terms are vague and abstract. Moreover, Eliot does not import a dogmatic adherence to naturalism (i.e., materialism) along with the metaphor, as Foerster does when he suggests that the ethical issues are, in fact, reducible to the mechanical forces of nineteenth-century physics. His humanism thus becomes indistinguishable from behaviorism, a humanism without the human. In either case, his physics is, as Eliot pointedly remarks, "old-fashioned." By 1928, Eliot was fully aware that Einstein's revolt had been successful in toppling Newtonian physics. The mechanistic premise was no longer fully tenable even within physics, much less in human affairs.

Another example of a critic whose thought is unbalanced by scientism is I. A. Richards, who declares in *Science and Poetry* that the old magical religious beliefs are no longer held and so cannot be the basis of poetry. Richards tries to offer a kind of scientific psychology in place of religion. Eliot reviews this book in an essay entitled "Literature, Science, and Dogma" and takes Richards to task:

> If one is going to consider philosophically the nature of Belief, it is as dangerous to be a scientist as to be a theologian; the scientist, still more—in our time—than the theologian, will be prejudiced as to the nature of Truth. Mr Richards is apt to ask a supra-scientific question, and to give merely a scientific answer.[45]

Richards admits that science "can tell us nothing about the nature of things in any *ultimate* sense," but Eliot finds that Richards does, in fact, accept scientific truths as ultimate ones when he regards them as having discredited religious beliefs.[46]

What inspires Eliot's most caustic wit is Richards's ethical claims, which reduce all values to scientific quantities instead of spiritual qualities:

> The difference between Good and Evil becomes therefore only the "difference between free and wasteful organization": Good is Efficiency, a perfectly working Roneo Steel Cabinet System. The best life for "our friend" (whom we wish well) is one "in which as much as possible of himself is engaged (as many of his impulses as possible)." St Francis (to take a figure in the public eye at the moment) might have chosen a life in which *more* of his impulses were engaged, than in the life which he did choose; he might have chosen a life in which his impulse toward fine clothes (not in itself a bad impulse) might have been included.[47]

Quantification of values that can be justly considered only qualitatively is one sure mark of abstract materialism, and Eliot here shows how it leads to ordinary consumer materialism. *Science and Poetry,* he concludes, is merely an updated version of Arnold's *Literature and Dogma,* for Richards, like Arnold, thinks that a new kind of poetry, "detached from all belief," can save us when religious belief no longer functions.[48] Richards gives *The Waste Land* as an example of this new type of poetry—bad timing given that the poet was confirmed as a Christian just when this book was published. Yet it is not only his religious conviction that causes Eliot to react to Richards: he consistently criticizes the use of mathematical science as a metaphysical basis for literary criticism or any other branch of humane studies.

The deleterious effects of scientism are observable in literary art as well as in criticism. For example, Eliot writes of Thomas Hardy,

> The philosophy, such as it is, of Hardy's novels, seems to be based upon the mechanism of science. I think it is a very bad philosophy indeed, and I think Hardy's work would have been better for a better philosophy, or none at all.[49]

Eliot's quarrel with Matthew Arnold is implicitly based largely upon the same deficiency: Arnold, and nearly all the Victorians, were too ready to accommodate their ideas and their art to the mechanistic assumptions of contemporary science—or, at the other extreme, to take refuge in a vague aestheticism, as Swinburne does. Even when the writers of the period resist scientific materialism, Eliot finds, their thinking is muddled by it, as is the thinking of Tennyson's *In Memoriam,* where "The hope of immortality is confused (typically of the period) with the hope of the gradual and steady improvement of this world."[50] An entire generation of literary artists in the late nineteenth century had struggled to come to terms with an expansionist science that appeared to be on the verge of conquering all the known realms of thought. The only options appeared to be irrational defensiveness or surrender. Eliot's generation found that science had not, in fact, been able to hold the humanist territories it had invaded and that leading scientists were themselves sounding the retreat.

The real scientist (unlike the Victorians, Norman Foerster, I. A. Richards, and the unnamed imperfect critic) sets aside the laws of nature when considering objects which are not purely natural—that is human and supernatural ones. The true scientist is one who is able to keep these distinctions clear. For example, the epitome of the Renaissance Man, Leonardo, "turned to art or science, and each was what it was and not another thing."[51] The prime exemplar of the true scientific mind, Aristotle, brings his scientific acuity to the writing of the *Poetics,* but he never attempts to make poetry into one of the natural sciences. As Eliot puts it in the Clark Lectures, "The only writer who has established a literary criticism which both sticks to the matter at hand and yet implies the other sciences, is of course Aristotle. . . ."[52] So, too, with Pascal: although he applies in the *Pensées*

> the same powers which he exerted in science, it is not as a scientist that he presents himself. He does not seem to say to the reader: I am one of the most distinguished scientists of the day: I understand many matters which will always be mysteries to you, and through science I have come to Faith; you therefore who are not initiated into science ought to have faith if I have it. He is fully aware of the difference of subject-matter, and his famous distinction between the *esprit de géométrie* and the *esprit de finesse* is one to ponder over. (*SE,* 366)

This passage sums up the difference Eliot constantly observes between legitimate and illegitimate extensions of scientific thought into other areas. To his mystical meditations, Pascal brings the "powers" of mind he developed in the discipline of mathematics, the intelligence of the scientist. However, he does not seek to extrapolate laws of nature into the supernatural realm; rather, he approaches that realm with his refined ability to observe it and discover its own laws. Paradoxically, the unified vision Eliot seeks can be achieved only by one who constantly recognizes the boundary between scientific and humanistic disciplines.

HISTORY OF SCIENCE: THE CARTESIAN SPLIT

The history of science was of great importance to Eliot. He knew well that the prime focus of pre-Socratic philosophy was physics. He was intensely aware of the way Aristotelian physics had dominated the European worldview throughout the Renaissance. He contemplated the scientific revolution of the seventeenth century, in which natural philosophy separated itself from the rest of philosophy and restricted itself to a purely empirical and mathematical method. As we have already seen, he immediately recognized the significance of the contemporary revolution in physics. He thought about how these changes in physical theory had affected other intellectual activities, especially philosophy and poetry.

The great turning point in the history of science is, of course, the seventeenth century. For Eliot, the importance of Pascal is that he offered a way the scientific revolution might have gone, a way that would have avoided the fragmentation of thought—precisely by maintaining a boundary between natural science and philosophy. Instead of following Pascal, the world followed his celebrated contemporary, Descartes. Eliot compares them, proclaiming that Pascal "succeeds where Descartes fails; for in Descartes the element of *esprit de géométrie* is excessive" (*SE,* 367). He quotes the passage in which Pascal himself says, "*Je ne puis pas pardonner à Descartes.*" Eliot could not forgive him either.

The unpardonable act of Descartes was, of course, to force a dichotomy between mind and matter and locate all reality with only one of the two. An idealist and a religious man, he chose mind: *cogito* is being; the sensory world is illusion. In the Clark Lectures, Eliot speaks at length about Descartes, calling his philosophy "a true Copernican revolution which occurred centuries before Kant was born, a difference which marks the real abyss between the classic scholastic philosophy and all philosophy since" (*VMP,* 80). He thus associates the Cartesian revolution with the scientific revolution initiated by Copernicus, and he traces the subsequent effects to Kantian subjective idealism and, hence, to the whole subjectivist turn of modern philosophy. After the Cartesian revolution, "Instead of ideas as meanings, as references to an outside world, you have suddenly a new world coming into existence, inside your own mind . . ." (*VMP,* 80). It is just this subjective philosophy that produces the solipsism Eliot describes in the final section of *The Waste Land* by the image of "each in his prison" and glosses in the Notes by quoting Bradley's analysis of the purely subjective level of experience, in which "the whole world for each is peculiar and private to that soul."

Descartes arrives at a subjective idealist position by denying the necessary existence of objects, of bodies. Eliot quotes a passage from Meditation VI in which Descartes says,

. . . quoique j'examine soigneusement toutes choses, je ne trouve pas néanmoins que, de cette idée distincte de la nature corporelle que j'ai en mon imagination, je puisse tirer aucun argument qui conclue avec nécessité l'existence de quelque corps.[53]

To this declaration, Eliot reacts violently: "This extraordinary [*sic*] crude and stupid piece of reasoning is the sort of thing which gave rise to the whole of the pseudo-science of epistemology, which has haunted the nightmares of the last three hundred years" (*VMP*, 81). The belligerent tone of this response fits with the rhetorical approach identified in Eliot's early *Athenaeum* reviews by Jeffreys, who concludes that "It was a necessarily aggressive and consistent rhetoric that helped Eliot to begin his meteoric rise, within the space of a decade, to the status of literary authority figure."[54] However, as Jeffreys shows, the earlier essays affect a cool and dispassionate tone even in their attacks. In the Clark Lectures, on the other hand, Eliot indulges in several passionate outbursts. Here, he completely loses his temper. The passage from Descartes, with its total skepticism as to the existence of bodies, is evidently, in his view, the beginning of all our modern insanity.

Up until the seventeenth century, Western philosophy had generally maintained that the physical world was, in some sense, real and that the mind (which was also real) could know that world more or less well. Indeed, particularly in the Aristotelian tradition, the world of objects was considered to have great significance to the mind, and the soul was considered inseparable from the body. The mimetic theory of poetry was based on such ideas. The Cartesian doubt as to the very existence of the corporeal world inaugurated a period in which epistemology became the primary branch of philosophy, since the possibility of any common knowledge became questionable. As a result, poetry became alternately rationalistic (as in the eighteenth century) or emotional (as in the nineteenth).

It might at first seem surprising that Pascal and Eliot would find Descartes's idealism so repugnant, but it was his way of framing the question that caused all the trouble. The Cartesian split is the assumption that since matter and spirit are totally inimical, one must be real and the other unreal—winner take all. William Skaff rightly connects Eliot's view of Descartes with his critique of Romanticism: "Eliot finds both Descartes's epistemology and his ontology, the spirit as self-consciousness within a body of matter, to lead directly to the dialectic of Romanticism."[55] Clearly, Eliot blames the Cartesian split for the divisions of the nineteenth century, of which the rift between faith and reason was prime. He also sees it as closely related to the split between subject and object, which scientific objectivity requires. Jewel Spears Brooker and Joseph Bentley, following Holton's *Thematic Origins of Scientific Thought,* locate the turning point in Kepler's *Dioptrics* (1611), which enjoined the observer to be completely objective—that is, to stand completely outside the object.[56] Physics from ancient times through the Renaissance had made no radical division between mind and matter but had sought instead to locate points of intersection. Pascal might remain aware of the difference in subject matter between physics and theology, but he did not declare that only one of these disciplines studied something real. From his point of view, and from Eliot's, the Cartesian split was a gap through which all the demons would enter the modern world.

One of those demons was the "dissociation of sensibility," which Eliot saw as the manifestation in poetry of the Cartesian split. I believe Sanford Schwartz was the first critic to suggest such a connection. He points out in a note that

> The "dissociation of sensibility" corresponds both chronologically and thematically to the mind/body dualism of Western philosophy from Descartes to the early twentieth century. While Eliot makes no explicit connection between Cartesian dualism and the "dissociation of sensibility," his knowledge of the history of philosophy may well have influenced his understanding of the history of literature.[57]

This is a critical insight that identifies the exact point at which Eliot's physics and his poetics intersect, and I will have more to say about it throughout this study. Given Eliot's attacks on Descartes in the Clark Lectures and elsewhere, there is little reason to doubt that the prime reference for his notion of the dissociation of sensibility is the Cartesian split.

Once Descartes (or perhaps we should say the spirit of the time, which is manifest in Descartes) forced the dichotomy, some were bound to favor the material side and deny reality to mind. Descartes was an idealist, but Eliot calls him (in his review of Jacques Maritain's *Three Reformers: Luther, Descartes, Rousseau*) "one of the ancestors of materialism as well as of irrational faith, of the antinomy of faith and reason."[58] Some such dualism is, Eliot goes on to say, the source of every heresy, "for all important heresy has two sides to it." Thus,

> . . . Descartes remains the great typical figure of modern "heresy" in the generalized sense of that word. Whatever the aberrations of individual philosophers in the Middle Ages, and they had been many; whatever their narrowness or ignorance, still the Greek philosophy of Plato and Aristotle had maintained its influence toward balanced wisdom, had prevented human thought from flying to peripheral extremes. In the simple, lucid, and persuasive writings of Descartes the various elements are, so to speak, released from each other, so that you need only to press one aspect of his philosophy or another to produce the extremes of materialism and idealism, rationalism and blind faith.[59]

Eric Sigg comments on this passage, writing that "Eliot focused on what he considered a dissociative, centrifugal habit in secular philosophy, which lacked the theological means to combine principles not easily reconciled logically or rationally."[60] Just so, and since the material and spiritual principles are the ultimate opposition, what Eliot says here may be read as his summary history of physics. Aristotle and Plato (who was not, in Eliot's view, responsible for the tradition of Neoplatonic dualism) recognized the dualities of life but integrated them. Christian theology found itself compatible with this philosophy and so took it as foundational throughout the medieval and even early Renaissance periods. Descartes and other seventeenth-century thinkers dissolved this integrated vision, and their dualism dominated thought until some scientists (Einstein, Bohr, et al.) and philosophers (Bergson, Bradley, et al.) of the twentieth century began the difficult task of recovering a unified vision. When Eliot speaks here of the "balanced wisdom" of the ancients, he is implicitly defining "wisdom" as the capacity to integrate the opposites. By this definition, philosophy after Descartes ceased to be the love of wisdom and instead gave itself to exposition of one or other extreme view.

One of the seventeenth-century proponents of the materialist extreme was Thomas Hobbes. Eliot speaks of him in his piece on Bishop Bramhall published in 1927:

> Hobbes's philosophy is not so much a philosophy as an adumbration of the universe of material atoms regulated by laws of motion which formed the scientific view of the world from Newton to Einstein. Hence there is quite naturally no place in Hobbes's universe for the human will; what he failed to see is that there was no place in it for consciousness either, or for human beings.[61]

Eliot has no quarrel with Newton, a great scientist who did not presume to extend his scientific discoveries into psychology and philosophy. Hobbes, on the other hand, is an early example of the kind of pseudoscientist who extends those discoveries to all areas. The result, Eliot points out, is "determinism," the doctrine that claims any event is completely determined by previous material events through a mechanical causality (*SE*, 312). Eliot's naming of Einstein should again remind us that determinism had, by the time he wrote this, been called into question even in physics. Even before Einstein, Eliot maintains, there was no justification for transposing Newtonian mechanics into laws of ethics and politics. The results of doing so were disastrous: "Materialistic determinism and absolutist government fit into the same scheme of life" (*SE*, 315). In one stroke, Eliot traces the modern concept of the absolute state to scientific materialism. It may be necessary to note that the monarchist position he himself adopted at about this time does not see the state as absolute: for one thing, Eliot's monarch must answer to God and to man for his conduct as ruler. Only given a materialist worldview can the state become absolute and law become a simple expression of power. Hobbes's totalitarian political philosophy is a striking example of the harm which has been done by the scientistic notion that came into being in the seventeenth century.

Eliot follows this principle consistently. Even when science seems to support his philosophy, he declines to accept the scientific evidence as proof for his belief. Though Eliot welcomed Einstein's theories, he chided people who claimed that those theories supported religious belief. When the Anglican bishops at the Lambeth conference of 1930 rejoiced that "there is much in the scientific and philosophic thinking of our time which provides a climate more favourable to faith in God than has existed for generations," Eliot suggested a less grateful tone:

> I do not disagree with the literal sense of the pronouncement which I have just quoted. Perhaps it is rather the tone of excessive amiability that I deprecate. I feel that the scientists should be received as penitents for the sins of an earlier scientific generation, rather than acclaimed as new friends and allies.[62]

He goes on to mention two of the scientists in question: one is Whitehead and the other is Sir Arthur Eddington, who had led the 1919 eclipse expedition, which yielded the first solid empirical evidence in support of Einstein's gravitational theory. Eddington, a member of the Society of Friends, wrote a number of books which emphasized the compatibility of the new physics with religious belief. Eliot writes, "I do not wish to disparage the possible usefulness of the views set forth by Whitehead and Eddington and others. But it ought to be made quite clear that these writers cannot confirm any one in the faith; they can merely have the practical value of removing prejudices from the minds of those who have not the faith but might possibly come to it: the distinction seems to me of capital importance" (SE, 327). He uses nearly the same words (but adds Sir James Jeans as an example) in a radio broadcast published in *The Listener* the following year (1932).[63] Though he is still careful not to base beliefs about the supernatural on scientific evidence, we should note that his statement really is substantially the same as the bishops', with a definite modulation of tone. He avoids introducing scientism into his own profession of belief, but he does recognize that these new findings remove prejudices that have been for many a hindrance to faith. Though Eliot also avoids making scientific discoveries into metaphors in his poetry, I will suggest (in chapter 5) that much of the imagery of *Four Quartets* is redolent of the new physics and would not have been conceived of before Einstein.

Having clarified, as I hope, Eliot's basic attitude toward science and his basic understanding of the history of science, I would like to review some of the major influences in his formative years, with an eye to their ideas about the physical world.

BIBLICAL PHYSICS

To begin with, we must recognize that Eliot, born in 1888, was a child of the nineteenth century. Raised in a Unitarian household, he came to consciousness in a somewhat rationalistic and progressive atmosphere. In fact, he was to note much later that "Herbert Spencer's generalized theory of evolution was in my childhood environment regarded as the key to the mystery of the universe."[64] Thus, Eliot's adoption of an anti-rationalist position had the force of a conversion. He was breaking with both his biological and intellectual forebears.

Unitarian progressivism was founded, as Sigg has pointed out, on a rejection of the doctrine of Original Sin: "Original Sin offended the sense of justice among Unitarians, who refused to consider themselves bound by punishment for acts they did not perform."[65] As a matter of fact, modern liberalism in all its varieties is based on a belief in the perfectibility of humanity and hence on a rejection of this dogma. As Sigg further says, Unitarians, in denying Original Sin, also denied the necessity for a divine sacrifice and rejected belief in the Incarnation. This latter denial is particularly significant for the present study, for the Incarnation is the model of resolving the spirit-matter duality. Lacking that model, religious belief tends either toward a radical immanentism (pantheism) or a radical transcendentalism (deism).

Of course, there were other influences in the Eliot household, and one of the most important was the Bible, which would no doubt have been read selectively and critically in a Unitarian household but read nonetheless. It would be needless to say, if we were not so apt to forget it while pursuing many other sources of Eliot's ideas, that Scripture had a profound effect on Eliot's poetry and on his conception of the world. This effect had little to do with the Unitarian interpretations of the Bible he would have heard. In fact, the poetic effect is in many ways contrary to Unitarian ideas, for the developing poet picked up the powerful concreteness of biblical imagery and the accompanying sacramental conception of the physical world, which his Unitarian forefathers had rejected. Gradually, Eliot realized that the relation between spirit and matter described in the Bible was quite incompatible with Unitarian thinking.

Let us, then, consider very briefly the principles of biblical physics. Spirit is, of course, the first and final reality there: "In the beginning God created the heaven and the earth." Matter comes forth ex nihilo at the word of God. The world has an existence of its own, but created matter continues to respond instantly to the commands of the Creator. Waters part; rain begins and ends; fire comes down on the wicked, and manna on the just; the sun stands still—all perfectly respondent to the will of God. If there is any concept of laws of nature, they are laws which can be—and frequently are—set aside. In short, it is a cosmos dominated by transcendent spirit. The Psalmist rejoices, "The voice of the Lord is upon the waters: the God of glory thundereth: the Lord is upon many waters. . . . The voice of the Lord divideth the flames of fire. The voice of the Lord shaketh the wilderness . . ." (Psalm 29:3,7–8).[66] This passage also demonstrates the fact that the Hebrew cosmos was composed of the same elements as the Greek—the air in which God's voice sounds, the waters, the fire, and the earth of the wilderness. In the New Testament, Christ exercises this same power over the elements, producing the miracles that so embarrassed nineteenth-century commentators, including Arnold, as well as Eliot's Unitarian forebears. Paradoxically, the sense of God's transcendence, which is experienced in miraculous transformations of matter, is arguably responsible for the birth of empirical science. The argument is that as long as the material world was seen animistically no one dreamed of studying it and experimenting with it; but once it came to be seen as something created by Spirit but not itself spiritual, it could be approached rationally and empirically. Such is the claim of Father Stanley Jaki in *Cosmos and Creator* and other books.[67]

There is another side to the story, however: there are signs of God's immanence in the material world. This is not, of course, a pantheistic immanence in which the divine is indistinct from matter; it is rather a teleological immanence in which all parts of creation long to serve God. They originally partake of His goodness, and their capacity to serve is only damaged, not destroyed, by the Fall. God not only speaks to the chosen people as pure voice, spirit-to-spirit, but manifests Himself materially—in a burning bush or a whirlwind. His angels frequently appear in human form: they eat, and even wrestle, with men so that Jacob can say, "I have seen God face to face" (Gn 32:30). This willingness of God to be embodied culminates, of course, in the Incarnation. Consequently, Christians believe that their own entrance into spiritual fulfillment will be in body, for the Apostles' Creed proclaims "the resurrection of the body." Since Unitarians do not subscribe to the Christian doctrines expressed in the Apostles' Creed, it was from the Bible itself and Dante and books about Christian mysticism that Eliot eventually came to this understanding, not from his church and family. There is a pervasive sense in the Bible that the physical world is no mere illusion but has a definite part to play in salvation history, and this very notion of salvation history sanctifies the four-dimensional, temporal world, since history takes place in that world. In the Judeo-Christian revelation, the world of the senses is not merely Maya, and personal identity is of soul and body together. It is this profound sense of union for which the Fathers of the Church fought, in opposition to the various dualistic heresies. Throughout Eliot's life, we find an instinctive antidualist tendency that derives largely from, and leads him back to, the biblical tradition.

Another way in which the physical world unites with the spiritual in the Bible is through the symbolic value of material objects. Since all that is has been created by God, each thing has a definite character that is meaningful to the mind. The symbolic significance of various objects is not arbitrary and conventional but divinely ordained. A creature such as the lamb, for example, is a natural symbol for a sacrificial victim not only because it was what the Hebrews happened to have available for that purpose but because the lamb is by nature harmless and helpless. Lambs were created in such a way that it was inherently meaningful for Jesus to be called the Lamb of God.[68]

In the biblical view, the basic elements of the created world are themselves seen as creatures with particular natures designed to correlate with certain spiritual events. Water purifies by cleaning or (more radically) by drowning the old self. God appears in a burning bush or as tongues of fire because fire partakes of the nature of divine intellect flashing out. Air is symbolic of the Spirit because the Spirit moves whither it will, affecting all invisibly. The literalness of biblical symbolism derives from a belief that the concrete objects are connected, from the beginning, with spiritual realities. This belief produces the sacramental idea in Christian theology. Eliot's family would not have read the Bible as a validation of belief in the sacraments, but they would have read the Bible, and eventually the poet came to accept this ancient view of symbolism, however naive it might have appeared to others of his time who were asserting that all symbols were conventional and arbitrary. That assertion, he recognized, was itself a manifestation of scientism, a naive faith that teaches that the world is not composed of significant elements but of meaningless bits of stuff that combine by random collisions to produce all we perceive. I will argue that Eliot's poetic theory was, from quite an early period of his career, close to the biblical and sacramental sense of symbolism.

PRE-SOCRATIC PHILOSOPHY

Eliot's Hellenism was, of course, as strong as his Hebraism. He had a classical education and became adept in both Greek and Latin. He studied ancient philosophy both as an undergraduate and as a graduate student at Harvard and Oxford. Recent critical studies have been immensely help-ful in clarifying Eliot's relation to modern schools of philosophy but sometimes at the expense of neglecting his classical philosophical founda-tion. We must look more closely than has been done at this foundation, particularly if we are to understand why Eliot chooses to organize his two greatest poems in sections corresponding to the four (or five) elements of classical physics.

The pre-Socratic philosophers are especially relevant to Eliot's physics because, for all of them, physics was virtually all of philosophy. Their single-minded interest in cosmology and the constituents of matter has earned them the title of "materialists," but that may not be entirely accu-rate. The division between materialists and idealists had simply not been made. When they wrote about *phusis,* the pre-Socratics did not think they were leaving out *psuche:* the mind-body question had not been asked. Put another way, there was as yet no specialization into different branches of philosophy. Metaphysics, politics, and ethics were all connected to phys-ics (none of these terms having been used in the modern sense). Eliot's lifelong fascination with the pre-Socratics focuses on the fact that they were the first analytic philosophers, but they still had the undivided primi-tive consciousness, in which the dualities that came to plague philosophy did not exist.

What did trouble the pre-Socratics was change, the mutability of the cosmos. They searched for the prime substance that gave permanence to the changing world. Aristotle calls this substance the *arche;* but for the pre-Socratics, the word *phusis* itself referred to it. So says John Burnet in his *Early Greek Philosophy,* the standard text in Eliot's student days: "Those early cosmologists who were seeking for an 'undying and ageless' something, would naturally express the idea by saying there was 'one *phusis*' of all things. . . . The term *arche,* which is often used in our authorities, is in this sense purely Aristotelian."[69] Eliot's notes on Bur-net's book are preserved in the Houghton Library, and this is one passage he recorded, adding, "Early Greek philosophy not conceptual; its 'being' was physical being."[70] This absence of abstraction attracted Eliot, espe-cially Eliot the poet.

Thales was the first to declare which substance was the *arche,* and he chose water. Burnet speculates that this seemed sensible because water "is familiar to us in a solid, a liquid, and a vaporous form, and so Thales may have thought he saw the world-process from water and back to water again going on before his very eyes."[71] As this comment, along with Eliot's note, indicates, this was not a philosophy of abstraction but of direct apprehension. The pre-Socratics were aware, from ordinary obser-vation, that matter exists in what are now called three states: solid (*earth,* in the old terminology), liquid (*water*), and gas (*air*). Thales, trying to account for the change of states, noticed that water easily entered solid and gaseous states, as ice and vapor. His water was not simply material, however. Eliot's notes from J. H. Woods's graduate course in ancient philosophy categorize Thales' philosophy not as materialism but as "hylozoism" (the doctrine that life is inseparable from matter). Eliot records Professor Woods as saying that water "is merely the title for the unknown source. This *water* is either spirit or matter, as you choose to take it. The separation between spirit and matter not yet made."[72] As the water is both spiritual and material, it is also changing yet permanent. Eliot's lecture notes continue, "All this sequence of perceptible change is a transmutation of something beyond ourselves. The only thing which makes this change thinkable is that it is the expression of something beyond change."[73] This way of thinking about change echoes through Eliot's poetry, especially *Four Quartets*.

Air was the element chosen by Anaximenes as the *arche*. Burnet points out that Anaximenes also used the word *pneuma*, which associated air with breath and wind; that air turns into the other elements by condensation and rarefaction; that it holds both the cosmos and the body together; and that it is called divine.[74] Air is more naturally conceived of as spiritual and is evidently the breath of life itself. Anaximenes gives philosophic definition to a belief rooted in primitive sympathetic magic, that the microcosm of the body is structured much as the macrocosm is. This belief in a connection between inner and outer worlds ends only with the scientific revolution and the "dissociation of sensibility" in the seventeenth century. Eliot's class notes on Anaximenes have it that "The breath breathes in us; we do not breathe it. . . . Our bodies are nourished by compressed air. Air is however the divinity. . . ."[75] Again, the spiritual nature of the physical element is stressed.

Even the grossest element, earth, was championed as the *arche* by one philosopher. Xenophanes says, "All things come from earth, and in earth all things end."[76] Evidently, this choice is based on the agricultural cycle. It may also be influenced by Hesiod's Gaea, first of all beings. Again, Eliot's class notes emphasize the quasi-spiritual nature of the *arche:* "Xenophanes appears to be thinking of the earth rather than the whole of Parmenides. The earth has no motion from without: it limits itself. You must think of this divinity as *round*. It is both material and thought."[77] The chief criterion for the prime substance was that it be the cause of all motion, all change, yet be unmoving and unchanging in itself. We see here a premonition of Aristotle's unmoved mover.

Eliot's favorite was, of course, Heraclitus. His notes say that "His philosophy is one of intuition. Poetic."[78] Eliot found Heraclitus's gnomic style particularly compatible with a modern poetic in which fragmentary statements somehow form an emotional whole. Burnet speculates as to

Heraclitus's choice of fire as the *arche:* "The quantity of fire in a flame burning steadily appears to remain the same, the flame seems to be what we call a 'thing.' And yet the substance of it is continually changing. It is always passing away as smoke, and its place is always being taken by fresh matter from the fuel that feeds it."[79] Like the other pre-Socratics, Heraclitus bases his choice on common observation. There is an important difference, though. Each of the other elements is seen as being transformed into the others, usually by a process of condensation and rarefaction. Fire, in contrast, is not itself transformed but rather transforms the other elements: earthy fuel is made into airy smoke by the fire, which remains itself.

Heraclitus seems to have concluded that there were only three ordinary elements (or states) and that fire was something different: though it is a thing, as Burnet says, its nature is less in its substance than in its activity of changing the others. Heraclitus thus leaps to the modern realization that matter is transformed from one state to another by heat. Still, he sees the fire as being substantial, which does not quite fit with the laws of thermodynamics developed in the mid-nineteenth century. In those formulations, energy and matter are radically different. However, the quantum theory of Eliot's time discovered, at a deeper level, an identity of energy and matter, leading Werner Heisenberg to name Heraclitus the ancient philosopher who had most closely predicted the laws of modern physics.[80] In chapter 5, I will explore the relation between Heraclitean and quantum physics in the context of *Four Quartets.*

The transformation of elements in the Heraclitean system is also seen as an exchange: "All things are an exchange for Fire, and Fire for all things, even as wares for gold and gold for wares."[81] Burnet comments that "In the fragments we find nothing about rarefaction and condensation. The expression used is 'exchange' (fr. 22), a very good name for what happens when fire gives out smoke and takes in fuel instead."[82] The notion of exchange also lies behind the statement that opposing elements live each other's death (Fr. 25), and this offers a new way of thinking about opposites. Eliot's class notes say that "Heraclitos is originator of the idea of reciprocal relation of opposites. . . . He shows that the opposites do not neutralize each other, but may sometimes be the same thing."[83] Thus, there is discovered an identity of opposites, an identity grounded in their ability to exchange with each other. When water turns into earth, it does not lose its identity, because it will become water again. Heraclitus applies this principle to all the antinomies: day and night, good and bad, men and gods. He insists on a union of opposites within the opposition rather than beyond it, an immanent principle of unity.

That principle is, of course, the fire, but even more than the other elements, fire was considered by common mythical belief to be divine.

Burnet states that "by God, or the 'one wise' there is no doubt Herakleitos meant Fire," and Eliot's notes on Burnet's book paraphrase this statement unequivocally: "By *God* he meant *Fire*."[84] The divine fire is also associated with the *Logos*. G. T. W. Patrick, in his translation of Heraclitus (which Eliot read) defines the *Logos* as "the element of order or law in the ever-shifting world."[85] He says of this divine law, "As fiery essence, it was identified with the universe and became almost material. As Order, it approached the idea of pure mathematical Relation or Form. As Wisdom, it was pictured as the intelligent power or efficient force that produces the Order."[86] Thus, Heraclitus conflated a number of concepts and identified them all with his fire.

Heraclitus also identifies the fire with the stuff of the heavens in mythic cosmology, the *aither*. In fact, the root of this word, *aithein,* means to "kindle" or "burn," and the aether was commonly thought of as a more refined fire in the upper reaches of the sky. As the source of Heraclitus's Fragment 63, Patrick gives a passage from Strobaeus that mentions the aether: "Heraclitus declares that destiny is the all-pervading law. And this is the etherial body, the seed of the origin of all things, and the measure of the appointed course."[87] The "measure" here is the *Logos,* and it is "etherial." The idea of a higher, heavenly fire was commonplace. Anaxagoras, who spoke of air and aether as infinite elements surrounding the world, also associated the aether with fire.[88] We find the idea still standard enough for mention in Spenser's "Cantos of Mutabilitie" many a century later. There we are told that a god claims sovereignty over each of the elements:

> As Vesta, of the fire aethereall;
> Vulcan of this, with us so usuall;
> Ops of the earth; and Juno, of the ayre;
> Neptune of the seas; and nymphs, of rivers all. . . .
>
> (*Faerie Queene* VII.vii.26)

Vulcan's ordinary fire ("this, with us so usuall") is distinct from Vesta's "fire aethereall." The aethereal fire will be important to my interpretation of both *The Waste Land* and *Four Quartets.*

Like the other pre-Socratics, Heraclitus finds the divine immanent in the material world. Patrick strongly emphasizes this point in his introduction. He terms Heraclitus a pantheist and claims he had no idea of a "Transcendent Reason," a concept that arose first with Anaxagoras:

> To the latter belongs the credit or the blame, whichever it may be, of taking the first step towards the doctrine of immateriality or pure spirit, which has influenced not only philosophy, but society to its foundations even to the pres-

ent day. Heraclitus was guiltless of it. To him the world intelligence itself was part of the world material—itself took part in the universal change.[89]

Patrick makes it clear that, to his mind, Anaxagoras merits blame, not credit, for introducing pure Mind (*Nous*) and thus conceiving of a dualistic world. Patrick's whole analysis has overtones which make it seem likely that he was a romantic pantheist himself—a position that always elicits scorn from Eliot. Nevertheless, Eliot was attracted to the antidualistic stance in this reading of Heraclitus. He continually rejected all forms of dualism, even the form it takes in the philosophy of his friend Paul Elmer More, with whom Eliot is otherwise in close agreement. There is, however, another way besides Patrick's to interpret the immanence of divinity in Heraclitus's teaching: focusing on the *Logos,* one can see it as a pagan prefiguring of Incarnation. In Christian doctrine, God becomes one with nature, not out of necessity, but out of love; and He preserves His transcendent divinity totally even as He becomes completely natural. Eliot clearly came to read Heraclitus this way—at least by the time of *Four Quartets,* but likely earlier. From the outset, he sought a nondualistic philosophy, and he found one in the teachings of Heraclitus that, lacking a clear statement of doctrine, could be fit with other philosophies and had great potential for poetic elaboration.

What did Eliot take with him from his intensive study of the pre-Socratics? Herbert Howarth, writing of Eliot's undergraduate studies, suggests, "May not one recurrent thought of his have stirred first when he read the Pre-Socratic philosophers with Palmer?—the thought of the form that is within the flux and the stillness that is within the form."[90] Indeed it may have, and this thought is part of a fundamental philosophical commitment. Eliot read the pre-Socratics as presenting an undissociated philosophy just prior to the advent of Platonic dualism. He would not have agreed with Patrick's deification of instinct and Nature, but he was largely sympathetic to Patrick's synopsis of the history of philosophy:

> It was, to be sure, not Socrates' fault that his method was afterwards abused, but as a matter of fact it took in later history a pathological turn that has resulted in wide-spread evils. Over self-consciousness, too much inwardness and painful self-inspection, absence of trust in our instincts and of the healthful study of Nature, which in ethics are illustrated in modern questions of casuistry, and in philosophy in Cartesian doubt and the skepticism of Hume, characterize our worst faults. The philosophy and ethics of Heraclitus, as we have seen, stood in vital opposition to all these traits.[91]

In Patrick's view, a misunderstanding of Socratic philosophy gave rise to radical idealism (that of Philo, the Gnostics, Origen, and ultimately Plotinus), which denied any reality to the material world. Descartes restated this unbalanced idea, seeking only in the inwardness of his own *cogito* for the real. We have seen that Eliot shared this view of Descartes.

In another passage, Patrick identifies German idealism with this ancient idealist tradition.[92] He sees the renewed interest in Greek philosophy as a healthy reaction. In "The Perfect Critic," Eliot dismisses German idealism for similar reasons. Pascal and Russell, he says, affirm that "the mathematician deals with objects"; Hegel, in contrast, operates by "dealing with his emotions as if they were objects" and by taking words to be realities. As an example of the latter tendency, he recalls with a satiric smile Professor Eucken (who gave a lecture at Harvard when Eliot was there) pounding on the table and exclaiming, "*Was ist Geist? Geist ist . . .*" (*SW*, 9). At this point, philosophy is nothing but words and inward speculation, proposing absurdly to define Spirit once and for all. The other extreme, of course, is materialism. Eliot agrees with Patrick that one finds in Heraclitus a philosophy that is not caught on the horns of this dilemma. Such an integrated philosophy is especially important to the poet, who must give to airy nothing a local habitation as well as a name.

ARISTOTLE

An integrated, nondualistic philosophy is also what Eliot finds in Aristotle, and Aristotle's approach is finally preferable in that it does not depend on any sort of hylozoism or pantheism, as the pre-Socratics' systems tend to do. As we have seen, Aristotle is the perfect critic because he is the perfect scientist. Eliot would readily reverse the formula: Aristotle is the perfect scientist because he is a critic (and ethicist and theologian)—that is, his science is not materialistic.

Recently, several scholars have done excellent work in explaining the influence of modern philosophy on Eliot; but in the process, they have (more or less inevitably) paid little attention to Aristotle. An exception is Richard Shusterman, who declares that

> In philosophy's recent dissatisfaction with the Cartesian tradition, there has been a renewed appreciation and application of Aristotelian ideas, particularly in philosophy of mind and ethics. Eliot seems to anticipate and manifest this move both by repudiating Cartesianism and . . . by his frequent praise and implementation of Aristotelian doctrines and strategies.[93]

Shusterman gives Aristotle a very high place among philosophers influencing Eliot. He focuses especially on Aristotle's idea of practical wisdom, relating it to Eliot's nontheoretical, nondoctrinal approach to literary criticism. I will be concerned rather with Aristotle's physics and metaphysics and their influence on Eliot's poetry. The connection Shusterman notes between Eliot's rejection of Cartesianism and his adoption of Aristotelianism has, as we have already seen, everything to do with physics.

Another philosopher who has written, even more recently, on Eliot's Aristotelianism is William Charron, whose essay "T. S. Eliot: Aristotelian Arbiter of Bradleyan Antinomies" gives a fine overview of the subject. Charron finds that Eliot's dissertation undermines both materialism and idealism. He concludes that

> Wisdom as Eliot comes to think of it—wisdom in the face of interminable human conflict and the inherent inconsistencies of life itself—requires thinking in a logic that assiduously avoids the fallacy of the false dichotomy. In the Aristotelian (not Hegelian) dialectic, wisdom requires uncommitted review of contrary opinions with the aim of gathering the partial truth each may contain.[94]

My own emphasis is on Aristotle's physics, and on a resolution of opposites beyond the relativism of opposites, but I believe Charron's analysis is essentially compatible with mine.

Though Eliot expressed passionate interest in the great philosophers of the day—Bergson, Bradley, James, Russell, et al.—Aristotle loomed large in his philosophical studies, beginning with Palmer's Harvard undergraduate course. When he returned from his Bergsonian year in Paris to graduate studies at Harvard, he enrolled in J. H. Woods's course, which covered the pre-Socratics and ended with Aristotle. Even when he was beginning work on his dissertation on Bradley at Bradley's Oxford (1914–15), he studied Aristotle. With H. H. Joachim, a disciple of Bradley's, he read the *Nicomachean Ethics*, which he proclaims the preeminent ethical system in his essay on "The Relationship between Politics and Metaphysics."[95] In the fall of the same year, Eliot attended R. G. Collingwood's lectures on the *De Anima*. William Pratt, in a recent essay on Eliot's year at Oxford, notes the importance of his Aristotelian studies in that year and asserts that "Eliot did not regard Bradley as the ultimate philosopher; that accolade he reserved for Aristotle. . . ."[96] A look at unpublished writings from this period supports this assessment: of the essays Eliot wrote during his postgraduate studies, a surprising number are wholly or largely on Aristotle.

In all of these courses and in the essays written for them, there was an emphasis on Aristotle's nondualistic approach to the material world. Woods asserted, according to Eliot's notes, that in Aristotle's thinking

"There is no suggestion of opposition between the sensible world + that of ideas." In other words, there was no dissociation of sensibility. This was in contrast to Plato:

> Plato would say that the ideas never fully exemplify themselves in this world. But for Aristotle matter is not an obstacle but a favorable factor—ready and willing to be formed—Instead of being non-existent and illusory. When the material is married to actualities of forms you have beauty.[97]

This is, of course, a commonplace contrast between the two. Literary artists have generally preferred Aristotle to Plato not only because Plato banished poets from the Republic but because he (allegedly, at least) disparaged the physical world, which is the immediate source of all art. Woods adds, however, that Aristotle did see in matter a limiting factor: " . . . the failure of form to realise itself—this also is due to the nature of matter. Matter makes the form possible but makes the final (perfect) form impossible." This qualification sets Aristotle apart from the pre-Socratics as well: for him, divinity does not simply reside in matter.

Aristotle explains the connection of material and ideal worlds by his famous doctrine of the four causes: each event has a material cause, an efficient cause, a formal cause, and a final cause. There is never a chunk of pure matter waiting for some force (efficient cause) to give it form, nor is there ever a purely ideal form waiting to give shape to some stuff. The union of these causes has a corollary in the union of potential and actual. As Woods puts it, "The potential acts upon us only because it is in a sense actual. It is real in God, the final cause. . . . The proof of the existence of God is the movement toward the ideal." This alludes to the idea of the unmoved mover, Aristotle's answer to the dilemma of change and permanence. God, since perfect, must be unmoving and immaterial. So how could he (or rather "it," for Aristotle's God is impersonal) set the material world in motion? The famous answer is that everything in the world is moved by love, desire for the divinity, the final cause. We will hear this note sounded in *Four Quartets,* where "the drawing of this Love" is the motive force of the whole cosmos.

In a paper entitled "On Matter," Eliot defends the Aristotelian concept against modern charges that there is a contradiction in his view of matter and substance. He uses the Bradleyan notion of "degrees of reality" to make Aristotle's idea understandable, which suggests that he viewed Bradley's idealism as compatible with Aristotle's realism. In fact, in the concluding chapter of his dissertation, Eliot writes, "We may draw, I believe, certain inferences as to the nature of reality which will forbid us to accept either an idealistic or a realistic philosophy at its full value"

(*K&E*, 153). His quest is for a combination of realism and idealism, which he finds in both authors.

The real incompatibility of either system is with materialism, and Eliot labors to distinguish Aristotle's view from scientific materialism: "the *hyle* of Aristotle is not to be identified with 'matter' in the colloquial or pseudo-scientific sense, although it may be said to include this. Admitted that the matter of Aristotle is usually the matter of physical objects, yet the nature of matter is not conceivable merely on analogy of touch and sight."[98] Eliot further refers to "Aristotle's conviction of the insufficiency of a thorough-going materialistic hypothesis in metaphysics. . . . In the end, any matter is realised in the form for which it is fit, and this fitness is Aristotle's teleology." The ideal is beyond matter, but it is simultaneously present in matter teleologically, as the final cause or end or fitness. In his 1916 essay on Leibniz, Eliot again comments on Aristotle's balanced approach, saying, "Aristotle is too keen a metaphysician to start from a naive view of matter or from a one-sided spiritualism."[99] In this way, Aristotle avoids the tendency of modern philosophers toward one extreme or the other: "Aristotle is neither an idealist, in the modern sense, nor a pragmatist."[100] Thus, Eliot affirms Aristotle's union of realism and idealism, immanence and transcendence, matter and spirit—and always as a remedy for the post-Cartesian dissolution.

Eliot contrasts Aristotle's integrative notion of causality with the "pseudo-scientific" or "materialistic" one, which traces each event in space to another event at the same place but at a preceding point in time. He eventually identifies the Aristotelian view with the Christian one. The concept of God as the final cause was embraced, of course, by Scholastic philosophy, and by the greatest poet of that philosophical period, who is also Eliot's favorite poet. In writing of the *Vita nuova,* Eliot uses this terminology: "The attitude of Dante to the fundamental experience of the *Vita Nuova* can only be understood by accustoming ourselves to find meaning in *final causes* rather than in origins. . . . The final cause is the attraction towards God."[101] Here we can see how Aristotelian physics is taken up by Christian theology and becomes an important element in Dante's poetics, which Eliot in turn adopted.

In another essay, "Matter and Form," Eliot further emphasizes the inseparability of the four causes, and he shows how this idea transcends our usual time-bound notion of causality: "The final cause, like the efficient, starts from a separateness in time which it proceeds to refute. . . . this particular movement toward this particular end cannot be accounted for except by the concept of fitness."[102] This Aristotelian theory of causation is a previously unrecognized source for the intersection of time and timelessness in *Four Quartets.* The "end" of "In my beginning is my end" is (on the philosophical level) Aristotle's final cause.

Parallel to the dichotomy of matter and form, and intimately connected with it, is that of body and soul, which is the question addressed by Aristotle's *De Anima* and treated in Collingwood's lectures at Oxford. Eliot's notes confirm the correspondence: "Since we distinguish soul and body, and matter and form, the two distinctions probably correspond, body to matter and soul to form. Soul is the form of which body is the matter."[103] Here is a conjunction of physics with psychology that reduces neither to the other. Chapter 3, according to Collingwood's synopsis, deals with the *Timaeus* and argues the "Impossibility of abstracting soul from body," thus taking issue with Plato's idealism. Chapter 2, according to Eliot's notes, "amounts to crit. of 2 assumptions, 1. the mechanical, 2. like = like, mind must be homogeneous with what it knows—assumption of idealism (in the Cartesian sense) and materialism." Again, we find Aristotle contrasted with both extremes, and we see that Eliot's quarrel is more with Cartesian than with Platonic idealism.

Collingwood (as recorded in Eliot's notes) goes on to emphasize further the integration of opposing views in Aristotle's notion of the soul:

> You might conceive a science of pure matter (*physics*, abstracts as far as possible from spatiality, while geometry abstracts from matter). Mechanics concrete. There might be abstract psychology and abstract physiology, treating respectively soul and body abstracted from each other. But neither of these sciences really exists. The two are truncated parts of one ideal science—the de Anima.

In the "science of pure matter," geometry abstracts from matter, reducing it to "spatiality," from which physics makes a further abstraction. The terminology of spatialization and abstraction may reflect the influence of Bergson on Collingwood's reading of Aristotle, and the idea that materialistic science is also highly abstract foreshadows Whitehead's approach. We may also recall Eliot's poem about the unreality of space and time: the mechanistic concepts of space and time are unreal just because they are abstractions from reality rather than immediate experience. This modern method of abstracting finally separates a science of mind from a science of body and is therefore judged inadequate in comparison with Aristotle's dynamically unified science.

In the Leibniz article, Eliot reasserts the Aristotelian doctrine of body and soul: "Soul is to body as cutting is to the axe: realizing itself in its actions, and not completely real when abstracted from what it does."[104] Ten years later (in 1926), Eliot declares once more his adherence to the Aristotelian view in criticizing that of Sir John Davies:

> The poem of *Nosce Teipsum* is a long discussion in verse of the nature of the soul and its relation to the body. Davies's theories are not those of the later

seventeenth-century philosophers, nor are they very good Aristotelianism. Davies is more concerned to prove that the soul is distinct from the body than to explain how such distinct entities can be united.[105]

Good Aristotelianism would, of course, do just this: explain how these "distinct entities can be united." Eliot places the blame on Davies' definition of form, and it is clear that he regards Aristotle's uniting of form and matter as the key to resolving the soul-body duality. Eliot is evidently thinking that the failure of Davies and other sixteenth-century thinkers to cling to that resolution opened the door to the theories of the seventeenth century, which dissolved the marriage of body and soul.

In accepting Aristotle's answer to the mind-body problem, Eliot moved toward Christian doctrine. To be sure, Christian thinking has been affected by a Neoplatonic tendency, but the credal dogmas are much closer to Aristotle—as Aquinas and most other medieval theologians avowed. The hypostatic union of God and man in the Incarnation, Christ's bodily resurrection and ascension, and the "resurrection of the body" confirmed by the Apostles' Creed all speak to a central mystery in which body and soul are inseparable. In the Clark Lectures, Eliot quotes a passage from the *Summa theologica* on the relation of body and soul. Aquinas, following Aristotle, says that " . . . inasmuch as the soul is the form of the body, it has not an existence apart from the existence of the body, but by its own existence is united to the body immediately."[106] Eliot comments that "The effort of Aquinas is obviously to reconcile the theological necessities of the soul with the Aristotelian view . . ." (*VMP*, 113). Eliot's Christian conversion was thus a continuation and deepening of his Aristotelian thinking.

It was, of course, Aristotle who fixed the conception of the cosmos that dominated Western physics through the Renaissance and has dominated Western poetry to the present. Joachim touched on Aristotle's cosmology a number of times in the course of his lectures on the *Ethics*. The *Physics*, he says (according to Eliot's notes), deals with the general question of matter and form, while "The rest of the treatises treat of various species of natural bodies. *de Caelo* treats of the simple bodies. 5 of these: the ether, earth, air, fire + water."[107] It was Aristotle who first conceived of the aether (I use the ancient spelling to distinguish it from the modern chemical compound) as an entirely separate element rather than a rarefied form of fire or air. From then on aether was known as the fifth element (*quinta essentia*, or quintessence), which makes it numerically appropriate as the ruling element in the fifth part of *The Waste Land* (see chapter 4). It is also appropriate there in that it is the element of which the heavens are composed.

Aether is important to Aristotle's theory of movement, change, and time. According to Eliot's notes, Joachim says that Aristotle defines change as movement between two poles, "But as regards the stars and the sun situation is different. They are eternal and changeless. They are incapable of alteration, but they do move in space." This movement of the aethereal bodies in perfect circles is intermediate between the stillness of the unmoved mover and the chaotic, linear movement of the sublunary world. The aether itself may be seen, then, as a point of intersection between time and eternity. Aristotle's idea of an eternal and perfect celestial motion closely tied to earthly movement also fits, and indeed was probably influenced by, the sense of eternal recurrence within primitive fertility cults.

In Joachim's lectures, Eliot encountered again the interpretation of Aristotle that emphasized his resolution of the immanence-transcendence polarity: "God is (J. thinks) a self-existent spiritual activity transcending the world, and yet it is a divine life pervading all things." It is significant that this was spoken by a devoted follower of Bradley. Evidently, close students of Bradley's philosophy found it compatible with that of Aristotle on this basic point. As we will see, Eliot follows this line of thought.

BERGSON

As is well known, Henri Bergson was famous in intellectual circles during the first decade of the twentieth century, and Eliot attended his lectures at the Collège de France during his year in Paris (1910–11). Eliot was cured of his Bergsonism quite quickly and said many critical things about Bergson, but he was the starting point in Eliot's quest to find a modern philosophy of science compatible with Aristotle's.

Bergson is important to the present study because his entire philosophy was a critique of intellectual, abstract thought and because he regarded science as the epitome of that mode of thinking. Intellect, he argued, chops the world up, analyzes it. In particular, it chops up time, spatializing it so that it appears as discrete instants in a line, rather than as a constant, unbroken flow—*durée réelle* (real duration). The opposite mental faculty, intuition, apprehends the world as it is and experiences time as duration.

As William Skaff points out, Bergson accused science of giving only a partial view of reality because it restricts its view deliberately to part of reality. This criticism agrees with Bradley's statement that taking scientific discoveries to be final realities is "barbarous metaphysics." Skaff further points out that Bergson's authority derived from his own familiarity with science:

What made Bergson's philosophy even more persuasive to an audience that was anxious to escape the materialism of science and yet at the same time dependent upon its empirical method as a criterion for truth was that Bergson frequently incorporated theories and evidence from biology and the other sciences into his philosophical arguments, a procedure Eliot termed "the use of science against science."[108]

This approach is particularly evident in *Creative Evolution*, which enters into the details of scientific debate over evolutionary theory. In *Bergson, Eliot, and American Literature*, Paul Douglass also points to Bergson's search for a "new empiricism."[109] His ability to move between science and philosophy made Bergson appear Aristotelian to Eliot, who later concluded, however, that Bergson's union of the two fields tended toward scientism after all.

As I have already suggested, we see Bergson's influence even in lectures at Oxford on Aristotle. Referring to the *Physics*, Joachim says "the 'now' is related to a period of time as the point is related to a line. Point is no part of a line, even an infinity of points could not make up a line. Every part of a line is itself a line. Every period of time includes a duration or lapse. In my experienced now there is a continuous flow of present into past."[110] Here, Aristotle and Bergson merge completely.

Eliot's notes on Bergson's lectures record ideas which would remain valid for the poet long after he renounced the French philosopher. At the very beginning of the notes, for example, we find the following:

Dans la [*sic*] monde de la matière la matière plus complexe s'explique par la plus simple: dans le monde de l'esprit le complexe se fait du plus complexe.[111]

[In the world of matter the more complex matter is explained by the more simple: in the world of spirit the complex is made of the more complex.]

This passage is, of course, an indictment of scientific reductionism. Bergson goes on to discuss nineteenth-century associationist psychology, which tried to explain the mind, he says, in terms of physics and chemistry. With this critique of psychological reductionism Eliot was in complete agreement, as his occasional snipes at J. B. Watson attest.

In spite of their broad agreement as to the dangers of scientific rationalism, Eliot did largely reject Bergson, and it is important to know why. His most frequent criticism is that Bergson is too optimistic or progressive.[112] This criticism addresses the Bergsonian faith in the constructive thrust given to the flux by the famous *élan vital*. Douglass suggests that Eliot's quarrel was more with disciples of Bergson (like J. Middleton Murry) than with the master, but Eliot did attribute this fallacy to Bergson himself.

During the Paris year or immediately after, Eliot drafted a paper on Bergson in which he is already voicing criticisms, and this paper gives the best explanation of the disagreement. The essay expresses Eliot's disappointment at finding that Bergson did not consistently achieve the goal he set himself, which was similar to Aristotle's. Eliot refers to Bergson's "attempt in M + M [*Matter and Memory*] to resolve the antinomy." He finds at some points in *Creative Evolution,* on the other hand, that Bergson's "Reality, though I should judge *one* at bottom divides itself into a Cartesian dichotomy—the way up, consciousness, and the way down, matter."[113] Eliot uses the Heraclitean terms as a contrast; in Bergson, the way up and the way down are not the same. Rather, there is an "almost Manichean struggle between life and matter." Connecting the ancient theological dualism of Mani with the modern scientific dualism of Descartes, Eliot finds Bergson trying to resolve the split but falling unconsciously back into the abyss.

Later in the essay, Eliot returns to Bergson's statement in *Matter and Memory* of a desire to find a middle ground between "extension" (corpuscular matter) and "in-extensive consciousness": the mediating term is "immediate intuition." Eliot approves of this approach but finds a phrase in *Creative Evolution* inconsistent with it: "Life is primarily (avant tout) a tendency to act upon brute matter—*une tendence à agir sur la matière brute.*" Clearly, it is the occasional outbreak of dualism in Bergson's writing that disturbs his young student. Bergson is being measured against the consistent antidualistic stance of Aristotle.

Eliot also reacts in this essay to Bergson's use of science. "Bergson," he writes, "appeals to the motions revealed by physics as the basis of matter. His assertions of universal motion rest largely on these physical theories. And just in making this appeal to science he seems to me to throw up his case against science. Return to the immediate, he says; science gives only abstractions. But when science gives motion, he accepts it." Let us note in passing that the "return to the immediate" links Bergson to Bradley. However, the former's use of science against itself seems to backfire, and Bergson is caught (Eliot finds) in a scientism of his own. Eliot insists that science cannot explain the ultimate cause of motion: for that he always returns to Aristotle's idea that the universe is set in motion by an immaterial force, love.

In this paper, then, Eliot argues that Bergson's philosophy is "a kind of pluralism, and a kind of realism." He is emphasizing this side of the case, he says, because "it is the side which I am interested to oppose." The other side is represented by "many other statements . . . which intimate a much more monistic point of view." Here Eliot declares his dedication to a monist philosophy—though it is not an unqualified monism, for he elsewhere states that monism is complementary to pluralism. As Douglass says of Eliot's essay on Bergson, "Eliot's chief criticism, in this essay, is that Bergson has failed to make good his 'claim to mediate between idealism and realism.'"[114] Douglass goes on to say that Eliot is "insisting on this disjunction" and that he criticizes Bergson because the latter "denies the polarity." My reading of the essay, with the support of the statement just quoted, suggests that Eliot complains for exactly the opposite reason: because Bergson sometimes gives up the aim of mediation between the two poles.

Eliot ends his graduate school essay on Bergson—the only careful, extended analysis he ever wrote on the topic—with a suggestion that Bergson's philosophy could be made coherent. To achieve this goal, it would have to be purged of scientism: "In such a system—Bergson Resartus—science in the narrower sense of the word would of course find short shrift." Douglass, commenting on this passage, says that "Science is Eliot's real target here," not Bergson's basic tenets; and that is quite right if we remember that it is "science in the narrower sense," science that takes the materialist assumption as a metaphysical given. Douglass rightly concludes that Eliot's essay "is not a straight attack on Bergson, for it does not condemn the philosopher's views, but strives to adjust them."[115] Even though he later called some of Bergson's views "heresy" and "gross superstition," it is accurate to think of Eliot as adjusting rather than rejecting Bergson's basic ideas. Eliot certainly continued to accept Bergson's critique of scientism and especially (as we will see in chapter 3) his critique of popularized Darwinism.

Bergson gave Eliot a good starting point in a number of ways. For one thing, as Skaff points out, he was somewhat mystical:

> . . . Bergson's attempt to integrate intuition into a philosophical explanation of existence indicated to Eliot that an intellectual justification of such a seemingly emotional experience as mysticism might after all be possible. Thus Eliot began a study of Bradley receptive to its potential for validating mystical contemplation.[116]

To be sure, Eliot was critical of Bergson's attack on intellect, but he was moving toward the idea of a union of thought and feeling, and Bergson contributed to this movement. Other students of mysticism, such as Evelyn Underhill, found Bergson's philosophy congenial. Bergson himself moved gradually toward beliefs similar to Eliot's, declaring at the end of his life that he would have become a Catholic except that it was the time of Nazi occupation and he chose to suffer with the persecuted.[117]

BRADLEY

There are two primary ways of looking at Eliot's career: one sees him adopting a certain philosophy for a time and then rejecting it and adopting another; the other sees him melding various schools of thought. Douglass takes the latter, eclectic approach and criticizes Piers Gray for organizing his book (*T. S. Eliot's Intellectual and Poetic Development, 1909–1922*) in such a way as to imply that Eliot's intellect "grew by digesting and then expelling philosophies and literary devices whole."[118] Gray's book, fine though it is, does give this impression, as does Shusterman's. The latter sketches an early shift from Bradley's idealism to Russell's objectivism, which he sees waning in its turn (in the mid-1920s), to be replaced in the 1930s by "a growing acceptance of the subjective and the personal in criticism."[119] This trajectory is compellingly documented; nevertheless, Douglass seems closer to the truth in finding a more cumulative development, the beginning still present in the end. Bradley is a good example of a thinker whose influence on Eliot faded but whose ideas nevertheless established a pattern that Eliot continued to seek and find in other concepts. A number of critics have demonstrated the compatibility of Bradley's thought with other systems that influenced Eliot, and I will emphasize those connections here. Much scholarly effort has been spent explaining Eliot's understanding of Bradley, and I will draw freely on those explanations while attempting to show that the primary framework for Eliot's analysis of Bradley is the philosophy of science.

In *Essays on Truth and Reality,* Bradley describes his notion of immediate experience: "We in short have experience in which there is no distinction between my awareness and that of which it is aware. There is an immediate feeling, a knowing and being in one, with which knowledge begins; and though this in a manner is transcended, it nevertheless remains throughout as the present foundation of my known world."[120] Bradley's use of the phrase "immediate feeling" in place of "immediate experience" here gives an important clue to the Bradleyan basis of what Eliot calls "feeling." The hallmark of this primal experience is the union of subject and object. This unity is what attracted the Harvard philosophy student, because as Skaff says, "The tendency to unify, to establish and then resolve a dialectic, is in fact an essential quality of Eliot's mind. . . ."[121]

What has not been sufficiently recognized is that the breakdown of the immediate experience is described by Bradley and Eliot in terms of physics. Eliot writes, "Immediate experience, we have seen, is a timeless unity which is not as such present either any*where* or to any*one*. It is only in the world of objects that we have time and space and selves"

(*K&E,* 31). Space and time are the fundamental dimensions of Newtonian physics, which takes account only of the world of objects apart from the selves and which thus claims to be objective. It is this cosmos of space and time that the sage declares unreal in Eliot's preparatory-school poem quoted at the beginning of this chapter. Reality, as perceived in immediate experience, is a continuity of self and object. "By the failure of any experience to be merely immediate," Eliot continues, "by its lack of harmony and cohesion, we find ourselves as conscious souls in a world of objects" (*K&E,* 31).

Bradley's work must be seen in historical context, as a reaction to British philosophy after the scientific revolution. Locke began with the assumption that objects and our sensory knowledge of them were real. Berkeley responded by arguing that we cannot test the correspondence of idea and thing because we can never get outside our minds—a thoroughgoing idealism in response to Locke's thoroughgoing materialistic realism. Hume adopted the skeptical side of both theories and denied reality to both subject and object, creating an impasse that modern philosophy has tried in various ways to break through.[122] The proper starting point for this history is, of course, the Cartesian dualism from across the Channel, for all these British philosophies accepted as a given the dichotomy between mind and matter.

Eliot finds one early attempt at resolving the Cartesian split in the monadism of Leibniz, but it is ultimately unsatisfactory:

> The ancient distinction between matter and form does not correspond to the modern distinction, since Descartes, of matter and spirit. And the dichotomy is as strongly marked in Leibniz as in Descartes. His solution of the difficulty marks the wide gulf that separates modern from ancient philosophy. For Aristotle matter and form were always relative, but never identical. For Leibniz matter and spirit are absolute reals, but are really (as for Spinoza) the same thing.[123]

Eliot admires Leibniz for his effort to resolve the duality but maintains that it must not be done by denying the duality. The Aristotelian approach is to point out that the opposites are not absolutes but are always relative to each other: there is no matter without form, no form without matter. They are integrally related. Leibniz is caught from the beginning when he accepts Cartesian absolute dualism as a premise.

Bergson's solution to this problem was to say that the whole story is a fabrication created by the severance of the intellect from the intuitive faculty. Intuition—being, by definition, an immediate, unconscious knowing—experiences no such division. Bradley's solution was, as Ann Bolgan says, a "New Idealism," which is termed "objective idealism" in contrast to the "subjective idealism" of Berkeley.[124] In his dissertation,

Eliot explicitly rejects subjective idealism (*K&E*, 100). Such a phrase as "objective idealism" would have been considered an oxymoron before, but Bradley's answer (not unlike Bergson's) was to grant reality to both subject and object. In Eliot's history of philosophy, this was the closing of the Cartesian split.

Like Aristotle, Bradley begins by arguing that the opposites are not absolutes but are relative to each other. Eliot explains in his dissertation that any attempt to isolate the pure subject or the pure object fails:

> Cut off a "mental" and a "physical" world, dissect and classify the phenomena of each: the mental resolves itself into a curious and intricate mechanism, and the physical reveals itself as a mental construct. If you will find the mechanical anywhere, you will find it in the workings of the mind; and to inspect living mind, you must look nowhere but in the world outside. (*K&E*, 154)

Similar expressions are to be found throughout the dissertation, for this is its central thesis. Inner and outer, mental and physical, subject and object—there is never one without the other any more than there is matter without form or body without soul in Aristotelian philosophy. The mind is relative to the physical world, and this implies that mind is *related* to the world, able to know something outside itself, a claim that, if accepted, ends the squabbles of epistemology and has great importance for poetic theory as well, for it supports an essentially classical mimetic theory of poetry.

As several Eliot scholars have shown, Bradley developed a scheme in which there are three stages of knowledge. First comes "immediate experience," the primal unconscious state of mind in which subject and object are one. The second stage is consciousness, which means the mind's consciousness of separation from the objects it contemplates. This "relational" awareness quickly becomes the ordinary state of mind for all people, which presumably accounts for the false assumption that subject and object are necessarily separate. Finally, a third state of mind is posited in which one would transcend consciousness and achieve a resolution of the dichotomy again. This third stage is the Absolute.[125] Immediate experience is lost almost from the beginning, but as Brooker and Bentley point out, it continues to be carried on in ordinary relational consciousness, so the correspondence between subject and object is never entirely destroyed.[126] One might also say, using the key terms of Eliot's criticism, that immediate experience is a union of thought and feeling, which then separate in ordinary awareness and need to be reunited. Thus, the dissociation of sensibility is what occurs, as Bolgan suggests, when conscious thought arises from immediate experience.[127]

Now, it is practically self-evident that Bergson's "intuition" names virtually the same concept as "immediate experience." As Douglass says, "For both Bradley and Bergson, primary experience is something with which we almost immediately lose touch, a nonverbal darkness out of which consciousness emerges mysteriously."[128] Bergson's "intellect" is thus parallel to Bradley's "relational consciousness," an awareness of a gap between subject and object—one of whose extreme manifestations is scientific objectivity, the attempt to remove the subject altogether from our knowledge of objects.

Bradley is more convincing to Eliot because Bergson tends to end up with the dichotomy rather than the resolution: he seeks the suppression of intellect and exaltation of intuition rather than their complementary interrelation. In fact, Eliot commonly complains that Bergson rejects intellect, even while creating an intellectual system: "Bergsonism itself is an intellectual construction" (SW, 45). As Skaff remarks, "while Bergson's attempt to find a place for both the intellect and the emotions in our quest for knowledge only continues the Romantic dichotomy between empiricism and intuition, Bradley's philosophy asserts that the intellect and the emotions are originally one faculty. . . ."[129] Bergson's Romanticism is also visible, Skaff remarks, in his attack on science: "Whereas Bergson's critique of science is really based on the nineteenth-century opposition between the intellect and the emotions, Bradley's critique of science forms part of an overall criticism of knowledge in general."[130] For Eliot, who was also partially trained by Irving Babbitt, any hint of Romanticism was anathema, and there was more than a hint of it in Bergson. In sum, Bergson and Bradley were attacking the same problem in analogous ways, but Bradley was more comprehensive and consistent: he avoided falling right back into the habit of choosing sides.

At the same time, Eliot finds, as I pointed out earlier, that Bergson unwittingly ends up adopting some assumptions of science. Bradley's philosophy, in contrast, "is a *pure* philosophy: it borrows none of the persuasiveness of science, and none of the persuasiveness of literature. It is, for example, a *purer* philosophy than that of either of his most distinguished (but younger) contemporaries: Bergson and Bertrand Russell. For Bergson makes use of science—biology and psychology—and this use sometimes conceals the incoherence of a multiplicity of points of view, not all philosophic."[131] Like Aristotle or Pascal, Bradley applies to his philosophy a disciplined focus on fact that could be called scientific, but unlike Bergson, he does not use scientific findings and terminology for their persuasiveness. Eliot seems to suggest that when one operates dualistically, as Bergson does, forcing a dichotomy, his thought may be unconsciously tainted by the element he intends to oppose. The same thing happened to Descartes, who, in totally negating the reality of the material world, gave birth, in Eliot's view, to the whole movement of modern materialism. This lingering dualism is the part of Bergson that Eliot does in fact leave behind as he moves on to Bradleyan discipleship.

Eliot found Bradley's thought compatible with his own interest in primitive mentality. Brooker and Bentley point out that "In the growth of the race, primitive experience would be analogous to immediate experience, and in the growth of the individual, infancy would be the corresponding stage."[132] Anthropologists had been pointing out the absence of a subject-object distinction in tribal cultures. Eliot had studied, in Josiah Royce's seminar, Durkheim's notion of *représentations collectives* and Lévy-Bruhl's *participation mystique,* both of which bear comparison with immediate experience.[133] It is thus through what Eliot called the "mythical method" that Bradley's philosophy takes shape in Eliot's poetry and particularly in *The Waste Land* (see chapter 4).

For similar reasons, as has already been suggested, Eliot found Bradley's ideas congenial to his fascination with mysticism. The mystical experience is a paradoxical state in which one is aware of oneself but is also totally absorbed in God. While at Harvard, Eliot took notes on Delacroix's *Etudes sur le mysticisme,* Inge's *Christian Mysticism,* and Underhill's *Mysticism.*[134] Skaff points out that Inge identifies God with the Absolute, though Bradley himself consistently denied that he equated the two.[135] Eliot's eclectic mind probably accepted the likeness as an exciting analogy. In any case, Eliot found Bradley's philosophy compatible with this mysticism. Conversely, he found in the mystics an experience that verified what Bradley was describing abstractly, an experience in which all the dualities of ordinary consciousness momentarily unite. Eliot's poetic career is a long attempt to create such experiences.

Another philosopher must be taken into account in relation to Bradley. Shusterman argues forcefully that Eliot turned from Bradley's idealism to Russell's realism shortly after completing his dissertation. It is certainly true, as Shusterman says, that Eliot's "early postdoctoral criticism . . . insists on firmly distinguishing objectivity, shared public truth, and 'Outside Authority' from the private subjectivity of 'the Inner Voice', elevating the former and violently repudiating the latter."[136] While Eliot may have been able to integrate something of Russell's empiricism into his view, however, there is little evidence that he adopted this view as a guiding idea in place of Bradley's. Repudiating the "Inner Voice" means repudiating Romanticism's subjective idealism, not Bradley's objective idealism.

Eliot's emphasis on the "object" in criticism of this period need not be incompatible with Bradley's philosophy. Gray points out, for instance, that Bradley did not reject facts; rather, he insisted that facts always be considered within a system.[137] The emphasis on system would be incompatible with Russell's logical atomism, which attempts to start from separate irreducible facts and develop objectively verifiable statements from them. The fact or object, however, is not denied validity. In short, Russell's emphasis on the object may fit within Bradley's scheme, and it is more accurate to say that Eliot integrated elements of Russell's objectivism than to say that he renounced Bradley's philosophy in favor of it. Moreover, as we have seen, Eliot's realism was derived mostly from Aristotle, and it is to the ancient philosophers that we now return to end our consideration of Eliot's Bradleyan thought.

Brooker and Bentley suggest that the similarity between the first and third stages of Bradleyan cognition—immediate experience and the Absolute—is reminiscent of Heraclitus's statement that the way up is the way down.[138] Quite so—the transcendence of relational thinking in the Absolute is a return to the primal, undifferentiated state of mind in which we began. Eliot may even have seen in pre-Socratic philosophy as a whole, with its hylozoism and its lack of differentiation into separate sciences, a kind of immediate experience that philosophy had soon lost and was seeking in the twentieth century to recover. By such analogies, Eliot no doubt linked the modern and skeptical Bradley with the ancients, and it is significant that near the end of his year at Oxford he wrote to Professor Woods at Harvard saying that he wanted afterward to go somewhere where he "could profitably continue work on Greek philosophy, and perhaps on other periods in the history of philosophy."[139]

In Joachim's lectures on the *Ethics,* we find the hint of a connection between Aristotle and Bradley. According to Eliot's notes, Aristotle says, "there are no ready formed innate ideas in the mind, but our mind has a capacity for grasping immediate truths, wh. is given in the simplest sensation."[140] Thus, Aristotle rejects Platonic innate ideas, but he certainly does not move to an empiricist or objectivist sort of realism on the opposite end of the spectrum. Instead, he speaks of some capacity of the mind to grasp "immediate truths" in sensation, some correspondence between mind and matter. We can assume that this capacity derives from Aristotle's basic theory of physics, in which matter is never formless and the soul is not separable from the body. Eliot later concludes his essay on Bradley by paying him the highest compliment, identifying him with Aristotle: " . . . Bradley, like Aristotle, is distinguished by his scrupulous respect for words, that their meaning should be neither vague nor exaggerated; and the tendency of his labours is to bring British philosophy closer to the Greek tradition."[141] For Eliot at least, this was the manifest tendency of Bradley's work.

ELIOT'S POETICS

Eliot's interest in theories of physics and the philosophy of science had a profound effect on his poetic theory and practice. We will now take a closer look at the theory; the rest of the book will attend primarily to the practice.

Poets have always been aware that the tools of their trade (words) were, as Eliot says, "imprecise." They were not waiting for Jacques Derrida to tell them so. The beginning of scientific linguistics in the late nineteenth century no doubt made poets of that time face this problem more consciously than ever before. Words, they now knew theoretically as well as practically, were arbitrary symbols. At the same time, they were being told by scientists that the objects they described with those words were also illusory—no longer composed of the four elements, they were finally only atoms and void. Thus, there was a dilemma on both sides of the poetic conjunction. Part of the response to the problem of words was a search for nonverbal meaning in poetry. Douglass says that "For Bergson and Eliot the effect of any arrangement of images must be to evoke a nonverbal moment—an intuition. . . ."[142] Many others were coming to this conclusion at the time, and we should again emphasize that this was only a heightening of a long-standing awareness—expressed, for example, in the Horatian motto, often quoted in the Renaissance, *ut pictura poesis,* poetry is like painting.

Eliot connected the problem of words with the problem of objects and worked gradually toward a solution in which words pointed toward nonverbal and nonarbitrary objective symbols. These symbols are the traditional ones that derive their meaning from our immediate intuitive experience of physical reality (as opposed to scientific analysis). Among the most basic of these symbols are the classical elements themselves, which are also central to religious symbolism.

This assertion leads us willy-nilly onto the battleground of modern linguistic and literary theory. Other recent critics have suggested a connection between Eliot's ideas and those of Hans-Georg Gadamer, Richard Rorty, Jacques Derrida, and others.[143] Manju Jain's response to such suggestions is on the mark: "His vision, in his early philosophical work, may have approximated to that of Derrida's 'bottomless chessboard', but he looked for a meaning beyond it. Unlike Derrida, Heidegger, and Gadamer, Eliot does not rest at a critique of foundational knowledge."[144] In fact, even in his early writing, Eliot does not accept any antifoundational critique as the final word. Any attempt to make him a proto-poststructuralist is doomed to failure. My own choice of a contemporary theorist compatible with Eliot is Paul Ricoeur, who is, not accidentally, a thinker who has been heavily influenced by Aristotle. The keynote of Ricoeur's theory of symbolism is the idea that symbols have one foot in reality, that is, in physical reality. The other foot is, of course, in ideality. This theory presents a resolution of the opposition between idealism and realism, subject and object, soul and body that is, as we have seen, at the heart of Eliot's

Aristotelian and Bradleyan philosophy. Ricoeur exposes the half-truths of poststructuralism by reminding us of the preverbal side of sacred symbolism, ritual. In doing so, he turns to a writer of Eliot's day, Rudolf Otto, who, in *The Idea of the Holy*, concentrates on the preverbal nature of religious experience. Of course, behind this realization of the nonverbal ritual connected with religious story (myth) is the work of Frazer, whose basic method was to explain myths, such as the death of Balder or the golden bough of Aeneas, by reference to ancient and modern rituals. Also in the background is the work of Cornford, Harrison, and others showing the origins of Greek drama in religious ritual. These writers are central to the debate in Eliot's "A Dialogue on Dramatic Poetry" (*SE*, 32). In fact, as Robert Crawford has shown, this anthropological interest is central to most of Eliot's writing, particularly in the early years.[145] My contention is that his fascination with primitive religion led Eliot to a belief in a preverbal level of symbolic meaning.

Ricoeur, following this line of thinking, starts from the observation that ritual is an essentially "non-linguistic dimension of the Sacred." The religious symbolism of the ritual, he says,

> functions as a logic of correspondences, which characterize the sacred universe and indicate the specificity of *homo religiosus's* vision of the world. Such ties occur at the level of the very elements of the natural world such as the sky, earth, air, and water. And the same uranian symbolism makes the diverse epiphanies communicate among themselves, while at the same time they also refer to the divine immanent in the hierophanies of life. Thus to divine transcendence there is opposed a proximate sacred as attested to by the fertility of the soil, vegetative exuberance, the flourishing of the flocks, and the fecundity of the maternal womb.[146]

This points to important connections Eliot was beginning to make when he wrote *The Waste Land*. He saw that the classical elements were powerful symbols, and that they were powerful because they were physically objective, not arbitrary. He saw, further, that they were essential (so to speak) to the religious view of the cosmos, at least to that of the fertility cults.

Of course, our experiential response to these physical realities may be *ambivalent,* and most primal or archetypal symbols do have both positive and negative charges. Rocks may be foundational or else fatal—one may build on them or die on them. The rock out at sea in *The Dry Salvages* is a "seamark" to guide oneself by in good weather, but "in the sombre season / Or the sudden fury, is what it always was." One might say that rocks have different valences, but they are never soft; they always mean the same thing to people because their meaning is a matter of physical experience, not abstraction. Nowhere will rocks ever come to have a conventional meaning suggesting softness, lightness, or instability.

As is well known but not often considered, Eliot's understanding of symbolism was deeply affected at an early stage by Arthur Symons's *The Symbolist Movement in Literature*. This book can be understood only in relation to turn-of-the-century science, for its initial premise is that the symbolist movement ousted scientific materialism from poetry and replaced it with mysticism. Symons begins by announcing that

> . . . after the world has starved its soul long enough in the contemplation and the re-arrangement of material things, comes the turn of the soul; and with it comes the literature of which I write in this volume, a literature in which the visible world is no longer a reality, and the unseen world no longer a dream.[147]

He goes on to explain that the age of Flaubert and Zola was "the age of Science, the age of material things; and words, with that facile elasticity which there is in them, did miracles in the exact representation of everything that visibly existed, exactly as it existed." One might keep this passage in mind when considering Eliot's focus on the object in his criticism: it is not this empirical kind of objectivism Eliot has in mind. Symons complains particularly about Zola, who "is quite sure that the soul is a nervous fluid, which he is quite sure some man of science is about to catch for us, as a man of science has bottled the air, a pretty, blue liquid."[148] The idea of bottling up one of the cosmic elements, and even the blue of the sky itself, epitomizes the arrogance of scientism. It was such a reduction of the elements and of the soul that the symbolists resisted.

Symons begins his definition of symbolism in the beginning: "Symbolism began with the first words uttered by the first man, as he named every living thing; or before them, in heaven, when God named the world into being." The aim of the movement must be, accordingly, to recover the primordial unity in which there was no gap between the creative word and the creatures it brought into being. Word and object were identical. Symons goes on to acknowledge that human words are imprecise and conventional—raising the problem of language's arbitrariness—but he also expresses hope of success:

> And we see, in these beginnings, precisely what Symbolism in literature really is: a form of expression, at the best but approximate, essentially but arbitrary, until it has obtained the force of a convention, for an unseen reality apprehended by the consciousness. It is sometimes permitted to us to hope that our convention is indeed the reflection rather than merely the sign of that unseen reality.[149]

This hope is not expressed by Symons in a very sanguine way, but it is there as the ultimate goal.

The theory in Symons's book is basically Romantic, but with ideas which could lead to mysticism rather than pantheism. We see the Romantic strain in Carlyle's definition, quoted early on, in which the symbol always achieves "some embodiment and revelation of the Infinite."[150] The "infinite" standing in for God is a Romantic deity, yet the notion of "embodiment" edges toward a more orthodox theology. Symons, like Arnold, hopes literature will save us: " . . . in speaking to us so intimately, so solemnly, as only religion had hitherto spoken to us," he proclaims, the symbolist revolt against materialism "becomes itself a kind of religion, with all the duties and responsibilities of the sacred ritual."[151] Eliot was never tempted to think literature could substitute for religion, but he found in these lines again the connection between poetry and ritual, with its nonverbal actions and icons. The symbolists, Symons points out, were seeking a literature which was more than words. Mallarmé, in particular, is said to have "aspired after an impossible liberation of the soul of literature from what is fretting and constraining in 'the body of that death,' which is the mere literature of words."[152] This aim must be achieved by symbols, which are embodiments of the ideal and hence able to communicate something nonverbal, a physical image or experience.

Symons was no philosopher, but he recognized that the union of spiritual and material worlds he was describing had been given a philosophical explanation by Aristotle: " . . . guided always by the rhythm, which is the executive soul (as, in Aristotle's definition, the soul is the form of the body), words come slowly, one by one, shaping the message."[153] Eliot frequently emphasizes the rhythm of poetry, one of the nonverbal elements. In speaking of Dante, he even goes so far as to claim that on occasion genuine poetry communicated accurately to him even when he did not know the words (*SE,* 200). Eliot's quest for nonverbal, nonconventional meaning in poetry is guided by Aristotle's theory of the soul, which he also mentions in the Dante essay.

This quest for extraverbal meaning also led Eliot to give an important role to incantation. Ronald Bush points out Eliot's praise for "the beauty of incantation" in *The Rock* and connects that with the poet's deliberately incantatory style of reading his own verse.[154] The idea of incantation further identifies poetry with religious ritual, which is normally accompanied by some type of chanted words. As Bush says, " . . . Mallarmé's symbolist aesthetic fits Eliot's Anglican beliefs like a well-made glove."[155] In Bush's view, Eliot's poetics changed as he proceeded toward conversion and as he reread Mallarmé. Without disputing that, I would emphasize a continuity between Eliot's earlier and later theories. Let us return for a moment to his dissertation and consider some implications of the ideas expressed there.

In his dissertation, Eliot employed a theory of symbolism that closed the gap between symbol and referent, much as Bradley's theory closes the gap between subject and object. The terms, however, are taken not from Bradley but from Charles Sanders Peirce. Eliot writes,

> I mean here by symbol both what Mr Peirce calls by that name and what he calls an eicon; excluding the index. Symbol, I mean, in the sense of the real (or rather objective) end of a continuity which terminates at one end in an *intended existent* or *subsistent* and at the other end in an object (*erfassbar*, apprehensible) which must have both existent and subsistent aspects. (*K&E*, 103)

By "symbol" Peirce meant signs with conventional meanings; an "icon," on the other hand, was a sign that did not entirely depend on convention for its meaning, one that had characteristics similar to those of the object or idea it symbolized. As the term implies, many religious symbols are among the primary examples of icons. They are symbols that have some universal significance and convey that meaning nonverbally. Eliot's definition of "symbol," then, combines the categories of conventional and universal symbols, implying that, in his view, most symbols have both kinds of meaning. This seems a wise combination, since it is difficult to find symbols whose meaning is completely immediate and universal, and it is also hard to find symbols whose meaning is entirely conventional and culturally specific.

Eliot's definition of symbol suits the Bradleyan project of integrating subjective and objective realities. "It must be emphasized," Eliot writes, "that there is properly speaking, no relation between the symbol and that which it symbolizes, because they are continuous" (*K&E*, 104). The continuity of symbol and symbolized would be true of Peirce's icon, but by combining that category with Peirce's conventional symbol, Eliot grants this objective continuity to virtually all symbols. Later, he restates this point emphatically, making it clear that this theory of symbolism is necessary to his general thesis:

> It is essential to the doctrine which I have sketched that the symbol or sign be not arbitrarily amputated from the object which it symbolizes, as for practical purposes, it is isolated. No symbol, I maintain, is ever a mere symbol, but is continuous with that which it symbolizes. (*K&E*, 132)

Thus, the symbol does not have a meaning that is arbitrarily and conventionally assigned but rather derives its meaning from a continuity with what is symbolized. This is so because subject and object can never be completely separated. It is hard to imagine that Eliot meant to include such clearly arbitrary symbols as numbers and most words, but he does emphasize that no symbol completely lacks continuity with that which it symbolizes. This must mean that even when highly abstract symbols are assigned meaning arbitrarily and conventionally, continuity is established with that which they symbolize. Such a theory of symbolism is roughly compatible with the one Symons had articulated and with the thinking of Ricoeur. Needless to say, it is completely antithetical to the poststructuralist denial of reference.

Or rather it *should* be needless to say that Eliot's theory is antithetical to poststructuralism. It is, unfortunately, necessary to say it emphatically, given the suggestions to the contrary in several recent essays. It has even been asserted that Eliot's brief discussion of Peirce is precisely a denial of referentiality. Michael Beehler—following Derrida's very brief (mis)-reading of Peirce in *Of Grammatology*—concludes that "both the icon and the symbol are for Peirce signs that can function in a differential field of signification without the identity of an object, and both are reflected in Eliot's term *symbol*."[156] Derrida and Beehler lump together two terms Peirce was at pains to differentiate. Beehler quotes Peirce's statement that an icon "is a sign which refers to the Object that it denotes merely by virtue of characters of its own, and which it possesses, just the same, whether any such Object exists or not."[157] Certainly, this distances the iconic sign from the object, and Eliot explicitly excludes the type of sign that is absolutely tied to the object, Peirce's "index," but the icon resembles the object (even if it is an imaginary object) "by virtue of characters of its own." In other words, it has its own characteristics, which are not infinitely malleable, and which have a certain meaning in themselves.

I take it Peirce's definition implies that the icon is itself partially an object or has objective qualities. In any case, the icon stands between the subjective "symbol" on the one hand and the objective "index" on the other (and even this formulation makes the symbol more arbitrary than Peirce would allow). "Icon" is a middle term that can no more be appropriated to symbol than to index. Yet this appropriation is precisely what Beehler performs when he collapses the categories of symbol and icon and claims that both "the icon and the symbol acquire their significance in a differential relationship with other signs."[158] We must insist that when Eliot combines the two terms he does not ignore their difference—one that the champions of difference seek to dissolve.

Beehler admits that what he takes to be Eliot's interpretation of Peirce is at odds with Eliot's position in the rest of the dissertation, as well as in his later writings; yet Beehler insists that Eliot does shift to this incompatible position during his very brief discussion of Peirce.[159] Eliot was not averse to a certain amount of inconsistency, but I suppose we should take him at his word when he says, one page after the passage about Peirce, that the symbol and that which it symbolizes are "continuous." If Eliot does combine the two categories, it is to give the term "symbol" some of the objective qualities of the "icon," not the other way around.

As we have seen, the idea of nonverbal symbolism—important to Symons, Otto, and others—is closely connected with the modern interest in primitive ritual. I will have more to say on this in discussing *The Waste Land,* where Eliot deliberately employs the "mythical method," but I must here emphasize how important his early study of anthropology was to his poetic theory. The "mystical participation" of the primitive mind with the whole community and with nature was accomplished through symbols and symbolic acts. The underlying assumption is animistic, the sense that the world itself is ensouled. As a more recent writer, Mircea Eliade, explains it, for the profane, irreligious mind "the universe does not properly constitute a cosmos—that is, a living and articulated unity." On the other hand, "the primitive always puts himself in a cosmic context."[160] Ricoeur makes the same point and connects it with his theory of symbolism:

> Within the sacred universe there are not living creatures here and there, but life is everywhere as a sacrality, which permeates everything and which is seen in the movement of the stars, the return to life of vegetation each year, and the alternation of birth and death. It is in this sense that symbols are bound within the sacred universe: the symbols only come to language to the extent that the elements of the world themselves become transparent. This bound character of symbols makes all the difference between a symbol and a metaphor. The latter is a free invention of discourse; the former is bound to the cosmos.[161]

This sense of being a part of a living system pertains also to religions that have abandoned animism: some essential attitude of mythic consciousness remains.

So we find the later Eliot writing, in *The Idea of a Christian Society,* "We may say that religion, as distinguished from modern paganism, implies a life in conformity with nature. It may be observed that the natural life and the supernatural life have a conformity to each other which neither has to the mechanistic life. . . ."[162] This statement is not made in a literary context, but it is significant for Eliot's poetics. The mechanistic world view of the "modern pagan" sees no connection between matter and spirit; the modern religious person is in this closer to the ancient pagan, who always saw the connection. Symbolism, in attempting to reconnect the two, inevitably draws near religious awareness and becomes either a substitute for religion or a way back to it.

One might suppose that mysticism would lead in a different direction, away from the natural world altogether, and many critics have pointed to Eliot's asceticism as leading to a disgust with the physical world (or vice versa). Mysticism, however, is full of paradoxes, and there are at least some mystics whose asceticism was combined with a profound sense of God's immanence in creation. In Eliot's collegiate notes on Underhill's *Mysticism,* we find a discussion of two different mystical doctrines: emanations and immanence. The latter may degenerate into pantheism but is clearly legitimate. Some mystics hold both views, especially Christian mystics: "Christianity, by means of the Trinity, harmonises both; non-Christian mystics usually reject one or the other."[163] The Trinity contains the incarnate Son, the wholly transcendent Father, and the Spirit who continues to penetrate earthly life, so immanence and transcendence are one.

Symons himself avows that he is moving toward mysticism, and he points to Maeterlinck as a symbolist poet who was also a traditional mystic.[164] Mysticism as he understands it connects higher and lower. For example, he says that Gérard de Nerval "realized that central secret of the mystics, from Pythagoras onwards, the secret which the Smaragdine Tablet of Hermes betrays in its 'As things are below, so are they above,' which Boehme has classed in his teaching of 'signatures,' and Swedenborg has systematised in his doctrine of 'correspondences'. . . ."[165] The *Tabula smaragdina* is actually an alchemical document, and it may be that Eliot took some interest in alchemy—as did Yeats, Charles Williams, and many other writers of the time. This famous alchemical formula would have reminded him of Heraclitus's statement that the way up and the way down are the same. The "correspondences" between things above and things below are revealed in poetic symbols.

One Christian saint who exemplifies the combination of severe asceticism with a profound love of creation is Saint Francis. Underhill speaks of him in this way and links him with Eastern mysticism:

"My little sisters the birds," said St. Francis, greatest adept of that high wisdom, "Brother Sun, Sister Water, Mother Earth." Not my servants, but my kindred and fellow-citizens; who may safely be loved so long as they are not desired. So, in almost identical terms, the dying Hindu ascetic:—"Oh Mother Earth, Father Sky, / Brother Wind, Friend Light, Sweetheart Water, / Here take my last salutation with folded hands! / For to-day I am melting away into the Supreme / Because my heart became pure, / And all delusion vanished, / Through the power of your good company."[166]

St. Francis's "Canticle of the Creatures," from which Underhill is quoting, addresses the four elements as the prime creatures. Though Francis withdrew from the physical world and mortified his flesh unceasingly, he venerated the very elements out of which the world was created—or rather joined them in venerating the Creator. In a holy literalism, he responded to the command "Rebuild my Church" by hauling stones to the little chapel of San Damiano where the crucifix had spoken those words to him and by beginning to repair the edifice. For Francis, all the elements were fellow creatures who obeyed the Creator's command that they bring forth life.

Thus, Eliot's study of both primitive religion and mysticism revealed to him a profound conformity between natural and supernatural. The theory of symbolism he eventually espoused and practiced has a religious basis. In his preface to Harry Crosby's *Transit of Venus* (1931), he says, " . . . symbolism is that to which the word tends both in religion and poetry; the incarnation of meaning in fact."[167] We may note here a continuing emphasis on "fact," but it is not the facts of Russell's objectivism. As Eliot's statement implies, belief in the Incarnation makes Christian theology particularly congenial to the use of symbols that are, in Ricoeur's terms, "bound to the cosmos." Sigg writes of the way Eliot identifies poetry with religion in this preface: "The symbol, it would seem, unites opposites the way the poet and the saint use the word. Moreover, Eliot here makes the church a kind of poet, or more likely, a kind of poem."[168] In fact, Eliot goes on to say, near the end of the preface to the Crosby volume, that " . . . no extravagance of a genuine poet can go so far over the borderline of ordinary intellect as the Creeds of the Church."[169] Thus, Eliot sees objects in the context of religious symbolism, which unites them with spiritual realities, and he sees such a union of opposites as the goal of poetic symbolism. Of course, Eliot was not a professed Christian when he first introduced such terms as the "dissociation of sensibility" and the "objective correlative" into his literary criticism in the years after the Great War. But I am suggesting that his early attempts to form a theory in which subject and object would be unified led him toward belief and melded with his later theology.

The dissociation of sensibility, as I suggested earlier, was, to Eliot's way of thinking, a side effect of the Cartesian split. If mind and matter are completely at odds, then thought and sensation must be too. Eliot introduced this concept in his famous 1921 essay on "The Metaphysical Poets," whose thesis is that later poets (particularly nineteenth-century poets), unlike Donne and the other metaphysicals, "do not feel their thought as immediately as the odour of a rose" (*SE*, 247). Brooker and Bentley point out that "immediately" here makes precise reference to Bradleyan immediate experience, in which subject and object are not dissociated.[170] Eliot regarded the Bradleyan continuity of subject and object as entailing also a continuity of thought and feeling: "There is no greater mistake than to think that feeling and thought are exclusive—that those beings which think most and best are not also those capable of the most feeling" (*K&E*, 18). Eliot would have encountered a similar idea in Symons, who says of Huysmans that he "is a brain all eye, a brain which sees even ideas as if they had superficies."[171] This is much like the "direct sensuous apprehension of thought" attributed to Chapman and Donne by Eliot (*SE*, 246). In fact, at the end of the essay on the metaphysical poets, Eliot explicitly identifies them with the symbolists. Laforgue and Corbière are, he claims, "nearer to the 'school of Donne' than any modern English poet" (*SE*, 249). It is the symbolists, and their English follower Eliot, who have begun the recovery of this integrated apprehension.

Another influence on Eliot's thinking about dissociated sensibility has been identified by Grover Smith, namely, Coleridge.[172] It was Coleridge, more than any other English critic, who defined the term "symbol" and brought it into common usage. Coleridge was, as George Bornstein has shown, the one writer Eliot spared when he attacked the Romantics.[173] Eliot twice quotes the following passage from the *Biographia Literaria:*

> This power . . . reveals itself in the balance or reconcilement of opposite or discordant qualities: of sameness, with difference; of the general, with the concrete; the idea with the image; the individual with the representative; the sense of novelty and freshness with old and familiar objects; a more than usual state of emotion with more than usual order; judgment ever awake and steady self-possession with enthusiasm and feeling profound and vehement.[174]

The power in question, is, of course, imagination, which "fuses" these opposites. It is easy to see how this theory would appeal to a later philosopher-poet who was constantly seeking a way to resolve life's dualities. In fact, the last pair of antinomies in this passage—"judgment" and "feeling"—is essentially the same as Eliot's own primary poetic antithesis between thought and feeling. Interestingly, Coleridge goes on to illustrate the idea with a passage from Sir John Davies concerning the relation of the soul to the material world, in which Davies claims that the soul "draws a kind of quintessence from things." Here is Eliot's ultimate concern with spirit and matter, and here is the "quintessence" as intermediate between the two.

The medium created by the imagination for this "reconcilement of opposites" is the symbol. Coleridge writes that the imagination "gives birth to a system of symbols, harmonious in themselves and consubstantial with the truths of which they are conductors."[175] The term "consubstantial" introduces a theological note, one which is not unusual in Coleridge's literary criticism. Indeed, his poetic symbol is finally an incarnation of an ideal universal in a concrete particular. In making a distinction between allegory and symbol, he says that the latter "is characterized by a translucence of the Special in the Individual or of the General in the Especial or of the Universal in the General. Above all by the translucence of the Eternal through and in the Temporal." The next clause is practically identical to the dogmatic definition of a sacramental sign: "It always partakes of the Reality which it renders intelligible. . . ."[176] This union of matter and meaning is possible because, as Coleridge believes, there is a natural correspondence between the mind and the material world. In other words, he is speaking of natural symbols. Eliot was increasingly drawn to such theories.

The dissociation of sensibility is a breakdown in these natural correspondences, a break between symbols and their meaning. After all, the rose Eliot invokes in speaking of Donne's mind is one of the prime natural poetic symbols. If the thought of the rose can be cut free from the physical, sensory experience of roses—if any other symbol can be made by conventional usage to smell as sweet—poetry suffers a great loss, for the rose no longer works symbolically: it becomes a mere metaphor. This is what the Cartesian split and the attendant scientific revolution of the seventeenth century do to the meaning of symbols.

Donne himself famously expresses this view of the scientific revolution:

> And new Philosophy cals all in doubt,
> The Element of fire is quite put out;
> The Sun is lost, and th'earth, and no mans wit
> Can well direct him, where to looke for it.
> And freely men confesse, that this world's spent,
> When in the Planets, and the Firmament
> They seeke so many new; they see that this
> Is crumbled out againe to his Atomis.
>
> ("The First Anniversary," 205–11)

The new philosophy is the natural philosophy of Copernicus, Galileo, Kepler, and others. Donne goes on to complain that "all Relation" is gone now that these scientists have destroyed the old model of the universe, for in that old model everything was interconnected. The physical world was meaningful in itself because it conformed to the supernatural realm. Donne says that the old elements are lost, even the chief of them, fire. The end of the passage suggests that he is thinking the elements have been supplanted by the atomistic theory, for he finds the world now crumbled into "Atomis." The great difference to a poet between elements and atoms is that the former have meaning based on immediate sensory experience, whereas the latter cannot be experienced by the senses and have no human meaning (see chapter 3 on Gerontion's "fractured atoms"). Thus, in this new universe, the poet's senses and his thought are divided. This is the dissociation of sensibility. By the time of the Clark

Lectures in 1926, Donne is no longer seen as the last example of the undissociated sensibility and is rather seen as the first example of the dissociated modern sensibility. However, this shift in Eliot's evaluation does not change the principles he was promoting in the earlier essay "The Metaphysical Poets."

Again and again in the early criticism, Eliot speaks of the "object" in poetry. In his essay on Swinburne (1920), Eliot writes that "Language in a healthy state presents the object, is so close to the object that the two are identified."[177] In a letter to Pound in 1915, Eliot exclaims, "I distrust and detest Aesthetics when it cuts loose from the Object and vapours in the void, but you have not done that."[178] Most famously, he speaks of the need for an "objective correlative," which he defines as "a set of objects, a situation, a chain of events which shall be the formula of that *particular* emotion; such that when the external facts, which must terminate in sensory experience, are given, the emotion is immediately evoked" (*SW*, 100). The objective correlative is not necessarily a traditional symbol: it is rather a subtle combination of elements which evokes a very specific emotion, such as Hamlet's madness. I would again argue, however, that this notion leads Eliot toward a traditional theory of symbolism.

Bolgan finds an important source for the idea in the writing of the Bradleyan idealist, Bernard Bosanquet, who speaks of "objective correlates." The idea is that the objective correlates with the subjective, approaching the unified awareness of immediate experience.[179] Skaff also takes Bradley to be the prime source. In order to remedy the fragmentation of ordinary consciousness, he suggests, "the poet must try to simulate unconscious immediate experience by once again unifying emotions with the objects that originally accompanied them into our world, that is, with the objects that tend to include the given emotion in his mind. . . ."[180] This formulation of the process implies that the objective correlatives are partially given, that certain objects originally accompanied the emotions the poet wishes to evoke. The idea that certain objects are right leads toward the idea of natural symbols. Eliot does not restrict his definition to such symbols or mention symbolism in relation to the objective correlative, but that idea finds its home in a traditional symbolic poetics by asserting that there are certain objects or sets of objects that evoke definite emotions in everyone. As Symons puts it, literature must build on a "confidence in the eternal correspondences between the visible and the invisible universe."[181]

The notion of an objective correlative may also, as Shusterman suggests, owe something to Russell's objectivist philosophy. But it is not an attempt, even in this brief period of Eliot's career, to establish a kind of scientific theory of poetry: that he consistently rejected. The scientific approach to physical reality is a very different combination of mental and physical dimensions from the symbolic one. It regards the ordinary experiences of the old order as illusory: the old elements are not elements at all but more or less complex conglomerations of atoms, which cannot be experienced directly. The symbols with which it designates the new elements are mathematical, wholly abstract, and hence totally meaningless by themselves. In the old physics, even these numbers were regarded as having profound human meaning, but now they are simply counters: "two" no longer means duality or division; it is simply the integer between one and three. It is of no human significance that the atomic number of hydrogen is two. These abstract symbols do not have one foot in ordinary bodily reality: they are not "bound to the cosmos" (Ricoeur). Nor do they have another foot in numinous reality, as the old symbols do.

At the same time, it is true that Eliot aimed for a theory of poetry that did not separate it entirely from genuine science. As we saw earlier, he thought that the poet must pay precise attention to the objective world much as the scientist does, for it is in the world of objects that poetic symbols are found. McDonald has shown that both Eliot and Pound saw poetry as uniting the analytic, scientific mode of thought with the intuitive, artistic mode: "Poetry, by Pound's and Eliot's definitions, is both analytic and intuitive, objective and subjective. . . . Pound and Eliot thus refuse the separation of the provinces of science and the imagination. Indeed they define the poetic imagination as a category that subsumes such definitions."[182] The combination of analytic and intuitive responses to the world is just what Eliot is aiming for when he seeks to unite thought and feeling in an objective correlative.

This way of including scientific thinking is, however, quite at odds with the approach that Eliot called "pseudo-scientific," and that he observed early in the century in the development of modern scientific linguistics. Linguists at that time began to ape the natural sciences by attempting a purely abstract description of language. They, consequently, made a radical change in the use of the word "symbol." It is a given for most linguists today that symbols are, by definition, arbitrary. Symons was already strongly aware of the arbitrary nature of words, as we have seen, but when this truth about linguistic symbols is transferred to all symbolism, it ceases to be true. A recent linguistics textbook, for instance, gives wedding rings as an example of an essentially arbitrary symbol.[183] Now, surely the gold of a wedding ring, in its perfect resistance to tarnishing, represents objectively the ideal purity of marriage, and the perfect circular shape of the ring is an objective correlative of the perpetual vow. A gold ring might be used to mean a number of things, to be sure, but its very form and material are naturally suited to this meaning because of their physical properties, not merely because of some arbitrary assignment of meaning by a particular culture. Pseudoscientific structural linguistics has made such indefensible suggestions as this one about the wedding ring commonplace by changing the definition of "symbol" in order to deny that any symbol is "bound to the cosmos," or that language can ever be (in Eliot's phrase) "so close to the object that the two are identified." In statements like this one, Eliot confronted the growing pseudoscientific assumption that all symbols are wholly conventional.

The structuralist assertion that all symbols are, by definition, arbitrary opens a gap in which poststructuralist theory thrives. Eliot was more aware than any deconstructionist of the gap between words and meaning, so it is not surprising that some critics have been tempted to see Eliot as a forerunner of poststructuralist thinking. Nevertheless, I believe the present analysis makes obvious the incompatibility of Eliot's theory with any version of poststructuralism. One true forerunner of postmodern theory is Descartes, with his denial of the body, for when everything is believed to be mental, it is more or less inevitable that someone will believe everything mental to be merely linguistic. Eliot consistently maintains, in contrast, that the psychic world can never be fully separated from the physical world. He also maintains that there are nonlinguistic ideas and that language itself is never separable from reality. In the dissertation, he asserts that "The idea, and its predication of reality, may exist previous to the articulation of language. It is not true that language is simply a development of our ideas; it is a development of reality as well" (*K&E*, 44). Such a statement is thoroughly inimical to poststructuralist theory.[184]

When Eliot complains of the Cartesian revolution that "Instead of ideas as meanings, as references to an outside world, you have suddenly a new world coming into existence, inside your own mind" (*VMP*, 80), he positions himself foursquare against the whole subjectivist tendency in the modern period—a tendency of which postmodernism is merely the *reductio ad absurdum*. Eliot's response to the arbitrary nature of words was to use them as precisely as possible and, more importantly, to use them to evoke images of physical realities that are not arbitrary but are natural universal symbols. From the beginning, Eliot sought symbols or objective correlatives that would close the gap between sign and meaning rather than widen it.

A somewhat more tenable suggestion about Eliot's poetics, but one with which I must still take issue, is Skaff's claim that Eliot adopted a surrealist poetic. Skaff may be right to connect metaphysical conceit with the surrealist tendency to use metaphors that link very different things, but he concludes improbably that Eliot's early poetic theory did not accept the symbolic approach of either Coleridge or the symbolists.[185] One might accept Skaff's formulation of the Romantic symbolic imagination as transforming "unconscious feelings into readily recognizable esthetic material that closely conforms, metaphysically speaking, to our everyday sense of reality" and his characterization of the surrealist metaphor as one that links "the ordinarily separate" and "defies natural order."[186] In short, the Romantic—and the symbolist—uses natural symbols, while the surrealist uses unnatural metaphors. To be sure, Eliot was attracted to the strained metaphors of the metaphysical poets, and some of his own early imagery seems to link "the ordinarily separate," but as I have tried to show, his goal of reconciling the spiritual and physical led him to precisely those theories of Coleridge and Symons that Skaff rejects. Eliot's early poetic practice has something in common with surrealism: the sense of disjointedness. Even his strangest images, however, usually partake of some common or traditional symbolism. If Eliot had a leaning toward surrealist theory, he never let on. In fact, he later wrote that "surrealism seemed to provide a method of producing works of art without imagination," making it the equivalent in art of logical positivism in philosophy, which "seems to provide a method of philosophizing without insight and wisdom."[187] I suspect that Skaff is led to grasp at this particular straw because of his apparent desire to have an agnostic Eliot; for he denies that Eliot ever held "a literal belief in Christian dogma."[188] In reality, it seems to have been the very literalness of Christian dogma that drew Eliot to it, much as the emphasis on natural symbolism in the theories of Coleridge and Symons drew him to them.

His search for a poetic union of spirit and matter led Eliot eventually to a theory of symbolism consonant with sacramental theology. Gregory Jay perceives in *The Waste Land* Eliot's "attraction to Catholicism" and suggests that the attraction was to the "transcendental poetics" made possible by Catholic theology: "In contrast to the iconoclasm of Hebrew, Protestant, and Puritan theories of sign, Catholicism reunites the letter and the spirit, signifier and signified, nature and culture, human and divine in the dogmas of the Incarnation, Passion, and Resurrection."[189] This expresses extremely well the essential connection between Eliot's religious and poetic convictions. The union of signifier and signified is total in the doctrine of the sacraments. Catholic theology, whether Roman or Anglican, claims that in the sacraments the symbol and the effect are not separable. The usual formulation is that "Sacraments effect what they signify." So the water of baptism symbolizes spiritual cleansing and effects that cleansing. The bread and wine of the central sacrament, the Eucharist, symbolize and really are the body and blood of Christ. In addition, traditional Catholic practice uses "sacramentals," signs that sanctify everyday life: the sign of the cross, blessings of houses and fields, habits for religious orders, rosaries, church buildings. Thus, all areas of ordinary physical life are symbolically connected with the transcendent.

Particularly important for the present study is the centrality of the classical cosmic elements in sacramental and liturgical ceremonies. For example, the church employs fire in candles and censers; water in the baptismal font, in the Asperges, and in blessings of houses, fields, and objects; air in the breath of the priest on the water at the Easter vigil and in the music of the pipe organ; earth in the stones of the church building and altar, and in all the objects used in services. The cosmic elements are seen by the church as creatures of God that speak His mind to us and that resonate with our own mind. The meaning, being nonverbal, is rich and not fully definable but, by the same token, is not arbitrary, for it is based on universal physical experience. As the soul is the inherent form of the body, the significance of a sacramental symbol is inherent in its substance. Therefore, sacramental symbols possess a perfect unity of sign and meaning and so become the epitome of the kind of symbolism Eliot sought.

This is, of course, the theology that informs the work of Eliot's favorite poet, Dante, who, as Ronald Schuchard has pointed out, eventually replaced Donne as Eliot's model of an undissociated poetic sensibility.[190] In the 1931 essay "Donne in Our Time," Eliot concludes that in Donne "there is a manifest fissure between thought and sensibility," while in Dante "there is always the assumption of an ideal unity in experience, the faith in an ultimate rationalisation and harmonisation of experience, the subsumption of the lower under the higher, an ordering of the world more or less Aristotelian."[191] Aristotle's divinity is pure thought and yet moves the universe by love; and it is such a union of thought and feeling that gives wholeness to medieval mysticism and poetry. Hence, it is not finally Donne's rose but Dante's which is the perfect symbolic ending to *Four Quartets.*

In Eliot's view, the Aristotelian synthesis of soul and body, integrated with Catholic theology by St. Thomas, largely accounts for Dante's ability to unify image and idea in his symbolism. The unification of idea and sense seems to be what Eliot is getting at in his essay on Dante in *The Sacred Wood* when he writes,

> The poet can deal with philosophic ideas, not as matter for argument, but as matter for inspection. The original form of a philosophy cannot be poetic. But poetry can be penetrated by a philosophic idea, it can deal with this idea when it has reached the point of immediate acceptance, when it has become almost a physical modification. (*SW,* 162–63)

The gift of the poet is to feel ideas as immediately as one feels physical objects through the senses—as immediately as the odor of a rose; thus, an idea becomes "*matter* for inspection" and finds an objective correlative. A philosophy yields "almost a physical modification." Eliot says this in the context of arguing that Dante had a peculiar advantage in this regard because the philosophy and theology of the time were more or less universally accepted, so there was little gap between philosophy and immediate lived experience.

In his later Dante essay, Eliot touches on the relation between the Catholic theology of the body and poetic meaning. He notes that Dante includes a fictional character (Ulysses) in the *Inferno,* along with all the historical figures there. The inclusion of a fictional character, Eliot writes, reminds us

> that Hell, though a state, is a state which can only be thought of, and perhaps only experienced, by the projection of sensory images; and that the resurrection of the body has perhaps a deeper meaning than we understand. (*SE,* 211–12)

The profound and mysterious doctrine of the resurrection of the body is here found to be integral to the highest poetic art.

In the Clark Lectures, Eliot identifies as one of Dante's three great poetic strengths "the gift of incarnation," making explicit the theological basis of his own poetic theory.[192] He also speaks of adequate poetic thought as "the *Word made Flesh*" and expands the idea by writing that "the characteristic of the type of poetry I am trying to define is that it elevates sense for a moment to regions ordinarily attainable only by abstract thought, or on the other hand clothes the abstract, for a moment, with all the painful delight of flesh" (*VMP,* 54–5). The power of reconciling thought and sensation, spirit and flesh, was just what Eliot sought in all the masters to whom he apprenticed himself—and what he found most fully realized in Dante's incarnational poetics. Eliot followed his Florentine Franciscan guide into the sanctuary where this artistic mystery is celebrated.

Curriculum Vitae Eius

In the remainder of this book, I will trace the development of Eliot's thinking regarding physics and poetics and the relation between the two, especially as this thinking finds expression in his poetry. What I find is that he continues throughout his literary career to deal with the issues I have discussed in this chapter, but that there is a definable progression in his treatment of those issues.

In the predominantly satiric *Prufrock* volume (1917) discussed in chapter 2, the poet shows modern, urban, scientistic people how they view themselves and the world around them. Given the turn-of-the-century dominance of scientific materialism, these people find themselves in a world that is no longer animated, or even haunted, by mysterious supernatural entities. They may turn to sentimentality about nature, as Prufrock does, or to sentimentality about art, as the Lady does in "Portrait of a Lady," but they are ultimately incapable of experiencing any conjunction of the natural and supernatural in human experience and art because their mechanistic assumptions preclude the symbolic dimension in which such a conjunction occurs. In other poems in this volume, the elemental world of ancient physics is suppressed and polluted by city life: earth is grime and mud; water is eau de Cologne and tea and dampness of soul; air is brown fog and hysterical gasps; and fire is a sputtering lamp or a battered lantern. There is no life-giving harmony of pure elements, as there is no genuine relation between human beings. The poet proposes no solution to this malaise and, indeed, has none to propose, yet his dark descriptions proclaim a desire to find out what has been lost.

In the 1920 volume, which is the topic of chapter 3, Eliot continues to satirize modern cosmology, but in a few places, he focuses on more precise issues raised by specific doctrines of scientific materialism. In "Gerontion," he asks what it is like to approach death if one has accepted as a final metaphysical truth the theory of atomism. This idea had been proposed, and largely rejected, in ancient times and then was apparently confirmed by modern chemistry. The old man in the poem expects to dissolve at death into "fractured atoms," and this belief accounts for his paralysis and isolation. He has no ghosts even, for he does not believe in any survival of the personality after death. Eliot also glances at the Darwinian doctrine of gradualist natural selection when he describes Bleistein as "a lustreless protrusive eye" staring from "protozoic slime." This is not so much Eliot's view of a Jewish-American tourist as modern man's view of himself. Similarly, "Apeneck Sweeney" and the "silent vertebrate" in "Sweeney among the Nightingales" are modern people seen in the light of Darwinian assumptions. The poems in this collection take a chagrined look at human existence stripped of meaning by scientific materialism, reduced to nothing but "birth, copulation, and death." Too commonly, these poems have been interpreted as revealing the poet's revulsion at life and his misanthropy, but even if there is some truth to this interpretation, the fundamental impetus of these works was to examine how educated people of the time thought of themselves. At this period, Eliot still has no answer to this mechanistic vision of humanity, but his poetic critique of dominant intellectual assumptions is more specific and explicit than in the first volume. He calls into question particular theories of mainstream nineteenth-century science, which had been uncritically adopted by many people as metaphysical dogmas.

The Waste Land, which is the subject of discussion in chapter 4, is transitional for Eliot's poetic thinking about physics, as it is for most major themes of his career. The poem continues to give a critique of the modern *Weltanschauung* in many of the images and characters. At the same time, however, Eliot takes a radically different approach to presenting the physical world in this poem. His philosophical search for a nondualistic understanding had led him back to Aristotle and the pre-Socratics, and he makes use of their physics here. This move is announced rather dramatically by the identification of the poem's five sections with the five elements. These ancient elements, because apprehensible in immediate experience and rich in symbolic meaning, offer a medium in which the Cartesian split may be resolved; hence, they provide an answer to the dilemma of modern life scrutinized in the earlier poetry. To be sure, the elements are not experienced as life-giving in most of *The Waste Land*. In fact, I find that their identification with separate sections enacts a separation of the elements, and when they are separate, they are deadly. Thus, each of the first four sections witnesses a death—by burial, suffocation, burning, and drowning—appropriate to earth, air, fire, and water. We are still in Eliot's *Inferno*. In the context of Frazer's fertility cults, however, death is routinely followed by rebirth, and this rebirth is at least potential in the poem.

The final section of *The Waste Land* is identified with the aether, the divine element that unites the four earthly elements. Here, the "aethereal rumours," the words of the thunder, revive the broken hero at least momentarily. Here also are images of the death of Christ and His resurrection, witnessed on the road to Emmaus. The figure encountered by the disciples in that incident is both spiritual and physical, an exemplar of resolved duality. This resolution is only glimpsed: the poem ends still in fragmentation. But Eliot has seen a momentary vision of the answer to his question about material and spiritual realities. He has begun to turn away from merely satirizing modern materialistic metaphysics and toward envisioning a metaphysics of integrated antinomies. He has arrived at his *Purgatorio,* where the suffering, though even more intense than before, is potentially redemptive.

In *Four Quartets,* Eliot gives his most complete response to the dilemma encountered in the early poetry, the duality of human experience. This poem is the subject of my final chapter. One could, perhaps, write another chapter examining his treatment of this theme in his plays. Some of the physical imagery certainly continues to appear in the plays—images of vacancy and void, for example. Eliot continues to take an interest in scientific concepts, as when he speaks of the "Heaviside Layer" (i.e., the ionosphere) near the end of *The Family Reunion*. This chapter, if it is ever written, will have to wait for another time and perhaps another writer. The picture I meant to paint seems to be complete with the chapter on *Four Quartets*. The issues I am taking up do not seem to be quite as important in the plays. As Eliot shifted to writing dramatic works in the latter part of his career, his primary thematic concerns shifted rather naturally to matters of human relations and away from relations between man and the cosmos. His dramas are mostly drawing room comedies, and their settings are nearly always indoors, though there are descriptions of key events out at sea or in the wilds of Africa. It seems to me that Eliot's final word on the ideas under discussion here is given in *Four Quartets*.

The classical elements again give this work its basic structure, for each of the four poems is identified with one of the four earthly elements. However, Eliot presents the elements in an entirely different way here. Where they were separated and fatal in *The Waste Land,* they are integrated and vital in *Four Quartets*. Though each poem is identified with one of the four, Eliot describes an interpenetration of the elements throughout. The primary cosmology invoked is that of Heraclitus, in which there is an exchange of earth, water, and air directed by the fire. This exchange accounts for the unending flux of events, but the divine fire creates a pattern within change, a pattern the poet glimpses now and again. In the Heraclitean system, the elements are actually transformed into each other in a rising and falling rhythm, so the elemental opposites are not ultimately separate entities but only different manifestations of the *Logos*. For example, the "ground swell" experienced out at sea is evidence of a fundamental identity between earth and water. There is not a separate section for the fifth element in this work, because for Heraclitus the fire and the aether are identical. It is, thus, the aether that performs the meaningful transformations of the elements and fills the void between earthly entities. Since Heraclitus also identifies the aethereal fire with the divine *Logos,* Eliot is able to merge his cosmology with Christian theology in the poem.

Each of the separate poems is also identified with one of the four seasons, but as with the four elements, these actually interpenetrate in surprising ways. For instance, there are blossoms of snow in "midwinter spring"; and in May, flowers look like snow on the hedges. The seasons, like the elements, are found to possess a likeness, observable occasionally by the poet's eye. The similarity is the pattern or form given to all the seasons by the *Logos*.

Even as he is returning to pre-Socratic philosophy, Eliot turns also to modern physics for imagery and concepts. He recognized that modern physics had overthrown the mechanistic and deterministic assumptions of nineteenth-century science, thereby reopening the question of relations between spiritual and material dimensions of the world. Einstein's theories affect Eliot's images of light, his conception of time, and his contemplation of entities that are neither matter nor spirit, "neither flesh nor fleshless." The poem also shows the poet's awareness of the other major branch of modern physics, quantum theory. One of the leading lights in this school, Werner Heisenberg, has declared that the philosopher who came closest to the insights of quantum physics was Heraclitus, and Eliot apparently reached the same conclusion. As Heraclitus speaks of one element being transformed into another by fire, Heisenberg describes the same sort of transformation being effected by what modern physics now calls "energy." Quantum theory calls into question the determinism that was often associated with Newtonian physics, and the poet experiences an indeterminacy in the world: "I can only say, *there* we have been: but I cannot say where." The new physics goes so far as to suggest that the physical world is affected by conscious observation, and this idea finds expression in the roses that "Have the look of flowers that are looked at." Even the idea of the aether, which had been definitively rejected after Michelson's measurement of the speed of light at the turn of the century, is resurrected in modified terms by the new physics.

Eliot refused to look to science for confirmation of his faith, but he recognized that twentieth-century physics was much more compatible with faith than the dominant theories of his younger years had been. His early poems attack the mechanistic world view but have nothing positive to offer in its place. *Four Quartets* puts forward a positive vision of a physical world that is also spiritual, a world whose laws of physics are consistent with the doctrine of the Incarnation and with sacramental theology.

2

Polis and Cosmos in
Prufrock and Other Observations

Throughout his early poetry, Eliot describes in satiric or ironic tones city dwellers whose urbanity and immersion in society cut them off from both nature and the supernatural. He is placing himself in the tradition of Juvenal congratulating a friend on his escape from Rome in the Third Satire and of Samuel Johnson translating the same sentiments into the London locale. Though he is urging us to leave the Unreal City, however, Eliot is himself the most urbane of city dwellers, so he cannot simply wander with Wordsworth over the hills of the Lake District. He is, in fact, simultaneously taking part in the symbolist reaction to the Romantic "egotistical sublime" mode. He reacts to the industrialized city much as the Romantics did, and he admits in his 1930 essay on Baudelaire that "a poet in a Romantic age cannot be a 'classical' poet except in tendency." The resulting "discrepancies between head and heart, means and end, material and ideals" are quite visible in the early poems.[1] In fact, George Bornstein has shown convincingly that Eliot displayed important Romantic tendencies in all his poetry, even while attacking Romanticism mercilessly in his prose.[2] In this first volume, Eliot reacts as a Romantic to the city, but he writes as a classical satirist, lampooning the inadequate Romantic response along with the social setting itself. Eventually, in *Four Quartets,* Eliot will return to the natural places of his youth and his ancestry, but even then it will be something closer to a Renaissance or Augustan retreat to a civilized country estate (Jonson's Penshurst, Marvell's Appleton House, or Pope's Twickenham Garden) than the permanent cottage residence of the Lake poets.

Thus, in his reaction to modern urban life, Eliot takes up one of the primary themes of Romantic poetry but then eschews the Romantic view in which nature reflects the poet's mind, taking on subjective rather than objective meaning. Instead, he adopts the classical mode of seeking to harmonize civil and natural life—polis and cosmos. It is not certain that Eliot had read "To Penshurst" at this period, but let us take it as an exemplar of the pre-Cartesian response to civil society and nature. Jonson praises Penshurst for avoiding the vanity of country houses "built to envious show." Instead, he writes, "Thou joy'st in better marks, of soil, of air, / Of wood, of water; therein thou art fair." The elements there are pure, and the house that joys in them rather than in the artifice of "marble" and "polished pillars" offers the true civility Jonson goes on to describe, from a bounteous board to a moral and happy family life centered in religion. Like Jonson, Eliot finds that regard for the natural elements combines with reverence for the Creator who transcends nature. With models like this in mind, he is beginning to search in his early poetry for what he will find at Burnt Norton and Little Gidding. As yet, he can only show the lack of such a place in the cities as he knows them.

"The Love Song of J. Alfred Prufrock": City Rooms and Sea Chambers

The opening of the "Love Song" promises a Romantic retreat from Boston, only to dash the mood upon an unnatural simile:

> Let us go then, you and I,
> When the evening is spread out against the sky
> Like a patient etherised upon a table. . . .

C. S. Lewis criticized this for being an unimaginable metaphor: "For twenty years I've stared my level best / To see if evening—any evening— would suggest / A patient etherised upon a table."[3] Surely, though, the strange inadequacy of the metaphor is the point: the natural Romantic diction of the first two lines suddenly is translated into something artificial and mundane. Fine sentiment yields to total lack of sentience in the anaesthetized impersonal "patient"; Romanticism proves impossible in the face of modern life, depersonalized by medical science. As Hugh Kenner has pointed out, the pattern of dashing Romantic idylls is contained in the title itself, where the name of the would-be lover undercuts the idea of a love song.[4] Marion Montgomery compares these opening lines with Wordsworth's "It is a beauteous evening calm and free." Montgomery, better than any other critic I have read, captures Eliot's ambivalence toward Wordsworth:

Eliot, as we know from his criticism, does not accept Wordsworth's emotional involvement with nature such as we see it revealed in "It Is a Beauteous Evening." Still, he is aware of a decline in the possibility of such involvements on the part of our wasteland world. Prufrock may be taken as an ironic commentary on that inability. . . .[5]

The Romantic discovery of human value in nature is a reaction to the idea of a meaningless material world—an idea promulgated by mechanistic science. Whitehead would write that the Romantics offered a kind of immediate and total experience of the world as an antidote to abstract materialism: "Berkeley, Wordsworth, Shelley are representative of the intuitive refusal seriously to accept the abstract materialism of science."[6] Eliot has the same reaction, but he finds the Romantic response inadequate in that it simply overemphasizes the opposite pole. Prufrock attempts a Romantic response to the evening, but it does not work: the only metaphor that will come to mind is a scientific one.

Nevertheless, the ether simile does work imaginatively in the way Lewis demands if we read "etherised" in the ancient sense, in which *aether* ordinarily means (in both Greek and Latin) "sky." To be "etherised" in this sense could mean to be "spread out against the sky." For instance, it is the word Virgil uses when he describes Jupiter looking down from the highest heavens:

> Et iam finis erat, cum Iuppiter aethere summo
> despiciens mare velivolum. . . .
>
> (*Aeneid*, I.223–24)

[Now all was ended, when from sky's summit Jupiter looked forth upon the sail-winged sea.][7]

After being visited by Mercury, Aeneas calls to his men,

> deus aethere missus ab alto
> festinare fugam tortosque incidere funis
> ecce iterum instimulat.
>
> (IV.574–76)

[A god sent from high heaven, lo! again spurs us to hasten our flight and cut the twisted cables.]

Another Virgilian example, from the *Georgics*, almost seems to be echoed in *The Waste Land*, though the contexts are quite different. "What is that sound high in the air / Murmur of maternal lamentation," Eliot writes. Virgil describes bees going forth to battle:

> aethere in alto
> fit sonitus, magnum mixtae glomerantur in orbem
> praecipitesque cadunt. . . .
>
> (*Georgics*, IV.78–80)

[in high air arises a din; they are mingled and massed in one great ball, then tumble headlong.]

"In high air a sound is made" would be a more literal translation. It seems unlikely that Eliot's line is directly derived from this one, but his reading of the classics in their original languages settled such translations in his ear, so that when he writes "high in the air" or "spread out against the sky" he inevitably has aether in mind.[8]

This pun in the opening lines of the poem reinforces the shock of the un-Romantic metaphor: to be etherized in the modern sense is to be rendered unconscious, or as Eliot will put it in *East Coker,* "under ether, the mind is conscious, but conscious of nothing." From intimations of the egotistical sublime in the first two lines, we are jarred into a deprivation of both ego-consciousness and sublimity, becoming aware of nothing. In the later poem, this mindlessness has potential for becoming "the way of ignorance" traveled by the mystic, but there is little hope of that here. The epigraph tells us we are in the infernal regions, not the heavenly ones. All the same, since Dante returned in spite of Guido's assurance that no one could and since there is a reference to "Lazarus, come from the dead, / Come back to tell you all," there is at least a hint of such hope, though Prufrock seems entirely incapable of following it. Piers Gray suggests an interesting reading based on Bergson's idea that being unconscious frees the mind to travel in memory. The unconsciousness induced by ether might then be seen as liberating in this way.[9] Eliot's notes on William James's *Varieties of Religious Experience* record a suggestion that ether can induce a positive religious experience: "*Nitrous oxide* (+ ether) stimulate mystical consciousness."[10] Thus, "etherised" may suggest dimly the possibility of a truly poetic and spiritual experience.

Other lines in the poem echo the opening image of the immobilized and negatively etherized persona. There are

> The eyes that fix you in a formulated phrase,
> And when I am formulated, sprawling on a pin,
> When I am pinned and wriggling on the wall,
> Then how should I begin. . . .

This image is in horrible contrast to the Romantic vision of the evening spread out against the sky. The Romantic poet would find his own soul merging with the evening. Eliot disliked the Romantics, to be sure, but his reaction to them was partly a sorrowful recognition that such a merging with nature was impossible to imagine in the scientific age in which nature had been explained away reductively. Prufrock is a would-be Romantic who keeps coming up against two harsh realities, social and scientific, which prevent his union with the cosmos. Here the social challenge, "the eyes that fix you," modulates into the scientific dissection of reality, including himself. Like a zoological specimen, he is pinned on the wall, and here we should recognize the patient on the table. The word "formulated" may recall the formaldehyde used to preserve specimens in biology laboratories. The word also suggests the way mechanistic science threatens to reduce human nature to a formula, to physical laws that do not allow for the act that our antihero is struggling to perform, an act of free will. At the same time, the "formulated phrase" suggests the reduction of human language to formulaic scientific terms.[11] This image captures the essence of the behaviorist psychological theory, which was gaining momentum at the time, an attempt to abolish man, as C. S. Lewis was to put it, by reducing what has been called "human nature" to a deterministic stimulus-response formula. Perhaps Prufrock's incapacitating self-consciousness also reflects the other materialistic reduction of human nature, the Freudian one, which was already producing many sophisticated people who could not act without analyzing themselves and yet had little hope that they could really choose their actions.

Another line closely related to the opening image also debunks Prufrock's Romantic impulses: "But as if a magic lantern threw the nerves in patterns on a screen." The magic lantern could easily become a way of joining the natural and human worlds in a Romantic synthesis. One thinks of Coleridge's Eolian harp, which intones "the one life, within us and abroad, / Which meets all motion, and becomes its soul." Instead, this magic lantern is a scientific instrument, an X-ray machine that throws the nerves, the material explanation for what we have traditionally called "soul," onto a screen. Robert Crawford has reproduced an illustration of just such an X-ray lantern from an article entitled "Seeing the Brain" published in the *St. Louis Globe-Democrat* of 17 January 1897.[12] Where in an earlier world the aetherized person might have felt his soul lifted to the heavens in union with God and nature, in the modern world of science and society, he actually ends up being pinned to a wall, cut open on a table, or projected on a screen.

If we glance for a moment from "Prufrock" to the "Preludes" in the same volume, we find Eliot again thinking of a literal image of a person "spread out against the sky" like the evening:

> His soul stretched tight across the skies
> That fade behind a city block,
> Or trampled by insistent feet
> At four and five and six o'clock. . . .

Here, too, the artificial world cuts off the natural, as the skies fade behind the houses, and the focus quickly shifts in both poems from the heavens to the streets. The "Love Song" continues, "Let us go through certain half-deserted streets." A brief, tortured glance upward is all the protagonist can manage: what he sees there instead of the heavenly aether holding the stars in their courses is his own intolerable emptiness.

The earthly elements also figure in "Prufrock," but they have been degraded by human manipulation and pollution:

> The yellow fog that rubs its back upon the window-panes,
> The yellow smoke that rubs its muzzle on the window-panes
> Licked its tongue into the corners of the evening,
> Lingered upon the pools that stand in drains,
> Let fall upon its back the soot that falls from chimneys. . . .

The fog is a natural mixture of air and water, but it is also polluted by soot and smoke from the chimneys, the sole source of fire in the sunless world of this poem, except for the *fiamma* from which Guido speaks in the epigraph. The pools of water cannot hold life, for they are standing pools, stagnant, with no wind moving over them. By contrast, there will be in *Burnt Norton* a "dry concrete" pool that is suddenly "filled with water out of sunlight" in a moment of elemental union. In these city pools, no such transformation is imaginable.

Part of the problem with the material surroundings in the city has to do with work. There is no work going on, nothing being done or made. There will be "time for all the works and days of hands / That lift and drop a question on your plate," but dropping a question is not the work of hands. This is a purely intellectual world, in contrast to the agricultural world of Hesiod's *Works and Days*. Work with hands is always a procreative act because the worker must cooperate with the created matter at his disposal in order to make something new. The temptation of the intellect, to which Eliot saw many modern intellectuals succumb, is to remake the world in whatever image it fancies, toying with "a hundred visions and revisions" that are all out of touch with reality. This attitude leads to a grandiose notion of being able to "murder and create," but not to real creative work within the limits of human nature.

The traditional agricultural life, on the other hand, has the potential for correspondence with the reality of both the natural and supernatural orders, as Eliot claims in a passage (quoted above, chapter 1) in *The Idea of a Christian Society:* "We may say that religion, as distinguished from modern paganism, implies a life in conformity with nature. It may be observed that the natural life and the supernatural life have a conformity to each other which neither has with the mechanistic life. . . ."[13] This "mechanistic life" is the modern urban world, designed by the intellect in triumph over nature and in scorn of religious truth: the work of mind and machine, not soul and hands. At the time when he was writing the poems in this volume, Eliot was reacting to this mechanistic world in a purely negative or satiric way, having, as it were, nowhere else to go. By the time he writes *The Idea of a Christian Society* and *Four Quartets,* he will have found somewhere else. Instead of "time yet for a hundred indecisions," the poet will find in the more real world of *East Coker* time ordered by the physical cosmos and Hesiod's peasants working productively in concert with it: "The time of the seasons and the constellations / The time of milking and the time of harvest." Instead of time measured by coffee spoons, the poet will find no time that is "oceanless." Instead of assuming that time runs in a straight line, as one does in "The *Boston Evening Transcript*" by imagining that "the street were time" and by marking its passage artificially with the appearance of the evening edition of the newspaper, Eliot will find time looping back on itself in the cycles of natural time marked by the four seasons in the *Quartets.*

When Prufrock later sighs, "I should have been a pair of ragged claws / Scuttling across the floors of silent seas," he reveals his lack of real identity, but in another way, this could be a healing image. His instinctual desire is to start over, to devolve and begin again as a truly unconscious creature in the real ocean, the "silent seas" where life originates. As Crawford comments, "The presentation of a reversion to the primitive evolutionary history of the race promises an escape from the complexities of civilized life."[14] Like Phlebas the Phoenician of "Dans le Restaurant" and *The Waste Land,* Prufrock might pass "the stages of his age and youth" and be given the possibility of rebirth. The crab suggests this movement. Hamlet says to Polonius, "you yourself, sir, should be as old as I am, if like a crab you could go backwards" (II.ii).[15] The "silent seas" also hold promise, for moments of true silence may produce contemplative renewal, which is impossible in the "muttering retreats" of the city. Should he really give himself to the dissolution of the sea rather than to whatever dissolute social visit he is intent on, Prufrock might come through a sea change to a state he has envisioned but despairs of experiencing, one in which the sexual relation would recover something of its elemental purity. If the opposing elements can dissolve, be purified, and recombine, so can the sexes.

In the vision of the mermaids at the end of the poem, the elements are natural and potentially life giving:

> I have seen them riding seaward on the waves
> Combing the white hair of the waves blown back
> When the wind blows the water white and black.

These beautiful lines set up, as Bornstein has pointed out, a "contrast between the sea and tea worlds."[16] The sea world is one found in Roman-

tic poetry, yet there is also a new note introduced, more biblical than
mythical. In contrast to "the pools that stand in drains," this water is
living because the wind is moving over it, as in Genesis, where "the Spirit
of God moved upon the face of the waters" (1:2). Hence, it is not fully
adequate to interpret this passage the way Bornstein does, as an eruption
of Romantic lyricism the author fears and wishes to control. It may be
just that to the poetic persona, but the poet himself is introducing a new
symbology which will eventually make it possible for him to resolve the
Romantic dichotomy between subject and object, man and nature.

Prufrock has heard the mermaids, apparently meeting one of the impossible challenges set by Donne in his "Song": "Go and catch a falling
star, . . . Teach me to hear mermaids singing." He is ill-prepared, however, to discover the one wonder Donne refuses to believe, that there is
anywhere "a woman true, and fair." Unlike both Donne and Marvell, the
metaphysical poets alluded to in the poem, he has not even imagined
testing a woman's virtue. The women seem to him impossibly distant and
self-possessed, talking of Michelangelo or responding (with perhaps a
sense of linguistic arbitrariness) "That is not what I meant, at all." Even
though he has heard the mermaids, he does not think they will sing to
him. Here is a man so cut off from the rest of the world that even the
mermaids have no wish to lure him to his death! Again, the Romantic
impulse is dashed against some kind of strange modern social reality.

The best thing that could happen to this man, as we have already seen
in the vision of the crab going backward in silent seas, would be to drown
and dissolve, because that would give the chance of rebirth. On the psychological or spiritual level, this means that to become his real self, he
would have to give up his self-consciousness. The mermaids' song would
draw him toward such a death, if he could even believe they sang to him.
A person aetherized in the old sense would be similarly dissolved in the
aether, but the modern drug produces only a mock dissolving of self.
Though "We have lingered in the chambers of the sea" with the "sea-
girls," the realities of the modern world made too conscious by science
and scientific psychology will not permit us to yield to this call from the
unconscious depths of nature. The final line is a total reversal of the
expectation (both Romantic and classical) that the protagonist will be
lulled into a slumber by the singing and drowned. The drowning now
happens when "human voices wake us," recalling us to the urban society,
to all the attenuated human voices in the poem: "Talking of Michelangelo," "muttering retreats," "a formulated phrase," "talk of you and me,"
etc. The city is full of talk but poor in speech directed to another person,
heart-to-heart speech. Singing comes from the heart as well as the head
and is thus quite different from all these intellectual, social voices. Just
as one can be "redeemed from fire by fire," one could be saved from

drowning in the babble of voices by being drowned in the singing and the sea, in the natural and mythic world.

Mankind's relation to the cosmos is in question in this poem: "Do I dare / Disturb the universe?" Kenner comments that "the switch from social to cosmic" in this line is "typical."[17] Indeed it is, for throughout the poem one comes across ironic contrasts between the social setting and the natural one. Let us explore the direction of this irony for a moment. Prufrock wishes to "have squeezed the universe into a ball." Marvell's words were "Let us roll all our strength, and all / Our sweetness up into one ball," which would be consolidating the personal, social relation of persona and mistress, not the universe, but which would give them some power over the latter: "Thus, though we cannot make our sun / Stand still, yet we will make him run." Scientism does not allow for such fancies. There is no connection, even fanciful, possible between macrocosm and microcosm now that the uncreated universe operates according to quantitative laws rather than hierarchical qualitative correspondences. In the Renaissance cosmos, one can imagine affecting the course of the sun through one's own actions (especially in relation to another), by rolling all the strength and sweetness of self and beloved into a ball. In the modern cosmos, the mechanist might hope "to have squeezed the universe into a ball," reducing it by force of intellect into something manageable. The earlier attitude is more humble and playful; the later, more proud and somber. This is Prufrock's despair, to be caught between the two worlds—a poetic temperament stranded in a social, rational, mechanical world.

"PORTRAIT OF A LADY": LIFE INDOORS

The "Portrait of a Lady" continues, in a yet more subtle and equivocal way, the satire of modern society cut off from nature and human nature. Like Prufrock, the Lady thinks in Romantic modes but lives in society, indoors, quite out of touch with the elements.[18] There is no sun but only "four wax candles in the darkened room," recalling Juliet's tomb. The inner flame of the poet-persona is correspondingly weak: "My self-possession flares up for a second. . . . My self-possession gutters; we are really in the dark." The impulse to get out and breathe—"Let us take the air, in a tobacco trance"—is frustrated by the realization that the outside air is also impure. Even if there is, at the end, an imagined moment outside and away from the Lady, the air is expected to be polluted: "Well! and what if she should die some afternoon, / Afternoon grey and smoky." Of course, Boston and other cities at that time *were* smoky because houses were heated with coal. Today, even the famous London fog is not so yellow and oppressive as it was in those bituminous days. This smoky air and the weak candle flames comprise the whole range of the natural elements in this claustrophobic poem—except for the brief, quickly stifled, whiff of spring in Part II.

The first part takes place in December, but at the beginning of the second part, the Lady has lilacs—it is April. The hope these flowers might occasion is soon strangled, though, as she "twists one in her fingers while she talks." She continues twisting it unconsciously while addressing her young visitor: "Ah, my friend, you do not know, you do not know / What life is, you who hold it in your hands." What she says seems true of the young man, but it is more obviously true of herself, for she holds life in her hands and does not know it, with the result that she damages it. Still, she momentarily becomes conscious of the outer world and is reminded of a better time:

> Yet with these April sunsets, that somehow recall
> My buried life, and Paris in the Spring,
> I feel immeasurably at peace, and find the world
> To be wonderful and youthful, after all.

There is still something artificial about the expression, but real feeling comes into her voice for a moment.

Matthew Arnold's "The Buried Life," alluded to here, begins with a similar desire to drop the social responses of the public persona and speak from the "hidden self":

> We know, we know that we can smile!
> But there's a something in this breast,
> To which the light words bring no rest
> And thy gay smiles no anodyne.

The "light words" here become the "velleities" (slightest of desires, barely willed) of Eliot's poem, and the smiles become those of the persona: "My smile falls heavily among the bric-a-brac"; "I feel like one who smiles, and turning shall remark / Suddenly, his expression in a glass"; "And should I have the right to smile?" These smiles are the most common way "To prepare a face to meet the faces that you meet" (in Prufrock's words). Arnold asks his beloved that they drop this mask, at least with each other, because he is aware even in "the world's most crowded streets," of

> A longing to inquire
> Into the mystery of this heart which beats
> So wild, so deep in us.

For a moment in the "Portrait," while listening to refined music, the persona becomes aware of his own heartbeat: "Inside my brain a dull tom-tom begins / Absurdly hammering a prelude of its own." Is the tom-tom the name of the poet himself, his own hidden self?[19] It is a primal rhythm, which contrasts with the Chopin Preludes to which they listen, the type of rhythm that is conjured up by what Eliot calls the "auditory imagination," which he defines as "the feeling for syllable and rhythm, penetrating far below the conscious levels of thought and feeling, invigorating every word; sinking to the most primitive and forgotten, returning to the origin and bringing something back, seeking the beginning and the end." The auditory imagination, he adds, "fuses . . . the most ancient and the most civilised mentality."[20] In Eliot's theory, if one's refined ideas are to become poetry, they must fit the simple primeval rhythm of the tribal drum. In these early poems, the deep music of the verse does hold our attention to the twisting and turning ironies. The tom-tom is, then, Arnold's wild heart and Tom Eliot's "hidden self," whose dull rhythms keep his auditory imagination attuned to deeper patterns amidst the complexities of his mind, preventing the separation of thought and feeling, consciousness and the unconscious, modern and primitive.

Arnold is not with a spinster socialite but with his wife, and they are able to touch hands and speak from their true selves. When they do, nature enters the poem:

> A man becomes aware of his life's flow
> And hears its winding murmur; and he sees
> The meadows where it glides, the sun, the breeze.

When he is true to his own nature for a moment, he sees the nature of the world, earth, fire, and air in their essential purity. Because human nature is compacted of the elements, his life flow becomes the watery element gliding through the meadow. Finally, Arnold envisions the union of his nature (at birth and death) with the elements:

> And then he thinks he knows
> The hills where his life rose,
> And the sea where it goes.

Eliot's persona in the "Portrait" hears the beating of his heart, but in the artificial setting, it can only seem a "false note." In the spring section, he too is aware of nature, but like Prufrock, he is unable to think it has to do with him. He remains "self-possessed," hidden behind his smile,

> Except when a street piano, mechanical and tired
> Reiterates some worn-out common song

> With the smell of hyacinths across the garden
> Recalling things that other people have desired.

Though it is mechanical, this song hits a "false note," like the tom-tom of his heart, and it similarly awakens more in him than does the music of Chopin, as it is preciously interpreted by "the latest Pole," who transmits it "through his hair and fingertips." The song blends with the smell of hyacinths, which are also common and reiterated every year, yet alive. Here is an elemental vision of release into a garden of innocence and fruitfulness, but just as Prufrock thinks when he hears the mermaids that they will not sing for him and just as the man in Part I of *The Waste Land* "could not speak" to the woman of the hyacinth garden, this young man rejects the vision as something "other people have desired."

For people in such a state of mind, April is indeed the cruelest month, for then they cannot quite ignore the stirrings of life to which they are nevertheless powerless to respond. The Harvard student is already caught in the effete reactions of the sophisticate to all that is common, and no doubt the more negative connotation the Renaissance gave to the word— as in Hamlet's "Aye, madam, 'tis common"—is heard. Hence, he cannot respond to the "common song" and the common desires so many others have felt. His is the intellectual indecision of Prufrock: "Are these ideas right or wrong? . . . And should I have the right to smile?" Answers could come only from what is most common: the elements, the seasons, love of woman, "things that other people have desired." They will come in *Four Quartets,* whose first epigraph from Heraclitus cautions that "Although the Logos is common to all, most men live as if each had a private wisdom of his own"—especially men like Prufrock and the young man in the "Portrait," who are engaged exclusively in their own thoughts. Answers will come in *Little Gidding* when he meets the "familiar compound ghost" of previous poets and walks with the ghost "compliant to a common wind." Only in relation to the elemental realities, to the common wind or the tom-tom that beats through world and self, can one know oneself. Only thus can one know the other as well and enter genuinely into the "friendships" the Lady pretends to have with her young visitors: "Without these friendships—life, what *cauchemar!*" As the poem ends in October with thoughts of her death unlamented by the cold young man, we realize that the poet has indeed taken us into that nightmare.

OTHER OBSERVATIONS: GRIMY SCRAPS IN VACANT LOTS

The "Preludes" are titled in contrast to the Chopin Preludes heard in the "Portrait," and the "Rhapsody on a Windy Night" is similarly contrasted with beautiful Romantic music, which Eliot was finding impossible to hear in the Unreal City. Guided by the symbolists, he was searching to capture a more troubled beauty—broken in many ways, yet still suggesting wholeness and primal meaning.

The Parisian images of these two poems are more sordid than the Bostonian ones that dominate in the rest of the volume. The problem is essentially the same—the artificial world of the city removing people from both the true physical world and their true selves, from nature and human nature—but the Parisian artificiality is less proper and also less *propre* in the French sense, less clean. There is an overwhelming awareness of what happens to the "earth" or "soil" of the forests and farmlands when a city is built upon them. As fields become "streets" and "lots," the fertile "soil" becomes "dirt." We find ourselves in a world of "dingy shades" indoors and "grimy scraps / Of withered leaves" outdoors. A woman clasps "the yellow soles of feet / In the palms of both soiled hands." In *East Coker,* the "earth feet, loam feet" of the farmers will be totally identified with the land, made of the dust into which they will return. City feet are presumed to be distinctly human, never really touching the earth to be reminded of their origin, yet inevitably the dust is there, and the feet are yellowed by it, taking on the same dingy, sickly color as the polluted yellow fog. As when unconscious complexes are not confronted, the reality of the element is experienced in an uglier way when it is ignored: "loam feet" become merely "muddy feet." In the same way, the urban hands reject their connection with the soil, in which they have never worked, yet they are "soiled," experiencing the fertile earth only as filth. In the "Rhapsody," a woman's dress is "stained with sand," and one is aware of "dust in crevices."

This sense of filth is even stronger in one of Eliot's sources, discovered by Grover Smith. Charles-Louis Philippe writes in *Bubu de Montparnasse,*

> At noon, in the hotel room of the rue Chanoinesse, a grey and dirty light filtered through the grey curtains and dirty panes of the window . . . and there was the unmade bed where the two bodies had left their impress of brownish sweat upon the worn sheets—this bed of hotel rooms, where the bodies are dirty and the souls as well.[21]

In the "Preludes," the grime and sordidness may be unrelieved but they are not presented as all that exists or could exist. Eliot is not, of course, already projecting *Four Quartets* as an answer, but he is aware of the city's dirt as a perversion of something real rather than as something in itself. The natural world hovers somewhere beyond the rooflines. As in "Prufrock," the first prelude begins with evening, a Romantic natural reality, and then yields to mundane artifice: "The winter evening settles down / With smell of steaks in passageways." Instead of being the quiet fading of the day into rest, the evenings in this city are "The burnt-out ends of smoky days." In the morning, too, there is a glimmer of reality:

> And when all the world came back
> And the light crept up between the shutters
> And you heard the sparrows in the gutters. . . .

Nature might be about to assert herself in her fullness: "all the world," the whole cosmos beyond the passageways and streets, comes back. But the light barely creeps between the shutters, being mostly kept out, and one hears only sparrows, city birds, in the (no doubt dirty) gutters—not larks in the sky or robins in the trees or the thrush of *Burnt Norton* leading us "Into our first world" (*BN,* I). The real world is almost imminent in these cityscapes. Eliot is not merely attempting realism or naturalism in his mundane descriptions but is precisely revealing that all this is unreal, a denial of "all the world," which keeps coming back all the same. The "blackened street" is "Impatient to assume the world," but this means only assuming the weight of the "insistent feet" that will tread on it. "The world" means only people, not the encompassing cosmos, which is not assumed to exist by those who walk down the street. At the same time, these human beings are merely extensions of their material surroundings. As Eric Sigg puts it, the poem works by "inviting us to apply the qualities of their circumstances to the people themselves. The connotative shift from inanimate to human subjects constitutes the poem's psychological method."[22] Scientific materialism both cuts modern man off from nature and reduces him to it.

Let us look more closely at the beginning and end of the "Preludes," the passages that frame this sordid place. After the opening lines in which the evening falls,

> a gusty shower wraps
> The grimy scraps
> Of withered leaves about your feet
> And newspapers from vacant lots;
> The showers beat
> On broken blinds and chimney-pots. . . .

The waste land might be renewed by this "gusty shower," which will appear at the climax of the later poem as "a damp gust / Bringing rain." In both poems, it is the spiritual wind that breaks the spell of dryness. Whereas in Part V of *The Waste Land* the rain is coming to a place in the mountains, however, in the earlier poem it falls on no fertile soil but on grimy scraps of leaves, newspapers, blinds, and chimney pots. The only natural objects, the leaves, are covered in city grime and have not been composted in soil. All else is artifact: earth has been made into earthenware chimney pots (the pipes projecting from the tops of chimneys). The vacant lots are fruitful only in litter. The elements seek to act in their natural harmony, with wind bringing rain to earth that will be warmed to life by the sun's fire, but the earth is not there—or only enough to produce a little mud that clings to the feet. Nor is the sun: the opening passage ends with "the lighting of the lamps," a poor artificial substitute.

The vacant lots are a pathetic analogue to the vast "vacant interstellar spaces" of *East Coker.* These grander cosmic vacuities seem to have been in the poet's mind early on: the "spaces of the dark" in the "Rhapsody" also seem to point toward them, as do the "vacant shuttles" that "weave the wind" and the "fractured atoms" (with the implied vacuum between them) which are "whirled / Beyond the circuit of the shuddering Bear" in "Gerontion." Eloise Knapp Hay, in her insightful book focusing on Eliot's negative way, follows Lyndall Gordon in confirming that the young poet was thinking much about vacancy:

> Exploration of the void, either as a stasis or as a "way," was already a project of Eliot's during his philosophical studies and in his first poetry notebook, before he began to publish professionally, as Lyndall Gordon has recently shown. His resolute turn from Western forms of "affirmative" religions to the study of Buddhism and primitive religions paralleled philosophical movements in the first two decades of the twentieth century which also were probing the uses of negation.[23]

In thinking of the void, however, Eliot would have been aware of the dictum of scholastic physics, that "Nature abhors a vacuum." He knew that everyone except the Greek atomists and their latter-day scientific descendants had assumed that the divine quintessence, a substance both material and spiritual in nature, filled the void. The vacant lots of the "Preludes" should be so filled with the Word but are instead littered with words, words, words—newspapers. The implicit cosmic analogue to the vacant lots intensifies the pathos and the satire of the description.

The poem ends in these vacant lots, with more hints of another order of being: "The worlds revolve like ancient women / Gathering fuel in vacant lots." The lots would correspond in the microcosm of the city to the apparently empty space in which the worlds revolve above, except that the modern city has not been consciously constructed as a microcosm, the way many ancient cities were. In *Four Quartets,* the tension of boarhound and boar on the earth is seen as "reconciled among the stars": the violence of the lower world is resolved in peaceful yet dynamic tension above. In this early poem, however, the reverse happens: the worlds imitate the ancient women, just as the evening in "Prufrock" takes on the character of the etherised patient. The women of "Preludes" are not only old but "ancient," reminiscent of some bygone culture in which they would perhaps have been enacting a kind of ritual dance affirming the connection between the human world and the cosmos. Such a mythic consciousness of dynamic totality has been quite lost in the world Eliot now describes, where the purpose of the old women is strictly human and material: they seek not wood for a sacred bonfire that will relume the sun but mere abstract "fuel"—perhaps processed bits of wood, newspapers. In Eliade's terms, this is a strictly profane world:

> From the point of view of profane existence, man feels no responsibility except to himself and to society. For him, the universe does not properly constitute a cosmos—that is, a living and articulated unity; it is simply the sum of the material reserves and physical energies of the planet, and the great concern of modern man is to avoid stupidly exhausting the economic resources of the globe. But, existentially, the primitive always puts himself in a cosmic context.[24]

Eliot often uses language that places his descriptions in the sacred, mythic context, while making it clear that this context remains inaccessible to the characters within the poem. These ancient women should be part of the cosmic context of which Eliade speaks, but they remain in the narrowly circumscribed material lots of the profane city.

When the four elements are degraded and secularized, the fifth is completely forgotten. In the heavens of the ancients, aether filled the vacancy between the stars as myth filled the mind's mysteries, but these vacant lots and the minds of the human beings inhabiting them are truly empty. The world view of abstract materialism sees no hierarchy and no *telos,* only a material equivalency of certain actions (revolving, for example) on different scales. Hence, the likeness between women and worlds is not that of microcosm and macrocosm, connected analogically and spiritually, but a flat material resemblance. A profound symbol becomes a mere metaphor. At the same time, Eliot the symbolist is attempting to renew the symbolic connection, even as he describes its disintegration, for his description of the women does evoke a certain sense of depth and power.

In the rest of the poem, there is a strange reversal of roles between animate and inanimate. The physical world has consciousness: "The morning comes to consciousness"; the street "hardly understands" a vision but implicitly could be imagined to understand it; the street has a "conscience" and is "Impatient to assume the world." On the other hand, the people hardly seem conscious. They are reduced, as Smith points out, to parts of themselves: "muddy feet that press / To early coffee-stands" and "the hands / That are raising dingy shades" and "short square fingers stuffing pipes" and "eyes / Assured of certain certainties."[25] When there is some incipient consciousness, as in these eyes which know something certain, the consciousness is really strictly of material matters, and this is, I think, the point of the reversal. Eliot is envisioning human beings who really are completely determined by their material environment, as various modern deterministic ideologies claim they are. Hence, we find that the very soul is only a collection of images from its surroundings:

> You dozed, and watched the night revealing
> The thousand sordid images
> Of which your soul was constituted. . . .

The night does the revealing; the soul is passive, being merely a sum total of its experience. This concept of the self is that of many modern philosophers, beginning with Locke, whose soul is a tabula rasa on which experience writes, and leading to the associationist school of psychology. Behaviorism owes much to Locke's views on the psyche, and many people were beginning to take its scientific pretensions very seriously in the early part of the century.

For a moment, when the sun creeps in between the shutters and the sparrows chirp, the soul seems to become something more: "You had such a vision of the street / As the street hardly understands." Smith finds even here no real distinction between the woman and the street: "Prufrock, while cringing immobilized before the actual, does not relinquish the preferable ideal; but the woman and the street not only do not have any such ideal in reserve but, indeed cannot have—for their consciousness and the external scenes are identical."[26] Smith is identifying the same problem of a consciousness totally determined by its environment, but it does seem to me that there is a momentary escape from it here. Perhaps it would be better to say that the merging of consciousness with the external world has here a positive potential for uniting subject and object in Bradleyan immediate experience.

Finally, no Romantic retreat to the country will relieve the horror of this poem. The only way out is through the depths of hell, so the only real hope in the poem is in the "infinitely gentle / Infinitely suffering thing." This is still a "thing," a material body, but it must also be a person, for there is no true suffering without consciousness. Hay is mostly right in emphasizing that the negative way of the early poetry is not the redemptive mystical way of the later poems, but surely this *infinitely* suffering one is one appearance in a very early poem of the Suffering Servant, though only as yet a half-conscious "fancy" or "notion." Sigg has it right, I think, when he says that "It would be difficult to argue that 'Preludes' portrays Christian faith" but adds, "More likely it renders that awkward if not uncommon state, a Christian sensibility without Christian belief."[27] Eliot glances sideways here at the Christian resolution of the divisions he is examining. By becoming a "thing," a body in the objective world, the Redeemer may save both the fallen soul and the fallen world, restoring them to their Edenic harmony. In other words, the Incarnation symbolizes the total union of subject and object.

"Rhapsody on a Windy Night" contains many familiar Eliot images but has always struck me as an anomaly. Perhaps the young poet only borrowed from Laforgue here, failing to steal. The ironic treatment of the Romantic moon is certainly a close study of the French symbolist. Nevertheless, Eliot does continue to contemplate poetically the relations between natural and human worlds.

It is the dead of night, and the fire of the sun is notably absent. Instead, the poem is punctuated by the sputtering and muttering of the streetlamps until the lonely wanderer returns to his apartment house, where "The little lamp spreads a ring on the stair." In "The Fire Sermon," fire will be similarly artificial and dim, especially when the "young man carbuncular" leaves his typist and "gropes his way, finding the stairs unlit." The corresponding inner fire is also dim in both poems. Even the fires of lust barely smolder as the young clerk finds his advances "unreproved, if undesired" and the protagonist of the "Rhapsody" (a passionate genre) apparently turns away from the prostitute shown to him by the streetlamp.

Presumably the moon is shining, but "She winks a feeble eye"—no real light or passion shines from her either. She recalls, in fact, the "Portrait of a Lady" as "Her hand twists a paper rose, / That smells of dust and eau de Cologne." This image captures the morbidity of the natural elements. Even the lilacs twisted by the Boston Lady are now only an artificial paper rose or the "sunless dry geraniums" a few lines later. The earth in which a real flower might grow is, of course, only dust; and the water needed by the plant is present only as a kind of artificial social water, eau de Cologne.

There is a shift in the sense imagery from sight to smell. Most of the poem is visual: "Regard"; "you see"; "Remark"; "I could see"; "I have seen"; "She winks a feeble eye." However, the next-to-last passage shifts to the sense of smell with "the old nocturnal smells" that cross the moon's brain:

> Smells of chestnuts in the streets,
> And female smells in shuttered rooms,
> And cigarettes in corridors
> And cocktail smells in bars.

Now, smell has always been regarded, at least from Plato on, as the lowest of the senses and sight as the highest. Smell is physical, primal, animal, while sight is intellectual, social, human. In this sunless city, the eyes are enfeebled and the nose takes over. The "divisions and precisions" of the rational visual memory break down, leaving only olfactory "reminiscence" crossing and crossing the brain chaotically. If these smells were at least natural, they might inspire deeper, truer responses, as happens in *King Lear* when Gloucester finds his way better after he is blinded and told to smell his way to Dover. In Eliot's city, however, the smells are mostly of indoor social settings. The "female smells in shuttered rooms" prefigure the "room enclosed" and the "strange synthetic perfumes" in Part II of *The Waste Land*. The "Windy Night" of the title might bring new smells, but it is shut out, much as the wind is kept outside the door in "A Game of Chess." The wind carries odors to the lowest of the senses, but it is also the spirit blowing where it will. In both its lower and higher functions, it is kept out of the enclosed rooms.

The tension between sight and smell reflects a struggle between the rational, daytime memory and the midnight "lunar synthesis":

> Twelve o'clock.
> Along the reaches of the street
> Held in a lunar synthesis,
> Whispering lunar incantations
> Dissolve the floors of memory
> And all its clear relations
> Its divisions and precisions,
> Every street lamp that I pass
> Beats like a fatalistic drum,
> And through the spaces of the dark
> Midnight shakes the memory
> As a madman shakes a dead geranium.

If Eliot desires a mythic or mystic experience of totality, this "lunar synthesis," which breaks down mental divisions, would seem promising. The problem is that this witching-hour synthesis overwhelms and dissolves divisions rather than integrating them. Poetry is created, Eliot later wrote, when incantation blends with thought. Here the memory, with its clear relations, stands for thought, while the "fatalistic drum" of the "lunar incantations" sounds the primal rhythm that must carry the thought.

However, no such harmony is achieved in the mind of the poetic persona. At the end of the poem, it is 4:00 A.M., and memory reasserts itself as the night wanderer returns to his room and day approaches:

"Here is the number on the door.
Memory!
You have the key,
The little lamp spreads a ring on the stair.
Mount.
The bed is open; the tooth-brush hangs on the wall,
Put your shoes at the door, sleep, prepare for life."

The last twist of the knife.

He returns hopelessly to number and order, conscious arrangement. Memory's artificial compartmentalizing is deadly here; but it need not be, for memory is the mother of the muses and ought to be, by rights, a kind of stabilizing element in that lunar synthesis. After all, memory unifies time as well as dividing it up, so it has a synthetic function too, but one that tries to maintain continuity in time. Something has gone all wrong: the midnight rhapsody, instead of playing fancifully with the memory to make new combinations appear, "shakes the memory / As a madman shakes a dead geranium."

The "spaces of the dark" between streetlamps represent the mundane equivalent of the interstellar spaces, and it is here that one might experience the aethereal paradox; but here, as in all the early poems, those spaces are experienced as simply empty. So is the mind of the child who automatically steals a toy: "I could see nothing behind that child's eye." The intangible but real mind that must be there seems not to be, as the child is motivated by "automatic" responses rather than mind. This child with the tabula rasa mind is a behaviorist's dream, perfect for the brave new world of Walden II. As in the "Preludes," there seems to be no more consciousness in humans than in their surroundings, a parody of the necessary synthesis of conscious and unconscious, subject and object.

When the memory is shaken by the night, it throws up "twisted things" that perversely seem to reveal cosmic mysteries:

A twisted branch upon the beach
Eaten smooth, and polished
As if the world gave up
The secret of its skeleton,
Stiff and white.

One might hope that the crossing of lunar incantation and solar precision might yield a glimpse of the world's foundations, but there is no integration, only the precisions twisted. What appears is only an image of the reductive science that denies the mystery. When asked how the world came to be, science will "murder to dissect." It vomits a stiff, white

skeleton, rather like the nerves projected on a screen in "Prufrock"—the
dead skeleton of the world, not its living form. It is merely a mechanist's
nightmare. The hidden form of the world is "A broken spring in a factory
yard, / Rust that clings to the form that the strength has left. . . ."

In "Conversation Galante," the persona expresses a similar sense of
impotent emptiness in relation to lunar, rhapsodic art:

> And I then: "Someone frames upon the keys
> That exquisite nocturne, with which we explain
> The night and moonshine; music which we seize
> To body forth our own vacuity."

This entire early collection of poems is much concerned with the puzzle
of integrating night and day. "Morning at the Window," "The *Boston
Evening Transcript,*" Prufrock's evening, the "winter evening" of the
"Preludes," "The troubled midnight and the noon's repose" in "La Figlia
Che Piange"—all these point to an unresolved tension between night's
fanciful, rhapsodic, mythical, synthetic, unconscious state of mind and
day's ordered, clear, composed, rational, conscious state. In terms of
physics, night corresponds to the void and day to the substantial elements. Matter and void appear as an irreconcilable duality, because there
is no spiritual element in the physical void, and because, in the corresponding mental vacuity, there is no soul made in the image of God.

THE FOUR ELEMENTS

At the risk of falsifying the meaning by ignoring the subtle contexts of
individual poems, I would like to consider the remaining poems of the
Prufrock volume together and examine the elemental images in them,
taking each of the elements in turn. The advantage of the procedure will
be to see patterns that lie behind all of them.

Earth is typically reduced, in "Morning at the Window," to "the tram-
pled edges of the street," and we continue to be aware of the streets as
covering the earth in most of the poems. There is something "sprouting,"
from this artificial ground, but it is only "the damp souls of housemaids"
or (in the following poem) the readers of the *Boston Evening Transcript,*
who "Sway in the wind like a field of ripe corn," waiting to be cut down.
Human and vegetable are confused, not as in the mystical union of Marvell's poem, in which everything is reduced to "a green thought in a green
shade," but rather in the Darwinian leveling, which sees all species as
filling some accidental environmental niche, effectively denying any hierarchy of being. At the same time, no real fertility exists, no real harmony

of elements. Earth mixed with water makes for "muddy skirts," not fertile soil, and it also pollutes the air, making "brown waves of fog."

Cousin Nancy, on the other hand, ventures into the country and encounters earth:

> Miss Nancy Ellicott
> Strode across the hills and broke them,
> Rode across the hills and broke them—
> The barren New England hills—
> Riding to hounds
> Over the cow-pasture.

The hills are barren, as is the unmarried Nancy. A New England cow pasture, though not as rich as a Missouri corn field, would not really be barren; yet the use it gets by Miss Nancy, who knows it only as a locale for her highly social and artificial sport, the fox hunt, makes the pasture barren. It is perhaps in this sense that she breaks the hills when she strides across them. She simply fails to recognize them as the ground of her life and nurture. It is also likely that Eliot was thinking of the atomistic view of matter, which would be the view of the educated New Englander, Miss Nancy. Henry Adams, whom Eliot takes as the epitome of the culture that produced both Miss Nancy and Eliot himself, is much concerned with the concept in *The Education of Henry Adams*. Eliot reviewed a new edition of the book in 1919, three years after writing "Cousin Nancy," and deplored Adams's "demolition" of myths. Eliot writes that "Wherever this man stepped, the ground did not simply give way, it flew into particles."[28] Perhaps Cousin Nancy is following in the footsteps of Adams, whom Eliot calls "A Sceptical Patrician," in which case she breaks the hills because her modern scientific notions do not regard the hills as something solid but rather as hosts of indivisible particles moving randomly in a vacuum. When Nancy dances the modern dances it is not on the earth, and she is unaware that hers are "earth feet," like those of the farmers to be described later. Lacking this humble insight, she cannot dance a ritual dance that would connect her with creation and Creator, with the dance of the stars. Hers is the dance of a passing fashionable moment, not the timeless dance of life.

In the presence of Mr. Apollinax, the mind of the poet escapes the tea party and imagines a fertile land with birch trees and "Priapus in the shrubbery." The elemental world is always a mythical world because one senses spirit in its mysterious patterning. With Priapus present, the "lady in the swing" will likely not be barren either, which makes a direct contrast with Miss Nancy—as does the image of the centaur's hoofs, which do *not* break the "hard turf." Here also is a vision of "coral islands," lands rising from the sea and thus likely to be full of life.

In "Hysteria," the poet is drawn into "dark caverns," which might be places of initiation and revelation but that they are only the throat of his companion. The human world again supersedes or absorbs the natural one. A waiter suggests they "take their tea in the garden," probably in the hope that the natural setting would bring the hysterical woman down to earth.

One unusual thing about "La Figlia Che Piange," the last poem (and last-written) in the collection, is that the couple *are* in a garden. She may "Lean on a garden urn," suggesting life, a cornucopia. She stands in the open, "Her hair over her arms and her arms full of flowers," and here the implicit likeness between hair and flowers is not a submerging of human identity in the vegetable world but true connectedness with nature. As many critics have pointed out, this is the hyacinth girl. She flings her flowers to the ground when she realizes the fellow is leaving her. The whole scene is made up ("So I would have had him leave"), but she is utterly natural, the only lovable figure in the whole volume.

Instead of air, these poems contain only the polluted fog, the "gasps" of hysteria, and (if you will) the social "air" of the woman in "Conversation Galante": "your air indifferent and imperious." We do hear that "The readers of the *Boston Evening Transcript* / Sway in the wind like a field of ripe corn," but this simile hardly introduces the pneumatic element. On the contrary, people are seen as vegetative. Evening is "Wakening the appetites of life in some"—arousing at least the Aristotelian "appetitive" or animal soul—but to the people we meet in the poem it is bringing the paper, whose title transcribes the natural evening into a verbal artifact. In their artificial, quasi–intellectual world, these people do not know the wind over a corn field, and as a paradoxical result, they become reduced to plant level.

The only one who holds plants without twisting them is the *Figlia,* and she is, as I say, the only character who has human responses. There is one more mention of air: from his window, the poet-observer sees tossed up to him "An aimless smile that hovers in the air / And vanishes along the level of the roofs." This suggests the capacity of the air to carry communication, but the smile, which is never real in this book of poems, is aimless and so communicates nothing to no one, rather like the twisted things thrown up by memory in the "Rhapsody." As the skies themselves "fade behind a city block," the air carrying this smile ends at "the level of the roofs," not at the aethereal sphere.

Water turns dirt to mud, not parched lands to gardens. The "brown waves of fog" are a kind of perverse merging of earth, water, and air, the right combination in the wrong place. In the inner world, water is also in a harmful combination. The housemaids have "damp souls," an image Smith finds "barely plausible."[29] It is quite plausible, though, as William Blissett has pointed out, within the system of Heraclitus, who taught that people who were in poor spiritual health had damp souls.[30] The soul, being composed of the aethereal fire, should be dry: "A dry soul is wisest and best" (Fr. 118).

Mr. Apollinax, however, inspires visions of the sea. His laughter is

> submarine and profound
> Like the old man of the sea's
> Hidden under coral islands
> Where worried bodies of drowned men drift down in the green
> > silence.

His head is imagined "With seaweed in its hair," like Prufrock's mermaids. Death by drowning is the way out. Drifting down in the vital contemplative "green silence," Phlebas may pass backwards through the stages of his life and perhaps become, like Apollinax, both the old man of the sea and "an irresponsible foetus" floating in the womb. In opposition to this oceanic vision, Professor and Mrs. Channing-Cheetah offer cups of tea. In the rest of the poems, the only other living water is the implicit tears of the crying girl, "La Figlia Che Piange."

Fire remains weak or absent. There is only the moon, which is likened to "an old battered lantern" in "Conversation Galante." In "Hysteria," the laughing woman's "teeth were only accidental stars with a talent for squad drill." She is all the world to him in an extremely negative sense that has become familiar in this analysis: the human, social world engulfs the self and seems to supersede the physical world but does so at the price of becoming mindlessly inhuman. Her head contains stars and caverns—but no mind.

There are also stars *manqué* at the end of "Cousin Nancy," where

> Upon the glazen shelves kept watch
> Matthew and Waldo, guardians of the faith,
> The army of unalterable law.

The artificiality of "glazen" shelves points up the problem with this law: it is man-made. Miss Nancy is a proto-deconstructionist whose fundamental principles are "socially constructed," and knowable only in "texts." Moreover, Arnold and Emerson do not actually agree on very much and are most alike in that neither could be described as a guardian of the faith in any traditional sense. The last line is from Meredith's sonnet "Lucifer in Starlight," in which the archrebel is humbled before the stars, which are the "army of unalterable law." Lacking real awareness of Nature's starry sphere, the Ellicotts (that is, the Eliots) lack an abiding belief in natural law and are left with nothing but the opinions of the great writers of the previous century, a faith as modern as Nancy's dance steps.

The only genuine sunlight in *Prufrock and Other Observations* is in that last poem, "La Figlia Che Piange," which clearly longs for something beyond the world of the other poems. Twice the incantation is repeated, "Weave, weave the sunlight in your hair." As with the conjunction of hair and flowers, this is emphatically not a loss of human identity in the material world but a weaving together of the two. The poem scarcely works, for it is nearly impossible to imagine a young man so perverse that he would reject such a vision because "I should have lost a gesture and a pose." Probably it *is* just a vision, or daydream, toyed with by one who lives only in fantasy: "So I would have had him leave. . . ." Eliot here presses the limits of his technique by letting a beautiful reality shine in the poem but still making his persona pull back into his mental world. The vitality of woman and garden and sunlight will not easily release the speaker: "She turned away, but with the autumn weather / Compelled my imagination many days." The weather, the operation of the "elements" as we say, awakens his true imagination and his natural desires, the "appetites of life" directed at the "things that other people have desired." In this first collection, Eliot explored the connection between our subjective awareness of our own humanity and our objective awareness of the world about us. In the Unreal City he found the connection broken.

3

Physics and Metaphysics in *Poems* of 1920

As many readers have recognized, most of the poems in this volume contrast the modern age with earlier times. Northrop Frye points out (disapprovingly) that Eliot subscribed to the view of history that sees it as a gradual disintegration.[1] It seems to me that Eliot recognized rather a pattern of decay and renewal in history, with high points reached in Golden Age Athens, Augustan Rome, and medieval and Renaissance Europe, but there is no doubt that he saw our own time as a time of disintegration. When Eliot compares a contemporary scene with a scene from the past, he seems to mean it as a sharp contrast between the ignoble and the noble. Even though the characters from the past have their own flaws, they are tragic flaws as opposed to banal ones.

This most recent historical decline results, in Eliot's view, from the dissociation of sensibility in the seventeenth century and hence from the false philosophical interpretation of the scientific revolution that produced the Cartesian split. In this 1920 volume, Eliot shows his concern for the split between material and spiritual elements in the psyche and the cosmos. He sees the split resulting in thinkers taking sides, becoming either strict materialists or strict idealists. From this perspective, we will see that "Gerontion" dramatizes life and death in the material world of the atomists, both ancient and modern. In this world, the old man has "no ghosts" because he believes that his dead acquaintances are now only "fractured atoms"—as he too will soon be. In some of the other poems, we will find satirical allusions to the most influential materialist of the modern era, Darwin. On the other hand, we will find the idealist strain represented primarily by Emerson, seen as a secularized version of Origen and other Neoplatonic theologians. Bergson rejected this idealism as "finalism," the teleological error opposite to materialism. Paul Elmer More saw it as another monistic view, incapable of accounting for the mysterious dualism of our experience. When we concentrate on the contrasts in these poems between the Renaissance world and the modern one, we can see that the main thing that has changed is mankind's understanding of the relations between spiritual and physical worlds. Eliot's deprecation of the modern is often thought to result from a vague nostalgia for the ancient. However, if we read these poems while keeping in mind the quite legitimate criticisms that several thinkers and poets of the time were aiming at scientism and at the complementary transcendentalism, we may see that his critique of the modern world view is pointed and cogent.

FRACTURED ATOMS: THE ATOMIST APPROACHES DEATH

I wish to argue that the phrase "fractured atoms" is the key to "Gerontion," identifying the old man as a convinced atomist and thereby invoking the long history of an idea. Eliot was acutely aware that the atomist theory was not new. Leucippus, Democritus, and others of their school had asserted anciently that the world was composed not of the traditional elements but of tiny particles they called "atoms" (literally, unsplitables). Part of what other philosophers found abhorrent in this idea was the necessary corollary that the spaces between atoms were entirely vacant, for if the atoms were the smallest particles, there obviously could be nothing between them. All the other physical theories had assumed that some supersubtle, quasi-spiritual substance must be filling the apparently empty spaces in the cosmos—either the aether or the Stoics' *pneuma*. In rejecting this element, the atomists were renouncing common sense, which has always felt that "Nature abhors a vacuum and so rushes to fill it in" (an adage formulated by the scholastic philosophers of the Middle Ages). Any complete vacuum, no matter how small, would surely exert infinite force in sucking matter into it.

Perhaps more alarming, the atomists were rejecting the presence of spirit in the material world, for the aether was a kind of intermediary between matter and spirit. The atomists were thoroughgoing materialists who believed that the patterns we see in the world, and our very consciousness, all arose by chance. Naturally, other philosophers and poets have ever since found this idea horrifying. Sir John Davies, for instance, pauses for a moment in his celebration of the cosmic dance to attack the atomists:

> Or if this all, which round about we see,
> As idle Morpheus some sick brains hath taught,
> Of undivided motes compacted be,
> How was this goodly architecture wrought?
> Or by what means were they together brought?
> They err that say they did concur by chance;
> Love made them meet in a well-ordered dance![2]

As we have seen (chapter 1), Donne shares this view. He abhors the "new philosophy" because it puts out the elements and reduces the cosmos to "atomies." We have also seen that Eliot identifies Hobbes as the first thinker since Lucretius to base his metaphysics on the atomist view: "Hobbes's philosophy is not so much a philosophy as an adumbration of the universe of material atoms regulated by laws of motion which formed the scientific view from Newton to Einstein" (*SE, 313*).

Atomism became increasingly accepted in the eighteenth century, yet it still had its detractors. Swift, for instance, attacks the feeble atomist explanation of human consciousness as swerves (*clinamina*) of the atoms:

> Epicurus modestly hoped, that one time or another a certain fortuitous concourse of all men's opinions, after perpetual justlings, the sharp with the smooth, the light and the heavy, the round and the square, would by certain *clinamina* unite in the notions of atoms and void, as these did in the originals of all things.[3]

The materialist assertion that chance and a few basic laws of nature, rather than any sort of spiritual agent, constructed the world's forms is what troubles Davies, Donne, Swift, and many others.

In Eliot's time, the Platonic dualist Paul Elmer More found in the atomist explanation of free will as swerving atoms the same gross illogic Swift saw:

> A dualist may solve this difficulty by attributing mechanical chance to the material world and conscious choice to the realm of spirit; but no such division was legitimately open to a consistent monist. Apparently Epicurus undertook to bully the logic of the situation by a transparent device. His primary atoms are described, as a true materialist should describe them, in purely quantitative terms; they have size and form, but no qualities, no sensation, nothing inducive of sensation. Then, suddenly, by the mere fact of aggregation, they have become endowed with qualities and with sensation, and in the finer atoms which constitute the soul mechanical chance has become converted into conscious free will.[4]

This argument points up the natural alignment of atomistic materialism with quantitative reasoning (i.e., mathematics) and helps explain the apparent paradox in Whitehead's phrase "abstract materialism." It also shows how atomism denies that anything like Bradley's immediate experience can be valid epistemology. The qualitative experiences of our senses are, to the atomist, totally illusory—even though they are, ironically, all we have to go on.

Eliot apparently joined this long-standing battle between poets and atomists early in his career. In his 1911 poem whose opening lines were quoted earlier (chapter 1), he contrasts, according to Lyndall Gordon's summary, "the enlightened view of the universe, a scientific ordered structure of atoms and geometric laws, with his own comic fantasy of the Absolute with arbitrary powers sitting in the middle of a geometric net like a syphilitic spider."[5] In the enlightened, scientific view, "Each atom goes on working out its law, and never / Can cut an unintentioned caper."[6] Here the atom is identified with positivistic and mechanistic definitions of science. Given the quantifiable nature of the discrete atoms supposed to compose everything that exists, scientists can lay the universe out on paper, rationally, mathematically, exhaustively, clearly. Though their movements are in one sense random, the atoms follow immutable laws of physics and thus can never "cut an unintentioned caper." In short, this is a statement of scientism, not of science, for true science holds all its laws to be provisional and (as Thomas Kuhn emphasizes) continually looks for unintentioned capers that may require modification or rejection of those laws.

The second stanza is, as Gordon says, a challenge to this positivistic view, even though it is apparently spoken by the same voice:

> He said: it is a geometric net
> And in the middle, like a syphilitic spider
> The Absolute sits waiting, till we get
> All tangled up and end ourselves inside her.

Eliot suggests that, though we try to live by the clear geometrical description of the world, we inevitably find ourselves facing an irrational, immaterial reality, the Absolute, Bradley's ultimate unified reality beyond the contradictions of appearances.

Atomistic materialism achieved its most eloquent ancient statement in Lucretius's *De rerum naturae*. Lucretius tells us not to fear death, for after death we will simply dissolve into our constituent atoms and cease to be. Somehow this seemed cold comfort to many people, then and later. Near the end of the nineteenth century, Dalton, following Lavoisier, reintroduced the atomic theory with empirical evidence to support it. For Eliot's Gerontion, in 1919, atomistic materialism is not one competing theory but indisputable reality. "Gerontion" has rightly been read as a satire on modern urban society, but it is fundamentally an examination of the spiritual emptiness experienced by the modern atomist.

John Crowe Ransom calls "Gerontion" "a very important poem in the Eliot canon" and reports that Allen Tate liked it better than any other except *Four Quartets*.[7] The poem's importance to Eliot is apparent in the fact that he considered reprinting it as a prelude to *The Waste Land,* though Pound persuaded him not to do so. The opening of the poem does, in fact, situate it in the waste land: "Here I am, an old man in a dry month, / Being read to by a boy, waiting for rain." Here is the disharmony of elements that forms the physical premise of the later poem.

We find Eliot's beginning—the fundamental truths he was intuitively moving toward—in his end, his last poems. In *East Coker,* he tells what old men might be:

> Old men ought to be explorers
> Here and there does not matter
> We must be still and still moving
> Into another intensity
> For a further union, a deeper communion
> Through the dark cold and the empty desolation,
> The wave cry, the wind cry, the vast waters
> Of petrel and porpoise.

This exploration is inward, passing through the "dark cold and the empty desolation" of death before the body dies and finding in that very waste land "another intensity" related to "communion." For Gerontion, a man who has imbibed scientistic assumptions, there can be no paradoxical movement in his senescent stillness. There is also no intensity for him because his senses have decayed and, as a true follower of Locke and other modern teachers of sensationalism or associationism, he believes in no other way of knowing. Associationism was the modern atomist's version of swerving atoms. As Sanford Schwartz explains, "Bradley . . . joins Bergson and James in attacking the associationists for describing experience as a bundle of discrete atoms."[8] Gerontion's is a mind that has no "immediate experience" (in Bradley's terms) or sense of "real duration" (in Bergson's).

Given his notion of reality, Gerontion can only try with decreasing success to "Excite the membrane, when the sense has cooled, / With pungent sauces, multiply variety / In a wilderness of mirrors." The "wilderness of mirrors" alludes to a passage in which Jonson's Sir Epicure Mammon is planning how to use the wealth of the philosopher's stone. He will have "glasses, / Cut in more subtle angles, to disperse / And multiply the figures as I walk / Naked between my *succubae*" (*The Alchemist,* II.ii.45–48). This sensualism is the grossest variety of materialism, but Sir Epicure's first name identifies him simultaneously with the ancient philosophical materialism of Epicurus, who was an atomist. These images indicate the horrible solipsism into which the materialist falls. His world is made of randomly formed objects which have no essence, and people are such objects, too: like the housemaids whose souls "sprout" by the gates in "Morning at the Window," Gerontion's landlord was (in his reductive view) "spawned"; and the one who makes his tea is simply "the woman."

A source for the opening passage is found in a letter of the aging Edward Fitzgerald quoted in A. C. Benson's biography: "I really do like to sit in this doleful place with a good fire, a cat and a dog on the rug, and an old woman in the kitchen. This is all my live-stock."[9] Fitzgerald, as the erstwhile translator of the mystical *Rubáiyát* into a sensualist carpe diem poem, is close kin to Gerontion, who has also lived the life of the senses in the belief that no other life existed. For the modern sensualist especially, the things he encounters do not have being: they are merely sensations. The senses experience these objects, and that is all we know of them or of ourselves. Even the sexual encounter is not, then, a union of beings but a strictly sensual experience to be enhanced by intensifying what the senses perceive (e.g., by multiplying mirrors so as to see from all sides).

Even if his senses continued to function, Gerontion does not believe he could use them to achieve any sort of union: "How should I use them for your closer contact?" The "communion" of *East Coker* is with God and with the Communion of Saints; Gerontion's denial of those realities has isolated him from others long before death. He is like the other old men of *East Coker,* with "Their fear of fear and frenzy, their fear of possession, / Of belonging to another, or to others, or to God." Gordon suggests that Gerontion's failing senses are an allusion to Newman's sermon on Divine Calls: "Let us beg and pray Him day by day to reveal Himself to our souls more fully, to quicken our senses, to give us sight and hearing, taste and touch of the world to come."[10] Here is an epistemology radically different from the materialist's and yet even more corporeal. Newman's belief in the resurrection of the body leads him to pray for spiritually quickened bodily senses that will experience the physical reality of the world to come.

In Gerontion's thought, we see the coexistence of abstraction and materialism Whitehead identified. Matter is all there is, but it is impalpable because it is finally made up of those infinitesimally small particles we will never see or touch. The traditional elements are named out of "immediate experience," that direct, holistic experience of the world (intuitive rather than intellectual, in Bergson's terms), whereas the elements of the periodic table are identified by experiments and by number. In his essay on Bradley (1927), Eliot quotes a passage that shows that Bradley considered atomism antithetical to immediate experience:

> That the glory of this world is appearance leaves the world more glorious if we feel it as a show of some fuller splendour; but the sensuous curtain is a deception and a cheat—if it hides some colourless movement of atoms, some

spectral woof of impalpable abstractions, or unearthly ballet of bloodless categories.[11]

It was a commonplace that matter had no color. We can no longer say that the leaf is green; scientifically described, the leaf absorbs all other wavelengths of light except the one our eyes perceive as green. At the atomic level of reality, there is no such thing as color. Thought of this way, our sense perceptions are, as Bradley says, "a cheat." Opposition to atomism runs throughout Bradley's work. Hyatt Howe Waggoner summarizes Bradley's view thus: "All that we find in immediate experience must be attributes of nature, feeling as well as extension, color as well as mass. The dead world of kinetic atomic physics is by no means the real world, though it is an element in, an abstraction from, the total reality."[12]

A more recent restatement of this critique is Harmon M. Chapman's "Realism and Phenomenology." Chapman points out that distrust of sensation is "a logical consequence" of atomism. His essay is valuable because he goes on to point out the connection between atomism and the denial of sensory validity in the thinking of Descartes. The theory of Democritus and the other ancient atomists, Chapman writes, "was not again widely entertained until Descartes espoused it and for essentially the same reasons. For if the world be as science demands, namely a *res extensa,* then the senses must be thoroughly discarded and superseded."[13] This link between atomism and Descartes is important. It is at first surprising to think that a commitment to atomism, a materialist doctrine, could lead to Cartesian idealism, but the argument is convincing, and Eliot shows himself aware of it. He follows Bradley and Bergson in reacting against the atomists' rejection of our sensory experience (color and solidity) in favor of mathematical "bloodless categories" (wavelength and atomic number). It was just because of its denial of ordinary sense experience that "A purely 'scientific' philosophy ends by denying what we know to be true . . ." (*SE,* 403), and the prime scientific philosophy was that of Descartes.

Thus, we find Eliot pointing toward an unholy marriage of the two extreme positions, materialism and idealism. In his unpublished graduate school essay on ethics, he finds that idealism has displaced materialism in philosophy, but he argues that it cannot do so permanently because it is one sided. The other side will reappear just when idealism triumphs, as it did in the case of Cartesian idealism. Eliot predicts that "a gigantic hand organ of atoms, grinding out predictable variations of the same tune, will fill the vast silences which idealism leaves empty."[14] Eliot's metaphor here implies a deep connection between idealism and atomic materialism: each creates a silence, a void, which the other then fills, only to create another void. Both lack a sense of dynamic balance and a sense of reality.

In his dissertation on Bradley, Eliot takes the paradoxical ideality of atoms as a given when he writes that " . . . the I is a construction out of experience, an abstraction from it; and the *thats,* the browns and hards and flats, are equally ideal constructions from experience, as ideal as atoms."[15] In atomic theory, then, radical materialism and radical idealism both take root.

From this perspective, the cooling of Gerontion's senses and the loss of their ability to help him contact another is attributable not only to decrepitude but to his own disbelief in the senses. He cannot touch anyone because he lives in a world of "impalpable abstractions." Though he is a materialist and hence a sensualist, Gerontion has not experienced the material world in its immediate elemental concreteness. He did not fight at the "hot gates" or in the "warm rain"—did not wield a cutlass while standing knee-deep in the marshes "Bitten by flies."[16]

With atomism comes also the notion that matter is random in its organization. It takes on certain forms according to physical and chemical laws but not in relation to any pattern or design. Form is seen as an anomaly in a world that is destined by the second law of thermodynamics to end in a dead stasis. Eric Sigg rightly connects the "fractured atoms" with the idea of entropy.[17] We see this idea of the cosmos reflected in the only bit of nature in Gerontion's locale: "The goat coughs at night in the field overhead; / Rocks, moss, stonecrop, iron, merds." Here is an encounter with the world of nature but not in its wholeness. As Ransom has observed,

We may take the iron to mean the scrap-iron of used-up metal gadgets tossed from the passing cars, and composing not a landscape but a litter; and merds are merds.[18]

This line presents an image of a chaotic nature, with piles of various objects having no organic relation to each other or to the man observing them. We glimpse the chaotic end to which the world is tending according to the scientist's laws.

Eliot had in mind one modern thinker who entertained—albeit unwillingly and skeptically—that view, for he had been reading and reviewing *The Education of Henry Adams* just before writing the poem. Smith points out a passage in which Adams looks at the world from the perspective of the second law of thermodynamics. Adams writes, "The kinetic theory of gas is an assertion of ultimate chaos. In plain words, chaos was the law of nature; Order was the dream of man."[19] Adams is here paraphrasing Karl Pearson's *Grammar of Science,* and though it is true as Smith says that Adams is also testifying to his own conviction, it is not a conviction that makes him happy, and Pearson's book is not one he admires. Adams goes on to imagine fearfully the world into which children would now be born:

> The child born in 1900 would, then, be born into a new world which would not be a unity but a multiple. Adams tried to imagine it, and an education that would fit it. He found himself in a land where no one had ever penetrated before; where order was an accidental relation obnoxious to nature; artificial compulsion imposed on motion; against which every free energy of the universe revolted; and which, being merely occasional, resolved itself back into anarchy at last.[20]

James Longenbach notes that in Adams's "Letter to American Teachers of History," he examined the possibility that the second law of thermodynamics might come to be taken as a model of historical change.[21] In this piece, as Longenbach further points out, Adams cautions that such laws of physics must not be taken as revealing ultimate truths about even the physical world. Adams writes of the law of entropy that "Instead of being a mere convenience in treatment, the law is very rapidly becoming a dogma of absolute Truth."[22] In the persona of "Gerontion," Eliot presents a man for whom this law of physics has indeed become a "dogma of absolute Truth."

The child of the entropic mechanistic age is later described by Graham Greene in *The Power and the Glory* (1940). Greene, who was received into the Roman Catholic Church a year before Eliot's reception into the Anglican Church, describes an army lieutenant fixated on finding and executing the last priest in his Mexican state, where religion has been outlawed:

> It infuriated him to think that there were still people in the state who believed in a loving and merciful God. There are mystics who are said to have experienced God directly. He was a mystic, too, and what he had experienced was vacancy—a complete certainty in the existence of a dying, cooling world, of human beings who had evolved from animals for no purpose at all. He knew.[23]

If the law of entropy is taken as gospel truth for the universe, the world will indeed end as in "The Hollow Men," with a whimper. Thermodynamics teaches that energy cannot be destroyed, but it constantly becomes less available for work or organization. These laws would lead inevitably to a universe in which the temperature was completely even throughout space. The last tiny blip of higher energy would be its last whimper. This entropic view of the universe is really the source of the spiritual hollowness experienced by the men who speak in this poem. They see themselves as living in a "valley of dying stars" or again "Under the twinkle of a fading star," because they have accepted the mechanistic second law of thermodynamics as the ultimate truth about their world. All the energy in this world is gradually dissipating, and the world itself is dying. There is no spiritual source of energy beyond this finite material system, and there is no spirit in their own dying bodies. Gerontion's chaotic jumble of "Rocks, moss, stonecrop, iron, merds" exhibits the hollow world's lack of organizing, working energy. So does his "decayed house," which is gradually disintegrating, like the old man, into "fractured atoms." Like Greene's Mexican lieutenant, he is one of the hollow men.

In *East Coker*, by contrast, houses suffer a more dramatic demise: "The houses are all gone under the sea." This decay is in the rhythm of nature, which rebuilds itself yearly, whereas Gerontion's tenement has no such potential. In *Four Quartets*, there is also the supernatural pattern, not subject to entropy. In this revealed plan, the world does end with a bang, in "a vortex that shall bring / The world to that destructive fire / Which burns before the ice-cap reigns." The use of present tense to describe both past and future in the last line indicates that this is an eternal fire, not one subject to the second law of thermodynamics. It will lead not to total entropy but to the indestructible houses of the New Jerusalem.

Adams submits to the findings of scientific materialism, but he remains somewhat skeptical nevertheless and expresses his bewilderment and his nostalgia for the old order. He laments that he cannot follow the mathematics and so cannot criticize the theories. He accepts them sadly. In his famous comparison of the Virgin and the Dynamo, he mourns the loss of a feminine force that expressed itself in fecundity and art. In place of that force he finds we have turned toward an impersonal masculine powerhouse whose energy is immense and immensely useful but meaningless and inhuman. Perhaps the faceless woman who makes tea for Gerontion, sneezes, and pokes the "peevish gutter" (the sputtering fire like the man's own feeble life) is the Virgin, now taken to be merely another organic object.

Adams himself, though he looked back longingly to the age of belief, took part in its "demolition," as Eliot said in his review. Though dismayed by the atomistic theory, Adams (whose name happens to sound like "atoms") bowed to it; and Eliot alludes to this acquiescence when he charges that "Wherever this man stepped, the ground did not simply give way, it flew into particles. . . ."[24] As we saw in chapter 2, the same idea lies behind his description of another skeptical New England patrician, Miss Nancy, who "Rode across the hills and broke them." The element that symbolizes solidity itself, earth, is breaking into particles under their feet not only because of their general skepticism but precisely because they have accepted the particle theory of matter.

In his review, Eliot goes on to say that Adams "was seeking for education, with the wings of a beautiful but ineffectual conscience beating vainly in a vacuum jar."[25] This vision of Adams connects him with the Sibyl of the *Waste Land* epigraph, who is trapped in her ampulla wishing to die. The idea of life in a vacuum also connects him with Gerontion's "vacant shuttles" and shows Eliot's awareness of the atomist's belief in the doctrine of a vacuum between particles, as well as his concern for the psychological implications of that belief.

Eliot quotes directly from another passage in *The Education of Henry Adams,* one that describes dogwood and flowering judas and then responds ambivalently to the scene:

> Here and there a negro log cabin alone disturbed the dogwood and the judas-tree, the azalea and the laurel. . . . The brooding heat of the profligate vegetation; the cool charm of the running water; the terrific splendour of the June thundergust in the deep and solitary woods, were all sensual, animal, elemental.[26]

Eliot writes, "In depraved May, dogwood and chestnut, flowering judas, / To be eaten, to be divided, to be drunk. . . ." Here is nature in all her richness and power. It is a deeply sensual experience, one Gerontion cannot really have. Thus, while some sort of communion is suggested, there is finally only ordinary eating and drinking. The fertility of nature seems depraved to the modern thinker because he is a denizen of the unreal city and sees nature subject to mathematics, not powerful and elemental; also, he finds no meaning in the scene, no presence of the Creator in the creation. Robert Crawford points out that Durkheim claimed communion, not worship, was the essential element of religion, and that the image of eating vegetation puts this passage into the context of communion rituals in fertility cults. For Gerontion, Crawford writes, "Both Christ and the fertility cycle seem terrifying."[27] To the urban man with his atomistic mentality, any sort of communion seems impossible and even terrible.

Hugh Kenner sees in this passage "Some rite, not innocent . . . some cosmopolitan Black Mass."[28] This inversion of the sacrament must have been associated in Eliot's mind with the Unitarian desacralizing of it and Emerson's abandonment of it. In defining "the Boston doubt" with which Adams was afflicted, Eliot writes,

> When Emerson as a young man stood in his pulpit and made clear to his congregation that he could no longer administer the Communion, he impressed upon them that he had no prejudice and passed no judgment upon those who continued in the practice, but that he could take no part himself—because (in his own words) it did not interest him.[29]

The transcendentalist is at the opposite pole from the materialist, but both renounce the sacrament because it asserts an indissoluble and inexplicable union of spirit and matter. Eliot, himself an inheritor of the Boston doubt, was already struggling with his realization that the modern dissociation of sensibility was connected with the Cartesian divorce of these opposites—and with a realization that Trinitarian Christian doctrine continued to proclaim a mysterious marriage of the opposites. The rejection by one of the "guardians of the faith" of sacramental religion and the cosmology on which it is based leads eventually to the rejection or perversion of the sacrament and ultimately to Gerontion's forlorn solitude.

Thus, into the middle of his modernist ruminations comes a momentary reflection on the faith Gerontion has lost:

> Signs are taken for wonders. "We would see a sign!"
> The word within a word, unable to speak a word,
> Swaddled with darkness. In the juvescence of the year
> Came Christ the tiger. . . .

Gerontion seems to be mocking the tendency of the credulous to see not just a sign but a wonder, something outside of the narrow bounds of scientific inquiry. When we first read his description of the Christ child, it seems to debunk the myth: the Word is unable to speak, just a baby. We know, however, that his words are from Bishop Andrewes's Christmas sermon delivered to James I in 1618; and for Andrewes, the babe's incapacity only heightens the wonder of the gift:

> Signes are taken for wonders: (*Master we would faine see a Signe*, that is, a *miracle*). And, in this sense it is a *Signe*, to wonder at. Indeed, every word (heer) is a wonder: . . . *an infant; Verbum infans*, the *Word* without a *word;* the *aeternall Word* not hable to speak a *word*. . . . He, that (as in the 38. of Job he saith) *taketh the vast bodie of the maine Sea, turnes it to and fro, as a little child*, and *rolls it about with the swadling bands of darknesse;* He, to come thus into *clouts*, himselfe![30]

The humble lamb has allowed himself to be swaddled in darkness, but he is still the power ("Christ the tiger") that wraps the sea in those bands. The modern rationalist rejects this wonder.

The sign is the Incarnation of the Word, and also the Eucharist, which reenacts that wonder each day. The Word is unable to speak a word, is deprived of language, yet He gives a sign through His physical presence, an undeniable nonverbal sign that speaks to all peoples. To the Pharisees who challenge him with "We would see a sign," Christ responds that they will be given only the sign of Jonah, the son of man three days in the

earth (Matthew 12:38–40). To those who believe, he gives a sign of life.
In Saint John's Gospel, the people who have been fed by the miracle of
the loaves and fishes follow Jesus, who has crossed the Sea of Galilee
to Capernaum:

> They said therefore unto him, What sign shewest thou then, that we may see,
> and believe thee? what dost thou work? Our fathers did eat manna in the
> desert; as it is written, He gave them bread from heaven to eat. Then Jesus
> said unto them, Verily, verily, I say unto you, Moses gave you not that bread
> from heaven; but my Father giveth you the true bread from heaven. For the
> bread of God is he which cometh down from heaven, and giveth life unto the
> world. (6:30–33)

The sign is Christ himself, "the bread of life" (6:35). It is this sacramental
sign that is perverted in Gerontion's mock-Communion.[31]

Over against Emerson's refusal to take part in Communion is the conclusion of Bishop Andrewes's Christmas sermon:

> *Christ* in the *Sacrament,* is not altogether unlike *Christ* in the *cratch.* To the
> *cratch* we may well liken the *husk* or outward *Symboles* of it. Outwardly, it
> seemes little worth, but is rich of contents; as was the *crib,* this day, with
> *Christ* in it. For, what are they, but *infirma et egena elementa,* weak and poor
> *elements* of themselves: yet in them find we *Christ.*[32]

The bread and wine are ordinarily referred to as "elements." In the Eucharist, these physical elements are inseparable from the spiritual being.
In Christian theology, the four elements of the cosmos are not seen as
united with God in this same way (that would be pantheism), but it is His
spiritual agency that forms them, as in the passage from Job to which
Andrewes refers. The ideas of creation, incarnation, and sacrament all
suppose a relation between spirit and matter that is denied both in Emerson's Unitarian transcendental idealism and in scientific materialism.

In its affirmation of the Incarnation and the sacramental Real Presence,
orthodox Catholicism is, in a certain sense, more physical than scientific
materialism. As Underhill writes, the mystic, "though he has broken for
ever with the bondage of the senses, . . . perceives in every manifestation
of life a sacramental meaning; a loveliness, a wonder, a heightened significance, which is hidden from other men. He may, with St. Francis, call
the Sun and the Moon, Water and Fire, his brothers and his sisters: or
receive, with Blake, the message of the trees. . . ."[33] Eliot's reaction to
atomistic science led him in this direction. In the essay on Bradley, while
distinguishing between Bradley's idea of the self and Arnold's, Eliot outlines a dichotomy between the notion of the self to which the atomist
inevitably subscribes and the concept of self consistent with Eucharistic

theology: "The distinction is not between a 'private self' and a 'public self' or a 'higher self,' it is between the individual as himself and no more, a mere numbered atom, and the individual in communion with God" (*SE*, 402). The perversion of the Eucharist in "Gerontion" and the persona's incapacity to achieve communion (or even "closer contact") with others, are both intimately connected with his atomistic assumptions.

Gordon suggests that "Gerontion's theological position recalls that of the American Puritan who sees himself without spiritual agency, abject, wholly at the mercy of divine omnipotence."[34] However, Gerontion has little in common with the Puritan; he has denied divine omnipotence but now in his last days has second thoughts:

> Think at last
> We have not reached conclusion, when I
> Stiffen in a rented house. Think at last
> I have not made this show purposelessly. . . .

Perhaps, he faintly hopes, in the end death is not the end. Perhaps his part in the show on the stage of life was not without purpose. But the old man cannot really believe that, having lived his life by another creed. He believes he is merely a highly structured concatenation of the "purposeless" matter Whitehead describes. By the laws of nature, the energy will pass out of him as heat, and his particles will lose the structure that energy had accidentally made.

Gerontion is "A dull head among windy spaces." The wind brings neither rain to earth nor inspiration to the mind. The spaces within and without are empty:

> Vacant shuttles
> Weave the wind. I have no ghosts,
> An old man in a draughty house
> Under a windy knob.

How can "an old man in a draughty house" have no ghosts? Critics have explained that Gerontion has failed to love and, therefore, has no connection with those he has known.[35] The present analysis finds in the phrase a literal meaning that complements this interpretation. In the penultimate stanza, Gerontion thinks of those he knew as having no ghost, no spirit:

> De Bailhache, Fresca, Mrs. Cammel, whirled
> Beyond the circuit of the shuddering Bear
> In fractured atoms.

Gerontion cannot be haunted because, following modern science, he has readopted the premise of Democritus, Epicurus, and Lucretius. After death, the body simply dissolves into its constituent atoms, and the person is no more.[36] Eliot must have remembered Zeller's book on ancient philosophy, which he read as an undergraduate. His notes on the section devoted to Democritus contain this passage: "Atoms' movement is without beginning, but not by chance; rather by necessity. Whirling movement."[37] Eliot knew that Epicurus also speaks of the "whirl" as the origin of all motion in the cosmos. The whirling that Gerontion invokes, then, is precisely the movement proper to the atoms of Democritus and Epicurus.

George Bornstein notes the imaginative intensity of this passage and argues that for the speaker such moments "come as chance epiphanies, having nothing to do with his ordinary self." This seems fine, but one may well question Bornstein's further assertion that such a passage is much the same for Eliot himself, "a revolt of imagination at the constraints of the intellect, which to Eliot appeared as an upheaval of violent and irrational forces."[38] Bornstein casts Eliot as a repressed Romantic afraid of his passions. There is no doubt some truth in this characterization, but it easily becomes caricature. Given the present analysis, it seems particularly clear that the speaker in this poem is quite distinct from the poet. Gerontion is a rationalist who fears and rejects both emotional and spiritual ecstasy. T. S. Eliot no doubt recognized himself in his character, yet he was rejecting not the eruption of imagination but the materialistic rationalism of the character that had made both imagination and belief seem useless.

Eliot's reaction to Gerontion's lack of ghosts may have been influenced by an essay in the *Little Review* of 1918 on "Henry James and the Ghostly," written by A. R. Orage. James's mission, Orage says, "was to act as a kind of Charon to ferry the understanding over the dark passage of the Styx and to show us that we are such stuff as ghosts are made of."[39] The "stuff" of ghosts must be at once spiritual and material, since ghosts have physical appearance but are spirits. The stuff of the atomic theory could never account for such beings. Eliot's later works, in contrast, are full of ghosts.

The vacant shuttles recall the atomist's assertion that the spaces between fractured atoms are entirely vacant. In that sense, Gerontion is a dull head among windy spaces—spaces that are merely void; wind that is woven by vacant shuttles rather than breathed forth by any ghostly force. Eliot alludes to Job, who in his tribulations did experience the emptiness in life:

My days are swifter than a weaver's shuttle, and are spent without hope. O remember that my life is wind: mine eye shall no more see good. The eye of him that hath seen me shall see me no more: thine eyes are upon me, and I am not. As the cloud is consumed and vanisheth away: so he that goeth down to the grave shall come up no more. He shall return no more to his house, neither shall his place know him any more. (7:6–10)

Here also is a man who has no ghosts: the dead shall go down and return no more to haunt their houses. Wind is symbolic of nothingness ("my life is wind"), much as it is when Gerontion speaks of his "draughty house" or the "windy knob." In the Book of Job, however, the wind will be rediscovered as *ruach,* spiritual breath, when the Lord answers Job's laments "out of the whirlwind" (38:1). The Creator challenges Job's knowledge of death: "Have the gates of death been opened unto thee? or hast thou seen the doors of the shadow of death?" (38:17). He proceeds to show that the dead not only continue to exist but can be brought back to life. No such revelation comes to Gerontion, who is not even complaining of his lot, since there is no one to whom he could complain. Instead of God's voice in the whirlwind, he hears only the chaotic and meaningless whirl of the atoms.

Eliot would have found death described as a void toward the end of *The Education of Henry Adams:*

> Every fabulist has told how the human mind has always struggled like a frightened bird to escape the chaos which caged it; how—appearing suddenly and inexplicably out of some unknown and unimaginable void . . . after sixty or seventy years of growing astonishment, the mind wakes to find itself looking blankly into the void of death.[40]

In ages past, this void was thought to be aethereal, somehow infused with spiritual substance. It was still frightening for most, but not hopelessly vacant. For the atomist, however, it is truly void.

Tennyson's "Lucretius" describes such an atomist facing death, and close phrasal echoes make it seem likely that this poem is a direct source that has not before been recognized. The dramatic monologue is spoken in his last moments by the philosopher who has written that death is nothing to fear since it is merely a dissolving of our selves. According to legend, his jealous wife gave him a love potion that tortured his mind with sensual visions until he committed suicide. Tennyson seems to admire Lucretius's strength of mind and unwavering commitment to his conception of the world but, at the same time, to question a materialistic philosophy which can offer no remedy to such a dilemma but suicide. He has Lucretius exclaim that in the coming destruction of the world

> momentary man
> Shall seem no more a something to himself
> But he, his hopes and hates, his homes and fanes,
> And even his bones long laid within the grave,

The very sides of the grave itself shall pass,
Vanishing, atom and void, atom and void,
Into the unseen for ever. . . . (252–58)

Gerontion's "windy spaces," "vacant shuttles," and "draughty house" reflect the Lucretian concept of the void. Like the homes Lucretius speaks of, Gerontion's house is decaying. His phrase "fractured atoms" echoes Lucretius's "atom and void, atom and void."

George Santayana's poetic analysis of Lucretius may be another source here. Santayana writes,

Vigorous and throbbing as are his pictures of spring, of love, of ambition, of budding culture, of intellectual victory, they pale before the vivid strokes with which he paints the approach of death—fatigue of the will, lassitude in pleasure, corruption and disintegration in society, the soil exhausted, the wild animals tamed or exterminated, poverty, pestilence, and famine at hand; and for the individual, almost at once, the final dissipation of the atoms of his soul, escaping from a relaxed body, to mingle and lose themselves in the universal flaw.[41]

The "lassitude in pleasure" is Gerontion's. The universal disintegration is the original notion of entropy. Tennyson, Santayana, and Eliot all seek to examine the sense of desolation inherent in this philosophy.

Gerontion's acquaintances whirling in the void of space are like the dead in *East Coker,* who "all go into the dark, / The vacant interstellar spaces." In the later poem there is (I will suggest in chapter 5) aether filling the void, and because of this divine substance, the empty darkness "shall be the darkness of God." In "Gerontion," however, Eliot merely shows, as did Tennyson in "Lucretius," that materialist physics yields despair at the approach of death. In Lucretius's modern descendant, there is not even the old philosopher's resistance to the sensual temptations, only regret that the senses can no longer respond. Nor is there Lucretius's noble defiance and conscious choice, but only "Thoughts of a dry brain in a dry season"—the inner and outer deprivation of elemental life that will be explored more expansively in *The Waste Land.*

In Gerontion's image of death, the spider and the weevil break the body into its constituent atoms, which are then whirled into space. The lines paraphrase Eliot's favorite lines from Chapman's *Bussy D'Ambois.* Bussy, about to die, orders his fame to proclaim his coming to the heavens:

Fly where the evening from the Iberian vales
Takes on her swarthy shoulders Hecate
Crowned with a grove of oaks; fly where men feel
The burning axletree, and those that suffer
Beneath the chariot of the snowy Bear. . . .

(V.iv)

As usual with Eliot's Renaissance allusions, the source is in stark contrast to the banal modern counterpart. These lines express a noble courage in the face of death. Bussy props himself up with his sword as he speaks them, refusing even to lie down as he is dying. He also expresses hope that his fame and his soul will continue after his death. Gerontion, on the other hand, believes the law of entropy dictates that the whole earth will eventually disintegrate as energy becomes unavailable for organizing matter. So for him Chapman's "snowy Bear" is a "shuddering Bear" beginning to fall apart.

Wind moving over water, which always recalls for Eliot the creative wind moving over the deep in Genesis, has just the opposite meaning for Gerontion:

> Gull against the wind, in the windy straits
> Of Belle Isle, or running on the Horn,
> White feathers in the snow, the Gulf claims,
> And an old man driven by the Trades
> To a sleepy corner.

The syntax itself breaks up in this passage, as wave and wind tear the world apart and the ocean gulf becomes the "gulf" in the sense of the "abyss." The lines quoted earlier from the end of *East Coker* ("Old men ought to be explorers . . .") seem a direct reply to these. There, wave and wind in the "empty desolation" bring forth life (petrel and porpoise) in greater intensity, leading to the final phrase: "In my end is my beginning." Here, the gull fighting against the wind is fighting the force of chaos and is reduced to "white feathers in the snow," just another disorganized pile of stuff like the rocks and merds.[42] These lines bear some resemblance to a passage in *Mysticism* in which Underhill has a scientist discover that atomist materialism is actually a kind of idealism:

"The red brick," says Science, "is a mere convention. In reality that bit, like all other bits of the universe, consists, so far as I know at present, of innumerable atoms whirling and dancing one about the other. It is no more solid than a snowstorm. . . . Moreover, these atoms themselves elude me as I try to grasp them. They are only manifestations of something else. Could I track matter to its lair, I might conceivably discover that it has no extension, and become an idealist in spite of myself."[43]

Underhill is trying to show science how much its materialism is (as Whitehead later says) abstract and hence ideal. Quantum physics was at this time (1911) beginning to call into question the atom's "extension," its very materiality. By the time of *Science and the Modern World* (1925), Whitehead can declare that the notion of matter with simple extension in space is no longer tenable. Compare Eliot's assertion (quoted earlier) that all "thats" are "ideal constructions . . . as ideal as the atom" (*K&E*, 19). Underhill's vision of the atomic world as a whirling snowstorm is much like the images of the "Gull against the wind" and the "White feathers in the snow" that reduce Gerontion to apathy.

The end of this poem is a kind of materialistic apocalypse in which all that is organic is claimed by the Gulf, the abyss, the inevitable entropic chaos, giving up its last bit of usable energy with a whimper. Gerontion expects to be dissolved back into the chaotic whirl of atoms, and this expectation has already reduced his psyche to a state of nearly total entropy in his "sleepy corner." Unlike Lucretius, who faces with a glowing mind the annihilation he expects, this modern old man has no philosophy, only a vague sense that the whole world has been scientifically proven to be a meaningless accident.

STARING FROM THE PROTOZOIC SLIME

Burbank and Bleistein are modern tourists visiting what was the greatest commercial and artistic center of the late Middle Ages and one birthplace of the Renaissance, Venice. Burbank takes part in a timeless drama, crossing over a bridge into the arms of a princess; but the scale of the drama has become diminutive (the bridge is little and the hotel is small), and Princess Volupine's *voluptas* is not that of one of the three Graces. Her "phthisic hand" might be the *gelida manina* of the operatic heroine, but that she seems to entertain all the heroes, instead of dying in the arms of her one true love. The poem is stuffed with such ironies.

The mock-tragic fall of Burbank is contrasted with the fall of Antony. Where Burbank's "little bridge" crosses over a canal that is not even mentioned, Antony and Cleopatra are defeated at sea. The "defunctive" or funereal music is found in Shakespeare's *The Phoenix and the Turtle* and implies a true love, though a doomed one. Cleopatra has taken Antony from his duty not just by the power of lust but with real beauty, so the warlike Hercules has abandoned him before the battle of Actium. Eliot will quote Enobarbus's breathtaking description of her barge again in *The Waste Land,* and there too it will be in contrast to the "synthetic perfumes" and other unnatural details in the setting. Here, the marvel of fire and water existing together in harmony (the barge burning on the water all the day) implies an elemental beauty far different from Princess Volupine's "blue-nailed" hands. The "music under sea" is like the music of the mermaids heard by Prufrock and Ariel's music heard on the shore by Ferdinand in *The Tempest,* leading him to Miranda. Now Princess Volupine entertains Sir Ferdinand Klein, Sir Ferdinand "small."[44] The primal elements of ancient mythological physics are full of power and significance in the world of Antony and Cleopatra; Burbank and Bleistein do not know they exist.

Though these modern characters are alienated from the elemental physical world and from their own bodies, they have been taught by popularized versions of Darwinism to view themselves as indistinguishable from brute matter. A telling allusion to Darwinism is to be heard in the description of Bleistein visiting a museum in Venice:

> A lustreless protrusive eye
> Stares from the protozoic slime
> At a perspective of Canaletto.

This is, as Crawford has noted, an "evolutionary joke," and Bleistein's "saggy bending of the knees" reinforces the Darwinian association.[45] The question is, who is the butt of the joke? I will argue that this is a sardonic image of the modern reductionist notion of humanity—not so much the poet's satiric view of his character or of modern man or of Jews but his satiric presentation of the human being as defined by dogmatic biologists. Waggoner noted some time ago the Darwinian overtone of this passage but read it differently: "The evolutionary movement is reversed in the description of Bleistein to make him at once repellent and modern."[46] Eliot's aim is not, I think, to make his character modern and repellent but to show how the modern world's scientistic beliefs define him. Waggoner has it right, I think, when he elsewhere explains Eliot's general approach: "Modern secular man . . . is hollow not simply because he has given up God, but because his own description of himself and of the world leaves no room for any other than hollow men."[47] This is just what Eliot is doing in this passage, giving an image of the human person as defined by modern scientistic dogmas. Instead of the clay of Genesis animated with divine breath, Bleistein must be made, according to the Darwinist dogma, of slime that accidentally became protozoic, filled with protoanimals. By further chance mutation, out of this organic ooze pops an eye and the consciousness behind it. Such an eye is naturally "lustreless" because it projects no inner spiritual light. Its awareness is supposed to be a strictly passive material phenomenon.

Eliot was aware that the eye is an organ that Darwin never felt he could explain and that had remained unexplained by all devout believers in natural selection via gradual changes. *On the Origin of Species* contains one section in which Darwin forthrightly confronts the problem of complex structures. There he admits,

> To suppose that the eye, with all its inimitable contrivances for adjusting the focus to different distances, for admitting different amounts of light, and for

the correction of spherical and chromatic aberration, could have been formed by natural selection, seems, I freely confess, absurd in the highest possible degree.[48]

He goes on to say that we can see in different species of crustaceans several stages of development, from a simple optic nerve with pigment over it to organisms with corneas and cone cells, concluding that it is reasonable to believe the eye did develop in this way.[49] However, he does acknowledge the difficulty and the insufficiency of his evidence to overwhelm the basic objection.

The eye is an extremely complex organ, comprising many highly differentiated types of cells and connected in no simple way with specialized brain centers. The problem for Darwin's theory is that any one of the countless mutations that would have to take place for such an organ to evolve in an eyeless creature is completely useless in itself. What good is a retina cell without an optic nerve or a cornea without an iris? How could such a thing evolve gradually, by tiny steps, when none of the tiny steps would give the organism an adaptive advantage?

For these reasons, Bergson had made the eye his test case when he set about demolishing the doctrine of natural selection in *Creative Evolution* (1907). It was only a few years after this work was published when the young philosopher T. S. Eliot came to Paris and attended Bergson's lectures at the Collège de France. In "Eeldrop and Appleplex" (1917), Eliot's materialist character refers to Bergson's fixation on the eye:

"The question is," said Appleplex, "what is to be our philosophy. This must be settled at once. Mrs Howexden recommends me to read Bergson. He writes very entertainingly on the structure of the eye of the frog."[50]

Crawford notes the importance of *Creative Evolution* to Eliot but sees this passage as part of Eliot's rejection of Bergson's "pseudo-science."[51] Though Eliot did come to see Bergson as a pseudoscientist, he was sympathetic to the Bergsonian critique of Darwinism, which also seemed to Eliot to become pseudoscience when it was adopted uncritically. The dismissive tone used here is that of Appleplex, who is identified as a materialist. In the essay Eliot wrote on Bergson after his year in Paris, he takes a more respectful tone in speaking of "the remarkable discussion of the formation of the eye" in *Creative Evolution.*[52]

The image of the "protrusive eye" popping out of "protozoic slime" is best read as a critique of Darwinism, echoing Bergson's critique. What Bergson says about the eye is this:

Whether the function be the effect of the organ or its cause, it matters little; one point is certain—the organ will be of no use and will not give selection a hold unless it functions. However the minute structure of the retina may develop, and however complicated it may become, such progress, instead of favoring vision, will probably hinder it if the visual centres do not develop at the same time, as well as several parts of the visual organ itself. If the variations are accidental, how can they ever agree to arise in every part of the organ at the same time, in such way that the organ will continue to perform its function?[53]

Darwin's tentative answer to this problem was that the variations were "insensible"—so slight that they do not affect function and can await the advent of the other necessary variations. Bergson answers, "Granted; but while the insensible variation does not hinder the functioning of the eye, neither does it help it, so long as the variations that are complementary do not occur. How, in that case, can the variation be retained by natural selection?"[54] Many scientists and philosophers have recognized this issue of complex organs as a serious logical difficulty for the theory of natural selection.[55] Eliot's image of the eye emerging from the protozoic slime with no intermediate stages of development presents exactly this problem.

While the biologist instances the complex organization of the eye as a challenge to Darwinism, the poet sees an additional symbolic dimension. At least since Plato's *Timaeus,* eyesight has symbolized mind. Our language for describing higher mental acts includes visual words, such as "insight" and "vision." Thus, Eliot's image not only questions how such a complicated organ could result from random mutations but how consciousness, or spirit, could arise by chance from matter. There is a similar image in the earlier poem "Morning at the Window," in which one sees "the damp souls of housemaids / Sprouting despondently." Here, too, the spiritual element in human nature is taken from the evolutionary viewpoint as an epiphenomenon of mindless vegetative growth. Thus considered, the modern soul is damp with protozoic slime, not filled with aethereal fire the way Heraclitus said it should be.[56]

Eliot had also found in *The Education of Henry Adams* some questioning of Darwinian theory. As Sigg points out, when Adams contemplated the Darwinian view of life, he "felt betrayed by the lack of morality or plan in the physical or metaphysical universe, in the lives of nations, or in his own life."[57] Adams reacts thus to Lyell's geological proofs of natural selection:

The vertebrate began in the Ludlow shale, as complete as Adams himself—in some respects more so—at the top of the column of organic evolution: and geology offered no sort of proof that he had ever been anything else. Ponder over it as he might, Adams could see nothing in the theory of Sir Charles but pure inference. . . . [58]

This is, of course, the argument about missing links—one that has been taken seriously by some biologists recently.[59] Adams also expresses another cogent criticism that has not been adequately answered. The lower creatures seem, in fact, to be just as well adapted to the environment as we are; there must be some other impetus besides natural selection pressing for the development of higher orders of creatures. That is, the zoological world is obviously hierarchical, but there is nothing in the idea of natural selection to explain the leaps to higher levels of being. Years later, still thinking about his ancestor the fish, Adams was still unconvinced:

> He wished to be shown that changes in form caused evolution in force; that chemical or mechanical energy had by natural selection and minute changes, under uniform conditions, converted itself into thought. The ganoid fish seemed to prove—to him—that it had selected neither new form nor new force, but that the curates were right in thinking that force could be increased in volume or raised in intensity only by help of outside force.[60]

This question of biological antecedents is expressed, as Crawford suggests, in a line from "The Death of Saint Narcissus": "Then he knew that he had been a fish. . . ."[61] Like Adams, Bergson concluded that there had to be some force at work directing life toward higher levels of organization, though Bergson tried to avoid Aristotelian vitalism and Christian teleology by defining that force as an initial impulse, the *élan vital*, rather than as an entelechy or a divine agent guiding evolution each step of the way toward some predestined goal.[62] He was attempting to develop a natural philosophy that was neither materialist nor finalist (i.e., teleological), and Eliot was also seeking some such middle ground at the time, though he scoffed at the vital force idea and found Aristotle's teleological approach compelling.

Another thinker who was seeking some sort of *via media* between transcendentalism and materialism (and who was led as Eliot was toward Anglo-Catholicism) was Paul Elmer More. Like Eliot, More recognized in Darwinism a new form of an ancient materialist philosophy, lumping it with Epicurean atomism, along with several other strains:

> Call it Stoicism or call it Epicureanism, call it science or deism or realism or mere indifference or what you will, the most insidious and obstinate enemy of religion was, and is, the subservience of the mind content to see in the world only a huge fatalistic mechanism or a heterogeneous product of chance or, as the modern Darwinians would have it, a monstrous combination of both. Whatever form the error may take, it is a denial of the Logos as the creative wisdom and purpose of God, a magnification of the creature, a refined, but none the less devastating species of idolatry.[63]

Eliot's thinking probably resembles More's even more than it does Bergson's. Upon More's death, Eliot wrote in the *Princeton Alumni Weekly* that it was not until the first two volumes of *The Greek Tradition* came out (in the early 1920s) that More became important to him but that he then discovered "an auxiliary to my own progress of thought."[64] As we saw earlier, More elsewhere criticizes the effort of the Epicureans to hold on to their materialistic monism by explaining free will as a swerving of atoms. Eliot and More could see in modern scientific psychology, Watsonian behaviorism, a similarly unjustified reduction of mind to matter, one that attempted to extend Darwinian materialism to the study of the human spirit.

In *Four Quartets,* Eliot would speak of popular Darwinism explicitly and critically:

> It seems, as one becomes older,
> That the past has another pattern, and ceases to be a mere sequence—
> Or even development: the latter a partial fallacy,
> Encouraged by superficial notions of evolution,
> Which becomes, in the popular mind, a means of disowning the past.

The superficial notions are evidently the ones that draw neat diagrams of inevitable, though random, development. The champion of this modern progressivist doctrine was, of course, Herbert Spencer, who, as we have seen (chapter 1) had a marked influence on the intellectual climate in which Eliot grew up. Bergson spends the final pages of *Creative Evolution* confronting Spencer's view.[65] Though Burbank in the earlier poem is "meditating on / Time's ruins," one feels certain that he is a progressive-minded person who needs to know no more of the past than Baedeker's guidebook will tell him. Bleistein's "lustreless" look disowns the past even while examining it. Canaletto's "perspective," on the other hand, is a highly conscious and visionary way of looking at Venice. The poet asks whether the artist's eye too is simply a random development of carboniferous slime or whether such a triumph of form must not have been aided, as Adams (though himself unbelieving) says, by some outside force that has given pattern to the past.

Another challenge to Darwinism is to be found in "Sweeney Erect." The title alludes to one scientific designation for mankind, *homo erectus,* and thus proposes to test the definition of humanity given by the ideology of scientific materialism, which has it that gradual mutations rather than the breath of God made us what we are. These poems show what we think of ourselves (and consequently become) when we see ourselves only from that perspective. At the point where the poem switches from classical images to modern ones, someone makes a "Gesture of orang-outang." Woman is reduced below the zoological level when she becomes a "withered root of knots of hair." Her mindless "clawing at the pillow slip" is evidently the result of an epileptic seizure but also of being in the Darwinian world, in which human nature too is "red in tooth and claw." Doris from down the hall also appears as an animal as she "Enters padding on broad feet." Several critics have noted the way Eliot reduces characters to the bestial level in these poems.[66] Some have attributed the motif to the theme of social alienation and some to simple misanthropy on the part of the poet. The latter view is expressed forcefully by Bornstein, who finds that "Sweeney Erect" and many of Eliot's poems express a "radical hatred of the human condition."[67] If we see these animal images of humanity in the context of a critique of Darwinian materialism, however, we will conclude that Eliot is not merely expressing disgust for humanity or even modern urbanites. He is showing how we think of ourselves in the Darwinian age and how we end up actualizing that self-concept.

In "Sweeney among the Nightingales," our hero becomes simply "Apeneck Sweeney," his body and mind showing traces of ancestry farther back than Ireland. He is also related to the zebra and the giraffe. In the same room is a "silent vertebrate in brown," a creature identified by zoological subphylum. The name "Rachel née Rabinovitch" may suggest the high value people place on genealogy. One definition of human beings is that we are the only creatures who know who our grandparents are, and this memory is mother of the muses. Rachel née Rabinovitch, however, is instantly reduced to her evolutionary ancestry as she "Tears at the grapes with murderous paws." Finally, given Darwinian assumptions, life in "Sweeney Agonistes" becomes simply "birth, copulation, and death." Eliot was working out for himself just what type of world a thoroughly secular and materialistic one must be, and he was finding it peopled by a species of intelligent creature that had no creator: Sweeney erect.

DUALISM: MATTER AND SPIRIT

Eliot sees Emersonian transcendental individualism as a complement to scientific materialism on the other side of the Cartesian split. Manju Jain has described a tendency in the Unitarianism of Eliot's time to reject transcendentalism and embrace empiricism. Yet, Jain adds, Darwinism was a stumbling block for them, and most of the debates in the Harvard philosophy department of Eliot's day were between religion and science. "With the disintegration of Unitarian philosophy under the impact of Darwinism," Jain writes, "the main concern of Harvard philosophers was still the defense of religious truths and spiritual values against the challenge of

Darwinism and the reconciliation of these with the new scientific, materialist view of the universe."[68] This was the setting of Eliot's philosophical education, and he himself sought fervently for a resolution of the duality. He did not find that any of his mentors at Harvard—Royce, James, Santayana—had honestly achieved the goal. For example, though he shared in the aestheticism of Santayana, as Sigg has shown in valuable detail, Eliot eventually determined that artistic beauty alone could not solve the problems of modern life. Sigg concludes that " . . . Eliot grasped how far culture fell short of forming an adequate foundation for society, morals, or manners. In 1927, he dismissed pure aestheticism, without a theological framework, in the most graphic terms."[69] Simply turning away from scientific and commercial materialism was not an answer but only an unbalanced reaction. In struggling to answer the questions raised by nineteenth-century science, the Harvard philosophy department split roughly into two groups, idealists and realists, and as Gail McDonald has pointed out, Eliot was eventually critical of both camps.[70] At the time these early poems were written, then, Eliot found himself in the middle of such philosophical divisions, and he could not yet see his way to an answer. The poems convey his sense that the mental world of modern man had split into a hopelessly unresolved dualism, with spiritualism and materialism locked in a perverse complementarity.

Eliot's Unitarian kin were badly caught on the horns of this dilemma. They attempted to cleave to transcendentalism on one side of their minds, while they accepted empiricism on the other side. Emerson remained for them a visionary who saw the ideal nobility of the human spirit. In "Sweeney Erect," Eliot answers Emerson's famous claim in "Self-Reliance" that

> He who knows that power is inborn, that he is weak because he has looked for good out of him and elsewhere, and, so perceiving, throws himself unhesitatingly on his thought, instantly rights himself, stands in the erect position, commands his limbs, works miracles; just as a man who stands on his feet is stronger than a man who stands on his head.[71]

"Emerson," Eliot responds, "had not seen the silhouette / Of Sweeney straddled in the sun." The cult of the self-reliant individual results not in miracles but in egoists like Sweeney, who goes on shaving while his mistress has an epileptic fit on the bed. In other words, as Sigg points out, Emersonian individualism tends to abandon any sort of social action: " . . . Emerson often yielded when tempted to condemn social considerations."[72] The amoral Darwinian notion of man as a species of animal that happens to stand erect and have a large brain tends toward the same point from the other side, as it were. Transcendentalism and materialism both end in a kind of antisocial attitude: either idealistic individualism or cynical social Darwinism. Perhaps the deeper connection between Emerson and Darwin is secularism, the idea of mankind apart from the divine. What has held us back, Emerson says, is the tendency to look for good outside ourselves, in our family, our culture, our Creator. History itself, he teaches, was created not by Providence working through peoples but by a few individuals. Emerson's transcendentalism insists on one side of human duality and ignores not only the animal side of human nature but even the physical side of Christianity, as when he declined to give Communion. Darwinism, on the other hand, insists exclusively on the physical side of human duality: Sweeney as orangutan; the "silent vertebrate" in "Sweeney Among the Nightingales"; life reduced in "Sweeney Agonistes" to "birth, copulation, and death."

Paul Elmer More would have labeled both the transcendental and the materialist views "monisms" and would have insisted that we accept the essential dualism of our experience. The core of More's philosophy was his constant insistence that

> . . . in every field of experience, if I push my analysis to the end of my resources, I find myself brought up against a pair of irreconcilable, yet interrelated and interacting, contraries, such as "good" and "bad," "mind" and "body," the "One" and the "Many," "rest" and "motion." The dualist is one who modestly submits to this bifurcation as the ultimate point where clarity of definition obtains. . . . He remains half-brother to the sceptic, whereas the monist is a metaphysical dogmatist.[73]

Eliot, at the outset, was essentially a monist seeking to resolve duality, but never by the expedient of denying either side of the dichotomy. In several of these 1920 poems, Eliot is applying a skeptical critique like More's to the modern world's complementary monist dogmas. "Sweeney straddled in the sun" is a "magnification of the creature," an idolatry which is encouraged from the transcendental plane by Emersonian individualism. What both the materialist and idealist varieties of modernism reject is the *mysterium tremendum,* which Rudolf Otto finds at the core of religious experience.[74] Neither feels the fear of the Lord, which is the beginning of wisdom, and neither acknowledges the mysterious unity of opposites in human experience. Neither can accept the mystery of the Eucharist.

Like "Burbank," "Sweeney Erect" presents a contrast between a mythic tale and a modern event. The heroine of Beaumont and Fletcher's *The Maid's Tragedy,* from which the epigraph and parts of the opening stanzas are taken, sees her betrayal in relation to Ariadne's betrayal by Theseus. Her maids are making a tapestry portraying Ariadne, and she directs them to take her as their model:

> Paint me a cavernous waste shore
> Cast in the unstilled Cyclades,
> Paint me the bold anfractuous rocks
> Faced by the snarled and yelping seas.
>
> Display me Aeolus above
> Reviewing the insurgent gales
> Which tangle Ariadne's hair
> And swell with haste the perjured sails.

As with Antony and Cleopatra, this story is tragic but has a certain nobility about it, and the natural setting corresponds to the human. It is an elemental vision of shore, rocks, seas, and gales. The Renaissance heroine can still see herself in the elemental, mythic setting, but the modern story takes place indoors and without any consciousness of models from the past that might give coherence. Where the winds of the god Aeolus tangled Ariadne's hair, a nameless woman is now reduced to "This withered root of knots of hair." The materialist standpoint perceives her as an impersonal organism defined strictly as a collection of limbs. The "perjured sails" hoisted by Theseus abandoning Ariadne are transmuted into bedsheets and the "pillow slip" clawed by the epileptic. In the mythic scene, there are "anfractuous rocks / Faced by the snarled and yelping seas"; in the modern one, Sweeney "wipes the suds around his face." Many levels of experience have been lost because they are integrally bound to one another. The supernatural world of Aeolus is inseparable from the elemental world of nature, and art needs both to locate meaning in human life.

Eliot's French poems in this volume also take up the issue of how material and spiritual worlds are connected. "Le Directeur" pits the social world against the natural in a way familiar to readers of the "Prufrock" volume:

> Le directeur
> Conservateur
> Du Spectateur
> Empeste la brise.

The highly civilized man "fouls the breeze." In "Coriolan," a row of ancestral busts have "Noses strong to break the wind." Both are images of the civil world in disharmony with the elemental, which is always both natural and supernatural.

"Lune de Miel" again presents American tourists who are doing the tour of Europe but failing to connect with the European tradition. Eliot describes brutally their night in a cheap fleabag hotel and points to the nearby monument of culture and religion they did not bother to see:

Moins d'une lieue d'ici est Saint Apollinaire
En Classe, basilique connue des amateurs
De chapitaux d'acanthe que tournoie le vent.

[Less than a mile from here is Saint Apollinaire
En Classe, basilica known by amateurs
Of acanthus capitals which the wind whirls around.]

The basilica of Saint Apollinaire is known by lovers (amateurs) of a kind quite different from the honeymooners. The highly artificial form of the capitals is yet a natural form, that of acanthus leaves. The wind moves freely here. The spirit still moves through the old church, which prefigures the "empty chapel, only the wind's home" in *The Waste Land*. In the industrial world, it is seen as a "Vieille usine desaffectée de Dieu" (an old factory disaffected from God), yet its stone retains spiritual form: "Saint Apollinaire . . . tient encore / Dans ses pierres écroulantes la forme précise de Byzance" [St. Apollinaire still holds in its crumbling stones the precise form of Byzantium]. Art and religion found the *Logos* in the element of stone, and that divine pattern is still apparent in the *Gestalt* of the basilica, though the place has been deserted and the stones are crumbling. The egoistic civility of "le directeur" or Coriolan's busts collides with nature, but the communal and traditional culture represented in the basilica finds a symbolist correspondence between the natural and supernatural.

The grotesque waiter of "Dans le Restaurant" recalls his own ancient history, his mythic past. It took place in the countryside, where the elements were, and are still, in vital harmony: "Dans mon pays il fera temps pluvieux, / Du vent, du grand soleil, et de la pluie; / C'est ce qu'on appelle le jour de lessive des gueux" [In my country it will be the rainy season, wind, bright sun, and rain; it is what we call the laundry day of the vagabonds]. The central event of his past was the moment of taking shelter from a storm with his hyacinth girl (a primrose girl in this case): "J'avais sept ans, elle etait plus petite. / Elle était toute mouillée, je lui ai donné des primevères" [I was seven, she was younger. She was all wet, I gave her primroses]. His tragedy was that he ran away when a big dog came after them. Now he has apparently moved to the city and ended as a garrulous waiter. In the old country, even the tramps had a laundry day when it rained; now he is so filthy that the diner specifies his tip should be used for a bath.

The Phlebas passage, which follows, may be seen as the type of bath the waiter (and probably the diner also) needs, a complete immersion which will drown him. It is a "sort pénible" [a painful destiny], but the submarine current "l'emporta très loin, / Le repassant aux étapes de sa vie antérieure" [took him very far, back past the stages of his former life]. This is just what the waiter instinctually desires, what he impotently seeks to do in his reminiscing. Eliot carefully avoids allusion to the sacramental meaning of such immersion, but he explores the primal experience of the watery element and finds its protosacramental efficacy. Only some such drowning could take the waiter back to the moment of his original sin and restore him to the primrose garden and his own full humanity.

THE TROUBLE WITH METAPHYSICS

Of course, Eliot was not at this time a believer. "The Hippopotamus" satirizes the Church (primarily identified with the Unitarian Church of a cousin) for translating its foundation "upon a rock" too literally, or rather too materially in the economic sense. It thus perverts its role as still point: "the True Church need never stir / To gather in its dividends." In "Mr. Eliot's Sunday Service," the same worship of Mammon is revealed in the young people "Clutching piaculative pence," purchasing pardon— and probably also in the "sapient sutlers of the Lord," the provisioners of the Christian soldiers. The poem also sets the creative potency of the Word over against the impotence of the eunuchs. Chief of them is Origen, whose name ironically plays on origins, genesis, but who took the Word literally and castrated himself. The Fathers of the Church are likened to bees, which are "epicene" (intersexual, having the same physical form for both sexes, which is a false union of opposites). They disseminate the Gospels as bees carry pollen, randomly, mindlessly. This is probably what is meant by calling them "Polyphiloprogenitive," progenitors of many lines—of many strange sects. Eliot's attitude toward Origen was no doubt influenced by G. T. W. Patrick, who, in his edition of Heraclitus, argues that true Greek philosophy upheld the idea of "the unity of man and Nature." Patrick blames Platonic transcendentalism for the demise of this view: "Philo the Jew, Plutarch the moralist, Valentinus the Gnostic, Origen the Christian, all yielded to it in greater or less degree. In Plotinus it reached its full fruitage. Porphyry, his pupil, relates that he was ashamed of having a body and was careless of its needs, so anxious was he exstatically to absorb his soul in the Supra-rational Transcendent One."[75] These are the "masters of the subtle schools" in Eliot's poem, those who have considered it necessary to deny the physical world entirely in order to seek the transcendent godhead.

The last stanza of this poem pits the metaphysical ponderings of these disembodied masters against the bodily reality of Eliot's favorite Irish pugilist:

> Sweeney shifts from ham to ham
> Stirring the water in his bath.
> The masters of the subtle schools
> Are controversial, polymath.

The attempt of the schoolmen to produce an all-encompassing "polymath" metaphysics results in the controversies of the plural "schools" and hence becomes "polyphiloprogenitive." Like Emerson, they indulge in transcendent philosophies (or, in Bergsonian terms, "finalist" philosophies) that take into account Christ's feet in the Jordan but not Sweeney's feet in the bath. The savior is a "Baptized God," not a God-man, and his "unoffending feet" are too angelic to be a convincing incarnation. Sweeney's hams are made strictly of *carne,* and he is no eunuch. The metaphysicians cannot account for his purely physical being. It is with such problems in mind that Eliot proclaims in his dissertation, "Metaphysical systems are condemned to go up like a rocket and come down like a stick" (*K&E,* 168).

The same confrontation of physical and metaphysical is the theme of "Whispers of Immortality," whose title challenges Wordsworth's facile discovery of spirit and self in nature. With Webster and Donne, Eliot begins with the obvious separation of soul and body at death. Instead of eyes, the sense organ identified with consciousness, Webster sees (with a comic touch added by Eliot) daffodil bulbs in the dead skull. However, Webster and Donne do find a connection beyond death. Webster "knew that thought clings round dead limbs / Tightening its lusts and luxuries"— not exactly the resurrection of the body, but not atomistic dissolution either. Donne "found no substitute for sense" because, as Eliot says in the essay on the metaphysical poets, "A thought to Donne was an experience; it modified his sensibility." The sensibility is a quasi-physical faculty, responding to the artistic medium and to physical reality, as well as to the thought. Conversely, Donne felt the "fever of the bone" was a quasi-spiritual fever incapable of being allayed by any "contact possible to flesh." The poem thus describes Donne's honest and difficult unifying of thought and experience as opposed to a metaphysical flight to quick resolutions. The "masters of the subtle schools"—both the less sensible medieval theologians and the Romantic idealists, such as Wordsworth and Emerson—retreat from immediate experience into idealist metaphysical speculation.

In place of Sweeney, Eliot introduces Grishkin as a challenge to the thinkers: "Uncorseted, her friendly bust / Gives promise of pneumatic bliss." As Kenner remarks, "'Pneumatic,' of course, evokes by its etymology the things of the spirit, though it is unlikely that Grishkin is one of the 'martyr'd virgins.'"[76] In fact, Grishkin is purely physical, with a "feline smell" more rank than that of the "sleek Brazilian jaguar," yet her physics is in some way closer to spiritual realities than "our metaphysics":

> And even the Abstract Entities
> Circumambulate her charm;
> But our lot crawls between dry ribs
> To keep our metaphysics warm.

I think it is clear here that the first person plural does not include Webster and Donne, whose thought was one with immediate experience, and that it does include Wordsworth, Emerson, and the schoolmen. Kenner introduces as a gloss on this poem Bradley's statement (already quoted earlier) about "impalpable abstractions" and "bloodless categories."[77] The physical world can be what Bradley calls "a show of some fuller splendour" if (perhaps only if) it is a world created by a deity who pronounced it good. The elements are thus always essentially reflecting the designs of the *Logos,* however much our relations with them may have become perverted. The masters of metaphysics, even when they are theists, tend not to experience the physical world this way: they see it strictly as an illusion, behind which lie abstractions if they are idealists, atoms if they are materialists.

Eliot held that Donne could have his unified sensibility because of his traditional religious belief and his traditional Aristotelian metaphysics. To the extent that Donne failed to maintain the Aristotelian approach, he represented the shift toward modern disjunction, which is how Eliot later came to regard him. If the world, including our own bodies, was created in such a way that matter and form were inseparable, and if the Word who created it also became embodied at a particular moment in history (in short, if one believes as Lancelot Andrewes does), then the symbols of poetry can express physical and spiritual reality simultaneously.

In reading Donne's meditations on death, Eliot began to think about the belief in the resurrection of the body. In this way, the poet moved toward the same end More approached via the study of Plato. In *The Catholic Faith* (1931), More would write characteristically,

If the future life is to be anything more than a vague abstraction of metaphysics to which we cling with a kind of cheerless hope . . . then surely we must think of the liberated soul as still possessing some center of activity in the vast expansions of space, some vehicle of self-expression, some medium of subtler perception and purer sensation, which may be regarded as an etherialized body.[78]

Here, More alludes to the ancient quasi-spiritual aether to imagine a resurrected body. From this point of view, what lies behind the appearance of the physical body is not a random conglomeration of atoms or some purely abstract form but an eternal spiritual body. Modern physics, which breaks down the dichotomy between matter and energy, might offer another way to explain spiritual bodies. The most ancient and the most recent physicists both thought of essences that are not strictly either material or spiritual. They dealt not in abstractions but in mysteries.

I would like to point out that Bradley, Eliot, and More did not become forerunners of the deconstructionists when they criticized metaphysics. More immersed himself in Plato, whose reliance on allegories, exemplars, and common sense he found antimetaphysical. Eliot found the same thing in Aristotle and in mythic and poetic symbolism. Both were drawn inexorably to the Apostles' Creed and to Catholic ritual as affirmation and enactment of mysterious realities. Deconstructionists define metaphysics much more broadly. For them, any notion of truth is metaphysical because they have begun by denying any "immediate experience." Experience is always mediated, they say. In fact, the mediating medium—and there is in their reductionism only one medium, written language—is all there is. Somehow this assertion is not regarded as a metaphysical statement about reality, evidently because it has been scientifically proven by the structuralists, whose scientific positivism is, of course, otherwise totally discredited by their intellectual offspring. One might call deconstruction "meta-metaphysics," for when Derrida abandons metaphysical abstraction he does not turn toward physical experience but tries to go beyond abstraction to abstractions about abstraction. Given the laws of nature, however, meta-metaphysics is bound to have a physical side. Deconstruction has as its obverse the crudest of material aims, power. It may deny the flesh but not the world.

Within Eliot's clarifying vision of the world, Grishkin's uncorseted bust may almost promise more genuine spiritual bliss than the abstractions of metaphysics. Eliot had not embraced Donne's religion at this time, but he had adopted the great divine's incarnational poetics as a way of escaping the tyranny of "bloodless categories." Grishkin is no martyred virgin, certainly, but in challenging abstraction, her breasts may almost be said to draw the poet toward "the barely prayable prayer" he will later address to the Virgin Mother.

It was initially under the influence of Bergson that Eliot rejected both materialist physics and transcendentalist metaphysics, though Paul Elmer More, F. H. Bradley, and Alfred North Whitehead were also thinking along similar lines. Bergson's solution to the dilemma did not satisfy Eliot, however, and he himself had in 1920 no positive suggestion to make.

He could only make critical or satirical reflections. In Dante and Donne and Andrewes, he was discovering a union of thought and sense that seemed the beginning of an answer to him. His response to the pre-Cartesian undissociated sensibility of these writers would lead him eventually to embrace their incarnational theology.

4

Elements and Sacraments in
The Waste Land

But it was all a mystery. Here we are,
  And there we go:—but *where?* five bits of lead,
Or three, or two, or one, send very far!
  And is this blood, then, formed but to be shed?
Can every element our elements mar?
  And air—earth—water—fire live—and we dead?
We, whose minds comprehend all things?
                    (Byron, *Don Juan,* Canto V, 39)

WHEN a materialist must finally face the mystery of death, he may
wonder, as Byron does here, how it is that the simple elements of which
our physical being is composed can turn against us and kill us; for each
element *can,* in excess, do so. This fatal potential of the four elements
becomes an organizing theme of *The Waste Land.* In the years leading
up to its composition, Eliot had been writing poetic studies of modern
materialists staring into the dark, notably in "Gerontion" and in
"Sweeney Among the Nightingales." Gerontion's is the hopeless death of
an atomist; Sweeney dies ignominiously, in contrast to the tragic death
of his classical counterpart, Agamemnon. However, there is a hint in the
latter poem of the ancient ideas of death, which Eliot would introduce in
The Waste Land as a counter to modern despair. The murder is to take
place under "Gloomy Orion and the Dog," stars whose appearance (according to the Egyptian calendar) presages rain and the flooding that
brings renewed fertility to the banks of the Nile.[1] The murder has ritualistic and mythic overtones: abundance of fruits, a man with a "golden
grin," nightingales singing near a convent. As critics have noted, the
"bloody wood" puts one in mind of Frazer's immense study of fertility
cults that practiced ritual sacrifice. The "stiff dishonoured shroud" at the
end even suggests the sacrifice of Christ and the shroud of Turin, which
remains a puzzle today. In this poem, and in *The Waste Land,* Eliot

describes the vacuity of the modern response to physical reality and to death in particular. At the same time, he begins to introduce the rich elemental symbolism with which ancient cultures have described the physical world and through which they have confronted the mystery of death.

In his earlier poetry, Eliot had satirized the profane modern view of the surrounding world. Partly as a result of reading Frazer, Weston, Harrison, Cornford, and others of their school, he began to recover a vision of the cosmos as symbolic and sacred. He recognized in Stravinsky's *Rite of Spring* such an attempt to speak of ancient mysteries in a modern idiom. In his review of the ballet, he thought about ways of taking Frazer's work: "In art there should be interpretation and metamorphosis. Even *The Golden Bough* can be read in two ways: as a collection of entertaining myths, or as a revelation of that vanished mind of which our mind is a continuum."[2] Eliot obviously was reading Frazer in the latter way. He appreciates (in the 1924 essay "A Prediction Concerning Three English Authors") what he perceives as a refraining from interpretation on Frazer's part:

> On the contrary, with every fresh volume of his stupendous compendium of human superstition and folly, Frazer withdraws in more and more cautious abstention from the attempt to explain.[3]

Thus, Eliot admits Frazer into the company of the true scientists, those who can focus steadfastly on facts. He takes the book essentially as a compilation of raw data related to the primitive mind.

However, when Eliot calls *The Golden Bough* a "compendium of human superstition and folly," he is really summing up Frazer's interpretation of all the facts he has gathered. As Robert Crawford puts it, " . . . to present the deeds of savages as 'folly' is a crucial act of theoretical interpretation which undermines all claims to be presenting mere 'fact.'"[4] On the other hand, when Eliot speaks of reading Frazer's work as a "revelation of that primitive mind of which our mind is a continuum," he gives an interpretation contrary to Frazer's. The great Scots scholar regarded all the myths and rituals he studied as so much superstition, and his beautiful closing paragraph, in which he describes himself standing in the grove at Nemi and hearing the bells calling people to pray the Angelus, implies that Christianity itself is just another version of the old fertility cults, with the Virgin taking the place of Diana, and Christ, that of the slaughtered priest of Nemi. He suggests as much as he concludes his monumental study, "Le roi est mort, vive le roi! Ave Maria!"[5] Frazer studied myth and religion from the progressive, rationalistic perspective, devoting his life to it so that he could explain away the irrational superstition and help interrupt the mental continuum, severing the modern mind from the primitive forever. Eliot was moving in the opposite direction, accepting the continuity of his mind with the barbaric mind and all of its magical, symbolic thinking. As Manju Jain has noted, Eliot had stated, in a much earlier essay for Josiah Royce's seminar, that Frazer, along with other folklorists and anthropologists, had actually given a "philosophical interpretation" of the facts, so as to support his "preconceptions."[6] In this case, his earlier view may be closer to his ultimate one than is the view expressed in "A Prediction." Of course, both views are partly true: Frazer did have strong preconceptions about his material, but he did present all the factual material, which then could be given other interpretations.

Eliot's reinterpretation of Frazer's material is one which was not uncommon at the time. For example, G. K. Chesterton addresses the same crux and points out in a similar way that one may look at the analogies between pagan myth and Christianity either as proof that all religion is a human creation with no objective truth to it, or as evidence that from the beginning man has had poetic inklings of the truth, leading toward the full revelation contained in Christianity. In *The Everlasting Man* (1925), he criticizes the reductive tendency of rationalistic professors of mythology and mentions Frazer's work:

> A really fine work of folk-lore, like *The Golden Bough*, will leave too many readers with the idea, for instance, that this or that story of a giant's or wizard's heart in a casket or a cave only "means" some stupid and static superstition called "the external soul." But we do not know what these things mean, simply because we do not know what we ourselves mean when we are moved by them. . . . Very deep things in our nature, some dim sense of the dependence of great things upon small, some dark suggestion that the things nearest to us stretch far beyond our power, some sacramental feeling of the magic in material substances, and many more emotions past finding out, are in an idea like that of the external soul.[7]

As Chesterton's words imply, the valuable feeling in mythology generally is that which senses a connection between material and spiritual phenomena; and it is valuable in that it leads toward Catholic sacramental theology. Chesterton's statement foreshadows what later writers like Eliade and Ricoeur would say on the subject (see chapter 1). Eliot was not putting the matter in religious terms at this time, but his recognition of the continuum of thought between the ancient mythic mind and his own was leading him where similar thoughts were leading Chesterton, who became a Roman Catholic the year *The Waste Land* was published.

Both Piers Gray and, later, Robert Crawford have analyzed in a detailed and careful way Eliot's thinking about the relation between primitive religion and Christianity. They find that he rejected E. B. Tyler's notion of "ancient savage philosophers," insisting, with Lucien Lévy-Bruhl, that early people were not simply rationalistic thinkers with very limited knowledge. Eliot leans toward Lévy-Bruhl's theory that primitive people had a "prelogical mentality" quite different from that of modern man.[8] This emphasis on the difference between ancient and modern minds would seem to contradict Eliot's statements about the continuity between the two. Bradley's thinking seems to have helped him with this difficulty by explaining that immediate experience, though it yields to relational thinking, is nevertheless carried along into the relational phase and may be accessible in certain states of mind. As we have seen, the central concern of Eliot's career was to bring together the prelogical *participation mystique* of immediate experience with the logical distinction-making function of relational consciousness. He saw that the sacramental worship of Christianity, though based on a relational, rational theology, sought to involve the prelogical mind in communal participation. By 1925, Eliot would conclude that within the Mass one experienced something of the primitive "Australian ceremonies" described by the anthropologists.[9]

In his paper on the scientific method written for Josiah Royce's seminar in 1913, Eliot praises Frazer for showing continuities between primitive and civilized: "No one has done more to make manifest the similarities and identities underlying the customs of races very remote in every way from each other."[10] At the same time, however, Eliot states in this essay that he "cannot subscribe . . . to the *interpretation* with which he ends his volume on the Dying God."[11] In that conclusion, Frazer reveals his rationalistic and positivistic assumptions: "Led astray by his ignorance of the true cause of things, primitive man believed that in order to produce the great phenomena of nature on which his life depended he had only to imitate them. . . . "[12] In this proclamation, Frazer makes exactly the same error Tyler does, assuming that primitive man held rationally formed beliefs, just as we do, that these beliefs were scientific beliefs concerning the phenomena of nature, and that they were wrong simply because they were based on inadequate knowledge. Thus, we can see that Eliot turned to Frazer for evidence of similarities between ancient and modern ritual but rejected Frazer's rationalistic interpretation in favor of a point of view influenced by Lévy-Bruhl and Bradley. Rather than dismissing both ancient and modern rites as magic, Eliot accepted both as authentic symbolic expressions.

Paul Elmer More is yet another who was reading anthropology the way Eliot was. In *The Catholic Faith* (1931) he writes,

Suppose a modern man more or less acquainted with anthropology to be confronted by the claims of revelation made for Christian theism and morality as embodied in the dogma of the Incarnation and the sacrament of the mass. One of two things may happen. If instinctively he is unsympathetic to those claims, or is prejudiced by certain fixed and incompatible intellectual axioms, he will reject them as nothing more than a prolongation of primitive ignorance and superstition. But, contrariwise, if instinctively he is sympathetic to the appeal of the supernatural and is sceptical of the finality of our scientific and rationalistic assumptions, then he will be inclined rather to judge the ancient myths of mana and tabu and the totemistic sacrifice in the light of their analogy with Christian dogma and will look to see in them clumsy gropings after a mystery finally revealed.[13]

Many people who were reading Frazer in his own rationalistic mindset naturally thought Eliot was one of their number when *The Waste Land* appeared. He was, however, like More, skeptical about the claims of rationalism. His fascination with pagan myth led him toward an Incarnational theology and a sacramental, ritualistic form of worship. It was the integration of physical and spiritual realities that attracted him to the story of the Fisher King—and then to the sacrifice and sacrament at the core of the story.

This understanding of the sympathy between pagan cult and Catholic Christianity is touched on several times by Jessie Weston, who seems to be slightly less inclined than Frazer to dismiss primitive rites as superstition. For instance, while discussing the worship of Mithra and of Attis, she argues that

> In both cults the final aim was the attainment of spiritual and eternal life. Moreover, both possessed essential features which admitted, if they did not encourage, an assimilation with Christianity. Both of them, if forced to yield ground to their powerful rival, could, with a fair show of reason, claim that they had been not vanquished, but fulfilled, that their teaching had, in Christianity, attained its normal term.[14]

Elsewhere, Weston makes it clear that among the "essential features" that establish this kinship is "the Sacramental idea."[15] This is essentially the notion that there is a real connection between physical substances and spirit—even, as Chesterton puts it, "a dependence of greater things upon small" (or as Thomas à Kempis said, "The higher cannot stand without the lower"). Weston several times emphasizes the relation between exoteric rituals aimed at "affecting the processes of Nature" and identical esoteric ceremonies "utilized for the imparting of high spiritual teaching concerning the relation of Man to the Divine Source of his being, and the possibility of sensible union between Man and God." Christianity, she goes on to say, recognized its affinity with the esoteric mystery cults:

The recognition of the cosmic activities of the Logos appears to have been a characteristic feature of this teaching, and when Christianity came upon the scene it did not hesitate to utilize the already existing medium of instruction, but boldly identified the Deity of Vegetation, regarded as Life Principle, with the God of the Christian Faith.[16]

This appropriation was natural because both pagans and Christians regarded rituals not as a "medium of instruction" but as a "sensible union between Man and God," as sacrament. This primitive religious sensibility is thus an undissociated one in which the symbol is simultaneously material and spiritual.

Eliot had read in Evelyn Underhill's *Mysticism* that even the Christian mystics, for all their denial of the sensual world, often find in their illumination an experience of immanence:

> Closely connected with the sense of the "presence of God," or power of perceiving the Absolute, is the complementary mark of the illuminated consciousness; the vision of "a new heaven and a new earth," or an added significance and reality in the phenomenal world. Such words are those of Julian, "God is all thing that is good to my sight, and the goodness that all thing hath, it is He," seem to establish the link between the two. . . . This experience, at its best, balances and completes the experience of the Presence of God at its best. That is to say, its "note" is sacramental, not ascetic.[17]

Underhill points out that such immanental mystics as Dame Julian are close to the poets, an observation Eliot may have recalled as he found himself becoming a poet rather than a philosopher or mystic—and which may have influenced his later use of Julian in *Four Quartets*. He appropriated the anthropological material with this sense of its compatibility with Christian sacramentalism and poetic symbolism.

The continuity Eliot saw between pagan and Christian religion was established by the continuation of certain natural symbols and patterns of symbolism. He further saw that it was possible for the modern poet to use the same perennial symbols and thus to reach the same ancient, prelogical part of the mind. He proclaimed, in 1918, "The artist, I believe, is more *primitive,* as well as more civilised, than his contemporaries, his experience is deeper than civilization, and he only uses the phenomena of civilization in expressing it. Primitive instincts and the acquired habits of ages are confounded in the ordinary man."[18] A year later, he wrote similarly that the artist is "the most *and* the least civilized and civilizable; he is the most competent to understand both civilized and primitive."[19] The primitive mind is more given to unconscious feeling and the civilized mind to conscious thought; the poet brings the two together.

Union of primitive feeling and civilized thought is the strength of the "mythical method" announced by Eliot in his famous review of *Ulysses:*

> In using the myth, in manipulating a continuous parallel between contemporaneity and antiquity, Mr Joyce is pursuing a method which others must pursue after him. . . . It is simply a way of controlling, of ordering, of giving a shape and a significance to the immense panorama of futility and anarchy which is contemporary history. . . . Psychology (such as it is, and whether our reaction to it be comic or serious), ethnology, and *The Golden Bough* have concurred to make possible what was impossible even a few years ago. Instead of the narrative method, we may now use the mythical method.[20]

Crawford argues that this should not be taken as a description of *The Waste Land*, for Eliot gives the themes of the poem "no firm significance which raises them above futility."[21] It will form part of my purpose in this chapter to maintain that the poem does give such firm significance to its themes, even though, as Ronald Bush has pointed out, the mythic structure was an overlay added by Eliot at the last hour to give some order to his chaotic poem.[22] Eliot uses primordial religious and cosmological symbolism, especially the symbolism of the elements, to establish a significant pattern beneath the sense of fragmentation. The mythical method as he employs it does not necessarily yield a clear resolution of the poem's dilemmas, but it does present the archetypal symbolic systems in which such a resolution has been found and in which it may perhaps be found again.

As he put the meeting with death into a mythic context, Eliot also inevitably put it into the context of the old cosmologies. In his early poems, he had shown himself and his readers what life was like in the modern urban world, in which there were no elements but only atomistic matter and artifacts. Of old, people had direct experience of the elements. Earth, water, air, and fire were not abstract notions but realities they all experienced constantly. In early agricultural societies, it was known bone deep that plant life, the basis of all life, would thrive only with a balanced blend of soil, rain, air, and sunlight. Since this experience is universal, these natural symbols are also universal. Eliot knew that Eastern philosophies speak of the same four elements, even adding occasionally the fifth element, space or aether. Besides being real in this very real sense, the elements are deeply symbolic. Prophetic writings are filled with references to these primordial essences, and all rituals employ them. It turns out that the most concrete description of the world is also the most symbolically rich.

The poet of *The Waste Land* longs to recover such a simple and vital relation to the world around him, rather as Coleridge does in *The Rime of the Ancient Mariner*. In fact, some rejected passages in the drafts of

"Death by Water," telling the tale of a ship driven by storm into the Arctic seas, are strongly reminiscent of Coleridge's sea tale. Eliot's poem thus becomes an initiation rite for modern man into the old mysteries. Through the ritual, fertility is renewed but only after bloody sacrifice. I wish to argue that in the poem's central symbolic narrative each of the elements in turn brings about the death of a sacrificial victim, but this death brings the scapegoat into a new union with all the elements. It is, I will maintain, with some such schema in mind that Eliot separates the four elements in the first four sections and then joins them momentarily in the last.

This poetic ritual is analogous to the art of alchemy, which sought to transform base matter into gold by dissolving it into its constituent elements and then joining them in a newly perfected balance: hence the alchemical motto *solve et coagula*. Again, Underhill may have introduced Eliot to the idea, for there is a section on alchemy in *Mysticism* that presents it as another esoteric system aimed at "the reordering of spiritual rather than material elements."[23] The notion of separating and then reordering is given due prominence: "As psychic uproar and disorder seem part of the process of mental growth, so '*solve et coagula*'—break down that you may build up—is the watchword of the spiritual alchemist."[24] Of course, this is such a universal pattern that one would not need to be an alchemist to write a poem that embodies it. Empedocles' idea of Strife (dissolving) and Love (coagulating) points to the same reality, but the alchemical dissolving is specifically of the four elements, so it may have influenced Eliot's treatment of them. *The Waste Land* is organized into sections corresponding to the old elements because it enacts such a dissolution of the elements, bringing about the death of the sacrificial victim and thus merging with the fertility rituals. The fatal chaos is followed by hints of a new resolution of the opposing elements, bringing about a revival or resurrection.

THE FIVE ELEMENTS

Eliot's interest in the classical elements runs throughout his work but is most obvious in his division of *The Waste Land* into five sections whose very titles name or refer to earth, air, fire, water, and aether. Of the four earthly elements, two are named in the titles "The Fire Sermon" and "Death by Water." Earth is evident in "The Burial of the Dead." Moreover, in the imagery of each section, the titular element dominates. Elisabeth Schneider has made this observation, further pointing out that the second section has a great deal of air imagery, though the title was originally "In the Cage" and finally "A Game of Chess," neither of which seems at first to allude to air. Schneider adds that "All the elements are brought together at last in 'What the Thunder Said,'" but she then drops her consideration of them with a dismissive footnote:

> I do not wish to make too much of this aspect of the poem's structure. It is incidental to the theme, and Eliot does not mechanically restrict each class of image to its assigned division; in particular, there are allusions throughout, for obvious reasons, to water or the absence of it. His structure somewhat resembles the much more rigid, smaller-scale structure of Shelley's *Ode to the West Wind,* where leaf, cloud and wave each takes its turn to dominate but together are cumulative, each caught up and translated, sometimes forcibly, into the imagery of the next, with, in the end, all recapitulated together.[25]

This comment has stood as the last word on the subject. The insight that the separate images are "recapitulated together" at the end points to a pattern with real significance, as we will see.

Actually, Northrop Frye had already addressed the topic in an earlier book. He writes,

> As later in *Four Quartets,* there is an elaborate imagery of the four elements. The cycle of water, from spring rains and the wet hair of the hyacinth girl to the Thames flowing out to sea, returning as the rains bringing new life to the parched land, is most prominent. According to Charles Lamb, Webster's "Call for the robin redbreast and the wren," and Shakespeare's "Full fathom five" are the great elegies of death by earth and water respectively in the language, and both are referred to in *The Waste Land.* In "The Fire Sermon," there is the implicit contrast between St. Augustine and Buddha who appear at the end, seeking "the fire that refines them" (the last line of Canto 26 of the *Purgatorio*), and those who are burning in their own lusts with heat but without light. The air is hidden in the "brown fog" of a London winter; it blows freshly towards home but leaves Tristan as far away as the Ancient Mariner or Ulysses; it stirs up and confuses the perfumes of the woman in "A Game of Chess"; it is the element of the fearful apparitions and mirages of the closing scenes.[26]

Frye, himself a great lover of things that come in fours, expresses in a compact and masterful way several of the insights I wish to explore more fully in this chapter. I would note particularly the idea of death by earth, water, and fire. I will argue that Eliot uses this elemental imagery to establish his basic structural and thematic pattern.

We may begin to see the pattern if we note that Eliot does not follow the order of the elements which is most common in ancient sources, wherein they were thought of as having different densities, the heavier falling to their natural level, and all four being logically listed from grossest to most aethereal: earth, water, air, and fire. Eliot employs an alternate schema (also common in classical writings, especially those of Empedocles), which emphasizes their opposition to each other. In this approach, each element is defined as a combination of characteristics from two pairs of opposites: cold vs. hot, and moist vs. dry. Earth is cold and dry; water is cold and moist; air is hot and moist; and fire is hot and dry. These antinomies appear in the elemental world of "Animula" as "dry or damp, chilly or warm." When the philosophers thus point to the strife between the elements, they pair each element with the one opposite to it in both qualities: earth (cold and dry) vs. air (hot and moist); fire (hot and dry) vs. water (cold and moist). Eliot arranges the sections of the poem in the oppositional order thus generated: earth, air, fire, and water. He is less concerned with the hierarchy of the four than with their strife.

In his introduction to a book on Empedocles, Marshall McLuhan briefly notes Eliot's focus on the classical elements and argues that it is primarily Empedoclean: "His devotion to the pre-Socratic philosophers is evident in his citation from them, but it is Empedocles whose vision pervades *The Waste Land* and *Four Quartets*."[27] Like other critics who have noted the importance of the elements in these poems, McLuhan does not elaborate. He is right to point toward the strife and love of the elements, but as we have seen, Eliot's favorite pre-Socratic thinker was, from the beginning, Heraclitus, and we will find that Eliot followed primarily the latter's system in *The Waste Land* and particularly in *Four Quartets*.

One reason critics have not attempted a more detailed analysis of the elemental structure in *The Waste Land* is that the poem has five sections, not four.[28] No one has previously observed that the fifth section also has its own element, the aether, which is associated in classical physics with the upper air and with lightning and thunder. This observation reopens the question of how Eliot used the elements in this poem and throughout his poetry, for the coming together of the elements under the influence of the quasi-spiritual aether is indeed integral to the poet's theme. Frye sees this resolution and suggests a Christian interpretation: "The dissolving and reforming of physical elements suggest that the reality of which they are an appearance is a spiritual substance, the risen Christ."[29] Just so; however, what prepares the way toward this Christian vision is the classical idea of a "spiritual substance," the divine aether.

The concept of aether seems to go back as far as that of the other elements. G. S. Kirk and J. E. Raven describe the popular conception of the cosmos in ancient Greece before the birth of philosophy: "The lower part of the gap between earth and sky, up to and including the clouds, contains *aer* or mist: the upper part (sometimes called the *ouranos* itself) is *aither*, the shining upper air, which is sometimes conceived as fiery."[30] In his essay on "Seneca in Elizabethan Translation" (1927), Eliot happens to quote lines that employ the word *aether* in a way that was common for the Roman poets, as a synonym of *caelo,* sky:

> The final cry of Jason to Medea departing in her car is unique; I can think of no other play which reserves such a shock for the last word:
>
>> Per alta vada spatia sublimi aethere;
>> testare nullos esse, qua veheris, deos.[31]

This denial that there are gods in the sublime aether shocks because it was assumed the aether was their natural abode and their very substance. As W. K. C. Guthrie puts it,

> The Greek word which approaches most nearly to the English "heaven", with all its associations, is not *ouranos* but *aither.* A Greek of any period would agree that it was in the *aither,* if anywhere, that the gods dwelt, and that the *aither* itself was divine, the epithet with which Prometheus addresses it in one of the best-known passages in Greek literature. In ordinary parlance, the *aer* belongs, as much as the earth itself, to the region of corruption and decay and mortality.[32]

Aristotle gave this concept the formulation it maintained through the Middle Ages when he called it the fifth element, the Latin phrase for which, *quinta essentia,* has remained in our language as "quintessence." The Philosopher described it as the more refined and stable element of the heavens.[33] Werner Jaeger says that Aristotle also identified the aether as the substance of the planetary deities, if not of the unmoved mover:

> The God to whom the world is subordinated is the transcendental unmoved mover, who guides the world as its final cause, by reason of the perfection of his pure thought. This is the original nucleus of Aristotelian metaphysics. Besides this, Aristotle described the ether as a divine body, or as a more divine body, as he does in the treatises; he certainly did not call it God. The divinity of the ether does not seem to fit very well with a strict transcendental monotheism, but below the unmoved mover were the stargods, whose matter was ethereal. There is no real contradiction in the fact that Aristotle called now the world and now the ether God, i.e. first the whole and then the part.[34]

For Aristotle and the other ancient physicists, the aether was at once material and spiritual. That is what makes it important to Eliot.

The poet must have become familiar with the notion of aether through his reading of the classics in the original languages and through his study of ancient philosophy at Harvard. This concept also continued in use in various contemporary writings. When Weston speaks of the Mithraic rites, she says (quoting Cumont) that "Mithra is the Mediator, who stands between 'the inaccessible and unknowable God, who reigns in the ethereal spheres, and the human race which suffers here below.' "[35] This function of mediation is frequently granted to the aether itself, in that it is considered to be both spiritual and material and is thought to penetrate all of space. Ezra Pound mentioned the aether frequently in his poetry, using it in the classical sense. For instance, his poem "Phanopoeia" (published in the *Little Review* in 1918, along with a piece by Eliot on Henry James) contains these lines:

> The swirl of light follows me through the square,
> The smoke of incense
> Mounts from the four horns of my bed-posts,
> The water-jet of gold light bears us up through the ceilings,
> Lapped in the gold-coloured flame I descend through the aether.[36]

He also writes of the aether often in the *Cantos*. In Canto XVI, we find "the blue banded lake under aether," and in Canto XX, the "Shelf of the lotophagoi, Aerial, cut in the aether." This association with the lotus eaters recalls Vivien Eliot's reported use of the modern gaseous ether. Eliot twice refers to this drug in his poetry—in "Prufrock" (see chapter 2) and in *Four Quartets* (see chapter 5)—both times with a play on the ancient meaning of the word.

Another association the word had for the poet comes from Underhill's discussion of the occultists' "Astral Light," defined as "an imponderable 'medium' or 'universal agent,'" which is described as beyond the plane of our normal sensual perceptions yet interpenetrating and binding up the material world." Underhill notes that these qualities are like those of "the ether of physics."[37] Eliot would have connected such descriptions with Weston's discussion of Mithra as mediator between the ethereal spheres and humanity, linking the fifth element with the core ideas of the mystery cults.

Since the aether is the upper air in Greek cosmology, the appropriate imagery for it is sky imagery: stars, space, thunder, and lightning. The title "What the Thunder Said" alludes to the aether. The thunder is the voice of the heavenly, divine regions. As a matter of fact, Eliot's beloved Heraclitus proclaimed, "It is the thunderbolt that steers the course of all things."[38] Kirk and Raven comment that "The pure cosmic fire was probably identified by Heraclitus with aither, the brilliant fiery stuff which fills the shining sky and surrounds the world: this aither was widely regarded both as divine and as a place of souls." They go on to say that this fragment "shows that Heraclitus' fire—the purest and brightest sort, that is, as of the aitherial and divine thunderbolt—has a directive capacity."[39] The poet makes this identification of the aether with the thunder's voice explicit in the line "aethereal rumours / Revive for a moment a broken Coriolanus" (416–17). These "aethereal rumours" suggest a transcendence, however uncertain or momentary, of the physical and spiritual fragmentation the poem describes. They heal the broken mind of Coriolanus, as well as the earth itself.

The Opening: April's Mixing

In *The Waste Land,* as in the earlier poetry, the elements are often adulterated, polluted, or perverted in various ways. Earth is again only dirt in "The broken fingernails of dirty hands" (303) or on the rat "Dragging its slimy belly on the bank" (189). The air is a "brown fog," both at dawn and at noon. Fire is reduced to the flame in the typist's stove (as artificial and passionless as her love affair), to "the sun's last rays" touching her laundry left to dry "Out of the window," to the "sad light" of the candles in Part II. The water of Spenser's "Sweet Thames" is littered in summer and "sweats / Oil and tar" (266–67).

The elements also appear in their pure forms in the poem, but they are not life-giving even then because they are not joined with each other. The early physicists generally agreed that the cosmos came into being and was maintained by some sort of alternation between opposing forces: chaos and order, separation and union, strife and love. Empedocles' notion of alternating love and strife between the elements is based on this primal mythic conception. Heraclitus pressed the idea further when he maintained that the opposites were really interchangeable and that "all things happen by strife and necessity."[40] Eliot quotes in *Little Gidding* a line that sums up Heraclitus's apparently paradoxical vision of a dynamic harmony of the elements, "United in the strife which divided them." The problem in *The Waste Land* is that the elements are not joined in the kind of loving strife the old physicists described. They are usually separated in a sterile way, and when they are mingled, the result tends to be adulteration rather than life-giving union.

The opening of the poem contrasts with Chaucer's cheerful *reverdie* at the beginning of *The Canterbury Tales,* yet we must not miss the fact that Eliot's opening *does* describe a regreening. "April is the cruellest month" not during the drought but when the rain falls, "stirring / Dull roots with spring rain." The "breeding" and "mixing" and "stirring" in the opening lines are the constant becoming of the world, Heraclitus's change that gives stability. The fertility cults Eliot had in mind after reading Weston and Frazer see the world in a similar way: only in the constant change of seasons is there an immutable pattern.

The opening, then, may describe the painful strife of the revolving seasons in the temporal world, but it is a strife-in-love, the experience of ordinary life—not the desert experience that the body of the poem describes. The sense of cruelty arises because mankind (especially mankind in the modern city) cannot endure much natural reality. The elements continue to be vital in the Bavarian scene:

> Summer surprised us, coming over the Starnbergersee
> With a shower of rain; we stopped in the colonnade,
> And went on in sunlight, into the Hofgarten,
> And drank coffee, and talked for an hour.
>
> (8–11)

The elements are in harmony: the wind blows the rain over the lake and onto the soil of the Hofgarten, where the sun shines. This potentially fruitful physical communion is reflected in a personal one, the quiet talk over coffee. Perhaps the harmony is already disturbed by the overheard conversations; certainly it is destroyed in the second verse paragraph, where there is already "only / A heap of broken images, where the sun beats, / And the dead tree gives no shelter, the cricket no relief, / And the dry stone no sound of water" (22–24). However, the opening of the poem gives a glimpse of a living harmony—transitory and even painful, but real and vital. Fragmentary memories of childhood in the mountains point toward the end of the poem, where we find ourselves out of the city and in the mountains.

THE BURIAL OF THE DEAD: EARTH

Suddenly wind and water disappear, and we find ourselves in the desert with sun beating on stones and rocks. It is a biblical desert, with echoes of Exodus, Ezekiel, Ecclesiastes, and Isaiah. As such, it is a desert in which the element of earth has been created by God and is totally subservient to Him. "The Order for the Burial of the Dead" in the Book of Common Prayer, to which the title of this first section alludes, includes these lines from Psalm 90: "Before ever the mountains were brought forth, or ever the earth, and the world were made: thou art God from everlasting, and world without end." When the people have been unfaithful, the Lord tells His prophet Ezekiel that He will strike the very mountains:

Son of man, set thy face towards the mountains of Israel, and prophesy against them, And say, Ye mountains of Israel, hear the word of the Lord God, Thus saith the Lord God to the mountains and to the hills, to the rivers and to the

valleys, Behold, I, even I will bring a sword upon you, and I will destroy your
high places. And your altars shall be desolate, and your images shall be broken:
and I will cast down your slain men before your idols. (Ezekiel 6:2-4)

As God does often in the Old Testament, He here reminds man that the
very elements are creatures that respond to His command. The broken
images alluded to by Eliot are fragments of artifacts that were worshipped
by their own creators, the Israelites. The Lord rebukes this arrogant
idolatry. There is hope in the passage, as there always is in the words of
the prophets. Water has been brought from the rock before in this desert
(Exodus 17:6). The shadow of the rock is found in Isaiah's prophecy of
the Savior: "And a man shall be as an hiding-place from the wind, and a
covert from the tempest: as rivers of water in a dry place, as the shadow
of a great rock in a weary land" (Isaiah 32:2). Nevertheless, these visions
of hope arise only momentarily in the gloom of chastisement. Isaiah returns to proclaiming the coming famine; Eliot's prophetic persona invites
us into the shadow of the rock to show us "fear in a handful of dust."
Without water, the most fertile earth is nothing but dust and so are our
bodies.

The hyacinth girl passage that follows presents the whole problem of
the poem in a complex way. Here earth and water are again joined, so
both nature and humanity are in blossom in the presence of the vegetation
goddess, but the persona fails to respond:

> —Yet when we came back, late, from the Hyacinth garden,
> Your arms full, and your hair wet, I could not
> Speak and my eyes failed, I was neither
> Living nor dead, and I knew nothing,
> Looking into the heart of light, the silence.
>
> (37–41)

No doubt Eliot is thinking of the Gardens of Adonis, baskets of flowers
that, according to Weston, grew and withered in three days at the festival
of Adonis.[41] The emphasis is on the fragility of life but also on its renewal.
Even though nature (and apparently woman) are full of life here, the man
who is speaking fails to respond, and from here on all the sexuality in the
poem is sterile or abortive. It seems that human infertility comes first in
the poem and causes the infertility of the land, as is the case in the Grail
legend and in the fertility cults, where the impotence of the king causes
the failure of the land. In classical terms, the Eros who unites people is
identical to the great Eros of Hesiod's cosmogony, who unites the
elements.

Two passages from *Tristan und Isolde* frame the events in the hyacinth garden. The first is from the beginning of the opera, just before the love potion takes effect. It corresponds to the earlier time ("a year ago") in the hyacinth garden. As in that paradisal garden, the elements are pure and life-giving. *Frisch weht der Wind*—the air is fresh over the sea they are sailing on. The stories of Isolde and the hyacinth girl are parallel, though the former is more grand. Both the opera and the hyacinth garden passage begin with fruitfully harmonious elements.

Oed' und leer das Meer comes from the last act of the opera and corresponds to the end of the hyacinth garden experience. Tristan is certainly not afraid to love, as his modern counterpart seems to be, but for tragic reasons he is unable to marry Isolde, and they never have a child. The passage resonates with one from a Grail romance quoted by Weston:

> Great is the loss that ye lie thus, 'tis even the destruction of kingdoms, God grant that ye be avenged, so that the folk be once more joyful and the land repeopled which by ye and this sword are wasted and made void.[42]

Perhaps this physical infertility is part of what is conveyed by the image of the empty sea: the womb of nature is as barren as the tragic love affair. At the same time, the emptiness is spiritual. *Oed' und leer das Meer* may simultaneously echo the biblical passage in which Elijah, having defeated the prophets of Baal, waits for the promised rain:

> And Elijah went up to the top of Carmel; and he cast himself down upon the earth, and put his face between his knees, And said to his servant, Go up now, look toward the sea. And he went up, and looked, and said, There is nothing. And he said, Go again seven times. (1 Kings 18:42–43)

At last, great black clouds and wind come, and it rains. The emptiness reported by a servant looking out to sea is not an expression of nihilism. It is recurrently in this void that the creative power of the Spirit works.

The hyacinth girl's would-be lover is not only afraid of women but is overcome by an experience of inner vacancy too powerful and too integral to Eliot's poetic vision to be seen as merely a kind of grandiose description of his fear of intimacy. It is, in fact, nearly identical to the experience of Tristan. When the shepherd reports that Isolde's ship has not appeared ("Waste and void the sea"), Tristan lies unconscious and half dead, "neither / Living nor dead." Immediately after the shepherd speaks, Tristan revives and describes an experience similar to that of the man of the hyacinth garden:

> Ich war,
> wo ich von je gewesen,

wohin auf je ich geh':
im weiten Reich
der Weltennacht.
Nur ein Wissen
dort uns eigen:
göttlich ew'ges
Urvergessen!

Stewart Robb translates these lines as follows:

I was
where I have been forever,
where I forever go:
the realm of night
which girds the world.
We have there one knowledge only:
godlike, endless
prime oblivion![43]

This passage expresses a Romantic longing for death, but it is finally more mystical than nihilistic.[44] Tristan's world-night in which there is only one divine thought has something in common with the darkness that "shall be the darkness of God" in *East Coker*. The "heart of light, the silence" connects the hyacinth garden with the mystic rose garden of *Burnt Norton*. Both Tristan and his modern counterpart in the hyacinth garden are truly hopeless, but their visions hold the potential for this kind of spiritual fulfillment. What Ronald Bush says of the emptiness in "The Hollow Men" and "A Song for Simeon" applies here as well: ". . . life is empty and yet paradoxically there is hope associated with vacancy."[45] "I could not speak" alludes to Psalm 39, which is part of the Order for the Burial of the Dead. The Hebrew singer confronts his own nothingness in comparison with God and admits that his only hope is in his Creator: "I became dumb, and opened not my mouth: for it was thy doing." The silent persona in the hyacinth garden is an impotent man incapable of love, but he is also a man who has a vision of his mortality. What I am suggesting is that the fall from grace in the hyacinth garden leads to a physical and spiritual desert but is potentially a *felix culpa* because the very emptiness of the desert is the place of mystical union, as it was for Moses and Ezekiel and many others.

In *Burnt Norton*, mystical vision comes when the separate elements combine suddenly and miraculously: water appears in a dry pool when the fire of the sun falls "through the vibrant air" upon the concrete. In *The Waste Land, Oed' und leer das Meer* may be translated as the words of Genesis: "And the earth was without form, and void; and darkness was upon the face of the deep." This void is what must directly precede the act of creation, which begins in the next line. Eliot quotes these lines in *The Rock:*

Waste and void. Waste and void. And darkness on the face of the deep
And the Spirit moved upon the face of the water.

(107)

Degenerate as the world of *The Waste Land* is, it is a world prepared by that very degeneration for a new creation. I do not wish to make it sound as though there were angel voices triumphantly singing "O happy fault" between the lines of the poem. The focus is on horror and suffering, and the renewal is yet to come at the end of the poem. Here, however, as throughout his poetry, Eliot finds in death, and only in death, the possibility of rebirth. The present analysis shows that Eliot holds physical nature and human nature analogous in this process. The separation and consequent sterility he describes between man and woman reflect the separation and sterility of the elements. Taken to the extreme, these separations leave us with a world and a mind that are waste and void. In that terrible vacancy, the mind and the elements are purified, returned to a primordial state in which they are capable of being reintegrated.

Christopher Ricks describes Eliot's fascination with vacancy in a section of his *T.S. Eliot and Prejudice* entitled "The Master of the Vacuum." He quotes Eliot's approving description of Joyce as "the greatest *non*-stylist, the master of the vacuum of personal style into which all things rush."[46] This comment gives a good idea of the positive effects Eliot expected from certain types of vacancy. Ricks also quotes the frequently cited statement in a letter of Eliot to More about "the void that I find in the middle of all human happiness" and comments, "The void and the vacuum can be positive in their very negativity. Nature abhors a vacuum. So does the religious supernatural, which yet loves to convert the human abhorrence of a vacuum into a spiritual incitement, driven by this sense of void."[47] Eliot's attitude toward vacancy is something like this. It is my argument that his expectation of finding something positive in the void finds its objective correlative in the idea that there is no true vacuum because the aether is everywhere, filling every apparent vacancy.

"Belladonna, the Lady of the Rocks" in Madame Sosostris's Tarot pack is the *Magna Mater* who presides over the death of the fertility godling. It has been suggested that Eliot was thinking of Walter Pater's impressionistic analysis of "La Giaconda": "She is older than the rocks among which she sits; like the vampire, she has been dead many times, and learned the secret of the grave. . . ."[48] Belladonna is "beautiful woman" but also a poison; she is the one Robert Graves calls the Triple Goddess. In her third manifestation as murderous crone she is Hecate, a chthonic goddess who indeed is one with the element of earth in deadly rocks and graves.

The "Unreal City"—a place already explored in Eliot's earlier poetry—is a place of death because the life-giving elemental harmony cannot take place in the city. Instead of the rain and sun and earth of the Hofgarten or the hyacinth garden, the crowd passes over London Bridge "Under the brown fog of a winter dawn"; the elements are muted and polluted. Once people remove themselves from Nature's harmony, they also cease to know their surroundings as a sacred place. They have lost the primitive sense of the sacrality of the cosmos described by Eliade:

> It matters little if the formulas and images through which the primitive expresses "reality" seem childish and even absurd to us. It is the profound meaning of primitive behavior that is revelatory; this behavior is governed by belief in an absolute reality opposed to the profane world of "unrealities"; in the last analysis, the latter does not constitute a "world," properly speaking; it is the "unreal" *par excellence,* the uncreated, the non-existent: the void.[49]

The elements of creation are not experienced in the city. It is uncreated in that it was built by man, not made by God. It is not built as many ancient cities were, with a center that makes it analogous to the cosmos. In the modern city, one has no awareness of the cosmos as a whole without a void. Eliot's city is unreal in this sense.

Physical reality nevertheless keeps breaking into this unreal and profane place. It seems that Stetson has a garden, a plot of real earth, and he has a real body buried in it: "That corpse you planted last year in your garden, / Has it begun to sprout?" A sentence from the *Criterion* of 1934 gives Eliot's key personal association with a buried corpse:

> I am willing to admit that my own retrospect is touched by sentimental sunsets, the memory of a friend coming across the Luxembourg Gardens, in the hot afternoon, waving a branch of lilac, a friend who was later (so far as I could find out) to be mixed with the mud of Gallipoli.[50]

Both here and in the poem, Eliot associates flowers and gardens with the body (Jean Verdenal's) gone back to its native earth. Where there is a garden, the world becomes both natural and sacred again, for there will be (inevitably, as it were) a fertility ritual. Weston talks about ritual burials:

> Thus, in many places, it is still the custom to carry a figure representing the Vegetation Spirit on a bier, attended by mourning women, and either bury the figure, throw it into the water (as a rain charm), or, after a mock death, carry the revivified Deity, with rejoicing, back to the town.[51]

Eliot derives macabre humor from picturing the burial of a real corpse, much as Shakespeare does in Ariel's song.

David Jones aims at something like the same grim humor when he connects the fertility rituals with the carnage of the Great War:

> Where his fiery sickle garners you:
> fanged-flash and darkt-fire thrring and thrrung athwart thhdrill . . .
>   harrow your vertebrae,
> bore your brain-pan before you can say Fanny—and
> comfortably over open sights:
>   the gentleman must be mowed.[52]

These lines are from *In Parenthesis* (which was originally published in 1937 under Eliot's editorship). The "gentleman" is John Barleycorn, the sacrificial victim in English harvest songs. One feels that both Jones and Eliot are introducing these grossly physical images of death from fertility cults into modern contexts so as to shock their urbanized and rationalistic contemporaries into awareness of their corporeal nature.

If the poets succeed, readers will become aware of their spiritual nature as well, because the natural and supernatural laws are analogues. In the Order for the Burial of the Dead, Saint Paul's words (from First Corinthians) describe the resurrection of the body as a sprouting: "So also is the resurrection of the dead; It is sown in corruption; it is raised in glory: it is sown in weakness; it is raised in power: It is sown a natural body; it is raised a spiritual body."

Hugh Kenner finds something sinister in the conversation with Stetson about a buried corpse, imagining it a talk between two murderers.[53] More likely, the friend who stops Stetson may be a ghost, for that is what ghosts do in Baudelaire's unreal city: "Fourmillante cité, cité pleine de rêves, / Où le spectre en plein jour racroche le passant" [Swarming city, city full of dreams, in which a ghost stops the passer-by in broad daylight]. I must disagree with Grover Smith when he says (commenting on the Baudelaire passage) that "The phantom accosting the passer-by is not found in *The Waste Land*. . . ."[54] Not only does this encounter have a ghostly quality about it, but Tiresias hovers like a ghost over the whole poem, and the passages quoted from *The Tempest* suggest the eventual reunion of Alonso and Ferdinand, in which each seems a revenant to the other. James Longenbach also finds that there are ghosts in the poem and points to Eliot's interest in the ghost stories of Henry James.[55] The humor of the Stetson passage prevents sinister overtones, I think. It is morbidly funny because the characters speak literally about something that normally is a spiritual analogy. There is certainly something disturbing in it, but it is an attempt to disturb modern complacency concerning the physical and religious orders of being from which we have, in our profane ingenuity, removed ourselves. Once one accepts the gross corporeal and elemental experience, Eliot was finding, a ritual religious response becomes natural too, and finally the literalism of Catholic sacraments affirms the continuity with the vanished mind of one's pagan ancestors. The sprouting body does suggest in a shocking way the Christian belief in the resurrection of the body, and it thus prefigures the resurrected body of the figure who accosts the disciples on the road to Emmaus in Part V—the ultimate ghost in the poem.

Perhaps this reading helps explain why Eliot alters Webster's "Keep the wolf far hence that's foe to man" to "Oh keep the Dog far hence that's friend to men, / Or with his nails he'll dig it up again" (74–75). The corpse must stay in the ground and return to dust if it is to "sprout" and "bloom." In this burial of a corpse in a garden, we may hear an echo of the Gospel of Saint John: "At the place where he had been crucified there was a garden, and in this garden a new tomb in which no one had yet been buried. Since it was the Jewish Day of Preparation and the tomb was near at hand, they laid Jesus there" (19:41–42). The fall from the edenic hyacinth garden leads to this burial garden; but since the corpse here is associated with the Hanged God, to whom Eliot refers in his note on the Tarot cards, this is a resurrection garden.

A GAME OF CHESS: AIR

Part II, "A Game of Chess," is the only one of the sections whose title does not indicate the element associated with it. Only once is the air explicitly present, when the odors of perfumes are "stirred by the air / That freshened from the window" (89–90). Actually, the element of air is conspicuous in this section by its absence. We find ourselves in "a room enclosed," in which the whole atmosphere is stifling. In the draft Eliot had written, "staring forms / Leaned out and hushed the room and closed it in."[56] The woman fears the air:

> "What is that noise?"
> The wind under the door.
> "What is that noise now? What is the wind doing?"
> Nothing again nothing.
>
> (117–20)

The wind is kept out. It can do nothing. Even should they go out, it will be an airless outing: "And if it rains, a closed car at four" (136). In this line, the air is identified with the rain that could renew the waste land, looking forward to the "damp gust / Bringing rain" (394–95) in the last section. This life-giving conjunction of elements frightens the loveless couple of Part II, and they shut it out.

Even the air that "freshened from the window" is merely polluted by the odors of "her strange synthetic perfumes" (87). As in "Burbank with a Baedeker" and other early poems, Eliot is here contrasting artificial modernity with natural antiquity. His modern scene is indoors, and as Kenner points out,

> All things deny nature; the fruited vines are carved, the Cupidons golden, the light not of the sun, the perfumes synthetic, the candelabra (seven-branched, as for an altar) devoted to no rite, the very color of the fire-light perverted by sodium and copper salts. The dolphin is carved, and swims in a "sad light," not, like Antony's delights, "showing his back above the element he lives in."[57]

Kenner's last example offers an instructive contrast because Antony's dolphin is a living creature who inhabits one element but jumps up into another momentarily and must do so to breathe. Eliot later mentions the porpoise, at the end of *East Coker*—thinking of it as an animal that lives at the boundary between water and air, as its companion the petrel lives in air and water. The dolphin here in *The Waste Land* swims instead in wood and up on the ceiling, completely out of his element. Possibly, Eliot alludes to Horace's criticism of the bad poet who, failing to be true to nature, "is like a painter adding a dolphin to the woods."[58] In any case, the passage is certainly loaded with artificiality.

In contrast, Enobarbus describes Shakespeare's Cleopatra thus:

> The barge she sat in, like a burnish'd throne,
> Burnt on the water: the poop was beaten gold;
> Purple the sails, and so perfumed that
> The winds were love-sick with them. . . .

> (II.ii)

This image of a barge burning on the water achieves a wondrous conjunction of the antithetical elements fire and water, and there is much of this type of imagery in the play, symbolizing the union of Mars and Venus, Antony and Cleopatra. In the modern version, "The Chair she sat in, like a burnished throne, / Glowed on the marble." The blazing fire of the sun reflected from the golden barge onto the water is transmuted into candlelight reflecting from a chair onto a marble floor. Where the winds became anthropomorphically lovesick with Cleopatra's perfume, the slight air from the window is now overwhelmed with perfumes and smoke:

> In vials of ivory and coloured glass

> Unstoppered, lurked her strange synthetic perfumes,
> Unguent, powdered, or liquid—troubled, confused
> And drowned the sense in odours; stirred by the air
> That freshened from the window, these ascended
> In fattening the prolonged candle-flames,
> Flung their smoke into the laquearia,
> Stirring the pattern on the coffered ceiling.
>
> (86–93)

The mixture of perfume and air is wrong because the perfume is synthetic (hence artificial), because the smoke pollutes it, and because there is too little air. The sense of smell (and the sensibility itself) is consequently confused, much as the sense of sight is when the smoky air stirs the pattern in the ceiling. Cleopatra's perfume had a more powerful effect because it cooperated with the airy element:

> From the barge
> A strange invisible perfume hits the sense
> Of the adjacent wharfs. The city cast
> Her people out upon her; and Antony,
> Enthron'd in the marketplace, did sit alone,
> Whistling to the air; which, but for vacancy,
> Had gone to gaze on Cleopatra too,
> And made a gap in nature.
>
> (II.ii)

This essence is "strange" in that it is invisible but has powerful effects, similar to the air itself. Antony whistles to the air, which can offer creaturely companionship as it performs its function of preventing vacancy, a gap in nature. We see here, incidentally, how air commonly was seen as having the same role as the aether itself, filling the void.

What appears to be another window turns out to be merely a painting:

> Above the antique mantel was displayed
> As though a window gave upon the sylvan scene
> The change of Philomel. . . .
>
> (97–99)

Eliot tells us that he took the phrase "sylvan scene" from *Paradise Lost*. A dozen lines after using that phrase, Milton describes Satan's approach to Eden:

> And of pure now purer air
> Meets his approach, and to the heart inspires
> Vernal delight and joy, able to drive

> All sadness but despair: now gentle gales
> Fanning their odoriferous wings dispense
> Native perfumes, and whisper whence they stole
> Those balmy spoils.
>
> (IV. 153–59)

As the paradisal "sylvan scene" is contrasted with the forest in which Philomel has been violated, these "native perfumes" contrast with the synthetic ones used by the inhabitants of the unreal city. The air in the opening of Part II is overfilled with the glow of marble, the glitter of jewels, the smoke of candles. It is as impure as Milton's Edenic air is pure. Satan's despair, incapable of being dispelled even by this aethereal atmosphere, seems to reign over the hearts of the people in Eliot's room as well.

Air, unlike the other three elements, can never be fatal in itself. This is a fact well known to the poets, particularly the Renaissance poets whose works Eliot had been reading carefully. Spenser's Mutabilitie, in describing the characteristics of the elements, holds that the purpose of air is "with subtill influence / Of his thin spirit, all creatures to maintaine, / In state of life" (*Faerie Queene* VII.vii.22). The traditional play on "spirit" makes the connection between the material element air and the spiritual world, much as Shakespeare does with Prospero's "tricksy spirit" Ariel. Maintaining creatures in "state of life" is animating them, ensouling them. In Renaissance psychology, the "spirits" link mind and body, neatly solving the old philosophical problem by positing subtle fluid substances, which are both spiritual and material. The physician attending Marlowe's dying Tamburlaine learnedly discusses such a substance:

> The humidum and calor, which some hold
> Is not a parcel of the elements,
> But of a substance more divine and pure,
> Is almost clean extinguished and spent;
> Which, being the cause of life, imports your death. . . .
>
> (*Tamburlaine* II.v.3)

While combining spirit and matter, this substance also unites the opposing qualities of moistness (humidum) and heat (calor). This life-giving stuff has much in common with Spenser's air and with the pure air of Milton's Eden.

Because air has this quality, the death-by-isolated-element pattern of the other sections is reversed. It is the *absence* of pure air, and the pollution of what air is present, that threaten death by suffocation. In his note to the line "The wind under the door," Eliot quotes Webster's "Is the wind in that door still?" The reference in Webster is to the last breaths in a dying person's mouth. In this context, it appears that the original title of this section, "In the Cage," refers to the claustrophobia of the enclosed room and obliquely to its airlessness. The cage reminds us of the jar (ampulla) in which the Sibyl hangs in the epigraph from Petronius at the beginning of the poem.[59] The Sibyl, like the sophisticated woman in this part of the poem, is one who knows too much about the degenerating society around her (Petronius's decadent Rome or Eliot's London) and is locked in an airless place suffering a kind of living death. James Karman writes of the Sibyl's wish for death, "She cannot die, however; nor, in *The Waste Land,* is there any kind of death that provides relief or offers regeneration. There is only perpetual disintegration."[60] This is true for the Sibyl and the woman in the closed room, but not for all deaths in the poem. The deaths by earth, water, and fire are all potentially regenerative. In fact, the useless disintegration is that of a culture that refuses to acknowledge the body and its death.

For Eliot, then, the air stands apart from the other earthly elements because it is breath, spirit—always a principle of life. As Guthrie points out, it is identified in ancient physics with the aether:

> The monist philosopher does not believe in the existence of more than one real substance, and those therefore who made *aer* the self-moved material basis of the whole universe must of course have believed that the *aither* is no more than this same substance in its purest (and thus, let us remember, its most divine) form; and secondly the religious and philosophic teachers who held that the *aer* which we breathe is the soul or life-substance, and that this substance is identical with the world-soul, so that the soul of each individual man is "a small portion of the divine", clearly based their doctrines also on the ultimate identity of *aer* and *aither* and considered the one to be only a base and contaminated form of the other.[61]

This is clearly the basis for Milton's notion of purer air. The air which is missing in Eliot's waste land is this aethereal air (or Stoic *pneuma*), which animates the physical world.

If the woman of Part II fears the life-giving wind, it is because she, like other dwellers in the waste land, fears its mystery and the emptying it effects. For, while air can never cause physical death, it is the element of spiritual transformation, which involves death to self. The wind is doing "nothing," and that is precisely the terror of it: submission to the spirit requires a *kenosis,* a self-emptying. Also, air is always vital, but wind can be powerfully destructive, invisibly tearing houses to shreds in an instant. Finally, the wind blows about the souls of the dead. In the draft, when the woman asks "What is the wind doing?" the man answers,

"Carrying / Away the little light dead people." Valerie Eliot glosses this line, identifying an allusion to Paolo and Francesca in the *Inferno:*

> . . . volontieri
> parlerei a que' duo, che insieme vanno,
> e paion sì al vento esser leggieri.
>
> (V, 73–75)

[willingly would I speak with those two that go together, and seem so light upon the wind][62]

This is indeed a fearsome wind, one which whirls the damned souls of the many who have loved passionately but illicitly, including Cleopatra. This passage describes a couple who are apparently married but whose passion has been killed by neurosis. Still, they know their souls to be light enough to be blown away by the same wind, and they do fear it. For a moment in *Burnt Norton,* the wind takes this role again, as Eliot describes "Men and bits of paper, whirled by the cold wind / That blows before and after time." The woman fears that this is the wind at the door.

The man in this autobiographical scene has entered half-consciously into the wind's fearful nothingness:

> "Do
> "You know nothing? Do you see nothing? Do you remember
> "Nothing?"
>
> I remember
> Those are pearls that were his eyes.
> "Are you alive, or not? Is there nothing in your head?"
>
> (121–26)

Like the man in the hyacinth garden, he is "neither / Living nor dead." Like the etherised mind in *East Coker,* his is "conscious but conscious of nothing." This is a state of mind Eliot described again and again, always with the experience of the mystics in mind. As St. Teresa describes it in a passage quoted by Underhill,

> In the prayer of union the soul is asleep; fast asleep as regards herself and earthly things. In fact, during the short time that this state lasts she is deprived of all feeling, and though she wishes it, she can think of nothing.[63]

It should be noted that Eliot was not an uncritical admirer of St. Teresa's. In the Clark Lectures, he goes so far as to say that she and St. John of the Cross, as well as other sixteenth-century Spanish mystics, "are as much psychologists as Descartes," contrasting their mysticism with that of the Middle Ages, which is in the Aristotelian tradition and hence has an intellectual element in it (*VMP*, 84, 165). Nevertheless, it is clear that he continued to find the *via negativa* of the great Carmelite mystics authentic, for he is still quoting from St. John of the Cross in *Four Quartets*. What Eliot describes in these lines is not conscious and deliberate contemplation, but it is an emptying caused by disease and despair that makes an opening where true contemplation could occur. As the state of sexual union gives a hint of mystic union, this state of sexual division gives a taste of the mystic's dark night of the soul that leads to union. The one thought Eliot's persona remembers here is of the transformation of the drowned man—with a pun on "remembering," which could be taken literally to mean putting the body's members back together. The nothing the wind is doing, the nothing in the man's head, point toward the central place of transformation in the poem, "the empty chapel, only the wind's home" in Part V.

Thus, Part II is unusual because air is partly identified with the aether of the conclusion. The closed room, dead as it is, bears a resemblance to the closed room in which the disciples of Christ cowered after the crucifixion. The Lord entered there, breathed on them, and told them to receive the Holy Spirit (John 20:19–23). Later on, at Pentecost, the Spirit did come to them:

> And when the day of Pentecost was fully come, they were all with one accord in one place. And suddenly there came a sound from heaven as of a rushing mighty wind, and it filled all the house where they were sitting. And there appeared unto them cloven tongues like as of fire, and it sat upon each of them. (Acts 2:1–3)

The second section of *The Waste Land* is a negative contrast to these biblical events, but it is also a reminder that inspiration comes in a moment of fear and death, the moment in the windy chapel of the last section and in the "draughty church" of *Burnt Norton*.

The pub scene is another indoor event, one that presents a lower-class version of sexual frustration and artificiality. As Kenner puts it,

> If we move from the queens to the pawns, we find low life no more free or natural, equally obsessed with the denial of nature, artificial teeth, chemically procured abortions. . . .[64]

Not unlike their more educated counterparts, these lower-class persons have granted to science—and particularly to medical technology—the highest authority over their lives. They do what their physicians and pharmacists tell them without demur, and having no active religious faith, they unconsciously adopt the modern faith in mechanistic and commercial solutions to human problems. For a price, one can have perfect teeth and can be rid of an unwanted pregnancy. Poor Lil finds out, though, that the modern priest is not infallible: "The chemist said it would be all right, but I've never been the same" (161). In the context of the ancient fertility cults, such deliberate killing of one's own children is, of course, unthinkable. In the biblical context, it is a direct affront to God the Father, the creator of all life.

Eliot presents Lil sympathetically. At least she has a name, an ordinary name. She should be a Lily, another hyacinth girl. She is the only fertile woman in the waste land. In the midst of squalor and war, she has borne children: "She's had five already and nearly died of young George" (160). In her motherhood, she has known real life and has come close to real death. She nearly sacrificed her life for a fifth child, George, whose name—derived from *geo,* "earth"—means "farmer" and whose patron saint is also England's. There could be nobility in Lil's life, but George is born in the city, not on the farm. In the urban commercial economy, he is a burden, not a blessing, and something must be done to prevent further accidents like him.

As Juan Leon points out in a recent article, Eliot glances here at the eugenics movement, which was extremely popular at the time. One of its most famous proponents, Margaret Sanger (foundress of the organization that came to be called Planned Parenthood), stated that her goal was to have "More children from the fit; less from the unfit." Leon points out that Bertrand Russell was himself committed to the idea of eugenics.[65] "Encouraged by the biological theories of Darwin, Weismann, and Mendel," Leon writes, "eugenicists and their sympathizers believed that the conscious control of human evolution was within reach."[66] Eliot shared the common concern for the rapid growth of the lower class, but referring to Eliot's review of Shaw's eugenicist introduction to *Back to Methuselah,* Leon says, "The optimism of eugenic reform, with its air of nineteenth century positivism and sweeping synthesis, Eliot regards with skepticism."[67] Though, as Leon emphasizes, Eliot's dismay at the rapid breeding of Lil's class is evident in this passage, so is his abhorrence of mechanistic solutions such as abortion. Eliot was childless himself and not one to romanticize large working-class families, but he saw the terrible danger inherent in exercising technological control over procreation.

As Kenner interprets the scene, "The chemist with commercial impartiality supplies one woman with 'strange synthetic perfumes' and the other with 'them pills I took, to bring it off,' aphrodisiacs and abortifacients. . . ."[68] Thus, science offers to increase pleasure while divorcing intercourse from its natural end, procreation. Lil's interlocutor asks in the most mean-spirited way, "What you get married for if you don't want children?" By placing this scene against the backdrop of Jessie Weston's fertility rituals, in which sexual intercourse means children and also means fertility for the land, Eliot asks the same question of the modern world. Once sexuality ceases to have procreation as its primary meaning, Eliot suggests, it comes to mean merely what Lil's acquaintance threatens to offer Lil's husband, "a good time." This devaluation of the physical act removes it from the cosmic and divine realms with which it had been connected and makes it what it is in *Brave New World*.

THE FIRE SERMON: FIRE

The title of the third section, "The Fire Sermon," explicitly designates its dominant element, but the opening passage takes us to the water:

> The river's tent is broken: the last fingers of leaf
> Clutch and sink into the wet bank. The wind
> Crosses the brown land, unheard. The nymphs are departed.
> Sweet Thames, run softly, till I end my song.
> The river bears no empty bottles, sandwich papers,
> Silk handkerchiefs, cardboard boxes, cigarette ends
> Or other testimony of summer nights.
>
> (173–79)

The passage makes an extended contrast with Spenser's *Prothalamion*. That title indicates a marriage song before the marriage. The poet describes himself going down to the river and seeing the river nymphs preparing for the double wedding soon to be celebrated:

> Calme was the day, and through the trembling ayre,
> Sweete breathing Zephyrus did softly play,
> A gentle spirit, that lightly did delay
> Hot Titans beames, which then did glyster fayre:
> When I . . .
> Walkt forth to ease my payne
> Along the shoare of silver streaming Themmes,
> Whose rutty Bancke, the which his river hemmes,
> Was paynted all with variable flowers,
> And all the meades adorned with daintie gemmes,
> Fit to decke maydens bowres,
> And crowne their Paramours,
> Against the Brydale day, which is not long:
> Sweet Themmes runne softly, till I end my song.

Spenser is setting the scene for a ritual that will unite mankind and nature as it unites husbands and wives. The bank is adorned with flowers that are like jewels. The wind is the god Zephyrus, the fructifying and spiritual West Wind. Eliot finds instead dead leaves in the riverbank and an "unheard" wind (one of which people are unaware) blowing over barren brown land. In place of procreative marriage, this section is full (and was even more full before Pound's editing) of illicit, perverse, and sterile sexual relations.

Spenser spots "A Flocke of Nymphes" who are "All lovely Daughters of the Flood thereby." They have human form but are daughters of the watery element itself, and the river is, no doubt, a demigod. The material, human, and divine realms are wedded in them. Weston, of course, associates the nymphs with various types of "fertility daemons."[69] Eliot, in contrast, comes to the river after the festivities. The nymphs are now "nymphos," promiscuous women with no connection to the elemental or the transcendent. They strew litter instead of flowers on the flood, and they do not marry the "loitering heirs" with whom they copulate. In Weston's rituals, by contrast, sexuality is connected with everything else: with the crops, with religion, with the community.

Spenser's young men take their brides "at th'appointed tyde." Human time is measured by the sea (for as Eliot says in *The Dry Salvages*, "We cannot think of a time that is oceanless"), and the human cycle of life takes part in nature's seasonal pattern. In these temporal patterns, the Renaissance mind finds something timeless. The modern lovers ignore all that but cannot evade time's companion, death: "But at my back in a cold blast I hear / The rattle of the bones, and chuckle spread from ear to ear" (185–86). Spenser comes to the river with a weary heart but finds cause for joy. Eliot weeps: "By the waters of Leman I sat down and wept" (182). The waters of Babylon and of the poet's Swiss retreat (with perhaps a pun on the Middle English "leman," mistress) replace the silver Thames. "White bodies naked on the low damp ground" might have been the ritual statuettes removed from the water, or they might have been men and women engaged in orgiastic rites that renewed the ground itself. Now they are simply bodies behaving instinctively and meaninglessly.

The central encounter between the typist and the clerk (one of the commercial clerks who have replaced religious ones) occurs as the weak winter sun sets for the day. It is at this time between day and night that Tiresias, who lives "between two lives" identifies himself at last:

> At the violet hour, when the eyes and back
> Turn upward from the desk, when the human engine waits
> Like a taxi throbbing waiting,
> I, Tiresias, though blind, throbbing between two lives,
> Old man with wrinkled female breasts, can see
> At the violet hour, the evening hour that strives

Homeward, and brings the sailor home from sea,
The typist home at teatime, clears her breakfast, lights
Her stove, and lays out food in tins.

(215–23)

Eliot plays the same trick that he used at the beginning of "Prufrock," beginning with a Romantic phrase and then undercutting it with dehumanized images. As in several early poems, we see only body parts (eyes and back), not a person. This is the view of the biologist, who has focused too much on the parts to see the whole. A mechanistic image comes next: man as automobile. These images and the attitude toward people they embody lead more or less inevitably toward the mechanical intercourse that is to happen. Given these assumptions about human beings, the typist has no reason to feel shame afterward: sexual intercourse is simply a physiological function. Where Goldsmith's Olivia wonders frantically "What charm can soothe her melancholy, / What art can wash her guilt away?" the modern mistress "smoothes her hair with automatic hand, / And puts a record on the gramophone" (255–56). She believes herself a complicated mechanism, nothing more, and her comfort is provided by a machine.

The description of evening bringing "the sailor home from sea" echoes, Eliot says, Sappho's poem about the evening star herding home "whatever / Dawn's light dispersed," including children returning to their mothers.[70] The coming of evening in the *Purgatorio* expresses the same longing for loved ones: "It was the hour that turns the memories / Of sailing men their first day out, to home / And friends they sailed from on that morning's breeze."[71] Sailors encounter the elements most directly and dangerously and know the value of love in a way that clerks and typists working always safely indoors scarcely can. After the lines about the sailors' longing to return, Dante goes on to describe the praying of evening prayer, compline, which begins, *Te lucis ante terminum* (To thee before the light is done). Angels come to guard the suffering souls through the night, and the angels' faces are so radiant that the poet cannot look on them. Prayer to the source of light and protection by fiery angels contrast with the typist's approach to night, lighting her stove. Her clothes hung out the window to dry are "touched by the sun's last rays." She does not know how precious the fire is. She does not turn to the setting sun and pray for a blessing, for protection until dawn.

Tiresias, however, "though blind . . . can see / At the violet hour." The evening hour is his time because he exists in a mysterious space between the antinomies. He has been both man and woman; he is blind but gifted with vision. Tiresias is everywhere in this poem, the author tells us, but he is mostly invisible. In this way, Tiresias defies the laws of mechanistic science. He might be explicable in terms of ancient physics, in which aethereal substances might be everywhere, penetrating the interstices of ordinary bodies; or in terms of modern quantum theory, in which matter does not occupy space continuously. The other theory of matter and spirit that may be significant here is that of the Hermetic tradition. Tiresias is transformed (in Ovid's account, quoted in the notes by Eliot) from male to female and back again when he encounters two serpents copulating. This is the symbol of Hermes, and in alchemy, Mercury is identified with the philosopher's stone, which effects the central transformation of base matter into spiritual gold. The alchemists pictured Mercury as a hermaphrodite, for the vertical duality of matter and spirit can be resolved only when the horizontal sexual duality is resolved.

In this transcendence of duality, Tiresias is identified with the Hanged God, whose physical death is physical rebirth. Eliot tells us he associates the Hanged God "with the hooded figure in the passage of the disciples to Emmaus in Part V." His is a body that, like that of Tiresias, is there but not there throughout the poem. He is the positive realization of the tortured state into which the protagonist falls after his failure in the hyacinth garden, "neither / Living nor dead," for he is both dead and living. In Part III, Tiresias still experiences his visionary androgyny as a torment: "I Tiresias have foresuffered all / Enacted on this same divan or bed" (243–44). But it leads directly to the Easter experience of Part V in which the apostle traveling to Emmaus says to his companion, "There is always another one walking beside you / Gliding wrapt in a brown mantle, hooded / I do not know whether a man or a woman" (363–65). The hopeless suffering of the waste land becomes redemptive in the central sacrificial act in which Tiresias or Christ consciously endures all. At that moment, the physical world is transformed, or rather the duality of matter and spirit is revealed as illusory.

After the typist passage, Eliot again returns to Spenser's Thames. The Fisher King is manifest partly as Shakespeare's Alonso, the (supposedly) drowned king, and partly as Ferdinand, who is mourning by the shore and surprised by aethereal music: "This music crept by me upon the waters" (257). The music comes from a spirit of the air who is moving over the empty waters. It is a Genesis moment, as the king's body is being regenerated. The "pleasant whining" of the mandolin, and the "chatter" of the "fishmen" in a pub are mundane but natural voices identified with Ariel's. Their vitality coexists harmoniously with the "Inexplicable splendour of Ionian white and gold" (265) in the neighboring church. One might say that the body of the king is identified with the body of St. Magnus, who was a martyred earl, and that his body has been changed into "something rich and strange" in the building of this splendid church.

The gold on the church walls symbolizes the great alchemical transformation and contains Heraclitus's transforming element, fire. Gold is what has been stolen from the Rhine in Wagner's *Götterdämmerung,* the inspiration for Eliot's lament of the three Thames-daughters. The first verse describes the Thames of the present, polluted with "oil and tar" and void of air: "Red sails / Wide / To leeward, swing on the heavy spar" (270–72). Without wind, the barges and logs drift aimlessly. Elizabeth's boat in the second verse brings golden fire to the river, as Cleopatra's barge did to the Nile: "The stern was formed / A gilded shell / Red and gold" (281–83). The "red sails" of the first verse are not golden and recall instead Conrad's *Heart of Darkness,* from which the original epigraph to the poem was taken. As fire and water come together with Queen Elizabeth's passage, air and water do too: "Southwest wind / Carried down stream / The peal of bells" (286–88). Nevertheless, the past is not entirely idealized here, for as Helen Gardner maintains, the flirtation between Elizabeth and Leicester was rather sterile and desperate.[72] Still, Eliot does describe the Renaissance as a time when there was at least the concept of an elemental conjunction enabling alchemical transformation. The aerial music carried over the waters proclaims it.

The time then shifts back to the modern Thames and another mechanical copulation ("I raised my knees / Supine on the floor of a narrow canoe") without ardor. Finally one of the Thames-daughters sings of Eliot's own experience when he was suffering extreme emotional distress at Margate, where part of the poem was written: "On Margate Sands. / I can connect / Nothing with nothing" (300–2). The sands of the seashore make a connection between land and sea, and that is part of their therapeutic virtue. This is one of the places in between, where Tiresias thrives—and where life itself thrives, at the point of elemental conjunction. However, the speaker's inability to respond sends him into the void, as it does elsewhere in the poem. He finds as yet no alchemical *conjunctio oppositorum,* no aether in the nothingness.

Fire in Part III is primarily the fire of lust, burning between the nymphs and their friends, Sweeney and Mrs. Porter, the typist and the pimply young man, the woman and man in the canoe. Mr. Eugenides (whose name, Leon points out, identifies him with eugenics), exhibits another kind of sterile and unnatural sexuality, homosexual activity.[73] The first line in the draft of this section begins with the source of all fire: "Admonished by the sun's inclining ray." The true fire is an admonition to the city. In the published poem, the elemental fire is muted and artificial: "the sun's last rays" on the typist's laundry, the lighting of her stove, "the stairs unlit" down which her lover "gropes his way." The life-giving fire of the sun barely reaches the "Unreal City / Under the brown fog of a winter noon" (208). At the very end, the ascetic masters offer the choice of another fire, but until then, the element is notably inoperative.

Saint Augustine's story is the prime exemplum of lust, and the section culminates with part of the sentence which opens Book III of the *Confessions:* "To Carthage I came, where a whole frying-pan full of abominable loves crackled round about me, and on every side." The sentence just before it, at the end of Book II, speaks of an inner waste land: "I slid away from thee, and I went astray, O my God, yea, too much astray, from thee, my Stay, in these days of my youth, and I became to myself a land of want."[74] However, the burning of lust gives way only a few pages later to a burning desire for God. Augustine describes the way his conversion began with reading Cicero: "How did I burn then, my God, how did I burn to fly from earthly delights towards thee, and yet I knew not what thou meanedst to do with me! For with thee is wisdom. That love of wisdom is in Greek called Philosophy, with which that book inflamed me."[75] Thus, in Augustine the fire of lust makes a waste land of the soul, but the fire of love for divine wisdom redeems. The Fire Sermon of the Buddha, who also had his lustful younger days, speaks similarly of the fires of the sensations and passions that one must escape.

For Augustine, the same element, and the same emotion, that destroys life can also give it. The mystical fire transforms, as does Heraclitean fire and the Pentecostal fire promised by John the Baptist: "I indeed baptize you with water unto repentance: but he that cometh after me is mightier than I, whose shoes I am not worthy to bear: he shall baptize you with the Holy Ghost, and with fire" (Matthew 3:11). In the Old Testament as well, the power of Yahweh is often manifest in fire, as in the burning bush or in the contest between Elijah and the prophets of Baal, when the fire of the true God consumes not only the bullocks but the water with which they were drenched and the stones on which they lay (1 Kings 18:38). To many Christian mystics, too, God has appeared as fire. Pascal sewed in his cloak a verse that recorded his vision: "From about ten-thirty in the evening until around half past midnight, Fire." Richard Rolle felt his heart burn "not imaginatively, but as it were with a sensible fire." St. John of the Cross teaches that "to renounce all those things, our love and inclination for which are wont so to inflame the will that it delights therein, we require a more ardent fire and a nobler love—that of the Bridegroom"—hence equating this refining fire, as Augustine does, with the love of Christ.[76]

In the line from the *Purgatorio* quoted in the final passage of the poem, the penitent soul leaps with somber happiness back into the fire: *Poi s'ascose nel foco che gli affina* (Then dived he back into the fire which refines them). As Herbert Howarth says, Arnaut Daniel "was the proper monitor for the anaphrodisiac poem because, the most illustrious love poet of his day, he leapt into the fire, *willingly,* to burn away his lusts."[77] The parting words of Virgil to Dante also refer to the two fires, *il temporal foco e l'eterno,* and these lines close Eliot's essay "What Is a Classic?" (*OPP,* 71). The end of "The Fire Sermon" already contains the truth Eliot will express in the powerful fire poem *Little Gidding:*

> The only hope, or else despair
> Lies in the choice of pyre or pyre—
> To be redeemed from fire by fire.

The fire beneath the "frying-pan full of abominable loves" (purely a material flame) burns in all the petty affairs of this section. The fire of divine love plucks Augustine out of that fire: "I entangle my steps with these outward beauties, but Thou pluckest me out."

The ancient elements of earth, water, and air have become in modern science the states of matter: solid, liquid, and gas. The fourth element, fire, is now seen as energy. However, as Helen Luke says, this view of fire leaves out its symbolic role as "the agent of transformation," which helped us "emerge from the unconscious of the animal world."[78] Heraclitus saw too that fire was different from the other elements and that it transformed everything, as when it turned wood into smoke. He saw it as the transforming principle in the human being and in the entire cosmos. Mechanistic science does reduce this creative force to mere energy, which can be controlled and set to work; but modern science again lets us see this energy as mysteriously connected with forms of matter: $E = mc^2$. In this section of the poem, Eliot calls upon the transformative power of fire.

DEATH BY WATER: WATER

Water is, of course, the element most often mentioned in this poem, for the people of the waste land are waiting for rain. Rain is water in its life-giving aspect, water that is falling upon earth, where the conjunction of these two elements with air and the sun's fire will produce vegetation. The fourth section of *The Waste Land,* however, concerns water in its deadly aspect. The sea is an immense body of water separated from earth. It is not even drinkable. Homer called it "barren." With its unrelieved horizon, the open sea is a frightful emptiness: *Oed' und leer.* The element thus isolated is fatal. Only thin planks keep the sailor from being engulfed and drowned, deprived of the animating element.

Throughout the poem runs Ferdinand's lament for his drowned father, who becomes one version of the Fisher King. "Death by Water" is a dirge for all drowned men and a memento mori to all of us: "Gentile or Jew / O you who turn the wheel and look to windward, / Consider Phlebas, who was once handsome and tall as you" (319–21).

Yet this death by water is precisely what will bring the life-giving rain and the rejuvenation of the king. Eliot's use of the Tarot is focused on watery death ("fear death by drowning") and on the fructifying power of water. Weston contends that "the original use of the 'Tarot' would seem to have been, not to foretell the Future in general, but to predict the rise and fall of the waters which brought fertility to the land."[79] Eliot is also aware of rituals Weston describes in which the effigy of the king was cast into the water and later retrieved with rejoicing.

The allusions to *The Tempest* are similarly regenerative, and no doubt Eliot was thinking of that play in relation to Weston's *From Ritual to Romance*. Romance, the genre of Shakespeare's final plays, requires people to die and be reborn: Marina in *Pericles* (subject of Eliot's later poem "Marina"); Perdita and Hermione in *The Winter's Tale;* Imogen and her brothers in *Cymbeline;* and both Alonso and Ferdinand in *The Tempest* (for each thinks the other dead). Several of these deaths are thought to be by drowning. Moreover, Shakespeare uses elaborate rituals within these plays to resurrect the supposedly dead characters: the unveiling of the statue of Hermione; the descent of Jupiter's eagle in *Cymbeline;* the masque of Juno and Prospero's dramatic revelation of Ferdinand to his father. It can be argued that the dramatic genius of the Renaissance, like that of ancient Greece, was born at a moment in history when ritual was capable of being integrated into secular drama without losing its spiritual force, and, indeed, this is just what Cornford's writings on drama had suggested.[80] Eliot goes so far as to say, through the interlocutor "E." in "A Dialogue on Dramatic Poetry," that "the consummation of the drama, the perfect and ideal drama, is to be found in the ceremony of the Mass. . . . Drama springs from religious liturgy, and . . . it cannot afford to depart far from religious liturgy" (*SE,* 35). In Eliot's reading, Shakespeare's romances were just such perfectly integrated ritualistic dramas. The union of ritual and drama becomes, then, another manifestation of the unity of thought and feeling that preceded the dissociation of sensibility. Eliot's scene of drowning seeks a renewal of the ritual and romance that made Shakespeare's final plays possible. Its undercurrents are, thus, a good deal more hopeful than many readers have perceived. In the world of fertility ritual, the sacrifice is always efficacious: death always leads to rebirth. In the world of Shakespeare's romances, those lost at sea always come back to life at the right moment, and kingdoms are renewed in peace and justice.[81]

Water is the universal solvent. Given time, it will dissolve anything. It dissolves Phlebas's body in a leisurely way: "A current under sea / Picked his bones in whispers" (315–16). This dissolution is prelude to a resolution, as in the alchemical motto *solve et coagula.* It reintegrates him with nature and thereby makes possible a new form of life. As the sea picks his bones "in whispers," human breath is suggested deep beneath the water, and connection is made with the "whisper music" of the final section, which may thus be said to be Ariel's song. "He passed the stages of his age and youth / Entering the whirlpool" (317–18): he is taken back in time, transcending ordinary time and space. Like Shakespeare's king, he is being turned into something strange, something not human; yet the king arises from the experience more human than before, perhaps because he has, like the Ancient Mariner, rediscovered his kinship with nature.

Similarly, in the context of Heraclitean philosophy, death by water is understood to be necessarily regenerative. Heraclitus insisted that the dry soul was wisest, yet he said elsewhere that "To souls it is joy to become wet." G. T. W. Patrick, in a note on this fragment, explains that " . . . it is a pleasure for souls to become wet, because pursuing the way down into apparent death, they attain their new birth of life in death."[82]

Psychologically and spiritually, drowning has always symbolized entering into a new consciousness or new state of grace. When Carl Jung was returning over the ocean from his visit to Harvard in 1909, he wrote to his wife, "The beauty and grandeur of the sea consist in our being forced down into the fruitful bottomlands of our own psyches, where we confront and re-create ourselves in the animation of the 'mournful wasteland of the sea.'"[83] The sea is always *Oed' und leer,* a waste land, a deep emptiness in which the mind encounters only itself, its own unconscious depths. There the psyche loses its persona, its surface identity. So Phlebas "Forgot the cry of gulls, and the deep sea swell / And the profit and loss" (313–14), all matters of life on the earth and in society. The drowned man enters entirely into nature and into the unconscious, and there transformation becomes possible.

In the Bible and in Christian ritual, water likewise symbolizes a total change, the death of one's old self and the birth of a new self. The Psalmist writes of trial by both fire and water: "Thou has caused men to ride over our heads; we went through fire and through water: but thou broughtest us out into a wealthy place" (Psalm 66:12). Crossing the Red Sea is read as a type of baptism, which becomes the first sacrament when John baptizes Christ in the Jordan River. Water in these events symbolizes not only cleansing but death, death of the old self and birth of the new. This and the other sacraments are said to "effect what they symbolize," so that there is no gap between symbol and reality. The water of baptism is a holy substance, a physical object which is spiritually efficacious. This sacramental theology springs from faith in the Incarnation. As spirit and matter were wholly wedded in one body in history, so they are at one in the holy water and in other sacramental substances. Eliot's tone in "Death by Water" is certainly not pious, but ultimately the religious context—

both of the fertility cults and of sacramental Christianity—is the *only* one into which this passage fits.

WHAT THE THUNDER SAID: AETHER

An excellent gloss on Eliot's conception of the elements in *The Waste Land* is to be found in a biblical passage not mentioned in his notes. In the First Book of Kings, the prophet Elijah, in utter despair, asks God to let him die. An angel comes to him and says, "Go forth, and stand upon the mount before the Lord" (I Kings 19:11). In this final section, Eliot takes us similarly up out of the city and into the mountains. On the mount, Elijah searches the powers of the elements for the Lord's voice, but his search is in vain—much as the poet has searched the separate elements identified with successive sections of *The Waste Land* and found them lifeless:

> And, behold, the Lord passed by, and a great and strong wind rent the mountains, and brake in pieces the rocks before the Lord; but the Lord was not in the wind: and after the wind an earthquake; but the Lord was not in the earthquake: and after the earthquake a fire; but the Lord was not in the fire: and after the fire a still small voice. And it was so, when Elijah heard it, that he wrapped his face in his mantle, and went out, and stood in the entering of the cave. And behold there came a voice unto him, and said, what doest thou here, Elijah? (I Kings 19:11–13)

Elijah is like the Sibyl here—a despairing prophet in a cave—but his prayer is answered. Though the wind, earth, and fire are set in motion by God's passing, He is not in them. He is in the "still small voice," in something spiritual that is barely there in the material world. There are many analogues to this still small voice in this last section of *The Waste Land* and in later poems—particularly "Ash Wednesday." The key reference is in the phrase "aethereal rumours," which identifies the small voice of the rumors with the voice of the thunder and with the quintessence. In the first four sections of the poem, the prophet watched the four material elements pass by, and the Lord was not in them. In the last, he encounters the spiritual element which animates the others.[84]

The still small voice is heard everywhere in the silences of "Ash Wednesday." The air itself is "thoroughly small and dry" as the speaker tries to pray. The "silent sister . . . bent her head and signed but spoke no word," and then a bird sings and the wind shakes "a thousand whispers from the yew." These images of small or silent voices all point to "the silent Word" at the center of the "unstilled world." The paradox of the silent Word coalesces with that of the unmoved mover who is "At the still point of the turning world" ("Coriolan"). The still small voice is the only cause of all motion and all spirited voice. It is in the dry voices of the crickets, which, Crawford points out, were heard as an appeal for rain in some primitive cultures studied by Lévy-Bruhl.[85]

In "Coriolan," small, insignificant creatures speak with this voice of the "hidden" reality:

O hidden
Hidden in the stillness of noon, in the silent croaking night.
Come with the sweep of the little bat's wing, with the small flare of the firefly
    or lightning bug,
"Rising and falling, crowned with dust," the small creatures,
The small creatures chirp thinly through the dust, through the night.

These lines sound the same note as T. E. Hulme's treatise on aesthetics, in which he proclaims that "It is essential to prove that beauty may be in small, dry things."[86] Eliot and Hulme have in common with the symbolists a belief that poetry ought to find beauty amid ordinary desolation, though, as Marion Montgomery points out, Eliot seeks the transcendent more than Hulme would allow.[87] In fact, Eliot's conception of the small dusty creatures may be influenced as much by Meister Eckhart's statement quoted by Underhill that to the pure soul "all creatures are pure to enjoy; for it enjoyeth all creatures in God, and God in all creatures."[88] Underhill, speaking of Saint Francis, that greatest mystic lover of small creatures, affirms that for the true mystic "the barrier between human and non-human life, which makes man a stranger on earth as well as in heaven, is done away. Life now whispers to his life: all things are his intimates, and respond to his fraternal sympathy."[89] A more recent student of St. Francis, Eloi Leclerc, sees in the "Canticle of the Creatures" the highest statement of a necessary communion with all creation:

The Canticle, uniting as it does the thrust toward the Most High and a fraternal communion with all creatures, represents a unitive grasp of reality. . . . The spiritual life cannot be built above, and in abstraction from, nature; neither can it be built in independence of the obscure region of our being and in contempt for our cosmic and psychic roots. . . . The man who wishes to be reborn of the Spirit must accept fraternal communion with water—and not only with water but with fire, wind, earth, and the other cosmic entities as well. He must enter, with a marveling and singing soul, into fraternal communion with all creatures, and even with the night and its darkling light.[90]

Eliot seeks beauty in the small dry things the way Hulme does, and even more the way Saint Francis does, uniting the immanental "fraternal communion" with the transcendent "thrust toward the Most High." To be sure, the primary note struck in Part V of *The Waste Land* is still fragmentation, not union. The small creatures here are scarcely lovable (though, for the matter of that, neither was the wolf of Gubbio), but Eliot challenges his protagonist and reader to approach a love of all creatures as the only way to regain spiritual health. He begins to find spirit in the small creatures who inhabit the emptiness of the waste lands, and he suggests that their thin chirping is akin to the mighty voice of the thunder.

The still small voice, then, makes some moments in Part V closer in tone and meaning to "Ash Wednesday" than to the rest of *The Waste Land.* It is to be heard in the "cicada / And dry grass singing," and again in the grass "singing / Over the tumbled graves, about the chapel"; in the "whisper music" of a woman's hair; in the sounds of the bats who "Whistled, and beat their wings"; and in "that sound high in the air / Murmur of maternal lamentation." The latter voice is heard at the festivals of Adonis, where women take a prominent place, weeping for the dead god all night long, then singing of his resurrection.[91] In the context of fertility cults, as well as Christianity, the small, impotent, mournful feminine voices inevitably herald the return of the divine presence—much as the still small voice does for Elijah. The cicada and the coming gust of wind may also hark back to Underhill's description of the illuminated soul: "The self then becomes conscious of the living reality of that World of Becoming, the vast arena of the Divine creativity, in which the little individual life is immersed. Alike in howling gale and singing cricket it hears the crying aloud of that 'Word which is through all things everlastingly.'"[92] As this phrase indicates, the small voice of the cricket is ultimately identified with the Word.

"What the Thunder Said" is thus the turning point, not only in this poem but in Eliot's poetic career. Perhaps A. D. Moody is cutting it too fine when he locates the turning point precisely in the water dripping song, especially since it is only what the speaker wishes to hear, not what is heard, but the section as a whole moves in a new direction.[93] No doubt the first critic to see this shift was Harold Hannyngton Child, who, in reviewing the poem at its first appearance for the *Times Literary Supplement,* proclaimed that "Students of Mr Eliot's work will find a new note, and a profoundly interesting one, in the latter part of the poem."[94] However, debate over the degree and nature of this change has continued, with many critics insisting that the last part is no less desolate than the rest. These critics are ignoring a fairly obvious change in tone and imagery. Even the process of composition, as described by the poet himself, was quite different. As Longenbach points out, Eliot later admitted that his description of mystical experiences in his introduction to Pascal's

Pensées drew on his own experience in writing this last section.[95] Bush's description of the change is excellent:

> There is no question that "What the Thunder Said," much of which was written in a sudden fit of emotional release, is enormously moving. Eliot's speaker is here removed from the "swarming life" of London and among the mountains. And even though "There is not even silence in the mountains," the change suggests a condition of momentary release from his recurring nightmare.[96]

Clearly, something happens here which is quite different from what we experience in the first four sections.

As I see it, the prophet-persona has at last left the city and gone into the real, elemental wilderness—up into the mountains—seeking a revelation. They are desert, drought-stricken mountains, to be sure, where there is "rock and no water," and even the thunder is "dry sterile thunder without rain," yet all God's prophets went up to such mountains. Just such a one is Mount Sinai, but there, on the figural morning of the third day, Yahweh greeted His people with thunder:

> And it came to pass on the third day in the morning, that there were thunders and lightnings, and a thick cloud upon the mount, and the voice of the trumpet exceeding loud; so that all the people that was in the camp trembled. And Moses brought forth the people out of the camp to meet with God; and they stood on the nether part of the mount. (Exodus 19:16–17)

Eliot's prime allusions here are biblical, though eclectically conflated with other systems, especially Hindu philosophy and Greek physics. As the poem moves from the urban waste land to the desert mountains, Tiresias becomes a Hebrew prophet and Christian mystic. He is like Isaiah proclaiming, "Behold, the Lord maketh the earth empty, and maketh it waste, and turneth it upside down, and scattereth abroad the inhabitants thereof" (Isaiah 24:1), for he sees a waste land in which "upside down in air were towers." The destruction of cities releases the soul into a lonely emptiness where contemplation may be practiced. St. John of the Cross speaks of the soul entering "an immense wilderness without limits. And this solitude is the more delicious, sweet, and lovely, the more it is deep, vast, and empty." Richard Rolle likewise says, "In the wilderness . . . speaks the loved to the heart of the lover."[97] The sterile mechanistic desert of the urbanites in the first four sections becomes the fruitful contemplative wilderness as the poem moves physically and imaginatively into the real elemental desert.

The upside-down towers and the bats crawling head downward are analogous to the Hanged Man of the Tarot, who is always pictured hanging upside down. Did Eliot also know that the alchemists speak of the rising and condensing of vapors in their apparatus as "turning upside down"? Hermes is supposed to have said, "What is below is like that which is above," and this challenge to duality was sometimes symbolized in alchemical documents by a picture of a man upside down in a flask— a hopeful image which would answer that of the Sibyl in her ampulla.[98] I have found no evidence that Eliot had this kind of detailed alchemical knowledge, but it is a tantalizing parallel.

The Hanged Man of the Greater Trumps now becomes explicitly Jesus. The "silence in the gardens / After the agony in stony places" recalls the agony in the Garden of Gethsemane. The imprisonment and trial of Christ become "The shouting and the crying / Prison and palace." The coming thunder disturbs the elements at the moment of death: "reverberation / Of thunder of spring over distant mountains / He who was living is now dead." So in the Gospel of Matthew, after Jesus "yielded up the ghost . . . the veil of the temple was rent in twain, from the top to the bottom; and the earth did quake and the rocks rent . . . " (27:50–51). Jesus had spoken of the tearing down of the temple (meaning his body); the rent veil of the temple is a fulfillment, at the literal level, of that prophesy and connects the crucifixion in Eliot's mind with the "falling towers" of the European cities, predicted by the Tarot card that shows a tower beginning to crumble as it is hit by lightning. Eliot sees in this card the Heraclitean aethereal thunderbolt that "steers the course of all things" and is identified with the *Logos*. The self-sacrifice of the incarnate *Logos* in the Gospel calls forth this thunderbolt, which momentarily connects heaven and earth and begins a reordering of the earthly elements. Thus, the voice of thunder is the incarnate Word, the mysterious union of matter and spirit briefly made apparent. The earthquake at the moment of death is followed in Matthew's gospel by another earthquake, which rolls the stone back from the mouth of the sepulchre on the third day; an angel whose appearance is like lightning greets the women who have come at dawn to the tomb (28:1–3). One line in a draft of the poem makes the Christian meaning explicit: "I am the Resurrection and the Life."[99]

This opening epiphany does not save the inhabitants of the waste land. They remain hollow men, "dying / With a little patience." The silence and "thunder of spring" of Gethsemane and Golgotha are lost in mountains where "There is not even silence," and the thunder is dry and sterile, yet this does not necessarily deny the efficacy of the sacrifice. Rather, it re- enacts the doubts of the disciples themselves after Christ's death. When the women tell them on Easter morning that he is risen, they react skepti- cally: "And their words seemed to them as idle tales, and they believed them not" (Luke 24:11).

Given their natural lack of understanding, the disciples are scarcely able to recognize their risen master even when he appears to them in the flesh. For Eliot, who at that time shared their doubts, the story of two disciples meeting the risen Christ on the way to Emmaus expresses his own state of mind. The two tell the stranger who has joined them of the events that have taken place and the report that Christ has risen. He chides them for their distrust, showing them how the scriptures foretell precisely this event. He joins them for the evening meal, and in the re-enactment of the Eucharistic sacrament at the Last Supper, they recognize him:

> And it came to pass as he sat at meat with them, he took bread, and blessed it, and brake, and gave to them. And their eyes were opened, and they knew him, and he vanished out of their sight. (Luke 24:30–31)

They return to Jerusalem and tell the others how they knew him "in breaking of bread" (24:35). Christ then appears to them all and proves he is no disembodied form by letting them touch him and by eating with them. Removed from the draft were these lines explicitly referring to the Eucharist:

> When comes, to the sleeping or the wake
> The This-do-ye-for-my-sake
> To the sullen sunbaked houses and the trees
> The one essential word that frees.[100]

At the Last Supper, Jesus blessed and broke the bread and said, "This is my body which is given for you: this do in remembrance of me" (Luke 22:19). Eliot was focusing on the institution of the sacrament in this final part of the poem. The Word is "essential" not only in being indispensable but also in the sense of being an essence—the prime essence (or, I would want to say, the quintessence) from which all other essences derive their being. In the essential staff of life, their daily bread, the disciples recognize the Word.

The emphasis in this whole passage is on the resurrection of the body. Christ does not slough off the flesh and become pure spirit again but rises (and later ascends) in that same body. The touching and eating not only prove the reality of the event but demonstrate the integral corporeal nature of the first risen man. Calvin Bedient describes the mysterious third person as "The Inapprehensible rendered in the somehow apprehensible form of an aethereal shape," and "aethereal" is just the right word, for this is precisely an aethereal body, neither flesh nor fleshless. However, this precise, traditional understanding of the word is not what Bedient is thinking of, for he goes on to speak of the figure as "a shape more image than body."[101] In the Gospel account, it is precisely the bodiliness of the risen Lord that is emphasized in His walking and eating with the disciples. Here is the figural fulfillment of the macabre pagan sprouting corpse in the garden of Part I. This great mysterious union of spirit and matter resolves the strife of the elements figured in the earlier parts of the poem. Eliot associates this convergence of opposites with Tiresias's experience of both male and female natures in the same body ("I do not know whether a man or a woman"). More importantly, he associates it with the Christian sacrament, which locates spiritual reality in the physical realities of ordinary life. Eliot must have been moved by Underhill's comment on the Emmaus story: "So too for us the Transcendent life for which we crave is revealed, and our living within it, not in some remote and arid plane of being, in the cunning explanations of philosophy; but in the normal acts of our diurnal experience, suddenly made significant for us."[102] Such mysteries of psychosomatic being are essential to Eliot's movement at this time toward Anglo-Catholicism. This whole analysis leads me to side with those like Northrop Frye, who see Christ as the "spiritual substance" of the poem, and to disagree with those who, with Grover Smith, say " . . . I see no prophecy of conversion in the poem."[103] With Percival, Eliot has here entered the Chapel Perilous, asked the right question, and recognized the Lord in a glimpse of the Eucharistic chalice.

The anthropology of Weston and Frazer takes Eliot part way because it focuses on the physical nature of primitive religion and its symbolism: the death and rebirth of Adonis brings fertility to the land; the spear and chalice of the Grail romances are phallus and uterus in pagan cult. However, as we have seen, Frazer's conclusion from all this is that Christianity is simply a superficially spiritualized version of the fertility cult. Eliot, as I argued above, sees the connection in just the opposite way, finding in the fertility cults a prefiguring or partial realization of the sacramental idea. In "Exequy," written for possible inclusion in *The Waste Land,* Eliot speaks of adepts in some Mystery religion whose orgiastic fertility rituals are sacramental: "The Adepts twine beneath the trees / The sacramental exercise."[104] In Crawford's view, the context of this line implies that the fertility rite "has become a decadent pleasure, rather than a genuine ritual," and he later says that throughout this poem "The rituals of the past are perverted or decayed."[105] This is true enough, but we need not conclude as he does that *"The Waste Land* is a poem which leaves its readers in darkness."[106] Though the ancient rites are perverted or decayed for the half-characters who appear in the poem, the readers are led to imagine a potential purification or revival of ritual and a renewed connection of life and ritual. Moreover, in this final section, the rituals begin to become efficacious. The characters may not recognize the third one walking beside them, but the readers know who the third one is and know how the story ends. The physical resurrection of Christ, manifested with particular force in His walking along the road to Emmaus and eating with the disciples, is found to be a fulfillment and purification of the magical connection between physical and spiritual worlds in Frazer's fertility religions.

Eliot would become convinced that spiritual development is not merely a superstitious *Aberglaube,* as Arnold had it, sprung from material existence, but that it was inseparable from material existence. He found that symbols have, in Ricouer's words, "one foot in reality." In religion, this realization takes the form of sacramental theology, the teaching that sacraments are not efficacious without the physical "elements" used in their administration. The elements do not merely stand for spiritual realities: they are those. As the catechists put it, sacramental signs effect what they signify. Such was to become Eliot's attitude, expressed in the passage in *The Idea of a Christian Society* where he speaks of the conformity between the natural life and the supernatural life, a conformity that is evident when the disciples recognize their Lord in the breaking of bread.[107] The opening passages of "What the Thunder Said" are the turning point in Eliot's poetry and correspond to the conversion in his life, which led him, a few years later, to embarrass his wife and brother by falling to his knees at the entrance to St. Peter's.

The climax of the poem takes place not at St. Peter's but at the Chapel Perilous: "There is the empty chapel, only the wind's home / It has no windows, and the door swings . . . " (389–90). The very desolation of the place is paradoxically its potency: there is nothing here but wind, yet that wind is everything. In "Ash Wednesday," God says, "Prophesy to the wind, to the wind only for only / The wind will listen"; and certainly if this is the Pentecostal wind, that is all that matters. The chapel, with its windows out and its door swinging open, is the opposite of the enclosed room in Part II.

The very fact that its door and windows are broken or missing and hence unable to keep out the wind identifies this as the true Grail chapel, for in the Grail romances, it is typically described so. For example, Malory tells of Lancelot coming upon an "olde chapell" in the midst of a "waste londe." He goes to the door of the chapel and finds it "waste and brokyn."[108] Later, Gawain and Ector come upon "an auncyant chapell which was wasted, that there semed no man nor woman thydir repayred."[109] A decrepit, empty chapel with a broken door is precisely what the quester must find. Of course, neither Lancelot nor Gawain achieves the quest, and Eliot's quester may not either, but he is certainly in the right place. Galahad, too, comes to an empty old chapel at the beginning of his quest: "Than sir Galahad com to a mountayne where he founde a chapell passing olde, and founde therein nobody, for all was desolate."[110] It is not here that he sees the Grail, but he does hear a voice, which gives him true guidance, much as Eliot's quester does when he hears the voice of the thunder. With these parallels from the Grail romances in mind, I would not say, as George Bornstein does, that the quest does not reach a conclusion.[111] To be sure, there is an ambiguity in the conclusion, but the quester has finally come to the Chapel Perilous and the rain is coming.

The sound of thunder is also proper to the Grail quest in medieval romance. In Malory's account, the quest begins when the Holy Grail appears at the court of King Arthur, and its appearance is heralded by thunderclaps: "Than anone they harde crakynge and cryynge of thundir, that hem thought the palyse sholde all to-dryve" (521). The thunder threatens to destroy the castle, in a parallel to Eliot's "falling towers." Later in the tale, Percival's sister gives her life blood to heal a gentle-woman, after which Galahad, Percival, and Bors put her body into a barge covered with black silk and return to the castle of the woman who was healed—whereupon there is another thunderstorm: "Than they drew all to the castell, and furthewith there fylle a tempeste suddeyne of thundir and lyghtnynge and rayne, as all the erthe wolde a brokyn. So halfe the castell turned up-so-downe" (592). Percival's sister exemplifies the virtue of giving commanded by Eliot's thunder. His "falling towers" are again suggested by the castle turned half upside down.

Another potential Arthurian source for the image of falling towers is Edwin Arlington Robinson's *Merlin* (which was published in 1917, though I am not certain that Eliot had read it). Robinson writes,

> The king must have the state, and be the state;
> Or then shall we have neither king nor state,
> But bones and ashes, and high towers all fallen. . . .[112]

The bones and ashes are also, of course, images Eliot uses in his waste land, in which the bond between ruler and state has been severed (as in the case of Prospero or Coriolanus). Another echo is heard a few lines later, when Robinson writes of "a broken king," as Eliot writes of "a broken Coriolanus" in *The Waste Land* and of "a broken king" in *Four Quartets*.

Whether either Malory or Robinson is a direct source or not, Eliot's imagery of an empty, broken chapel and thunder threatening the towers of a castle is common in the Arthurian tradition and is associated with an eventually successful quest for the Holy Grail, the Eucharistic miracle that unites the physical world with the divine.

At the climactic moment of the poem, a cock stands on the chapel roof crowing in a new day:

> Co co rico co co rico
> In a flash of lightning. Then a damp gust
> Bringing rain.

(393–95)

The cock's crow reminds Kenner of the one that made Peter weep in repentance, and it thus continues the imagery of the crucifixion and resurrection.[113] The lightning flashes between sky and earth, connecting for a moment the aethereal and earthly realms. The four elements are again harmonizing, though in their typical strife. The lightning bolt releases the rain, which is borne on a gust of air and will be received by the earth. This "gust" is also a "ghost," the spiritual wind blowing whither it will, the *spectre en plein jour,* the ghostly presence of the resurrected master. Bedient rightly calls this passage "the first conjunction of wind and water in the poem since the Elizabethan passage," and one could say it is the first potentially fruitful conjunction of elements since the description of spring at the beginning of the poem. Bedient is not being inordinately hopeful when he says this "is promise enough."[114]

The thunder, voice of the aether, initiates and presides over this conjunction. The Hindu origin of this thunder has appropriately occupied those glossing the lines, but as I have suggested, Eliot was very likely thinking also of Heraclitus's statement that "It is the thunderbolt that steers the course of all things," where the thunderbolt is the aethereal fire (the two elements being identical in Heraclitus's cosmology). Patrick's edition of Heraclitus's fragments gives the sentence from Hippolytus that recorded this typically obscure fragment:

> And he also says that a judgment of the world and all things in it takes place by fire, expressing it as follows, "Now lightning rules all," that is, guides it rightly, meaning by lightning, everlasting fire. (Fr. 28)

Eliot's thunder is Heraclitean in that it guides, rules, judges. Heraclitus identifies the thunderbolt with the aethereal fire, which is also the *Logos,* the law or destiny that keeps order in the strife of the elements. Patrick translates Strobaeus as saying, "Heraclitus declares that destiny is the all-pervading law. And this is the etherial body, the seed of the origin of all things, and the measure of the appointed course" (Fr. 63). The "etherial body" is thus responsible for creating all things and re-creating them in each moment by maintaining the tension of opposites that is life. The lightning that flashes down on the chapel here is Heraclitus's aethereal body, identified with the "one essential word."

As I have maintained previously, the thunder is biblical, too. The speech of the thunderclap is particularly related to the thunder of the Book of Revelation, which is identified with the opening of the seals and the voice of the evangelist: "And I saw when the Lamb opened one of the seals, and I heard, as it were the noise of thunder, one of the four beasts saying, Come and see" (Rev. 6:1). In effect, the thunder symbolism is universal: whether over India or Palestine, it is experienced naturally as a divine locution.

The thunder commands us to sympathize. Eliot glosses his image of "each in his prison" with Bradley's description of a radical subjectivism in which "my experience falls within my own circle, a circle closed on the outside." Eliot's hastily concocted notes may at times lead us astray, but here I think he shows us the heart of his struggle.[115] The thunder commands us to transcend the alienation most of the poem describes. Sympathy can release us from the prison of subjective experience, releasing even the couple from their enclosed room and the Sibyl from her airless ampulla.

Sympathy becomes possible in *The Waste Land* because of the objective reality of the four elements out of which all things are made and especially because of the reality of the quintessence, which makes both physical and spiritual connections:

> Thinking of the key, each confirms a prison
> Only at nightfall, aethereal rumours
> Revive for a moment a broken Coriolanus.

(415–17)

Bedient has suggested that these "aethereal rumours" are "perhaps of the Aether," and indeed they are.[116] This identification is, I am maintaining, a key that unlocks the mystery of this entire final section of the poem. These rumors from the aether are related to the "Murmur of maternal lamentation" that sounds from "high in the air" (367–68). In fact, in the draft Eliot had first written "aetherial murmurs." As the faint voice of the aether can "reform" the city, at least incipiently or momentarily, it can "revive" Coriolanus. The draft has the aethereal rumors "revive the spirits of" Coriolanus, which makes more explicit the connection between the spiritual element in the cosmos, the aether, and the spirit of the human microcosm.[117] The spirit connects all the disparate parts of reality, as Josef Pieper explains in a later book for which Eliot wrote the introduction:

> . . . in the tradition of Western philosophy, the capacity for spiritual knowledge has always been understood to mean the power of establishing relations with the whole of reality, with all things existing; that is how it has been defined, and it is conceived as a definition more than as a description. *Spirit,* it might be said, is not only defined as incorporeal, but as the power and capacity to relate itself to the totality of being.[118]

Thus, the very capacity for communion is spiritual. The spiritual element revives Coriolanus by reconnecting him with others, as it reunites the physical elements.

As we have seen, the aether is identified by Heraclitus with the *Logos,* and in the image of a broken Coriolanus, we also see the incarnate Word whose bones were broken on Golgotha. In the fraction rite of the Mass, the consecrated host is broken as a reenactment both of the breaking of bread at the Last Supper and the breaking of Christ's bones. Paradoxically, these acts of fragmentation are necessary for the full Communion of God and His people to occur, unifying both the living and the dead in the Communion of Saints. Through this breaking (also related to the pagan *sparagmos*), is formed the wholeness of the Body of Christ. In the final section, this theological truth appears and gives a new meaning to the fragmentation the poem describes.

At the end of "Coriolan," the hero who stood alone in glorious triumph hears the maternal lamentation and desires union again: "Mother / May we not be some time, almost now, together." E. P. Bollier describes Coriolan this way: "Imprisoned in the private world of the closed circle of the Bradleyan self, perhaps he too refused to sympathize, to acknowledge that other selves also have an existence independent of his. . . . "[119] He stands among the busts of his forefathers, who stand forever alone, with "Noses strong to break the wind," but he begins to feel the "small wind" under the dove's breast, to experience what is "Hidden." Coriolanus begins to perceive the small unlikely creatures that communicate faint rumors from the indomitable breath of life, from the "Hidden." In other words, he begins to hear "the still small voice" of Elijah. As we have seen, all these small dry voices come to life in "What the Thunder Said," until, at the climactic moment, we hear the grass singing "Over the tumbled graves, about the chapel" and then the voice of the cock. All these speak with the same breath as the thunder, and they express a commonalty in the experience of all creatures—one derived, in fact, from their common creatureliness. Their voices are not heard earlier in the poem but only in this final section with its "aethereal rumours" that revive Coriolanus. The creative union of the elements is only momentary, and the poem ends in fragmentation, but the revelation at the chapel is that the directive capacity of the spirit, channeled through the aethereal dimension, can revive and recreate the material world.[120]

Much argument has taken place concerning the conclusion of this poem, and one must admit that it is characterized by a kind of ambivalence that fuels the argument. Some of the best commentary on the conclusion has located it neither in heaven nor in hell but in purgatory, pointing to the quotation from Dante's *Purgatorio* (428). Marion Montgomery says that in "What the Thunder Said" the "journey in the world of things and unhappy people is abandoned for high and arid hills that are of a world less anchored by the particulars of London and the English countryside than by Dante's ascent among the shades in Purgatory."[121]

This seems quite right, and the association gains more strength if we note that the rites of initiation in the Chapel Perilous are connected, according to Weston, with medieval narratives describing visits to purgatory.[122] Longenbach points out that even the quotation from Hesse's *Blick ins Chaos* included in Eliot's notes is part of a passage in which disintegration leads to a new birth.[123] Helen Gardner also hits the right note in her description of the poem's ending:

> At the centre of its spiral movement there is simply "the abyss", "the void" or "the overwhelming question," the terror of the unknown, which cannot finally be evaded. For all this its ending is not despair. Stripped of his illusions, his pride broken, man is left to face the final possibility. *The Waste Land* ends with the truth of the human situation as the religious mind conceives it: the beginning of wisdom is fear.[124]

The poem ends in chaos and disillusionment, but the "fear in a handful of dust" has become genuine fear of the Lord, the requisite feeling for entrance to the path of purgatorial regeneration.

Milton Miller puts it in a more positive way, emphasizing the sense of a sudden union with the divine coming about in the midst of the dark night of the soul: "For precisely at the height of disconnection and irresolution the reader perceives a transformation which makes of spiritual despair the very material for spiritual climax and resolution."[125] Miller perhaps goes too far when he suggests that the babble of voices at the end suggests the pentecostal glossolalia, and no doubt some readers will think I have gone too far toward hearing aethereal rumors in all the poem's empty spaces. I must insist, however, on Eliot's awareness that the purgatorial path leads inevitably (however painfully) to paradise, just as the empty chapel is inevitably the Grail chapel. Bornstein is not entirely correct in concluding that by the time of *The Waste Land* "Eliot had not yet found the active conception of suffering that Christianity later opened to him. . . . "[126] After all, the line from the *Purgatorio* describes Arnaut Daniel as he leaps willingly into the fire, knowing it is the way to the peace which passeth understanding. Arnaut's parting words to Dante before he returns to the fire are the last words spoken by any of the suffering souls in the *Purgatorio,* for Dante now enters the earthly paradise and leaves Virgil behind as he meets Beatrice. The line quoted by Eliot thus signals an impending release from purgatorial suffering. The entire finale seems touched with such a grim but solemn hope.

To put it once more in Heraclitean terms, let us glance at Patrick's comment on the doctrine of flux:

> It banished all permanence from the universe, and banished therewith all those last supports which men are accustomed to cling to. It introduced alarm into

philosophy, and set men, even to the present day, asking, what can be saved from this general wreck? What is there absolutely permanent in the universe? The question . . . did not trouble Heraclitus himself, for, consistently or inconsistently, he had a foundation rock in his Universal Law, Reason or Order, which was his theoretical starting-point. [127]

Eliot constructs *The Waste Land* according to this cosmology and consequently finds the strife-torn world reduced to a "general wreck." Mysteriously, in the midst of the ruins, he comes to know the Law, the *Logos*. [128]

As a foil to the present reading, let us return to I. A. Richards, who gave this poem as an example when he called for a new poetry free of all the beliefs science had invalidated. In a footnote, he credits Eliot with having shown how this could be done:

> . . . by effecting a complete severance between his poetry and *all* beliefs, and this without any weakening of the poetry, he has realised what might otherwise have remained largely a speculative possibility, and has shown the way to the only solution of these difficulties. "In the destructive element immerse. That is the way." [129]

Eliot's review of the book demolishes this view of poetry, linking it to Arnold's:

> Mr Richards thinks that the only thing that can save us from "mental chaos" is poetry, a poetry of the future detached from all belief. . . . "Poetry is capable of saving us," he says; it is like saying that the wall-paper will save us when the walls have crumbled. It is a revised version of Literature and Dogma. [130]

This obviously rejects Richards' reading of *The Waste Land*—a reading still frequently given to the poem today. Far from being detached from all belief, Eliot at this stage accepts any belief—Eastern or Western, pagan or Christian, Heraclitean or mystical—so long as it can connect the physical and spiritual realities and thereby fill the void left by scientific abstract materialism. It is curious that Richards quotes an alchemical dictum—"In the destructive element immerse"—when describing this as a poem without belief. The poem does effect something like the acidic dissolving he favors, and perhaps Richards turns to alchemy as the precursor of modern chemistry, which has dissolved all beliefs about matter in the experimental beaker. If Eliot is thinking of alchemy at all here, he turns to the spagyric art for precisely opposite reasons, seeing it as one of the symbolic systems that align physical and spiritual processes. Immersion in the destructive element prepares for a later stage of reintegration at a higher level. *Solve* is followed by *coagula* as inevitably as the *Purgatorio* is followed by the *Paradiso*. Eliot's dissolving of the four elements into the separate sections of the poem prepares for their reintegration as a more noble substance in the final section within the medium of the quintessence, which is identified in alchemy with the philosopher's stone.

Eliot thinks of the classical elements as a way of coming to terms with the apparent reality that the world is made up of opposites: earth and air, fire and water. This awareness of opposition was the essential insight of the pre-Socratics, summed up by Heraclitus's assertion that everything is strife. If these material elements are at odds, order is impossible without some formative principle, but if that principle is strictly spiritual, its introduction only shifts the dilemma to the ultimate opposition—between form and matter, or spirit and matter. At the level of the person this becomes the mind-body problem. Some philosophers have solved the problem by positing the existence of the fifth element, which is at once material and spiritual. In Eliot's poetry, the aether (along with several associated ideas and images: the hidden, the still point, etc.) represents whatever it is that makes possible the dynamic complementarity of opposites that we call creation. It is the paradox, the mystery, at the heart of life: the spirit moving over the waters, the miracle of bringing water from rock in the desert. For Eliot, vital order comes from the pattern or dance of opposites orchestrated by the Heraclitean aethereal *Logos* and achieves its ultimate mysterious verification in the incarnation of the *Logos* in the historical person of Jesus.

5

United by Strife: Ancient and Modern
Physics in *Four Quartets*

THROUGHOUT his poetry, T. S. Eliot continues to use the classical elements and attendant images to symbolize the structure of the cosmos, and in his two major works, he uses them to create thematic structure in the poems themselves. As has become clear in earlier chapters, the elements are for Eliot primordial, nonarbitrary symbols (or objective correlatives), which focus his thinking about the dualities of the created world: matter and spirit, body and soul, the many and the one.

As with the sections of *The Waste Land,* each of the *Four Quartets* has one of the elements assigned to it. Grover Smith made this observation some time ago, writing that "The symbolism of the four seasons and of the elemental quaternion, earth, water, air, and fire, maintained the subject of cyclical change in time, against which Eliot posed the idea of a stable eternity."[1] My interest is in seeing how Eliot's idea of the elements—informed by classical philosophy, the literary tradition, and Christian mysticism—helps him describe an integration of these opposing principles. I will show that Eliot does not finally oppose "stable eternity" and "cyclical change"; instead, he follows Heraclitus in finding the principle of stability within the cyclic change. I also will argue that Eliot finds this Heraclitean idea of immanence compatible with the discoveries of modern physics—and with the Christian view of the physical world.

Helen Gardner, in *The Composition of "Four Quartets,"* has shown that Eliot first decided on four poems associated with the four elements when he was working on the second poem. She quotes a letter from John Hayward to Frank Morley in 1940 that says Eliot is working on a second poem and refers to a plan for more. Gardner says,

> This confirms what Eliot stated more than once: that the notion of four poems based on the symbolism of the four elements and the four seasons, which seems so fundamental to the conception of *Four Quartets,* was a notion that came to him during the writing of *East Coker.*[2]

One of the places Eliot explained this process was a letter to William Matchett (in 1949). There Eliot writes that

> The idea of the whole sequence emerged gradually. I should say during the composition of *East Coker*. Certainly by the time that poem was finished I envisaged the whole work as having four parts which gradually began to assume, perhaps only for convenience sake, a relation to the four seasons and the four elements.[3]

Thus, Eliot acknowledges that he was consciously organizing the *Quartets* using these symbols but suggests that he did so for convenience. I hope to convince the reader that Eliot was partly playing Possum in this letter and that Ronald Bush is right to say that " . . . the development of the poem's formal relations was never merely 'convenient.'"[4] The fact that Heraclitus was central to Eliot's thinking in these poems makes it nearly impossible that elemental organization would be merely for convenience, since Heraclitus's whole philosophy is based on his thinking about the physical elements. Anyway, as David Huisman suggested to me on this subject, the "convenience" of a great poet may be something of real significance. Eliot's convenience may have been to use ancient symbols as the primary structural and thematic foci of his magnum opus. It seems clear to me that the elements were convenient to Eliot in this sense, rather as the topography of hell, purgatory, and heaven was convenient for Dante.

In her earlier book, *The Art of T. S. Eliot,* Helen Gardner had already pointed out the centrality of the elements in *Four Quartets:*

> The "thematic material" of the poem is not an idea or a myth, but partly certain common symbols. The basic symbols are the four elements, taken as the material of mortal life, and another way of describing *Four Quartets* and a less misleading one, would be to say that *Burnt Norton* is a poem about air, on which whispers are borne, intangible itself, but the medium of communication; *East Coker* is a poem about earth, the dust of which we are made and into which we shall return; it tells of "dung and death," and the sickness of the flesh; *The Dry Salvages* is a poem about water, which some Greek thinkers thought was the primitive material out of which the world arose, and which man has always thought of as surrounding and embracing the land, limiting the land and encroaching on it, itself illimitable; *Little Gidding* is a poem about fire, the purest of the elements, by which some have thought the world would end, fire which consumes and purifies.[5]

This is as fine a summary of the poem's thematic structure as one could ask for. An interpretation of this structure might well begin with Gardner's mention of the Greek thinkers who asserted that water was the "primitive material out of which the world arose," for this comment places the whole scheme in what was, for Eliot, its primary context. As a matter of fact (as we have seen), water was not the only element thought to be prime. While Thales argued for water, Anaximenes proposed air, Xenophanes championed earth, and Heraclitus chose fire. The pre-Socratics argued endlessly about what was the *arche,* the substratum of the physical world, and the argument had resumed in Eliot's time, carried on in new terms that gave renewed validity to ancient physics (as we will see later in this chapter). Such arguments lie behind Eliot's interest in the elements. Other critics—Russell Kirk, Thomas Rees, and Marshall McLuhan—have pointed to the association of *Quartets* and elements, but no one—Gardner not excepted—has attempted a reading of the poem that truly takes them to be what she calls them, basic symbols.[6] The first part of this chapter is such an attempt.

The imagery of the four poems does correspond to their assigned elements. In *Burnt Norton,* the "vibrant air" of the rose garden contrasts with the "faded air" of London. As Gardner points out, there is much here about communication, which takes place through the medium of air. *East Coker* starts out in an "open field," where fire returns "ashes to the earth." Here peasants dance with "Earth feet, loam feet." *The Dry Salvages* focuses on water, both the sea and "the strong brown god," the river. *Little Gidding* is dedicated, of course, to fire: winter sun and "pentecostal fire" and fire bombs and the fire that is the rose.

However, the association of different elements with separate sections is handled quite differently in this poem than it was in *The Waste Land,* where the elements were much more completely cut off from each other. In the earlier poem, the very titles of the sections gave the identifications, and one element clearly dominated the imagery of each section. Only in the fifth section did the four begin to coalesce under the influence of the fifth. In *Four Quartets,* the identifications of sections with elements are much less clear and static, which is probably why the critics have not thought more of them. The titles give no hint, and the leading element of each section is far from dominating the imagery. In fact, the point is that there is a resolution of the opposing elements in each poem, a resolution conceived of primarily in terms of the physical theories of Heraclitus.

Heraclitus saw that earth, water, and air were what modern scientists call "states" of matter (the modern terms being "solid," "liquid," and "gas"), rather than unchanging elements or essences. He also saw that fire was something else, a transforming force, which science today calls "energy." However, where Newtonian science uses the mechanical laws of thermodynamics to describe energy and matter, Heraclitus saw fire as a spiritual phenomenon. It is also, for him, *Logos* and aether. It does not transform the other elements randomly but does so in an eternal pattern, creating a world that is, like Spenser's Garden of Adonis, "eterne in mutability." In this way, Heraclitus finds the eternal and unchanging pattern immanent in the world's flux.

Eliot's whole theory of poetic meaning, especially the idea of the objective correlative, aims to bridge the gap between the objective material world and the subjective spiritual world. In this, he followed Coleridge especially, and also the symbolist poets. Edmund Wilson writes in *Axel's Castle*, "It is the aim and the triumph of the Symbolist poet to make the stabilities of the external world answer to the individual's varying apprehension of them. It is, indeed, his effect, if not his purpose, to lead us to question the traditional dualism which would make them out to be two separate things."[7] Having taken such an aim as his goal at the beginning of his poetic career, Eliot ended with a less subjective version of the same idea, one grounded not only in poetic principles but in physical ones. Where the symbolist poet forces subjective apprehension to fit the external world, Eliot asserts with Heraclitus that our apprehension is not entirely subjective because "the *Logos* is common to all." The *Logos*-aether orders physical and psychic worlds in the same way; thus, we can understand the harmony of the elements in *Four Quartets* only after we have looked in the poem for the harmonizing element.

The quintessence, which begins to appear only at the end of *The Waste Land*, is here present throughout. Gardner ends her brief but enlightening discussion of the subject on this note:

> We could then say that the whole poem is about the four elements whose mysterious union makes life, pointing out that in each of the separate poems all four are present; and perhaps adding that some have thought that there is a fifth element, unnamed but latent in all things: the quintessence, the true principle of life, and that this unnamed principle is the subject of the whole poem.[8]

Gardner does not tell us who has thought the fifth element was the subject of the whole poem, and I have not found the suggestion made in any other publication. She herself does not say anything more about it in her book.

The quintessence is not unnamed, and it is only if the name "aether" rings a bell and if we are aware of its Aristotelian function of filling the void that we will catch Eliot's oblique allusion to it in *East Coker*, where he plays on the modern anaesthetic ether as he did long before in "Prufrock":

> O dark dark dark. They all go into the dark,
> The vacant interstellar spaces, the vacant into the vacant,
> The captains, merchant bankers, eminent men of letters.

                                                              (*EC*, III)

Darkness is here the vacancy of the interstellar spaces, the vacancy filled by the aether in the classical (especially Aristotelian) cosmos. The lines further associate that physical vacancy of space with bodily death and with a mental or spiritual vacancy in men, similar to that of the etherized patient in "Prufrock" and that of several figures in *The Waste Land*. After thus dwelling on vacancy and death, however, the poet introduces a paradoxical hope:

> I said to my soul be still, and let the dark come upon you
> Which shall be the darkness of God.

At the very moment of dissolution, the spirit of God fills the dark interstellar spaces, perhaps recalling the paradox of a spiritual material that fills the void. Shortly after, Eliot likens death to the experience when a subway train

> stops too long between stations
> And the conversation rises and slowly fades into silence
> And you see behind every face the mental emptiness deepen
> Leaving only the growing terror of nothing to think about.

These modern travelers, having nothing to think about, must think about nothingness. Their experience is similar to that of the man in the hyacinth garden or the man in the closed room in *The Waste Land*.

A few lines later, Eliot compares this mental vacancy with the experience of the anaesthetic ether: "Or when, under ether, the mind is conscious but conscious of nothing." Like the mind of the patient on the operating table in "Prufrock," this mind is pathetically empty, yet here the play between the anaesthetizing chemical and the heavenly element is not as ironic as it is in the earlier poem. In the "vacant interstellar spaces" lies the darkness which *may* become, if the soul is able to wait, the "darkness of God." There is a way of thinking about nothing which is not the mind being "distracted from distraction by distraction" but is rather the mystical contemplation described a few lines later: "In order to arrive at what you do not know / You must go by a way which is the way of ignorance" (*EC*, III).

Eliot is thinking, of course, of the dark night of the soul in the writing of St. John of the Cross. He may also have in mind the anonymous *Cloud of Unknowing*, which he quotes in *Little Gidding*. The fourteenth-century mystic writes of his practice,

For at first when thou dost it, thou findest but a darkness, and as it were a *cloud of unknowing*, thou knowest not what, saving that thou feelest in thy will a naked intent upon God. . . . And therefore shape thee to bide in this darkness as long as thou mayest, evermore crying after him whom thou lovest. For if ever thou shalt see him or feel him, as it may be here, it must always be in this cloud and in this darkness.[9]

This biding in darkness is the essence of the *via negativa,* and it powerfully attracted Eliot, who once wrote to Paul Elmer More that he was astonished to find people who did not experience, as he did, the void at the center of life. To enter this void consciously, as the contemplative does, is to seek the experience of the mind under ether, "conscious but conscious of nothing." Eliot places this passage describing the psychic void near the one describing its cosmic analogue, the vacant interstellar spaces.

To be sure, the mind under the modern chemical ether is as sterile in its emptiness as the minds in the darkened subway train and the minds of the dying eminent men of letters. Eliot seems to suggest, however, that holy contemplation proceeds precisely from this experience of the emptiness of life. One who is able to face the terror of the void in the dark night of the soul will find that void filled with God. As the macrocosmic spaces are filled with the divine aether, so is the microcosmic mental void.

As Gardner suggests, the quintessence pervades *Four Quartets.* It is to be found in the "open field," the "empty silence," the "darkness," the "Thunder rolled by the rolling stars," the "dark cold and the empty desolation," the "Zero summer," the "hidden waterfall," and "in the stillness / Between two waves of the sea"—in all the dark, hidden, silent, empty, in-between, or intersecting places. In *The Waste Land,* the "aethereal rumours" and the voice of the thunder are heard only in the fifth section, but here no fifth section is needed because the fifth element is everywhere present. Since Heraclitus identifies the aether with fire, it is also present wherever there is fire or the transformation of the other elements effected by fire. This identification of fire and aether is a given even in the Renaissance. Sir John Davies writes in *Orchestra* of "That heavenly fire or quintessence divine."[10]

While filling the empty spaces of the universe, the aether provides a medium in which the four opposing elements (really only three in Heraclitus's scheme) can cohere and merge, allowing them to join, as Gardner says, in a "mysterious union" that "makes life." If we look at the opening rose garden passage, we find the elements united for a moment under the influence of the quasi-material fire of the sun: "And the pool was filled with water out of sunlight" (*BN,* I). Suddenly, the dry concrete is full of water, which has emerged from its opposite, fire. This may be a mirage, but it is taken as an experience of matter transformed at the "still point" that is "neither flesh nor fleshless." The real illusion is not the mirage but our usual sense that matter and spirit are inimical. This is a moment of reality in which they intersect as the opposing elements do.

Perhaps there is a similar sense of the elements in harmony under the influence of aether when Ezra Pound writes of "light air, under saplings, / the blue banded lake under aether, / an oasis, the stones, the calm field, / the grass quiet . . ." (Canto XVI). Here, too, the vision seems to be one of all the elements in fruitful conjunction under the aethereal heaven. As we saw in chapter 4, "aether" appears quite often in the *Cantos,* and in other writings by *il miglior fabbro.* The notion of aether was evidently in the air at the time.

With the role of the aethereal fire partly clarified, we may better understand the importance of Heraclitus's physical ideas to the symbolism in *Four Quartets.* The two epigraphs from Heraclitus are less enigmatic than some of Eliot's epigraphs and do tell us where he started in his search for answers to his central question about the relation between the temporal world of change and the eternal, changeless world. The first epigraph declares, "Although the Logos is common the many live as if they had a private understanding."[11] Heraclitus was apparently haughty, but he did not believe that truth was available only to a chosen few. Anyone who chooses to can know the *Logos,* he taught. This emphasis on a pattern in reality common to everything and knowable by everyone challenges the subjective state of mind described by F. H. Bradley, and it was precisely that sense of radical separation from all others (which Eliot seems to have experienced intensely himself) that the poet transcends in *Four Quartets.* On the physical level, the *Logos* is an eternal pattern lying just behind the apparent orderless flux of the elements; on the psychological level, the *Logos* is an understanding we have in common, if we choose to avail ourselves of it.

In other words, for Heraclitus, neither the individual elements nor individual people are really separate, but we have somehow come to think and act as though they were. He urged his students to see life whole: "The wise is one thing, to be acquainted with true judgement, how all things are steered through all."[12] The wholeness, however, is a dynamic pattern hidden in the flux of the world, not a static structure: "Things taken together are whole and not whole, something which is being brought together and brought apart, which is in tune and out of tune; out of all things there comes a unity, and out of a unity all things."[13] Heraclitus's emphasis on the underlying unity of the elements goes with an emphasis on the unity of knowledge in an objective natural law ordained by the divine *Logos.*

Eliot's second epigraph proclaims, "The path up and down is one and the same."[14] This fragment indicates the way Heraclitus explained the world's unity-in-diversity. Smith interprets the epigraph by reference to Heraclitus's view of the elements:

> In Heraclitus it refers supposedly to the transmutation of the elements, the cycle of earth, water, air, and fire, for which later philosophers cited Heraclitus as an authority. Heraclitus calls the flux "war" or "strife." The way up is from earth to fire, the way down from fire to earth; the cycle proceeds everlastingly. And since for Heraclitus the primary substance is fire, fire motivates the cycle. Indeed, in an extended sense, the cycle itself is fire. This is what Heraclitus sometimes means by his *logos*—an equivalence, practically speaking, with the flux itself.[15]

This analysis is exactly right. The *Logos*-fire is the flux, but since it is cyclic, it also has pattern. Because Heraclitus identified the flux with the *Logos,* he did not finally regard the flux as chaotic. The aethereal fire causes the transformation of the other elements, the flux, but it also directs it, orders it, patterns it: "Thunderbolt steers all things."

The second section of *Little Gidding* encapsulates this teaching. It begins with descriptions of decay, and the three stanzas conclude, "This is the death of air. . . . This is the death of earth. . . . This is the death of water and fire." Smith says this passage "finds no meaning" in the flux: "Here is represented only the downward tendency of material things, toward ruin."[16] The passage certainly describes nothing but decay, yet if we are faithful to the teaching of Heraclitus, must we not at this point assume that this downward way is also the way up? The passage alludes to a saying of the philosopher that speaks of life as well as death: "Fire lives the death of air, and air lives the death of fire; water lives the death of earth, earth that of water."[17] This fragment actually describes a very straightforward literal concept. Heraclitus sees the elements organized hierarchically, from finest and highest to grossest and lowest: fire, air, water, earth.[18] The highest, fire, dies (as it descends) and becomes air; air becomes water; and water becomes earth. However, the transformation goes in reverse order, too, so that substances rise from earth, through water and air to the fiery heaven. Heraclitus is describing what we would now call changes in the *state* of matter, from solid to liquid to gas. In the dynamics of the antinomies, however, this suggests to Heraclitus and Eliot that every death has its complementary birth among the elements, which are in that sense united by strife.

The exchange of elements—their transmutation into one another—is explicable in the ancient physics as an exchange of the four basic qualities: hot and cold, dry and wet. Each element is defined as a combination of two qualities—one from each of these pairs—and the four elements exhaust the possible combinations: earth, cold and dry; water, cold and wet; air, hot and wet; fire, hot and dry. Note that as we ascend or descend in the hierarchy of elements, each one has one quality in common with its neighbor above and one in common with its neighbor below. For example, water shares coldness with earth and wetness with air; thus, a change in one of the two qualities will transform an element one step upward or downward without making it completely lose its character. Eliot himself describes this system in his essay on Leibniz, in the context of explaining Aristotle's nondualistic metaphysics:

> The *materia prima* is not *actual,* because it has no predicates; the smallest number of predicates which an actual existent can have is two. That is, whatever is merely hot, or merely dry, is not a substance but is identical with the quality of the substance itself; but whatever is hot and wet or cold and dry, is a substance different from its predicates. These elements—the possible combinations of four qualities—are capable of transmutation into one another in a cycle which occurs in the exchange of qualities (the hot-dry becomes hot-wet, the hot-wet becomes wet-cold, etc.).[19]

This theory of physics is what enables Aristotle to avoid dualism in his metaphysics, but the terminology of "exchange" derives more properly from Heraclitus. It is precisely this cycle of exchange that Eliot has in mind when he speaks of the elements living each other's death and when he quotes Heraclitus's "The path up and down is one and the same."

What appear to be opposite entities, then, are really aspects of one reality: "And as the same thing there exists in us living and dead and the waking and the sleeping and young and old: for these things having changed round are those, and those having changed round are these."[20] What we think of as independently existing opposites actually extend from one another as ends of one continuum—or, in Heraclitus's metaphor, as ends of the string stretched out by a bow. It is only in the strife between elements that the world can be. *Logos* is the pattern of their transformation into one another. The isolation of the elements in *The Waste Land* breaks the pattern or denies it, while the interplay of elements living each other's death in *Four Quartets* reveals (as I hope to show) the life-giving pattern. This pattern is the dance of the elements—their circulation and exchange—which unites them in strife. Let us look at instances of the dance within the individual poems.

BURNT NORTON: AIR

Air is the prime reference in *Burnt Norton,* but when he wrote it, Eliot did not yet have the larger scheme in mind. He did have in mind, however, the Heraclitean flux of elements. The very title refers to fire, and the exchange of elements is worked out fairly completely in this one poem, particularly in the miraculous opening section, mentioned previously. Suddenly, the man and woman walking around the grounds of the old manor house find themselves accompanied by ghostly beings:

> So we moved, and they, in a formal pattern,
> Along the empty alley, into the box circle,
> To look down into the drained pool.
> Dry the pool, dry concrete, brown edged,
> And the pool was filled with water out of sunlight,
> And the lotus rose, quietly, quietly,
> The surface glittered out of heart of light,
> And they were behind us, reflected in the pool.
>
> (*BN*, I)

The "dry concrete, brown edged" is a familiar waste land image of rock without water: the earth is dead. All at once, the pool is filled with water, not from rain but "out of sunlight." Fire yields its complete opposite, water, and from this conjunction arises new life, the lotus. The vision ends as suddenly as it began, but it has given a glimpse of the deeper reality in which the opposites are one. There is a suggestion that the "formal pattern" of the rose garden assists this transformation, for pattern comes from the aethereal fire, the *Logos,* which forms the world out of the flux of elements. Perhaps there is also an allusion in the phrase "box circle" to the alchemical *coniunctio oppositorum.* The alchemists sometimes call their work "squaring the circle," which means, in part, taking the four elements (the square) and uniting them in an eternal circle. Eliot does occasionally mention as an example of an unreal or imaginary object the "round square," making the speculation slightly more plausible. As Nancy Hargrove points out, the "box circle" refers to a circular hedge of "evergreen boxwood," which "represents everlasting life." I am suggesting that the phrase "box circle" simultaneously evokes the idea of squaring the circle, which also stands for everlasting life.[21]

Another analogue is to be found in Sir Thomas Browne's interpretation of the quincunx pattern presumed to be found in ancient gardens. The quincunx has four points at the corners of a square and a fifth point in the center. Browne explains that lines drawn through the center from the corners form an *X,* symbolizing rectilinear earthly motion macrocosmically and the senses microcosmically. However, when the figure is spun on its center, it makes a circle, which symbolizes the perfect uniform motion of the first Orb (the *primum mobile*) and the divinity of the human soul. Thus, the union of opposites is symbolized by an identity of square and circle.[22] Perhaps Eliot's "box circle" in the garden at Burnt Norton is meant to evoke the symbolism of these ancient gardens.

The poet's vision of the pool might be an illusion: it goes away when a cloud passes in front of the sun. Yet it seems quite real, as do the ghostly visitors that precede it. Both are phenomena that hover between the material and spiritual worlds. The spirits are "Moving without pressure": that which moves is in the physical, temporal world, but that which exerts no pressure is spiritual. The poet is for that moment at the still point, "Neither flesh nor fleshless." The "heart of light" is the higher fire of Heraclitus, temporal and eternal at once.

The conjunction of elements appears at the moment both in and out of time, when one is aware of movement but also of the stable pattern underlying movement:

> To be conscious is not to be in time
> But only in time can the moment in the rose-garden,
> The moment in the arbour where the rain beat,
> The moment in the draughty church at smokefall
> Be remembered. . . .
>
> (*BN*, II)

Each of these visionary moments is associated with one of the three material elements: the rose garden with earth; the rainy arbor with water; the draughty church with air. Each element can evoke the aethereal dimension because each is continually connected with that dimension.

Burnt Norton has many images of lifeless or fatal elements. The air itself ceases to support life in the "Eructation of unhealthy souls / Into the faded air" (*BN*, III). The fourth section returns to the language of "The Burial of the Dead": "Will the sunflower turn to us, will the clematis / Stray down, bend to us, tendril and spray / Clutch and cling?" (*BN*, IV). The poem ends with a repetition of the rose garden experience: "Sudden in a shaft of sunlight / Even while the dust moves / There rises the hidden laughter" (*BN*, V). Here even the dust, symbol of dead earth, comes to life in the sunlight.

East Coker: Earth

The first section of *East Coker* is replete with earth images, which suggests that by the time Eliot completed it, he was quite definitely thinking of the elements as serious organizing symbols. The setting is an "open field," and a dance of "earth feet" takes place there. It is a marriage dance but also a funeral dance leading flesh inevitably back to the earth in "Dung and death." The section does not end there. Rather, it shifts suddenly to an image of the eternal sea. We are not left with the deadliness of one isolated element but with sudden conjunctions.

The opening passage describes the way up and down as a cycle of human building or natural growth followed by decay:

> In succession
> Houses rise and fall, crumble, are extended,
> Are removed, restored, or in their place
> Is an open field, or a factory, or a by-pass.
> Old stone to new building, old timber to new fires,
> Old fires to ashes, and ashes to the earth. . . .
>
> (*EC,* I)

Heraclitus speaks in these lines. Here is his notion that fire (as sunlight) transforms the grossest element into a living creature—timber—and eventually transforms that again, in the downward movement, to earth. In fact, it was probably just this cycle of wood growing in sunlight and dying in fire that gave Heraclitus his initial insight about the way up and down, and about the function of fire. "Timber" is the right word here because the Latin *materia* sometimes designates "wood" or "timber," while it means more generally "matter." Timber is one of the chief symbols of matter, signifying at once its solidity and its mutability. With wood there is "a time for building" something solid but also a time for the wind, the lightest of the three ordinary elements "to shake the wainscot." The real solidity in this world of vanity is in the fire, which will raise up new life and buildings as surely as it destroys them.

The "open field" is one of the empty places in the poem where one may find the creative aether. Here, "the light falls / Across the open field," the light being the subtle celestial fire. A curious line observes that "the sultry light / Is absorbed, not refracted, by grey stone." This is highly scientific language. It must be emphasizing the unmixed earthiness of the stone, for it is water that would refract light. Perhaps it is another way of saying that there is rock but no water here. In any case, the "empty silence" of this open field is bound to be full of something spiritual:

> In that open field
> If you do not come too close, if you do not come too close,
> On a summer midnight, you can hear the music
> Of the weak pipe and the little drum
> And see them dancing around the bonfire. . . .
>
> (*EC,* I)

The unnamed "them" must be like the spiritual presences of *Burnt Norton,* also called simply "they." Here they turn out to be dancing peasants; but if we stopped with these lines, we would surely expect fairies dancing round a magic fire to the tune of "weak pipe" and "little drum." They disappear if we come too close. In this empty field at midnight (the time-less moment between two days), we enter the spirit world. The dancing peasants are, for all their earthiness, spirit beings. In fact, they are the ghosts of those who danced in this field in the days of Sir Thomas Elyot.

Their "loam feet" identify the dancers with an earlier time before time and earth became fatal, the time of creation—for *Adam* (man) is made from *adamah* (soil, clay). Adam is also made in the image of God, so in him matter and spirit are one, though his sin puts them at odds. Eliot describes people who are made of earth but are dancing in a ghostly faery world.

Their fire is a "bonfire," which was originally, as Frazer observes, a "bone fire." It is a funeral pyre returning bones to ashes in the downward side of the cycle, toward "Dung and death." The marriage dance creates new life and then becomes the *danse macabre* to take it away, yet the cycle is not merely vanity, precisely because it is a cycle, a figure of wholeness.[23] The momentary reappearance of the ghost dancers assures us that what has once taken part in the dance of life never entirely ceases to exist. The "necessarye coniunction" of man and woman symbolizes the union of all opposites, while the Renaissance spelling taken directly from Elyot makes us think of the Renaissance passion for uniting opposites. Alchemy flourished during that era and took the marriage of Red King and White Queen as its symbol for the *coniunctio oppositorum.* Another favorite phrase of the period expressing the same idea was *discordia concors*—out of discord, concord (united by strife). Matrimony, Elyot says, "betokeneth concorde." The dancers are "joined in circles," mandalas that become ultimately the "crowned knot of fire" at the end of *Four Quartets,* the final symbol of integration.

This opening meditation on earth ends with a vision of water:

> Dawn points, and another day
> Prepares for heat and silence. Out at sea the dawn wind
> Wrinkles and slides. I am here
> Or there, or elsewhere. In my beginning.
>
> (*EC,* I)

The heat and silence of the open field transfer to the open sea. There is a conjunction of elements in the "dawn wind" (a sun wind) sliding over the sea. The usual analogy with the Spirit moving upon the face of the waters is reinforced by the final phrase—"In my beginning." The ending in dung and death immediately begins a new cycle of creation. At the same time, earth dies and water is reborn from that death.

In the second section of *East Coker,* comets "Hunt the heavens and the plains"—that is, the comets shoot between the aethereal sky and the earth, connecting them as the thunderbolt does. This rain of fire becomes "that destructive fire / Which burns before the ice cap reigns" (*EC,* II). At least the world will no longer end with an entropic whimper but with an apocalyptic bang. The present tense of "burns" places this event not only at the end of time but beyond time in an eternal present. It seems it is not a choice between fire and ice but a paradoxical combination of the two, as in the "frigid purgatorial fires" (*EC,* IV). Beyond the fourth dimension, these distinctions are inoperative.

Eliot deprecates all this as a "periphrastic study in a worn-out poetical fashion," yet the self-criticism may not be entirely ingenuous. Periphrasis means "circumlocution" (*peri,* around). If Eliot's subject is something ineffable, he cannot go right to the point. What he can do is to describe the cyclic movement of seasons and elements and dancers around that still point and thereby locate it. When he later acknowledges the same criticism—"You say I am repeating / Something I have said before"—he declares the fault unavoidable: "I shall say it again" (*EC,* III). "The poetry does not matter" because it can finally apprehend only matter; what really matters is the immaterial reality in the middle of the physical experience the poet describes. So he recalls his greatest master by beginning

> In the middle, not only in the middle of the way
> But all the way, in a dark wood, in a bramble,
> On the edge of a grimpen, where is no secure foothold,
> And menaced by monsters, fancy lights,
> Risking enchantment.
>
> (*EC,* II)

The "dark wood" is matter, recalling the "timber" earlier. The poet must go "all the way" into this earthly world, this grimpen. When he does, though, he finds it full of monsters and faery lights and enchantment, as in the open field earlier. In the final lines of this section, "The houses are all gone under the sea. / The dancers are all gone under the hill" (*EC,* II). This is the way down, but by now the way up is implicit. Houses disintegrate under the water to be remade into something rich and strange. Dancers under a hill foreshadow the already-dead people in the underground train in the next section. The faery dancers and ghosts also go back under the hill after a night of revelry, to return again the next night.

In Part III, going into the dark under the hill is analogous to going into the "vacant interstellar spaces." Heraclitus merges with St. John of the Cross, as the way down becomes the *via negativa:* "In order to arrive at what you are not / You must go through the way in which you are not" (*EC,* III). This is from *The Ascent of Mt. Carmel,* and Mt. Carmel may be the hill under which the dancers have gone. Burial in this earth is the only way to ascend. The prime reference for burial and rebirth comes just before in a description of one of the beautiful moments in and out of time:

> The laughter in the garden, echoed ecstasy
> Not lost, but requiring, pointing to the agony
> Of death and birth.
>
> (*EC*, III)

The rose garden of laughter requires the garden of agony—the Garden of Gethsemane. To get to that "echoed ecstasy," we must "go by a way wherein there is no ecstasy"—the way of the Cross. That is why, in spite of the agony, "we call this Friday good" (*EC*, IV). The "timber" and the "dark wood" are fulfilled in the cross, which God the Son accepted when he took an earthly body and became the second Adam; hence, His "bloody flesh" becomes "our only food"—our only way to spiritual communion. Because of the Good Friday suffering and death, "The whole earth is our hospital / Endowed by the ruined millionaire . . . " (*EC*, IV). The gross earth of which our bodies are made and to which they return has been discovered to have healing powers. The "wounded surgeon" of this passage is ultimately Christ, who heals us through His own suffering. The phrase may, at the same time, resonate with Heraclitus's statement (Fr. 58) about "physicians who cut and burn," which has to do with the paradox of healing by causing more pain and injury.[24]

In the final section, the timeless moment the poet is seeking is found to be earthly and historical. It is

> Not the intense moment
> Isolated, with no before and after,
> But a lifetime burning in every moment
> And not the lifetime of one man only
> But of old stones that cannot be deciphered.
>
> (*EC*, V)

The very grossness of earth makes it the most nearly timeless and immutable of the elements: the oldest forms we see in this world of change are "old stones." So, too, the oldest historical records we have are those written in stone, and Eliot may be thinking of the illegible gravestones in the churchyard of St. Michael's Church, East Coker. Even when we can no longer read them, these engraved stones inspire in us the ordinary sense of timelessness Eliot is trying to evoke here, the sense of continuity through time. The people who chiseled runes or cuneiform symbols in this stone thousands of years ago were not very different from us; they are yet living, in the stone and in us, their descendants. The dance of generations continues. This ordinary, earthly sense of timelessness is the one we feel in the "evening with the photograph album," a more recent way of imprinting a moment and preserving it for future generations.

In *East Coker*, then, Eliot reveals spiritual essence in earth itself. The fire "burning in every moment" is in the indecipherable stone. We should read this poem keeping in mind the Psalms, which frequently call God "my Rock," and keeping in mind Eliot's most overtly religious poetry, the choruses for *The Rock*. As the poet remembers here that he must enter the dark wood of matter, the artist is reminded there to be one with the stone:

> The soul of man must quicken to creation.
> Out of the formless stone, when the artist united himself
>   with stone,
> Spring always new forms of life, from the soul of man that
>   is joined to the soul of stone. . . .
>
> (The Rock, IX)

Stone seems to be "formless" matter. But the artist who will bring true form from it must know the form inherent in it, must know that it is a creature with its own essence or soul.

East Coker ends, as its first section did, with a water image; thus, the end of the earth poem is the beginning of the water poem, and water lives the death of earth:

> The wave cry, the wind cry, the vast waters
> Of the petrel and the porpoise. In my end is my beginning.

Wind and waters are again united in another genesis. The two elements are identical in their "cry," a barely articulate voice that registers the presence of the Word in both. Waves are caused partly by wind, so they take their patterning from the more spirited element. The creatures named here live in both elements: the petrel is a creature of air that lives by the sea; the porpoise is a water creature that leaps into the air and breathes air. Life flourishes in the interplay between the two substances.

THE DRY SALVAGES: WATER

The very title of this poem crosses our expectations in its reference not to water but to dry rocks (though "dry" may have been originally a corruption of *trois*), and the final line will be an earth image, too. The setting is not so much the open sea as the shore, where the poet observes the give and take between sea and land, each living the other's death. In this interchange, we again discover the *Logos* underlying and patterning both elements.

"I do not know much about gods," the poet informs us, "but I think that the river / Is a strong brown god" (*DS*, I). It is brown, of course, with the soil it has washed away from its banks—water full of earth. So the opening image is of a mixture of the opposing elements. These primordial waters bring out Eliot's pagan instincts. We are back in the world of *The Golden Bough,* and we will take, in the next section, a "backward half-look / Over the shoulder, towards the primitive terror" (*DS*, II), being reminded of the continuity between the primitive mind and our own, spoken of by Eliot long before in his review of *The Rite of Spring*. That continuity is nowhere more evident than in our responses of awe—of wonder and fear combined—in our encounters with the elements. Even now, Eliot says, the Mississippi seems inhabited, as all the rivers of ancient Greece were, by some demigod. Like Wordsworth, he would rather be "suckled in a creed outworn" and expect to hear over the waters "old Triton's wreathed horn" than live in the world of inanimate matter conceived by scientific materialism. Indeed, his immediate experience *is* of such an animated world. Therefore, he keeps to a Christian creed that does not entirely reject the pagan ones, a creed that finds God immanent in created matter.[25] Pagan animism is fulfilled rather than wholly rejected by the sailors' prayers in this poem to Mary, Star of the Sea, and by the primitive terror in *East Coker* of eating the "bloody flesh." Eliot acknowledges that the sacrament does have something in common with cannibalism. I will say more about sacramental physics later. For now, let us note that the poet is thinking from within an ancient religious consciousness when he senses a divinity in the river; and when he prays with the sailors to their sainted patroness, he finds Christianity a spiritualized and humanized fulfillment of that same consciousness.

The river was "at first recognized as a frontier," as a boundary. Like the sea, it is "the land's edge," cutting the continent in half. As people worked to connect the two halves, the river was no longer seen as a frontier or border but merely as "a problem confronting the builder of bridges" (*DS*, I). A bridge is, of course, an earthen extension connecting land to land across the water, making the water no longer an edge or frontier. In his preface to a 1950 edition of *Huckleberry Finn*, Eliot tells of floods that destroyed St. Louis bridges in his youth and speaks of Mark Twain as having respect for the god of the river: "It is as a native that he accepts the River God, and it is the subjection of Man that gives to Man his dignity. For without some kind of God, Man is not even very interesting."[26] It is the progressive and mechanistic mentality that reduces the strong brown god to an engineering problem: the river comes to be

"Unhonoured, unpropitiated / By worshippers of the machine." Eliot was not necessarily such a Luddite that he would object to having bridges that could withstand the Mississippi's flooding; yet he observes here that our technological solutions to physical limitations have brought a temptation to make those solutions into a religion, which they cannot be. The old pagan religions, he asserts here, were truer than this positivist faith in our ability to dominate nature, for the pagans knew that we were part of nature. As Eliot's comment on Mark Twain suggests, the trouble with failing to honor the old river gods is that we eventually fail to worship any gods at all. Ironically, the rationalists who argue that ancient gods were created by the human mind end up worshipping technological marvels which were indisputably created by the mind.

In his early poetry, as we saw in chapter 2, Eliot mourned the loss of spirit in the materialist cosmology. Prufrock, though a Romantic, knew that the mermaids would not sing to him from the sea. Now Eliot does not conclude with the loss of the river's divinity; instead, he reasserts the presence of the god, who is "unpropitiated" but still there, "watching and waiting":

> His rhythm was present in the nursery bedroom,
> In the rank ailanthus of the April dooryard,
> In the smell of grapes on the autumn table,
> And the evening circle in the winter gaslight.
>
> (*DS*, I)

The river, having taken soil from the land, gives something back. These are images poetry can capture of the water's extension into earth (plants growing in a yard), air (the smell of grapes), and even fire (gaslight). It is not simply the water itself that is present in these other elements, though, but the water's "rhythm," which, like the rhythm of the loam feet, is a manifestation of the patterning *Logos* within the changing elements.

We, too, are compounded not only of clay but of water, so "The river is within us." This is true in that our bodies are mostly water and constantly need replenishing with water but also in that our structure is homologous with that of the sea creatures, the "earlier and other creation." For there is continuity not only with primitive peoples but with the other creatures: "the whale's backbone" is not unlike our own. Finally, the river is within us as it is in the ailanthus or grapes or gaslight. The water has been transformed by the *Logos* into another substance, which yet retains the rhythm of water. We will return to this passage later in the discussion of the interplay among the four seasons, for they are also united here.

The opening section turns from the river to the sea but continues to focus on the interchange of earth and water: "The sea is the land's edge also, the granite / Into which it reaches, the beaches where it tosses / Its hints of earlier and other creation . . ." (*DS*, I). Eliot's ambiguous syntax forces us to see the shoreline with parted eye. Our normal tendency, being naturally land-dwellers, is to see the land as the sea's edge, but the erstwhile summer resident of Gloucester declares that "The sea is the land's edge also." The sea is thus "the granite / Into which it reaches." Here the "it" must be the land, but it could also be the sea, especially since these hints of earlier creation are sea creatures that could not have been tossed by the land into the sea. There is a blurring of reference as Eliot makes us see the negative of our usual beach picture, as if we were looking at one of those optical illusion drawings that can be seen as either a duck or a rabbit. We can suddenly refocus and see the land reaching into the sea. We can even observe that the sea is solid as granite, not to be moved by any earthly force. This reversal is another way of getting at the idea that the way up and the way down are the same; for in the scheme of relative lightness, water is up from earth, but here it becomes just as solid.

Like the river water in the dooryard, the sea water penetrates and permeates the land: "The salt is on the briar rose, / The fog is in the fir trees." This line forms a paragraph by itself and thus stands out as a sudden and central insight. The salt of the sea water is somehow on the rose; the sea water itself is transformed (by fire) into air (fog) and then comes back down onto creatures of earth, the fir trees. Life exists—roses and trees—where this elemental interchange takes place.

At the same time, the sea is penetrated by the earth and becomes earthy in the "ground swell" to which Eliot points as the oldest measure of time. Here again, it is not the material earth but the ground's rhythm or pattern (the *form* of the earth rather than its matter) that appears in the water. A certain type of wave may be called a "ground swell" either because its encounter with the ocean floor as it approaches the shore raises the swell, or because the rolling shape of the swell is like that of an earthen hill. Whatever the origin of the term, its use in this context calls attention to the fact that a term from the element of earth (in fact, synonymous with "earth") is used to describe a phenomenon in the element of water. This striking exchange of terms is possible because the same forms appear in both materials.

Eliot connects the exchange of the elements with the sea voices and with time. The voices are, as always for him, signs of spiritual presence. One of the voices is that of surf breaking on the shore, "The distant rote in the granite teeth." The word "rote" refers to this sound of breaking waves, but it is also the name of a medieval stringed instrument. The voice of the elements is rhythmic and hence musical. It is a music that is played by rote, from memory, repetitiously, with no variations, yet it is by the same token ancient and true, the very keynote of creation. The elemental conjunction in the ground swell is similarly musical, for, like the "ground" of a song, it rings the descant of a sea bell:

> And the ground swell, that is and was from the beginning,
> Clangs
> The bell.
>
> (*DS*, I)

The rhythmic clanging is the origin and source of music, and music is based on measures of time. In this complex of symbols, Eliot presents the world that has been "from the beginning"—that is, from the beginning of time, the beginning of motion in a three-dimensional physical world. This world is full of change and confusion, yet those very changes, produced by the exchanges between the primordial elements, retain the rhythms set by the Creator in the beginning and, therefore, mark time harmoniously. Their ancient rhythms remind us of "the primitive terror" perhaps, but also of the moment of divine creation.

The second section is dominated by the Annunciation, which is connected to the beginning because it is the only moment in time at which there was another creation *ex nihilo*, a generation of new life "Not in the scheme of generation" (*LG*, I). The sea bell rung by the ground swell now calls us to pray the Angelus, the "barely prayable" prayer announcing the definitive intervention of God in the temporal order.

In this context, Eliot revisits the issue of evolution. Gone is the satire of the early poetry in which, as we saw in chapter 3, Eliot had shown the modern materialist how he viewed himself, as a "lustreless protrusive eye" staring "from the protozoic slime" or as "Sweeney Erect," the trousered ape. Now he can accept evolution in a nuanced way, quietly rejecting the popularized and thoroughly materialistic version of the theory:

> It seems, as one becomes older,
> That the past has another pattern, and ceases to be a mere sequence—
> Or even development: the latter a partial fallacy,
> Encouraged by superficial notions of evolution,
> Which becomes, in the popular mind, a means of disowning the past.
>
> (*DS*, II)

The difference between superficial notions and deeper ones is expressed in the earlier passage about the sea creatures as "hints of earlier and other creation" (*DS*, I). We may be descended from the crab, but not by a strictly random process of material development. The crab is an earlier *creation*, not an earlier accidental variation. In short, Eliot believes in some form of creative evolution, more biblical than Bergsonian. Those who continue to promote the idea of natural selection as the sole mechanism of evolution do not acknowledge the great difference between mankind and the "other creation," the animals, for they deny the soul.

At the same time, Eliot points up in this passage a more important and opposite problem with the notion of accidental evolution. Even as it makes us a random result of past processes, it becomes a way of cutting us off from the past because we begin to believe in an inevitable progress. In his talk on "Religion and Science," Eliot had exonerated real science of the charges brought against it and had named this progressivist attitude as the actual enemy of faith:

> Many people assume that, if the Christian faith had been true, Europe would have stuck to it; and the reason why the majority of people, in the most civilised countries, have drifted away from it, must be that it is not true. But this belief goes together with another crude faith, the faith that progress in enlightenment and civilisation is something automatic, that to improve from generation to generation is natural to man. . . .[27]

Belief in automatic progress is heavily influenced by the superficial version of evolutionary theory, which assumes a totally accidental process that nevertheless leads inevitably to greater levels of organization.

When he speaks of superficial notions of evolution, Eliot no doubt has in mind the Social Darwinism of Herbert Spencer, who was one of the leading lights in the milieu of Eliot's upbringing. In 1938, William Harrison reviewed Geoffrey West's biography of Darwin for *The Criterion*. Harrison points out that some of the metaphysical excesses of Darwinism are to be charged not to Darwin but to followers like Spencer: "Even the phrase 'survival of the fittest', as we are prone to forget, was not his, but Spencer's; and Herbert Spencer, as the ardent disciple, moralized beyond the master's intentions."[28] Nevertheless, West calls Darwin himself a "fragmentary man," arguing that he was excessively specialized in his thinking and hence incapable of considering what implications his scientific theory might have in other areas. Harrison quotes the following passage from West's book: "The fragmentary man can only manifest a fragmentary truth. Darwin was incomplete, and Darwinism accordingly inadequate as a philosophy by which men may live."[29] Like many other writers of the time, West was describing the fundamental problem with scientism: scientific ideas, given their inherent limitations, cannot serve as "a philosophy by which men may live."

In Eliot's view, the overriding problem with popularized Darwinism is its faulty conception of time and change, for these do not produce progress:

We cannot think of a time that is oceanless
Or of an ocean not littered with wastage
Or of a future that is not liable
Like the past, to have no destination.

(DS, II)

Superficial evolutionists *can* think of an oceanless time, a time which is "mere sequence" or "development," moving from one isolated moment to another, with no Bergsonian "real duration" and no creative Word. The true time of the ground swell, by contrast, has no progressive sequence but instead a recurring pattern, visible at times even in the wastage. Time moves in waves, not in a line.

In this sense of time, we feel connected to the primitive—and even to the bestial. Another hint of our connection to the lower and earlier creatures comes in the next section of the poem, when the ear is called "the murmuring shell of time" (DS, III). This is evidently a seashell, which does resemble the whorls of the human ear and which murmurs when held up to the ear. It is the "shell of time" in that a seashell grows larger and adds more rings over time, but also in that it is much more ancient than the human and more lasting. The ear, however, is not homologous to the seashell because of being accidentally evolved from it: rather, it has the same pattern because the spiral is a form built into the natural world—by the Creator.

While Eliot acknowledges the likeness between man and beast, he also acknowledges—in the prayer of the Annunciation—the Spirit who created the pattern and can suddenly (that is, not developmentally) enter history to make a new and "other" creation. Curiously enough, the mechanistic evolutionist disowns the past, even while asserting that everything in the present is a mere development of what was there before. Meanwhile, both the Bergsonian creative evolutionist and the Christian who accepts some part of the evolutionary theory claim the radical intervention of either the *élan vital* or the Spirit in history yet accept and celebrate the profound connectedness of past, present, and future.[30]

In this section, we find another image of the sea's earthiness, the "shallow banks unchanging and erosionless" (DS, II). Sea "banks" are high plateaus of the ocean floor, and thus areas of relatively shallow water. However, the word is used on land, too, where "banks" are mounds or rising slopes along the edge of a stream. The word has to do with the meeting of earth and water, whether on land or at sea, and it becomes another instance of a form that exists in both elements. These watery banks are "unchanging"—strangely enough for anything in the restless sea. They are paradoxically even more permanent than earthen banks because they are "erosionless," being protected from erosion by the very element that erodes them on land. The water is, in this way, the granite into which the land reaches—something even more permanent than granite. This image of moving but constant sea shapes modulates into the human realm in which

> our own past is covered by the currents of action,
> But the torment of others remains an experience
> Unqualified, unworn by subsequent attrition.

(DS, II)

The torment of others is "unworn," like the erosionless sea banks. The reversal in which sea becomes more permanent than land is analogous to a psychological reversal here. We would normally expect our subjective experience to be more lasting in our memory than the experience of others, but Eliot says the reverse is true. We remember the pain of others more clearly, precisely because it was outside us and, consequently, somewhat objective.

The section ends with the deadly power of the river and the sea—flood and shipwreck. The image of "ragged rock in the restless waters" finds water and earth alike dangerous. The alliteration links them, and the raggedness of one must look like the restlessness of the other. Like the poet's words, the two antithetical elements have a common form or rhythm binding them in a pattern of creative order and giving them meaning. The rock out at sea can be a helpful "seamark" in good weather; but in the storm, it "is what it always was," hard and unyielding. The opposing elements, that is, can complement each other (with the sea speeding one's passage while the rock aids navigation), but they can also return to the chaotic battle they fight in Hesiod's *Theogony* before Eros joins them, and in that chaos nothing lives. These images of death by water are introduced by the observation that "Time the destroyer is time the preserver." These words have a Hindu ring to them, but they also become here another version of Heraclitus's up and down. With them in mind, we expect this tempest at the end of the passage to lead to a new cycle of life; and, indeed, any tempest in Eliot's poetry is Prospero's tempest and is thus a beginning as well as an end.

In the third movement of *The Dry Salvages*, Eliot gives the epigraph in English—"And the way up is the way down"—adding that the same is true in a horizontal dimension: "the way forward is the way back" (*DS*, III). This line introduces the passage in which trains are likened to ships: conveyance over earth and sea feel the same. The "sleepy rhythm" of the train is the light swaying of the car, a patterning of motion and time similar to the rolling of "the drumming liner" over the waves. The "rhythm" of the train and the "drumming" of the ship make music, which is essentially setting some object vibrating in time. However, that very conscious entrance into time is a way of transcending it momentarily by giving it shape and meaning. Both sea and land journeys make us intensely aware of the passage of time—so like the ship's "passage"—but the "sleepy rhythm" also puts us into a drowsy, half-conscious state in which time does not seem to pass. Still, time does pass. The travelers who arrive are not the ones who began the journey (a variation on Heraclitus's statement that one cannot step in the same river twice).[31]

Eliot notices, brilliantly, that the rails receding behind the train are a mirror image of the ship's wake:

> You are not the same people who left that station
> Or who will arrive at any terminus,
> While the narrowing rails slide together behind you;
> And on the deck of the drumming liner
> Watching the furrow that widens behind you,
> You shall not think "the past is finished"
> Or "the future is before us."
>
> (*DS*, III)

Land travel and sea travel are opposites in that the two rails appear to converge, while the two edges of the wake diverge; thus, they are images of the opposition between forward and backward. Yet the experience of looking back is identical, whether one is seeing convergence or divergence. Either way, there are two lines which are joined at one point and separate at all other points. There is confusion as to whether the point of convergence is in the present (as it is on the ship) or the past (as it is on the train), and there is further confusion as to whether what we are seeing behind us is going into the past (since it is where we were before) or into the future (since the lines are moving closer together or farther apart as time passes into the future). Therefore, the travelers cannot say that "the past is finished," since they still see the past developing; nor can they say that "the future is before us," since they are looking behind and yet seeing the future unfolding. The way forward is the way back.

Part of the meaning here is that we can approach the mystery of the fourth dimension only by observing simple motion in the pure, primordial elements of water and earth. Eliot is thus anything but the poet of abstractions he has often been taken for. He is seeking to express not abstractions but mysteries, and he does so with the simplest and most concrete images he can find. Land and sea journeys produce here opposite perspectives but the same pattern and the same state of mind. The elements are conjoined in one word as the wake becomes a "furrow"—a wave of earth turning behind the plow.

The passage then leaves the train and follows the ship, and as it does, we see the water connected with a third element, air:

> At nightfall, in the rigging and the aerial,
> Is a voice descanting (though not to the ear,
> The murmuring shell of time, and not in any language). . . .
>
> (*DS*, III)

The ship is moving through water and air at once. Its hull is in one element and its rigging in the other. The "aerial" is, I take it, a radio antenna, a slender bit of solid matter reaching up into the air of its name and receiving invisible and inaudible signals. It picks up a signal the ear cannot hear (either a voice or the signs of Morse code, which is "not in any language") and then translates it into an audible and meaningful sound. (Let it be noted that, if this reading is sensible, Eliot is using a modern technological marvel as a spiritual symbol—no dogmatic archaist, he.) Now, the "aerial" must recall Prospero's Ariel, an airy spirit who flames the rigging of Alonso's ship and then leads Ferdinand by descanting to him in a voice heard more by his mind than his ear. Much as Ariel represents the "spirits" of Renaissance physiology—the aethereal fluids connecting mind and body—this voice in the aerial is neither simply mental nor simply physical and moves from the immaterial air to the solid ship through the aerial. The word "aerial" also carries (in older usage) the meaning "aethereal," and the context here evokes that meaning.

This section ends with an apostrophe to all pilgrims: "O voyagers, O seamen." As "voyagers," we are following some *via* (the root of the word), some way. Krishna admonishes Arjuna to "fare forward" on his way, even though it seems the wrong way, the way down into battle. The way down into the chaos of the material world can be, if it is followed with detachment, the way up. A "voyage" can be any journey, but it has come to mean specifically a sea journey, so all voyagers are "seamen." This name for sailors can also be read as a reminder to all of us that we are creatures of the sea, for seamen are mermen and mermaids. In evolutionary terms, we are descended from sea creatures, and our form is like the form of sea creatures (our ear like the shell). The sea can easily claim us again, dissolving us in the primal flux of its dark abyss, and our way does inevitably lead down there, back to the place where we began. Eliot has made us feel in this poem that we are not merely creatures of clay sailing over the sea but truly men of the sea. In an unexpected way, the mermaids who would not sing to Prufrock have become our kin and have sung to us.

The fourth movement is a brief meditation on Mary as guardian of sailors. I will defer discussion of it until a later part of this chapter focusing on Christian theology.

The final movement of *The Dry Salvages* describes some of the false ways of seeking the upward path of spiritual fulfillment and then finds the real way (for anyone but the saint) to be the way down, into the physical world:

> For most of us, there is only the unattended
> Moment, the moment in and out of time,
> The distraction fit, lost in a shaft of sunlight,
> The wild thyme unseen, or the winter lightning
> Or the waterfall, or music heard so deeply
> That it is not heard at all, but you are the music
> While the music lasts.
>
> (*DS*, V)

One is in and out of time here because in and out of the material, four-dimensional world. Each of the images is of a physical event that is not merely physical. The shaft of sunlight is the aethereal fire of the sun taking definite physical form as a "shaft." The lightning is also aethereal fire shooting from heaven to earth and recalling Heraclitus's statement that "thunderbolt steers all," as well as the thunder and lightning at the end of *The Waste Land*. The "wild thyme unseen" is a humble plant, creature of earth, but one whose presence is sensed in an unspecified way—not by sight, but by a subtle odor in the air. The thyme (with a pun on "time") is there and not there. The waterfall presents another vertical image: like the sunlight or lightning, it goes down through the air to the earth, connecting higher and lower. These scenes inspire a visionary moment because they manifest "the impossible union / Of spheres of existence," whose prime instance is named here, the Incarnation.

Just as the earth poem ends with a sea image, this water poem ends with an earth scene far from the ocean:

> We, content at the last
> If our temporal reversion nourish
> (Not too far from the yew-tree)
> The life of significant soil.
>
> (*DS*, V)

Eliot has just referred to "daemonic, chthonic / Powers" which move dead matter in a purely material world. Those chthonic powers are of the earth but do not sanctify the earth. In contrast, the power who takes on a body of clay in the Incarnation renews the life of the soil itself. These final lines return us to "The Burial of the Dead" in *The Waste Land* but with a difference. The corpse is now buried in an English churchyard whose ancient yew tree symbolizes death and resurrection. The ground here is blessed, sacred.

Only in the sacred universe can the elements signify. As Paul Ricoeur says, "In the sacred universe the capacity to speak is founded upon the capacity of the cosmos to signify."[32] The meaning of words, then, depends on the capacity of the world itself to be meaningful. "Significant soil" is earth that is not merely material; it has an inbreathed form or nature. Such earth turns to dirt in the Cartesian world, where mind and body can have no concourse. Eliot's early poems scrutinize the modern city, suffering from the dissociation of sensibility, and in this place, the poet finds much "dirt." In *Four Quartets,* he goes to the country and finds soil, ground, earth—the living, animated element.

Significant soil can finally be apprehended only in a world that was created by a purely spiritual being out of nothing. There, even the basic elements are creatures. An example from another modern Christian poet may help. In his *In Parenthesis,* David Jones describes Private Ball pressing himself into "the white chalk womb" to escape "his" (i.e., the enemy's) fire: "inches below / where his traversing machine-guns perforate to powder / white— / white creature of chalk pounded. . . . "[33] For Eliot, as for Jones, the earth is a creature, an essence created with a certain nature by God. At this point, the Christian understanding of the elements goes beyond the ideas of the old philosophers, for whom the elements were essences but not created natures.

The Christian attitude is perhaps best represented by Saint Francis's "Canticle of the Creatures." Francis praises the omnipotent Lord who made the creatures, and the creatures he names are not the birds and wolves of Franciscan legend—rather, they are the heavenly bodies and the elements themselves: Brother Sun, Sister Moon, Brother Wind, Sister Water, Brother Fire, Mother Earth.

If we turn to a more immediate influence on *Four Quartets,* Julian of Norwich, we find the same idea of the elements as creatures whose natures were ordained by God. Julian speaks, for example, of the created elements at the moment of the crucifixion:

> . . . all creatures which God has created for our service, the firmament and the earth, failed in their natural functions because of sorrow. . . . God in his goodness, who makes the planets and the elements to function according to their natures for the man who is blessed and the man who is accursed, in that time withdrew this from both.[34]

Only such an omnipotent spirit can be one with the material world. Immortal but material demigods like Zeus alternate between standing aloof from mortal life and lusting after mortal women. Zeus takes mortal shapes for his pleasure, but he does not become truly incarnate, which (Francis's "Canticle" reminds us) means accepting also Sister Death. In the Christian view, the physical world is made good, falls along with Adam, and is redeemed by the second Adam. Julian is thinking of this historical cycle when she writes the words Eliot uses in *Little Gidding:* "For just as the blessed Trinity created all things from nothing, just so will the same blessed Trinity make everything well which is not well."[35] This is the paradox of Christian physics: it is the purely spiritual and omnipotent God who is able and willing to become a helpless mortal body. It is this theological understanding of the physical world that makes the soil, along with the other elements in *Four Quartets,* significant.

LITTLE GIDDING: FIRE

As we have seen, Heraclitus associated fire with the aether, with the *Logos,* and with God.[36] This cosmic fire, transcendant and yet everywhere immanent, has flashed forth at crucial moments in the other *Quartets* because it is the one that transforms the other three elements. This final poem is a meditation on the fire itself.

As the reader might by now expect, the poem begins not with fire but with its polar opposite:

> Midwinter spring is its own season
> Sempiternal though sodden toward sundown. . . .
>
> (*LG,* I)

The fiery sun is waning at the end of this shortest day, and water dominates the "sodden" season. We must remember that, for Heraclitus, water, being the element that quenches fire, is inimical to spirit—as in the "damp souls of housemaids" in "Morning at the Window." Here, however, moisture does not extinguish it because the fire appears in its eternal aspect, not as the mere opposite of water but as the divine fire, the omnipresent *Logos:*

> When the short day is brightest, with frost and fire,
> The brief sun flames the ice, on pond and ditches,
> In windless cold that is the heart's heat,
> Reflecting in a watery mirror
> A glare that is blindness in the early afternoon.
> And glow more intense than blaze of branch, or brazier,
> Stirs the dumb spirit: no wind but pentecostal fire
> In the dark time of the year.
>
> (*LG,* I)

Here is one of the poem's elemental conjunctions. Water has become as solid as earth, and the sun enflames this earth-water substance; thus, the antinomy of fire actually magnifies it, turning the "brief sun" into "a glare that is blindness," a "glow more intense than blaze or brazier." There are traditionally two types of fire, as Spenser says in the "Cantos of Mutabilitie," the earthy kind, which fights the water, and the heavenly kind ("the fire aethereall"), which lives in all things and lends them life (VII.vii.26). Clearly, this fire is of the latter variety, in contrast to the mundane fire of blaze or brazier. This passage recalls the one in *Burnt Norton* in which water is momentarily created "out of sunlight." In both cases—and throughout the *Quartets*—sunlight is the divine fire.

In *Little Gidding,* Eliot identifies the Heraclitean fire with the fire of the Holy Spirit. The glow in the icy ditch "Stirs the dumb spirit: no wind, but pentecostal fire." In equating the two, Eliot is baptizing Heraclitus, but he is also seeing the third person of the Trinity as a revelation of God's immanence in created matter. The Spirit can manifest Himself in such mundane settings as this sodden evening, or even in the horror of the fire bombs. The stirring of the dumb spirit here is a reprise of the opening section of *The Waste Land,* where dull roots are stirred by rain. There the stirrings of spring were painful and scarcely efficacious; here the stirrings are more spiritual, though not separated from the physical world, and the season is neither winter nor spring but a timeless moment between the two.

The next verse paragraph recalls the "broken Coriolanus" at the end of *The Waste Land* in speaking of a "broken king" (*LG,* I). The historical reference is to Charles I, but the suggestion is that the reader—everyone—might come to Little Gidding "like a broken king," and the archetype of this universal figure is the King of Kings, who, like Charles, was executed by his own people. The "aethereal rumours," which revive Coriolanus, momentarily become more Christian and effective here, for they become the Pentecostal fire, which folds the unfortunate adversaries in the civil war into "a single party" (*LG,* III), a party that would be properly called the Communion of Saints. The aethereal rumours are the faintly heard voices of these blessed dead:

> And what the dead had no speech for, when living,
> They can tell you, being dead: the communication
> Of the dead is tongued with fire beyond the language of the living.
>
> (*LG,* I)

The ghostly, aethereal voices speak with Pentecostal tongues of fire and are understood universally rather than being limited by particular languages. The momentary revival of the broken Coriolanus has become an eternal resurrection of the broken king.

The second movement of *Little Gidding* begins with the passage describing the elements "living each other's death." The transforming fire reduces roses and other living forms to ashes. Both a house and a mouse were made of "dust inbreathed"—that is, of earth filled with and animated by a spirited element, air. At the end of the story, we find the reverse, "Dust in the air suspended." Air and earth unite for a time in a creative synthesis, which inevitably disintegrates.

Earth and water strive with each other—"Dead water and dead sand / Contending for the upper hand"—causing either a surfeit of water or a lack of it, "flood and drouth." Similarly, "Water and fire succeed / The town, the pasture and the weed." They alternate with each other, destroying everything in the process. We are in the waste land, where the elements are at strife. Still, in Heraclitean physics, this very strife unites the elements in a creative pattern, for the *Logos*-fire enacts the strife. What appears chaotic to us may be merely a small swirl in a larger pattern, as recent expositions of "chaos theory" have suggested.

After the descent of the "dark dove with the flickering tongue," the poet is visited by a communion of sainted poets, a "familiar compound ghost." As Smith has pointed out, this phrase echoes the "affable familiar ghost" of Shakespeare's Sonnet 86. I think we also hear echoes of Shakespeare's plays in the line "The wonder that I feel is easy." When people are brought back from the dead in his romances, the dominant emotion is wonder. Miranda cries out, "O wonder! / How many goodly creatures are there here!" (V.i.181–82). In *The Winter's Tale,* a gentleman describing the miraculous events reports that "A notable passion of wonder appeared in them" (V.ii.15–16), and another proclaims, "Such a deal of wonder is broken out within this hour that ballad-makers cannot be able to express it" (V.ii.23–25). At the end of *Much Ado about Nothing* comes a line that expresses exactly the easy wonder Eliot is describing. As Hero comes back to life, the Friar says he will explain it all later and adds, "Meantime, let wonder seem familiar, / And to the chapel let us presently" (V.iv.70–71). Eliot has just used the word "familiar" of the ghost, who is the resurrected person in this scene. Not only the phrasing but the whole situation recalls Shakespeare's romances. This association is strengthened by the fact that Eliot had read with admiration G. Wilson Knight's interpretation of Shakespeare's last plays, as Bush remarks.[37] The title of one of Knight's pieces on the subject, "Myth and Miracle," indicates his adherence to the idea of a continuity between primitive myth and Christianity, an idea which is as central to *Four Quartets* as it was to *The Waste Land.* If, as many critics have suggested, *Four Quartets* is Eliot's *Paradiso,* it is also his version of Shakespearean romance.

Of course, Dante is the chief poetic spirit here, and the *Divine Comedy* gives another reference point for the fire symbol. "What! Are *you* here?" Eliot asks, quoting Dante's address to Brunetto Latini, whom he finds in hell. Then, near the end of the passage, while invoking Yeats, Eliot points away from infernal toward purgatorial fire:

> From wrong to wrong the exasperated spirit
> Proceeds, unless restored by that refining fire
> Where you must move in measure, like a dancer.
>
> (*LG*, II)

Fire may destroy, but it may also refine. In the *Comedia,* the way down into the inferno becomes the way up the purgatorial mountain. We are reminded of "The Fire Sermon," in which the fire of lust becomes, in Saint Augustine and the Buddha, the fire of holy love. We also remember Arnaut Daniel leaping back into the refining fire (*Poi s'ascose nel foco che gli affina*) in the *Purgatorio* and at the end of *The Waste Land.* This passage points to the later one where

> The only hope, or else despair
> Lies in the choice of pyre or pyre—
> To be redeemed from fire by fire.
>
> (*LG*, IV)

If we choose the base fire of earthly passions, it will become the infernal fire of torment. The purgational fire, which is also the fire of the Holy Spirit, is our only salvation.

The Communion of Saints theme continues in the third movement, which is also full of ghosts:

> See how they vanish,
> The faces and the places, with the self which, as it could, loved them,
> To become renewed, transfigured, in another pattern.
>
> (*LG*, III)

The view of death offered here sounds like a direct answer to the views of Gerontion. Like that old man, the dying here are losing sensory awareness and pleasure. They experience "the cold friction of expiring sense" (*LG*, II) and watch their acquaintances pass away. While Gerontion thought of the dead as being dissolved into "fractured atoms," however, one now sees the dead "transfigured." In Heraclitean physics, disintegration yields new and enduring patterns. Death is the ultimate strife separating elements and persons, but through death they are "touched by a common genius, / United in the strife which divided them" (*LG*, III). These lines combine Heraclitus's statement about the elements being united in strife with the poem's first epigraph: "Although the Logos is common to all, most men live as if each had a private wisdom of his own." The "common genius" is the Heraclitean and Christian *Logos*, a binding substratum for both physical and psychic life.[38] The *Logos* is revealed to the dead, who are "folded into a single party," the party of that common universal Word.

Dante's symbol of the Communion of Saints, the heavenly rose, becomes the central symbol of this poem and returns it to its beginning in the rose garden. Eliot first introduced the rose in relation to death: "Ash on an old man's sleeve / Is all the ash the burnt roses leave" (*LG*, II). Now he denies that he is merely trying to revive the past:

> It is not to ring the bell backward
> Nor is it an incantation
> To summon the spectre of a Rose.
>
> (*LG*, III)

He is not joining the occultists, who experimented with burning roses, seeking the form of the rose in the ashes. In another and more orthodox way, however, he is seeking the same thing, some assurance that the form transcends the disintegration of the body—that though "body and soul begin to fall asunder" they will not do so entirely. The "spectre of a Rose" is the ghost or spirit of the Rose (capitalized to indicate that it is a type rather than an individual object). The specter is the Rose's Platonic form in the ideal world. Eliot writes a few lines later that the united dead have left us "A symbol perfected in death." That symbol must be the Rose. It is perfected in death because its form or pattern is purified and universalized by its partial disembodiment. Like ghosts of people, the specter of the Rose is still physical but not grossly so. Eliot's Rose is not perfected by the occultists' experiments but by its apotheosis in Dante's *Paradiso*.

Here Eliot touches momentarily on the importance of symbols. Even in the divine order, he seems to suggest, symbols have a physical side. The rose is perfected, but not completely transcended, just as, in Christian theology, the resurrected body is transfigured or glorified but not left behind. Symbols have, as Ricoeur says, "one foot in reality," even though they are the best expressions of the ideal world. In a draft of *Little Gidding*, Eliot wrote, "The symbol is the fact. . . ."[39] One might imagine that abstract words would come closest to the ideal, but words are somewhat arbitrary in their meaning, as structuralist and poststructuralist critics remind us. Symbols, with their physical, literal side, are not fungible the way words are, though they may have a whole range of meaning and may be ambiguous. *Four Quartets* hints that everything in our world is an incarnation of spiritual reality. This notion is consistent with the thought of Heraclitus, for whom physics is not separate from metaphysics, as well as with Christian thinking about the physical world.

This section ends with words from Julian of Norwich: "All manner of things shall be well / By the purification of the motive / In the ground of our beseeching" (*LG*, III). The "motive" is love, the desire for God which moves everything in the universe in Aristotelian and scholastic physics; thus, it is another name for energy or fire. The motive is purified as our love becomes love of the Creator, known either through love of His creatures (immanence) or in place of that lower love (transcendence). In Heraclitean terms, this means the elemental fire becomes the aethereal fire of the *Logos*. Dame Julian calls God "the ground of our beseeching." Here the most grossly physical element, lowest and heaviest of the four—"ground"—is identified by normal theological language with pure spirit, the deity. Once again, Eliot emphasizes the continuity between lowest and highest.

In the fourth movement, the universal motive force is called by name:

> Love is the unfamiliar Name
> Behind the hands that wove
> The intolerable shirt of flame
> Which human power cannot remove.
>
> (*LG*, IV)

The love of Deianira is of the lower kind and thus destructive, yet it is continuous with the pure love that is God. Heracles' shirt of flame, like the Nazi fire bombs (or V2 rockets), is somehow one with the aethereal fire. The flaming shirt cannot be removed, but as we purify the motive it can become the refining purgatorial fire and, eventually, the "crowned knot of fire" in paradise.

In the final movement, we are reminded of the deadly nature of the elements when they are isolated: "Any action / Is a step to the block, to the fire, down the sea's throat." One may die by earth, fire, or water, yet we are reminded again that the dead "return, and bring us with them." The ghosts are still haunting the poem.

We return to the present moment "while the light fails / On a winter's afternoon" and to images of water: "the source of the longest river / The voice of the hidden waterfall." The water is now not sodden but spiritual. It is the water of "the beginning," the "source" (a word that is itself originally a water metaphor, meaning a "spring") of the long river of time. In the midst of the water, we hear the spiritual voice that haunts Eliot's poetry: the "voice of the hidden waterfall" which is also "heard, half-heard, in the stillness / Between two waves of the sea." This last is a powerful image of a stillness in the midst of motion. The waves move, but the space between them does not change. It calls up the idea of the aether filling the otherwise vacant spaces in the cosmos and giving the elements a medium through which to move.

In the final image, two prime symbols of *Little Gidding*—fire and rose—are seen as one. The petals of the paradisal rose are also the tongues of Pentecostal flame that have flickered throughout. In their archetypal forms, the two symbols unite because the underlying pattern established by the Word is identical in both.

THE FOUR SEASONS

As Smith and Gardner suggest, the *Four Quartets* are associated with the four seasons as well as the four elements. If we look more closely at the seasonal imagery, we find that the treatment is also analogous. As the elements interpenetrate and exchange, so do the seasons. There is one season loosely identified with each poem, but the whole point is that there is finally a complex dance of the four throughout. As in the case of the elemental exchange, this dynamic interchange of seasons is primarily understood in Heraclitean terms. Heraclitus says (Fr. 67), "God is day night, winter summer, war peace, satiety hunger; he undergoes alteration in the way that fire, when it is mixed with spices, is named according to each of them."[40] Thus, winter has one scent and summer another, but one who can perceive what is "common," the *Logos*-fire that burns the spices, finds a hidden likeness or attunement (to use another Heraclitean metaphor) in opposite seasons.

Since Eliot did not have the four-poem plan in mind when he wrote *Burnt Norton,* it is not so clearly identified with a particular season as the others. In a letter to Kristian Smidt, Eliot later acknowledged that the first poem became the poem of spring by default: "*Burnt Norton* then had to stand for spring in the sequence, though its imagery was perhaps more summery."[41] Then again, great poets have plans of which they are scarcely aware, along with a certain amount of luck and inspiration. As in the case of the elements, *Burnt Norton* works in part as a model for the whole, showing how the four seasons live each other's death. In the later poems, as he worked this theme out more consciously, Eliot continued to contravene expectations of a simple division and succession of seasons.

As it happens, *Burnt Norton* does begin in the spring of the year and the spring of life, "our first world." The rose garden evokes the original garden eastward in Eden from which four rivers flow out in the four directions. Here, in this beginning world, we hear the laughter of children in the leaves; yet, precisely because the associations are with the world's beginning, we are aware that this spring world is actually not present except as a vision of the past. The beings from the first world are "Moving without pressure, over the dead leaves, / In the autumn heat" (*BN*, I). The setting is really autumn; Tom Eliot and Emily Hale are already moving into the second half of life. Still, "autumn heat" suggests the early autumn, still summery, and the world can suddenly renew itself. The dead leaves come back to life in the trees, the pool fills with water, and the lotus rises from it. The autumnal future and the vernal past both "Point to one end, which is always present." This opening passage sets the tone for Eliot's treatment of the seasons throughout *Four Quartets*, a treatment that will become more conscious in the later poems.

In the second section of *Burnt Norton*, another season appears as we "Ascend to summer in the tree." This is after the passage about the "dance along the artery" being "figured in the drift of stars" and leads into the pattern of boarhound and boar "reconciled among the stars." As Northrop Frye often points out, the stars are the realm of higher nature in which there is movement but also the permanence of a recurring pattern. The stars move day by day but always return to exactly the same place a year later; thus, they are both "in and out of time." That sidereal cyclic pattern unites all the different moments of the year and holds the seasons in an eternal return—as in Spenser's Garden of Adonis, which is "eterne in mutabilitie." For Eliot, winter and summer are reconciled in the dance, as are man and woman. The opposites keep turning and, in doing so, take each other's place—becoming each other while remaining distinct.

Eliot describes the circulation of both seasons and elements a few lines further:

> To be conscious is not to be in time
> But only in time can the moment in the rose-garden,
> The moment in the arbour where the rain beat,
> The moment in the draughty church at smokefall
> Be remembered. . . .
>
> (*BN*, II)

The garden is earthy; the rain, watery; the draughty church, airy. Rose garden and rain are spring images, while the draughty church is autumnal, "smokefall" evoking the fall of the year. Those moments are of a particular element and season; yet there is a deep likeness between them so that each recalls the other, thereby transcending particularity without losing it.

The imagery of the middle sections of *Burnt Norton* is of autumn and winter. The animating wind becomes an

> Eructation of unhealthy souls

Into the faded air, the torpid
Driven on the wind that sweeps the gloomy hills of London. . . .

(BN, III)

The faded air and the wind sweeping gloomy hills are autumnal, and "the torpid" is autumnal, too, because the word refers to the stiffness of a dormant or hibernating animal. The "fall" is "the way down" in the seasonal cycle, which corresponds to sundown in the diurnal cycle:

> Time and the bell have buried the day,
> The black cloud carries the sun away.

(BN, IV)

The way down is also the way up because the dead of winter, the total torpor, turns inevitably into spring. At the end of *Burnt Norton,* the cycle is completed:

> Sudden in a shaft of sunlight
> Even while the dust moves
> There rises the hidden laughter
> Of children in the foliage. . . .

(BN, V)

Here again is the vernal conjunction of elements. Earth (dust) and fire (sunlight) are united in the air. Spring foliage and children arise from this union; thus, *Burnt Norton* presents the whole cycle and envisions the presence of all seasons in the still point at the center of the cycle. Later quartets seem to be more clearly identified with their seasons, but the main idea remains the integration of all four within each time.

East Coker begins "On a summer midnight" (*EC,* I)—summer is its season. More precisely, we are at midnight on Midsummer Eve, for there is a traditional celebration, dancing around a bonfire. As Shakespeare's *Midsummer Night's Dream* assumes, this night is the ideal time for the "necessarye coniunction" of matrimony figured in the dance around the fire. The June wedding is old pagan magic, for the Midsummer orgy will make the fields fruitful.

The celebration of summer recalls the past and the Midwinter yule fire, so it speaks of winter and death, as well as of summer and life. Those who have danced here before are now "Nourishing the corn," and the present dancers eventually will follow them. Therefore, the dance symbolizes not only matrimony but the cycle of the seasons, the cycle of life. The dancers are

> Keeping time,
> Keeping the rhythm in their dancing
> As in their living in the living seasons
> The time of the seasons and the constellations. . . .
>
> (*EC*, I)

One cannot "keep time" in the sense of keeping it from moving; one can merely keep time by marking its passage with the rhythmic movement of the dance. The "Feet rising and falling" mark not only seconds but seasons—the rising of spring, the falling of autumn—the way up and the way down. The dance of summer reminds us of "the time of harvest," when there will be another bonfire, but that is the time of "Dung and death." The repetition of seasons and generations has a mournful tone, and this passage, of course, echoes the sense of vanity in Ecclesiastes. Nevertheless, "the time of the seasons and the constellations" is also a kind of repetition, which we love because the opposites are reconciled in its eternal pattern. A few lines later there are "constellated wars" in which even the heavenly bodies are at war, but "constellated" means organized, orchestrated. The "Thunder rolled by the rolling stars" only "Simulates triumphal cars" in these wars, acting out the pattern in a perfected, bloodless strife. The Heraclitean thunder and stars are aethereal, so their very strife is creative.

Thus, even when this passage ends with the stars "Whirled in a vortex that shall bring / The world to that destructive fire / Which burns before the ice-cap reigns" (*EC*, II), the fire (being both Heraclitean and apocalyptic) destroys only to restore. In "the time of the seasons and the constellations," one cannot celebrate life without remembering death, for Midsummer Day is the longest but is, by the same token, the beginning of the winter cycle of shortening days. Then again, that winter dying is sure to bring back another summer.

The second section of *East Coker* begins with one of the passages that describe a communion of the seasons:

> What is the late November doing
> With the disturbance of the spring
> And creatures of the summer heat,
> And snowdrops writhing under feet
> And hollyhocks that aim too high
> Red into grey and tumble down
> Late roses filled with early snow?
>
> (*EC*, II)

Fall, like spring, is a time of disturbances, of change. Winter and summer, on the other hand, seem unchanging; they are the end points the two in-between seasons change from or into, so the disturbances of spring resemble those of November. Autumn is doing something to the summer creatures, transforming them. Summer and winter touch and exchange with each other in these transfigurations. Roses fill with snow, becoming momentarily paradoxical winter blossoms; snowdrops are summer flowers patterned after the snow. Immaterial forms unite the opposites in their strife. Later, summer again merges with its enemy in the "winter lightning" (*EC*, III). We will find other images of this *coniunctio oppositorum* in *Little Gidding*.

The Dry Salvages should be the poem of autumn, and it does tell of "The silent withering of autumn flowers" (*DS*, II). But the opening passage describes in a new way the seasonal commonalty. The river "Keeping his seasons" is the *arche* here, the uniting element, so all the seasons are his:

> His rhythm was present in the nursery bedroom,
> In the rank ailanthus of the April dooryard,
> In the smell of grapes on the autumn table,
> And the evening circle in the winter gaslight.
>
> (*DS*, I)

Thales probably thought water the prime element because it is essential to all life, so the ailanthus and the grapes must contain water. The river, however, is everywhere present in a deeper way, for it is not his substance but his rhythm that is present, the rhythm of the seasonal dance, the timing determined by the tide. Rhythm is form, the *Logos*, which appears in all seasons—here spring, autumn, and winter. The winter image is the most challenging because the river is manifest here as its elemental opposite, fire. Eliot is probably picturing the rippling effect of gaslight and the sense of a pool of light in the "evening circle"; thus, the mortal enemy of water becomes its alter ego as winter suddenly becomes summer.

In *Little Gidding*, we should come to winter, and indeed, the first word is "Midwinter," but the second word already asserts the interplay of seasons:

> Midwinter spring is its own season
> Sempiternal though sodden towards sundown,
> Suspended in time, between pole and tropic.
>
> (*LG*, I)

The juxtaposition of "Midwinter spring" is like the juxtaposition in Heraclitus's phrase "winter summer." Midwinter, the winter solstice, is (like Midsummer) an ancient time of festivals, for festivals are held at these times between seasons, these turning points. The feasts declare time momentarily stopped, caught at the still point in and out of time. Eliot finds continuity between this old idea of timeless moments between seasons and the new science, whose terminology he uses to describe the world suspended "between pole and tropic." The solstice is "the short day" but the turning point toward longer ones and thus the beginning of spring as well as winter. For this reason, it is the appropriate time for the Christmas feast, the fulfillment of the old Saturnalia.

If winter comes, spring cannot be far behind; but Eliot goes a step further and finds spring manifest in winter. "The brief sun flames the ice," mixing elements as it mixes seasons, and the cold becomes "the heart's heat." The glare of the sunlight on the winter ice is even more intense than the glow of spring sun. It is aethereal fire creating a pure, immaterial springtime, with "no earth smell / Or smell of a living thing." The form of spring, not its substance, penetrates winter.

As in *East Coker*, there are winter blossoms reflecting the summer:

> Now the hedgerow
> Is blanched for an hour with transitory blossom
> Of snow, a bloom more sudden
> Than that of summer, neither budding nor fading,
> Not in the scheme of generation.
>
> (*LG*, I)

This discovery of spring flowers in the midst of winter places us in a romance world much like that of *The Winter's Tale*. Shakespeare's tale of winter includes a scene in which the lost maiden, Perdita, reappears when least expected, giving flowers to an old king and renewing his line by marrying his son. Perdita is explicitly identified with Persephone, the one whose loss and recovery bring winter and summer. Eliot's snow blossom does not grow from a bud but materializes with the frost. In the scheme of generation, flowers can only come from flowering plants. There is no spontaneous generation (or, as the old philosophical axiom—first enunciated by Parmenides—has it, nothing can come from nothing—*ex nihilo, nihil fit*). In the scheme of Genesis, however, the world was created by the Word, *ex nihilo*. In a world so created, spontaneous generation is quite imaginable. Even without a miracle, there are bound to be moments like this when the pattern of creation transcends particularity and appears where we least expect it.

Just below, on his way to Little Gidding, Eliot discovers the reverse of Midwinter spring, a hint of winter in the midst of spring:

> If you came this way in may time, you would find the hedges
> White again, in May, with voluptuary sweetness.

In place of the old idea that one season conquers another, Eliot proclaims
that they reflect each other, being simply different modes or instantiations
of the same spiritual form.

The opening passage of *Little Gidding* ends with wintery summer:

> Where is the summer, the unimaginable
> Zero summer?

Lyndall Gordon questions the response of Eliot's friend John Hayward,
who thought this referred to the absolute zero of physics.[42] I think absolute zero fits rather well, for it is a state in which all movement (and
hence time) stops. Absolute zero is thus a modern scientific concept that
corresponds to Eliot's notion of a still point outside of time's covenant.
Then again, Eliot might have had in mind ordinary zero degrees Celsius,
the point "Between melting and freezing" in this passage. Be that as it
may, "zero" certainly is meant to recall winter, so as to mirror the opening
phrase. At the two ends of the passage are "Midwinter spring" and "Zero
summer," and in between are images in which the two seasons complement each other and exchange identities.

In this final quartet, the tone is considerably more positive than that
of the earlier ones. Particularly if we compare it with the seasonal images
in *East Coker,* we see a major shift. The earlier poem speaks of the turning
seasons in the language of Ecclesiastes. The idea of an eternal pattern
joining summer and winter is there, but there is little comfort in that
knowledge. In *Little Gidding,* on the other hand, there is a kind of solemn
peace in our awareness of winter and spring as mirror images of the
same forms:

> If you came this way,
> Taking any route, starting from anywhere,
> At any time or at any season
> It would always be the same. . . .
>
> (*LG,* I)

Clearly, the relation of the *Four Quartets* to the four elements and four
seasons is not merely "for convenience sake," as Eliot suggested it might
be in his letter to William Matchett. On the contrary, these *quaternios*
are the essential symbols Eliot uses to explore his Heraclitean and Christian vision of a unity within the multiplicity of the created world. It is not
a vision of transcendent unity beyond that world but of unity within its
very change and division. I suggest, then, an alteration in Smith's formulation. Instead of saying that the symbolism of the elements and seasons
"maintained the subject of cyclical change in time, against which Eliot

posed the idea of a stable eternity," I would say that Eliot described a stable eternity appearing within that cyclic change. More recently, Steve Ellis has found an opposition of the eternal and temporal in this passage. He writes, "Here it seems that heaven and earth are running on completely different timetables, so to speak, with heat, fruition, and fecundity all being posited as a total metaphysical inversion of the 'scheme of generation' that peaks in the summer."[43] In contrast, I am arguing that the eternal patterning of the *Logos* is presented as being perceptible within the chaotic flux of the "scheme of generation." Ellis later states that in *Four Quartets* "we have Eliot's relegation of the natural creation not only to a secondary status, but to one totally sundered from the spiritual except in the epiphanic moments of consciousness."[44] This is a good corrective to a certain kind of Romantic, pantheistic reading, but it seems more accurate to say that the epiphanic moments reveal a union of eternal and temporal that is always there.

The Age of Eliot; The Age of Einstein

If, as Russell Kirk says, the first half of the twentieth century was the age of Eliot in letters, it was even more obviously the age of Einstein in natural science. Inevitably, the poet was profoundly aware of what the physicist was saying. When Eliot was a boy, the American scientists Michelson and Morley were beginning the revolution by conducting a series of increasingly refined experiments to measure the speed of light. Their finding that this speed was invariable, whether the light beam measured was moving in the same direction as the earth or perpendicular to it, stimulated Einstein to develop a new theory based on this constant, and in 1905 he published his Special Theory of Relativity. Ten years later, in 1915, his General Theory of Relativity presented a new way of understanding gravity and space. By the time of *The Waste Land,* Einstein had been lionized and popularized.

Alan J. Friedman and Carol C. Donley, in their book *Einstein as Myth and Muse,* give an excellent explanation of the new theory and demonstrate the broad influence it had on writers. They deal with specific works of Eliot only passingly, but they offer a judicious estimate of his interest in these matters. They find him predictably reluctant to base his whole world view on scientific theories but deeply aware of those theories:

> Nevertheless, Eliot did not reject the new physics in itself—only its unwarranted extension into other disciplines. Among the major writers, Eliot was one of the most informed about the new physics, having studied and lived with

Bertrand Russell, and having read some of the works of Einstein, Whitehead, James Jeans, and Arthur Eddington.[45]

An earlier and more detailed account of Einstein's influence on Eliot was given by Steven Foster, who points out that Einstein's theory achieved acceptance by Russell and other writers in *The Monist* as early as 1915, and that Eliot's essays published in the same journal a year later speak of Leibniz's theory of space and time as "relativistic."[46]

Eliot translated an essay by Charles Mauron on Einstein and published it in *The Criterion* in 1930. This essay expresses strongly the view that scientific knowledge and experiential knowledge should be kept strictly separate. However, at the very end of the essay, Mauron shows how the new science has made room for other types of knowledge—room that was crowded out previously by mechanistic science. He observes that Einstein has discovered new limits to the observable universe, particularly the limit of the speed of light, beyond which empirical science cannot go.[47] At last, science itself was declaring that its investigations were inevitably limited.

Though Eliot rejected science as the final arbiter, he saw that the new physics performed a valuable service in demolishing the materialistic, mechanistic, and positivistic assumptions which had grown ever stronger in the popular reception of scientific findings, if not in the thinking of scientists themselves (the latter being typically modest in their metaphysical claims). Just as positivism reached its peak and it seemed only a matter of time and effort before science removed the last little discrepancies in the mechanical model of the universe (such as the very slight difference between the calculated path of Mercury at its perihelion and its actual path, or the stubborn resistance of light to revealing definitively whether it was made of particles or waves), and just as J. B. Watson prepared to begin explaining even human behavior in strictly mechanical terms, Einstein and Planck proved mathematically that the universe did not behave mechanically when objects approached the speed of light or the size of an electron. Just as the atomic theory of matter was proven beyond dispute, Rutherford discovered that the atoms were not the tiny little balls imagined by every materialist from Democritus to Dalton. They were not, in fact, unsplittable. This recognition that modern physics overturns materialist premises is the thesis of Whitehead's *Science and the Modern World*. Mauron, though he insists on strict separation of science and mysticism, ends his essay this way: " . . . who knows whether our successors will not see matter as invested with a new magic, more correct but stranger than the phantasmagoria of old? 'There are more things in heaven and earth, Horatio. . . . '"[48] Horatio's "philosophy," here, is the natural philosophy that put "all in doubt" in the time of Donne but which eventually claimed to be on the verge of achieving certain knowledge about everything in the universe. Einstein's theory draws a line beyond which this philosophy cannot go and thereby introduces mystery to the universe again. My thesis is that Eliot agreed with Whitehead and others in taking the new theories this way and that in *Four Quartets* he does see the new physics as compatible with his metaphysics.

I must disagree with Friedman and Donley when they conclude that

> For Eliot, modern science *does* indicate a universe in which truths are relative to the observer's reference frames; therefore, for him, a whole world view governed by such science is fragmentary, frightening, void of meaning. Eliot implies in "The Four Quartets" and in "The Rock" that humanity needs other truths, religious and artistic, which reach beyond the limits of science.[49]

While the last statement is consistent with Mauron's, and Eliot's, insistence on the limits of science, the assertion that Einstein's relativity theory revealed to Eliot a world devoid of meaning is just backwards. As previous chapters have shown, it was precisely the world described by the old mechanistic physics that Eliot found to be necessarily fragmentary and void of meaning, since it pictured a world of fragmentary atoms bumping randomly into each other in the void, and much of his early poetry satirizes such a world view. He recognized that it was this cosmology that the new physics shattered.

Steve Ellis also blurs the distinction between relativity and subjectivism. His interpretation of *The Waste Land* argues convincingly that the poem's "instantaneous teleportation between disparate events" reflects the theory of relativity in setting aside mechanistic causality. When he goes on to claim, however, that the poem's "metaphysical objectives" were to show that subjective experience is the only reality and to proclaim "the failure of absolutes to validate themselves," Ellis equates physical relativity with philosophical relativism.[50] In stating that the new science "demonstrated that the barrier between men and whatever ultimates might exist was impassable," Ellis extrapolates from science to theology, making science the final arbiter in just the way Eliot consistently repudiated.

Einstein's theory does not in fact indicate, as Friedmen and Donley claim, "a universe in which truths are relative to the observer's reference frames," though it does indicate a universe in which *time* is relative to the frame of reference. Einsteinian physics gives no real encouragement to metaphysical subjectivism or relativism.[51] As Bertrand Russell writes in his *ABC of Relativity* (1925),

> The "subjectivity" concerned in the theory of relativity is a *physical* subjectivity, which would exist equally if there were no such things as minds or senses

in the world. Moreover, it is a strictly limited subjectivity. The theory does not say that *everything* is relative; on the contrary, it gives a technique for distinguishing what is relative from what belongs to a physical occurrence in its own right.[52]

Henri Bergson also makes this distinction in his 1922 book on relativity, *Durée et simultanéité*, where he concludes that " . . . this theory, far from ruling out the hypothesis of a single time, calls for it and gives it a greater intelligibility."[53] Eliot surely would have read Russell's book and probably would have read Bergson's. We can confidently assume that he knew Einstein's relativity was not epistemological or metaphysical relativism.

In Einstein's theory, measurements of time are relative to the observer, but this is not a statement of skepticism. In fact, the relativism of these measurements is an objective reality, not a subjective state of mind, and the variation in measurement is exactly calculable, based on what Einstein declared a universal constant: the speed of light in a vacuum. This constant now defines the limit of the four-dimensional time-bound world we inhabit, for time theoretically stops at the speed of light. Thus time, which limits our own reality and ultimately brings us to death, is itself limited. There may be dimensions beyond the three we perceive in which extension in the fourth dimension does not appear as movement to any beings who live there but appears as something still, just as length, depth, and breadth do to us. Time is, for us, movement of three-dimensional objects, and Eliot attempts to find images representing a transcendent perspective in which the dimension of time is stable, unmoving. Augustine and Boethius tell him that time is not motion for God, who exists beyond time. Einstein tells him that science now recognizes a precise point at which time as we know it ceases to exist.

Eliot calls this intersection between time and timelessness the "still point":

> At the still point of the turning world. Neither flesh nor fleshless;
> Neither from nor towards; at the still point, there the dance is,
> But neither arrest nor movement. And do not call it fixity,
> Where past and future are gathered.
>
> (*BN*, II)

In the next paragraph, the still point takes on the image of "a white light still and moving." Light moves at a particular, very great speed, yet the hands of a clock moving at that speed would become still. The stillness of light is not "fixity." Time does not cease to exist, but it ceases to move sequentially: "past and future are gathered." Eliot identifies light more explicitly with the still point when he says "the light is still / At the still point of the turning world" (*BN*, IV). Of course, there are much older reasons to identify light with the still point, but Einstein's theory accounts for the paradox of stillness and movement nicely and is thus consonant with those older reasons.

The poem begins with that miraculous moment in the garden at Burnt Norton, which is suddenly transfigured into "our first world," the rose garden they did not enter in the past. The miracle takes place in sunlight, which suddenly fills the dry pool with water and shows them children reflected in the water (perhaps their younger selves, or the children Tom and Emily might have had). In this light, the past—and even the unrealized potential of the past—becomes present. Such a miracle is newly imaginable in the light of Einstein's theory. The miracle of light is repeated or remembered at the end of *Burnt Norton:*

> Sudden in a shaft of sunlight
> Even while the dust moves
> There rises the hidden laughter
> Of children in the foliage. . . .
>
> (*BN,* V)

Again, it is in the light that the past is gathered into the present, as it would be at the speed of light according to Einstein's theory.

At the end of *The Dry Salvages,* Eliot speaks in general of these rare moments when one suddenly apprehends timeless reality, and light is again the catalyst:

> For most of us, there is only the unattended
> Moment, the moment in and out of time,
> The distraction fit, lost in a shaft of sunlight. . . .
>
> (*DS,* V)

These mystical moments have become more comprehensible to the physical scientists, now that they no longer think of time as a simple movement from place to place at a particular instant but as a space-time "event," for while Einstein's Special Theory redefined time, his General Theory redefined space. Classical mechanics dealt with objects moved by outside forces through empty space. One located an object in the three dimensions of space and then determined its location in time independently. The world fit Euclidean geometry, in which the shortest distance between two points was a straight line. Einstein upset this conception of the cosmos when he used a non-Euclidean geometry to show that space and time were not separable determinants. An object's location in space affected its location in time. The shortest distance between two points in space-time was not a straight line but a geodetic line, which follows the curves in the space-time continuum. In this geometry, too, parallel lines can meet—as they do when "the narrowing rails slide together" behind Eliot's voyager (*DS*, III). This new concept of bending space-time pervades *Four Quartets*, unexpectedly connecting a particular time and place with other times and places, and with what is beyond time and place.

Russell shows how the mechanical notion of space and time has been set aside, resulting in strange possibilities of reversals in time sequence:

> There are now a number of ways of fixing position in time, which do not differ merely as to the unit and the starting-point. Indeed, as we have seen, if one event is simultaneous with another in one reckoning, it will precede it in another, and follow it in a third.[54]

Thus, sober scientists have suggested the potential for the intersections of past and future Eliot describes. The world becomes mysterious anew. It is no longer possible to identify positively one place at one time, as Sir Arthur Eddington writes in his 1920 book *Space, Time, and Gravitation:*

> The denial of absolute simultaneity is a natural complement to the denial of absolute motion. The latter asserts that we cannot find out what is the same place at two different times; the former that we cannot find out what is the same time at two different places.[55]

This uncertainty does not apply to events as long as they all take place within a very limited frame of reference, such as Earth, but earthly events located in the universal scheme would not be as neatly sequential as they seem to us. Ole Bay-Petersen has examined the influence of Einstein's theories on Eliot's sense of time and has concluded that " . . . Eliot's idea of eternity as forming a kind of pattern or design where all times coexist is remarkably similar to Einstein's space-time."[56]

Eliot finds ways of glancing at his visits to the locales of the *Four Quartets* from a universal perspective, and he finds unexpected connections across time and space. East Coker, for instance, was Andrew Eliot's beginning point in his seventeenth-century voyage; space-time bends, and it becomes his descendant's ending point. In the world of Einstein, such coincidences may be more than fancies.

The new understanding of space and time raised questions about causality and coincidence. The mechanist is necessarily a determinist. If the world is composed strictly of material moved by mechanical forces and if one could exhaustively describe the mass and momentum of an object and of other objects around it, then one would know absolutely what would happen to that object from then on. There would be no surprises. Positivists imagined that they would one day be able to do just that, but cause and effect are not so simply connected in the relativistic cosmos. As Sir James Jeans puts it in his *Physics and Philosophy* (1943),

> At the same time, the question of causality has assumed a new aspect. We can no longer say that the past creates the present; past and present no longer have any objective meanings, since the four-dimensional continuum can no longer be sharply divided into past, present and future.[57]

Jeans hastens to add that everything may still be determined—merely at another level by more complex laws—but relativity at least reopened the question of deterministic causality. Those who, like Eliot, believed that events were not entirely determined by preceding events could take comfort. Determinism was even more directly challenged later by the quantum theorists, as we will see.

The constant interpenetration of past, present, and future—or of the four seasons—in *Four Quartets* fits with a relativistic understanding of space-time:

> If you came this way,
> Taking any route, starting from anywhere,
> At any time or at any season,
> It would always be the same. . . .
>
> (*LG*, I)

This affirms, of course, a permanent reality residing in one place, the chapel at Little Gidding. However, the many paths through space and time that lead to this event may suggest Einstein's geodetic lines connecting time and space in unexpected and non-linear ways. The poet further claims that the journey is not ruled by deterministic forces:

> And what you thought you came for
> Is only a shell, a husk of meaning
> From which the purpose breaks only when it is fulfilled
> If at all. Either you had no purpose
> Or the purpose is beyond the end you figured
> And altered in its fulfilment.
>
> (*LG*, I)

The effect of this action is not what the rational mind predicted from what it knew of the prior situation. Innumerable lines have connected this action with others in different times and places, producing unexpected results.

One might even say that Eliot's poetic technique here would scarcely have been possible before Einstein. It is a poetic in which surprising acausal connections occur: Midwinter spring and Zero summer. Of course, the same could be said of a number of other modern poets. There were others who included overt references to Einstein's theories (such as Auden, Williams, and MacLeish), as Friedman and Donley point out. However, Eliot's very technique reflects the new physics more perfectly than anyone else's. We have become accustomed to hearing that he used this modern technique to convey old ideas, but the old ideas of Boethius and Augustine concerning time and eternity happen to fit rather comfortably with the new physics, as Eliot saw, and the striking novelty of his tone is not simply a matter of technique. What we hear is the new physics resonating with the old metaphysics in his verse.

The conception of time proposed by the new physics offered another challenge to the "superficial notions of evolution" Eliot dismisses in *The Dry Salvages*. With the demise of simple sequential causality, evolutionary theory came under renewed scrutiny. As Russell put it,

> The collapse of the notion of one all-embracing time, in which all events throughout the universe can be dated, must in the long run affect our views as to cause and effect, evolution, and many other matters. For instance, the question of whether there is progress in the universe, may depend upon our choice of a measure of time.[58]

Not everyone would agree with this statement, because the earth's history, though long, is set in an inertial frame in which the laws of classical mechanics remain accurate. Nevertheless, many thinkers who (like Russell) understood Einstein's theory well concluded in the twenties and thirties that it did call some principles of orthodox Darwinism into question simply because that theory tends to be identified with a thoroughly mechanistic assumption, which Einstein contradicts. In Russell's reference to "our choice of a measure of time," we hear something like Eliot's concern in *Four Quartets* for various measures that yield different experiences of time. There is the annual measure of the seasons; the eternal measure of the "drift of stars"; the diurnal measure of the sun, from dawn to dark; the artful measure of music and dance; the historic measure from war to war; the geographic measure of the traveler. Thus, he evokes poetically a sense of multiple frames of reference, which is incompatible with the usual evolutionary view of time as "a mere sequence."

If time is no longer a straight line through space, a sequential cause-effect development ceases to be the only way for new organisms to arise. From the universal perspective (or infinity of perspectives), it would not be immediately obvious even that the "other" creations (evidenced by starfish, crabs, and whale's backbone) were "earlier." From this theoretical point of view, recurring patterns, such as the homologous designs of different organisms (the whale's backbone and the poet's), may not prove that they developed gradually and randomly from common ancestors but rather that some organizational principle connects them through loops in space-time.

At the same time, the other revolution in modern physics, quantum theory, tends to suggest that the old adage *natura non facit saltum* (nature does not make leaps) is quite wrong. At least at the atomic level, nature does not do anything *except* by leaps. Whether this applies at the biological level is debatable, but it has certainly been seen as calling into question the assumption of gradualism in orthodox Darwinism. In fact, some biologists have more recently begun to speak of "punctuated equilibrium," lengthy periods of equilibrium punctuated by short epochs of dramatic change—leaps forward in evolution during which thousands of new species arose rather suddenly. By the time he wrote *The Dry Salvages,* Eliot had come to see the similarities between man and mongoose as evidence of divinely ordained patterns penetrating space-time, not as evidence of gradual development from one species to the next.

One other revolutionary finding of Einstein's is that expressed in the famous equation $E = mc^2$, which suggests that at the speed of light energy and matter—two traditionally antithetical principles—are identical, or at least transformable into each other. Discussion of this idea will be deferred until the quantum theory is introduced, for the latter arrives at the same notion from a different starting point.

HEISENBERG AND HERACLITUS

The other revolution in modern physics was less famous than Einstein's at first but may have raised an even greater number of philosophical questions as it became better known. Relativity theory sprang from the discovery of a constant in the infinite reaches of space and time, the speed of light; quantum theory sprang from the discovery of another constant pertaining to the infinitesimal actions within the atom. It is called Planck's constant, after Max Planck, who discovered it in 1900. The basic revelation was that atoms which are heated (or somehow excited) give off energy only in integer multiples of their frequency of vibration multiplied by the Planck constant. In other words, energy is not released in gradually increasing amounts as the excitation is gradually increased; rather, energy is transferred only in packets, or quanta. This somehow does not sound as earth-shaking as Relativity, but as a phalanx of physicists worked together (mostly over glasses of Tuborg in Copenhagen) year by year to elaborate the theory, it proved to challenge our basic conceptions of the material world just as radically as the companion theory. The two have never been connected to everyone's satisfaction. Niels Bohr's rather loose idea of Complementarity attempts to do so, but it is apparently more philosophical than mathematical—which is evidence of the state of affairs scientists have reached, leading more than one of them to write books called *Physics and Philosophy*.

One such scientist-turned-philosopher was Werner Heisenberg, whose Uncertainty Principle (or Principle of Indeterminacy), proposed in 1926, was the clearest sign that quantum theory was causing a major disturbance in scientific notions of the material world. His *Physics and Philosophy* was not published until 1958, but I will quote from it several times because it draws together in coherent fashion insights that were in the air throughout the time *entre deux guerres* when these strange revelations were breaking on the world, and the *Quartets* were incubating. In particular, Heisenberg makes the connections with ancient physics that (as I hope to show) Eliot was making.

In reviewing the history of physical theories, Heisenberg concludes that quantum theory overturns the materialist doctrines that had seemed so well established and validates the insights of some of the ancient philosophers whose ideas had long been considered pure fantasy. Significantly, he acclaims Heraclitus above all. Heisenberg notes that the agent of Heraclitus's change, the fire, is "both matter and a moving force." Matter and force, or matter and energy, were defined strictly as opposites in the atomism of Democritus and in Newtonian mechanics. The major revolution of modern physics is to see that these two principles are not ultimately separable, so Heisenberg responds enthusiastically to Heraclitus's fire as a resolution of the traditional opposition:

> This leads to the antithesis of Being and Becoming and finally to the solution of Heraclitus, that the change itself is the fundamental principle; the "imperishable change, that renovates the world," as the poets have called it. But the change in itself is not a material cause and therefore is represented in the philosophy of Heraclitus by the fire as the basic element, which is both matter and a moving force. We may remark at this point that modern physics is in some way extremely near to the doctrines of Heraclitus. If we replace the word "fire" by the word "energy" we can almost repeat his statements word for word from our modern point of view. Energy is in fact the substance from which all elementary particles, all atoms and therefore all things are made, and energy is that which moves. Energy is a substance, since its total amount does not change, and the elementary particles can actually be made from this substance as is seen in many experiments on the creation of elementary particles.[59]

Among the ancient physicists who chose one or another of the four elements as the *arche*, Heraclitus was closest to the view of modern science.

He saw that fire was the odd element in that it was the least substantial and the one that transforms the others. The fourth element is that which melts solids to make them liquid and causes liquids to evaporate and become gas. Even for ordinary chemistry, then, Heraclitus makes sense, but the ordinary chemist might complain that energy should not be seen as one of the four elements, since it is radically different from matter. Here, the quantum physicist enters and remarks that matter is not actually permanent, as the atomists had supposed, and it is not always distinguishable from energy. The weeping philosopher must be laughing at having been vindicated after all these centuries.

There is no explicit reference to the quantum theory in Eliot's poetry, but he must have seen the connection Heisenberg notes. I will argue that the new physics has influenced one idea we find running throughout *Four Quartets*, the idea that substances can be mysteriously transformed into energy or into other substances. As we look more closely at how the new physics fits with the ancient physics and at how this combination fits the images of the poem, we will see quantum physics as a pervasive influence.

One critic has previously explored these connections. In a brief article entitled "Eliot and the Particle Physicist," Marion Montgomery suggests, in his usual incisive manner, that Eliot's poetry shows an approving awareness of the new physics. Montgomery points specifically to Heisenberg's Principle of Uncertainty as an idea compatible with Eliot's philosophy and concludes that the main philosophical issue affected is the question of immanence versus transcendence:

> If the idea of immanence is the modern philosophy (as opposed to the medieval idea of transcendence) in the neoscholasticism of particle physics, we may be discovering the necessity of abandoning that idea to return to transcendence. Consider the question of the antiparticle out of which particles emerge; one is very close to the edge of creation *ex nihilo* in such a conception of matter.[60]

Indeed, it is precisely this question of the relation between ultimate spiritual reality and the material world that is raised in a new way by subatomic physics. I am suggesting that the new physicists are more neopre-Socratics than neoscholastics, but for Eliot's purposes, they are part of the same extended family. Eliot's answer to the question, however, is not entirely a return to transcendence. He fits the paradoxes of indeterminacy with those of Christianity and resolves the dichotomy between immanence and transcendence. In *Four Quartets,* both are true, as we will discover by following Montgomery's suggestion and taking a close look at the poem with these issues in mind.

Heisenberg singles out another of the ancients as a prophet of physics, Aristotle. The latter conceived of matter and form as inseparable. No object, he argued, could exist as pure matter without form. In fact, matter without form may be thought of as only a *potential* reality. Heisenberg again responds to the union of opposites in this approach. He explains that the creation of new subatomic particles in the atom smashers has shown that particles are not permanent but can change form:

> All the elementary particles are made of the same substance, which we may call energy or universal matter; they are just different forms in which matter can appear. If we compare this situation with the Aristotelian concepts of matter and form, we can say that the matter of Aristotle, which is mere "potentia," should be compared to our concept of energy, which gets into "actuality" by means of the form, when the elementary particle is created.[61]

Eliot's emphasis on "form" or "pattern" fits this concept of a dynamic interplay between matter and form. In the mysterious experience in the garden, for instance, unseen persons suddenly materialize enough to be somehow perceived:

> There they were, dignified, invisible,
> Moving without pressure. . . .
>
> (*BN*, I)

Here, there is also "unheard music," insubstantial forms on the verge of physical existence ("virtual" music, one might almost call it, using a newer term from physics). This notion of something hovering between ideal and material existence is authorized by quantum mechanics, which can only describe the statistical probability that a particle will exist in a certain place. Heisenberg likens this approach to Aristotle's:

> The probability wave of Bohr, Kramers, Slater . . . was a quantitative version of the old concept of "potentia" in Aristotelian philosophy. It introduced something standing in the middle between the idea of an event and the actual event, a strange kind of physical reality just in the middle between possibility and reality.[62]

This statement uses exactly the same terms as "The Hollow Men," in which we could say that the potential is never realized because the opposites remain apart:

> Between the idea
> And the reality
> Between the motion
> And the act
> Falls the Shadow.

In *Four Quartets,* on the other hand, the entities hovering between idea and reality frequently become momentarily real and unite the opposites.

One such quasi-ideal, quasi-material entity in the poem is speech, and another is music. These are forms with very slight—but not negligible—material substance; hence, the poet writes,

> Words after speech, reach
> Into the silence. Only by the form, the pattern,
> Can words or music reach
> The stillness. . . .
>
>   (*BN, V*)

Materialist theories of science discount the principle of form or organization. Eliot plays with the necessary interaction of material and formal causes in the world of his poem. There is the "wild thyme unseen"; the lightning that momentarily springs from potential (electrical potential, in fact) and then becomes merely potential again; dust that momentarily appears in a shaft of sunlight; the ashes on an old man's sleeve, which were a rose and may be one again; and the "spectre of a rose." In purgatory, "the flame is roses, and the smoke is briars," as the same form appears in different substances, and of course, this line is echoed in the final line of the poem, where "the fire and the rose are one." In such images, Eliot asserts the primacy of form in the material world and shows form and matter inseparably involved in a lively interplay. His attitude is Aristotelian, but with more dynamism, and this renewed formalism is informed by the new physics. As Eddington expresses it, "The relativity theory of physics reduces everything to relations; that is to say, it is structure, not material, which counts."[63] *Four Quartets* is a poetic investigation of the same newly recovered ancient truth.

Let us now look more closely at the new conception of matter and at how that resonates in the poem. Russell sums up the shift in thinking when he writes,

> The truth is, I think, that relativity demands the abandonment of the old conception of "matter," which is infected by the metaphysics associated with "substance," and represents a point of view not really necessary in dealing with phenomena.[64]

Note that relativity theory, like quantum theory, leads to this conclusion. Both theories change the definitions radically because they find an identity or interchange between matter and energy. As Russell explains,

> Mass used to be defined as "quantity of matter," and as far as experiment showed it was never increased or diminished. But with the greater accuracy of

modern measurements, curious things were found to happen. In the first place, the mass as measured was found to increase with the velocity; this kind of mass was found to be really the same thing as energy.[65]

Thus, the new physics sounded the death knell of materialism, at least of materialism as a metaphysical assertion. For three centuries, science had successfully pursued knowledge of the physical world by narrowing its focus to that world and carefully avoiding contamination by ideas concerning ultimate reality. Finally, however, this narrowing of focus to matter came to be taken by many scientists and lay people as evidence that the material world was all there was. The limitation of scientific inquiry was unconsciously turned into a metaphysical claim. As Jeans expresses it,

> The doctrine of materialism asserted that this space, time and material world comprised the whole of reality; it regarded consciousness as only a minor incident in the history of the material world, a somewhat exceptional episode in the haphazard muddle resulting from the chaotic movement of photons, electrons and matter in general. It interpreted thought as a mechanical motion in the brain, and emotion as mechanical motion in the body.[66]

Thus, the ultimate danger of scientific materialism is that it will attempt to reduce even our spiritual experience to mechanistic explanations. Jeans goes on to describe the radically different view necessitated by modern physics:

> The new physics suggests that, besides the matter and radiation which can be represented in ordinary space and time, there must be other ingredients which cannot be so represented. These are just as real as the material ingredients, but do not happen to make any direct appeal to our senses. Thus the material world as defined above constitutes the whole world of appearance, but not the whole world of reality; we may think of it as forming only a cross-section of the world of reality.[67]

The philosophical terminology of Eliot's dissertation on Bradley—appearance and reality—is now being used by the scientist. Appearance is not rejected as total illusion, but it is no longer accepted as total reality.

At the end of *The Dry Salvages* comes a passage that contrasts the two world views. Eliot has been describing the visionary moment "in and out of time," which has recalled the Incarnation:

> Here the impossible union
> Of spheres of existence is actual,
> Here the past and future
> Are conquered, and reconciled,

> Where action were otherwise movement
> Of that which is only moved
> And has in it no source of movement—
> Driven by daemonic, chthonic
> Powers.
>
> (*DS*, V)

The latter part of this passage describes the older, materialist view of pure mass, which "has in it no source of movement," no energy. It is, therefore, "that which is only moved." What moves it is force, whose origin is unexplained (hence daemonic) or explained as somehow material as well (hence chthonic, earthy). Force and mass are radically distinct realities. In the preceding lines, on the other hand, "the impossible union / Of spheres of existence" becomes "actual." This is the Incarnation, uniting spirit and matter. It happens to be consonant with the new physics, in which a number of oppositions are seen as collapsing at the limits of experience: energy is mass; light is made of particles (photons) but behaves like an electromagnetic wave; and subatomic particles also appear to be waves. All these resolved scientific dualities suggest the ultimate resolved theological dualities of matter and spirit, time and eternity.

For Eliot, the new physics respects his faith as it resolves the Cartesian split, source of the dissociation of sensibility. Jeans explains how quantum physics resolves the opposites:

> The new dualism of the particle- and wave-pictures is in many ways reminiscent of the old dualism of Descartes. There is no longer a dualism of mind and matter, but of waves and particles; these seem to be the direct, although almost unrecognizable, descendants of the older mind and matter, the waves replacing mind and the particles matter. The two members of this dualism are no longer antagonistic or mutually exclusive; rather they are complementary.[68]

Complementarity is a qualitative term the mathematicians have had to introduce to explain the mystery they have encountered. The particles do behave like particles (with mass, momentum, etc.), but they also behave like waves. These two are by definition, however, mutually exclusive "spheres of existence." The antinomies come to be seen as complementary aspects of a single reality we can never quite grasp in its singleness.

Eliot describes a number of interchanges between matter and energy in the poem. In the opening miracle, energy turns to matter as the pool is "filled with water out of sunlight." The still point, which (as we have seen) is identified with "a white light still and moving," is undefinable as either matter or not-matter: it is "Neither flesh nor fleshless." Later, when the day is buried and the sun disappears, the poet asks, "Will the sunflower turn to us . . . ?" (*BN*, IV). The word "sunflower" combines the pure energy of the sun with a material object, the flower: the fire and the rose are one. Sunflowers follow the sun in a mysterious way, suggesting that they are children of the sun who follow him of their own will. The flower is not the sort of matter that "is only moved" and "has no source of movement." It is a reality that better fits the Aristotelian notion that all the material world moves with desire—a desire, ultimately, for God. The image of the sunflower turning to us seems to be a macabre reversal in which, at night, the roots seek our buried bodies. We are back in the world of "The Burial of the Dead." But if we are in the place where the union of spheres of existence is actual, where flower and sun are one, the body can experience resurrection. This death "shall fructify in the lives of others" (*LG,* III).

Before the sun sets, "the kingfisher's wing / Has answered light to light." This is realistically only a reflection of light off the wing, but symbolically, it suggests a deeper correspondence between the organism and the source of its energy, as between sunflower and sun. The bird has sun within it to answer the great sun. Is this the Fisher King appearing again anagrammatically and giving an answer that will revive his land? Be that as it may, this is no waste land, for the sun is not gone, even after sunset: "the light is still / At the still point of the turning world." The light is stilled by the burial of the day, but it is also still in its timelessness, which is not ruled by the passage of day and night. Therefore, it is "still" there, *always* there (in the Renaissance sense which is ever in the word when Eliot uses it). From our new perspective, this means that fire-energy never leaves the world, even in the darkness, because matter itself (the sunflower, the kingfisher, the corpse) comes from this energy and is this energy. Another source for the idea that fire is both matter and energy was one Eliot encountered in his early reading at Harvard. He took notes on a book about Empedocles, Bodiero's *Principio Fondamentale e cui s'informa il sistema di Empedocle,* and his notes include this statement: "*Fire* is the point of transition between force and matter."[69] The same meaning inheres in the "winter lightning" (*DS,* V). Winter is the death of the sun, but out of the dark clouds the fire suddenly flashes as the energy inherent in matter is released.

The mysterious complement of the two spheres of existence accounts for all the in-between states in the poem. There is the moment between scenes in the theater or between stations in the tube. The poet is in the "middle way" between youth and age, between two wars, between end and beginning, between land and sea, "Between midnight and dawn." Ultimately, the poem places us between the way up (toward the spiritual) and the way down (toward the material) and finds that "the way up is the way down" (*DS,* III). Transcendent spirit is immanent in matter. Eliot's attention to what is in-between corresponds with the probability wave of quantum theory, which, as Heisenberg says, "introduced something standing in the middle between the idea of an event and the actual event, a strange kind of physical reality just in the middle between possibility and reality."[70]

The ghost who appears to him in *Little Gidding* moves easily in this in-between world. As a poet he has struggled to move from expressions appropriate for one time to new ones,

> For last year's words belong to last year's language
> And next year's words await another voice.

But now, in the world in and out of time, the right words for the present time come easily to express the unchanging realities. With a pun on poetic "passages" of words, he claims,

> But, as the passage now presents no hindrance
>   To the spirit unappeased and peregrine
>   Between two worlds become much like each other,
> So I find words I never thought to speak
>   In streets I never thought I should revisit
>   When I left my body on a distant shore.
>
> (*LG*, II)

One of the poets compounded in this ghost is Eliot's revered antagonist, Matthew Arnold. Arnold, writing at the height of scientific materialism, declared that he was "Wandering between two worlds, one dead, / The other powerless to be born." He could not make the passage to the new world. He imagined it would be a world without miracles, and try as he might, he could never fully embrace that world. As it turns out, the new world of physics is full of wonders. The poet is not stuck between the worlds of science and faith because they have "become much like each other." The ghost is not caught in a limbo between them: he is at his ease in both at once.

In "Gerontion," we may recall, a child of the age of scientism hovers between life and death. He "has no ghosts" because those who have passed on are merely "fractured atoms." The ghost in *Little Gidding* declares that he never expected to revisit his old haunts when he left his body, but it turns out he did not entirely leave it. At least he has some sort of body now, enough to be perceived by the living, and personal enough to be identified. The body and the psyche have not been sundered by death. Psychic energy is able to manifest physically, or the matter of the body is able to rise up. The two worlds have become much like each other; the two spheres of existence are united. The modern poet responds to this miracle, "The wonder that I feel is easy." His acceptance of the marvel is made easier in part by the revelations of modern physics, which suggest that supernatural events are not necessarily unnatural.

The new understanding of matter and energy is consonant with another physical phenomenon in *Four Quartets:* the transformation of one substance into another. The opening of *East Coker* describes such transubstantiations:

> In my beginning is my end. In succession
> Houses rise and fall, crumble, are extended,
> Are removed, destroyed, restored, or in their place
> Is an open field, or a factory, or a by-pass.
> Old stone to new building, old timber to new fires,
> Old fires to ashes, and ashes to the earth
> Which is already flesh, fur and faeces,
> Bone of man and beast, cornstalk and leaf.
>
> (*EC,* I)

The transformations here are natural and cyclic. The decay of one thing leads eventually to the life of another: "Houses rise and fall"; they are "removed, destroyed, restored." In the natural world, as Northrop Frye points out, time is cyclic: it is in this sense that it is both destroyer and preserver. The bones of man and beast, with the stalks of corn, do make the earth rich so that new life may arise from it. This natural cycle is what Heraclitus is thinking of when he speaks of change and strife as establishing a kind of permanence. Through the constant change, the *Logos* keeps re-creating the same forms.

As Heisenberg recognized (and, I am suggesting, Eliot as well), this idea is really quite compatible with the modern concept of energy. Heisenberg declares that

Since mass and energy are, according to the theory of relativity, essentially the same concepts, we may say that all elementary particles consist of energy. This could be interpreted as defining energy as the primary substance of the world. It has indeed the essential property belonging to the term "substance," that it is conserved. Therefore, it has been mentioned before that the views of modern physics are in this respect very close to those of Heraclitus if one interprets his element fire as meaning energy. Energy is in fact that which moves; it may be called the primary cause of all change, and energy can be transformed into matter or heat or light. The strife between opposites in the philosophy of Heraclitus can be found in the strife between two different forms of energy.[71]

Such an idea of energy and transformation was incompatible with classical mechanics, which considered matter to be made up of tiny balls of indestructible, permanent stuff. It turns out that, at the atomic level, matter is not permanent, and one type of matter can be transformed into another. Heisenberg continues,

> In the philosophy of Democritus the atoms are eternal and indestructible units of matter, they can never be transformed into each other. With regard to this question modern physics takes a definite stand against the materialism of Democritus and for Plato and the Pythagoreans. The elementary particles are certainly not eternal and indestructible units of matter, they can actually be transformed into each other.[72]

Of course, Heraclitus was not thinking in atomic terms at all. He was probably picturing ordinary sensory events like Eliot's burning timbers, but his insight goes far beyond such phenomena. The basic model of physics he constructs is strikingly similar to that of the modern scientist.

The notion of one element being transubstantiated into another is the focus of the passage describing the deaths of air, earth, fire, and water in *Little Gidding* (II). As we saw, this passage evokes Heraclitus's statement about the elements living each other's deaths. We are now able to see how the new physics is compatible with the notion of the physical world Eliot is presenting here. The lines describe the strife between opposing elements ("Dead water and dead sand / Contending for the upper hand"), which Heisenberg tells us "can be found in the strife between two different forms of energy" in modern physics. As one element dies, its opposite lives. Like the elementary particles, "they can actually be transformed into each other." This sort of discussion by the leading scientists of his time resonated deeply for Eliot.

As I mentioned previously, quantum mechanics tended to call into question the determinism that had been assumed in classical mechanics. The old physics is deterministic because it is mechanistic; that is, it assumes that one could describe the world at a given instant strictly in terms of masses and velocities. This is the world in which there is "movement / Of that which is only moved / And has in it no source of movement" (*DS*, V). If the physicist can describe one instant in this mechanical, three-dimensional world, then the next instant can be completely predicted and so on into the future, which is thus completely determined by the past.[73] This idea of causality naturally excludes any genuine mystery and any free will. Philosophers often opposed it, but as long as they began from the materialist assumptions of nineteenth-century science, they were trapped. Then science itself came to their rescue. Given the new discoveries, Jeans proclaims,

> There is no scientific justification for dividing the happenings of the world into detached events, and still less for supposing that they are strung in pairs, like a row of dominoes, each being the cause of the event which follows and at the

same time the effect of that which precedes. The changes in the world are too continuous in their nature, and also too closely interwoven, for any such procedure to be valid.[74]

It is not only because Eliot has grown older but because he has read this and other accounts that he finds the past "ceases to be a mere sequence" (*DS*, II).

When Jeans says that events are "too continuous in their nature" to support determinism, he uses a phrase that might have come from Henri Bergson, who has, in fact, been credited with foreseeing this turn of events. Friedman and Donley explain that

> Bergson denies the existence of any durationless instants. In so doing, he denies that any instantaneous cut can be made through a system. This fact (as later physically realized in the Uncertainty Principle) limits how much we can know about the state of that system. No instantaneous cut means no mathematically exact description of the position and momentum of a particle; hence no exact determination of its future position and momentum. In this way, Bergson challenged the classical determinism in a manner quite close to that of Heisenberg and Bohr some years later. De Broglie, who freely acknowledges his debt to Bergson, was particularly impressed by Bergson's argument in *Time and Free Will*, summarized in the line: "The effect will no longer be given in the cause. It will reside there only in a state of possibilities."[75]

De Broglie was the first to show that the position and velocity of sub-atomic particles could not be quantified exactly but could only be described as probability waves. This mathematical solution led to a questioning of established notions of causality by Heisenberg and all the members of Bohr's Copenhagen school. As Friedman and Donley point out, Bergson had posed the same questions. Physics and philosophy were meeting again after a long separation. Eliot would have been extremely aware of the way science was confirming what one of his early philosophical masters had said about time and causality. He follows both Bergson and Bohr as he confronts deterministic assumptions throughout the *Quartets*. Eliot finds human reason incapable of determining the outcome of events:

> Either you had no purpose
> Or the purpose is beyond the end you figured
> And is altered in the fulfilment.

(LG, I)

No instantaneous slice of an earlier moment would have predicted accurately the end to which it was leading. There are mysterious patternings involved that transcend cause-and-effect relations.

Exploration of quantum theory eventually led to the proclamation of a finding that directly challenged the deterministic model, Heisenberg's famous principle (made public in 1927). As everyone knows, this principle sets forth a law of physics which states that our inability to determine both the position and velocity of an electron is not merely a limitation in experimental techniques but is built into the scheme of things. Any experiment that can measure one of the two factors inevitably adds an element to the system that makes it impossible to measure the other. When other physicists accepted Heisenberg's reasoning, they admitted that there were some things science would never ever know for certain. We had reached an absolute limit in human knowledge. The physical world became mysterious again.[76]

The principle of indeterminacy suggests that the act of observation inevitably affects the object observed. Heisenberg describes one of the experiments in which light clearly acts as particles and just as clearly acts as waves, and he exclaims, "Now this is a very strange result, since it seems to indicate that the observation plays a decisive role in the event, and that the reality varies, depending on whether we observe it or not."[77] Jeans remarks that this discovery made it impossible for science to do what had been its first aim since the time of Bacon, the separation of subject and object to achieve a strictly objective finding.[78] Jeans adds that this is true only at the atomic level, but if it is true anywhere, it signals the end of positivism and determinism as philosophical ideas.

In 1930, a few years after Heisenberg's pronouncement, Jeans wrote one of his books about physics and gave it a title that would have been unthinkable for a book on that subject before, *The Mysterious Universe*.[79] Now, the reviewer in *The Criterion,* Hugh Sykes Davies, rather panned this book, finding it merely an exaltation of Jeans's own field of study, mathematics. Nevertheless, the editor of *The Criterion* lauds it, along with a book by Eddington, in his "Religion and Science" talk:

> Please understand that I am not criticising the attitudes of the eminent scientists themselves; nor am I criticising their more popular books, which even I can understand in part, and some of which I have read with pleasure and I hope profit. I instance Sir James Jeans' *The Mysterious Universe* and Professor Eddington's *Science and the Unseen World.* I am only criticising an uncritical attitude of the public towards these writers and their books, an attitude shared, I am sorry to say, by theological writers who ought to know better.[80]

Eliot's point in this piece is that religious thinkers should not turn to modern physics for a vindication of their beliefs. Another passage clarifies Eliot's attitude toward the new physics:

But it is clear that the popular attitude of hailing modern physical science as a *support* of religion is very misguided. To remove an obstacle is not the same thing as to raise a support. It is just the same old superstition of science: you are continuing to make the natural sciences the key to ultimate truth, though the key now unlocks a different door.[81]

Thus, we should not expect to find the poet embracing modern physics as proof of his faith, yet he does claim that this new development may "remove an obstacle," showing people that science never should have been used to question religious doctrines. The new science removes an obstacle by proclaiming the end of mechanistic determinism and acknowledging, as Jeans does in his title, the mysterious, indeterminate nature of the universe. This reawakened sense of the mysterious in the material world we do find in the poem.

Indeterminacy is everywhere evident in *Four Quartets*. It is at "the uncertain hour before the morning" that the poet meets a ghost who is "Both one and many . . . Both intimate and unidentifiable" (*LG*, II). Subject and object become confused:

> So I assumed a double part, and cried
> And heard another's voice cry: 'What! are *you* here?'
> Although we were not. I was still the same,
> Knowing myself yet being someone other. . . .
>
> (*LG*, II)

The still point passage in *Burnt Norton* seems to resound with the language of the particle physicist, who cannot exactly place a particular particle in both space and time:

> I can only say, *there* we have been: but I cannot say where.
> And I cannot say, how long, for that is to place it in time.
>
> (*BN*, II)

Because the still point is "Neither flesh nor fleshless"—neither particle nor wave—it is "neither arrest nor movement." Its position and velocity cannot be determined.[82] The still point is a state of consciousness, a contemplative state in which one is oneself but simultaneously completely united with the other. Heisenberg's way of talking about indeterminacy and about the inseparability of subject and object harmonizes with the ecstatic analogies of the mystics:

> Dawn points, and another day
> Prepares for heat and silence. Out at sea the dawn wind
> Wrinkles and slides. I am here
> Or there, or elsewhere. In my beginning.
>
> (*EC*, I)

Heisenberg points out that one of the basic rules of logic is violated by quantum physics. If we say, "here is a table," it is either there or not there: no third possibility exists (*Tertium non datur*).[83] However, in the new physics, and in these passages of *Four Quartets,* a new logic applies.

The idea that our observations change the object appears in Eliot's statement that "the roses / Had the look of flowers that are looked at" (*BN,* I). The flowers have been altered physically by "the unseen eye-beam." The correlation of subject and object is so unbreakable in Heisenberg's model that he declares the disappearance of the Cartesian split:

> It has been pointed out before that in the Copenhagen interpretation of quantum theory we can indeed proceed without mentioning ourselves as individuals, but we cannot disregard the fact that natural science is formed by men. Natural science does not simply describe and explain nature; it is a part of the interplay between nature and ourselves; it describes nature as exposed to our method of questioning. This was a possibility of which Descartes could not have thought, but it makes the sharp separation between the world and the I impossible.[84]

I have argued earlier that Eliot's "dissociation of sensibility" is another name for the Cartesian split. He surely recognized that the uncertainty principle reconnected mind and experience in a surprising way and that it encouraged his own efforts to reclaim a unified sensibility by which one could apprehend profound correspondences between mind and body, self and other, psyche and cosmos. Where Donne's ideas were once as immediate as the odor of a rose, the roses are now affected by his idea of them: they have the look of roses that are looked at.

The healing of the Cartesian split means also a healing of the split between arts and sciences. The split occurred when Descartes set out to base philosophy strictly on mathematics. Modern science became the enterprise of describing reality in quantitative terms, avoiding entirely the ambiguous qualitative judgments of ordinary language and philosophy. Suddenly, in the early twentieth century, the most thoroughly mathematical scientists in history realized that their mathematical language was giving ambiguous descriptions of reality—even contradictory ones. In attempting to explain to others, and even to themselves, what their formulas were revealing, they found themselves using ambiguous terms from natural language, such as Bohr's "complementarity." They found themselves reviewing the history of philosophy.

As he struggled to find words, Heisenberg became aware that he was not so different even from artists. "Both science and art," he writes, "form in the course of the centuries a human language by which we can speak about the more remote parts of reality, and the coherent sets of concepts as well as the different styles of art are different words or groups of words in this language." Both disciplines are finally out to describe "something that is probably quite ineffable" (*DS*, II), and they must deal in "hints and guesses" (*DS*, V). In their attempts to approach an understanding of the mysterious limits of reality, the scientists had begun speaking in paradoxes, as Heisenberg does here:

> . . . one may say that the concept of complementarity introduced by Bohr into the interpretation of quantum theory has encouraged the physicists to use an ambiguous rather than an unambiguous language, to use the classical concepts in a somewhat vague manner in conformity with the principle of uncertainty, to apply alternatively different classical concepts which would lead to contradictions if used simultaneously. In this way one speaks about electronic orbits, about matter waves and charge density, about energy and momentum, etc., always conscious of the fact that these concepts have only a very limited range of applicability.[85]

Eliot's paradoxical style derives first of all from the Bible and the mystics, and the metaphysical poets; but it has also been influenced by this unlikely source, the physicists. Perhaps it is better to say that Eliot is able to use the paradoxical style effectively again because the world has once again become paradoxical.

The famous passage at the end of *East Coker* about the struggle with words is in sympathy with the physicist's struggle. Eliot tells us that "one has only learnt to get the better of words / For the thing one no longer has to say," and Heisenberg avows that "The real problem behind these many controversies was the fact that no language existed in which one could speak consistently about the new situation."[86] If the physicist has discovered that he is a poet, however, the poet conversely finds himself using a scientific image in describing his words as "shabby equipment," conjuring up the untidy lab of the experimenter. When this equipment is said to be "always deteriorating / In the general mess of imprecision of feeling," we may think of the new admission of inevitable imprecision in science. Physics and poetry are speaking each other's language for the first time since the Middle Ages.

The end of *Four Quartets* returns, of course, to the beginning, the mystical moment in the rose garden. This time the ghostly "voice of the hidden waterfall / And the children in the apple-tree" is "half-heard, in the stillness / Between two waves of the sea" (*LG*, V). The still point is, as we have seen, the undefined, uncertain point between the antinomies: in and out of time, neither flesh nor fleshless. Modern science had given Eliot concepts that made such a state understandable not only as mystic transcendence but also as the real state of affairs in the physical world at the limits established by the absolute constants Einstein and Planck had discovered. The wave image used here also takes on additional resonance from these theories because both Einstein's light and Planck's electrons are paradoxical entities behaving at once like particles of matter and like electromagnetic waves. The atomic particles appear wavelike in the probability equations, which are therefore known as "wave mechanics." Eliot's wave is like a quantum wave in that the quantum theory says energy can be given off only in discreet packets, not in a gradual flow. The release of energy from an atom is like waves of the sea, not a river. The trough between waves is a perfect image here because it is "still but still moving": the space moves with the waves but remains fixed in relation to the waves before and behind. It is thus not "fixity" but a dynamic stillness in the middle of the most irresistible forces.

The final lines of the poem draw on Heraclitean fire, the Gospel account of Pentecost, and Dante's *Paradiso*:

> When the tongues of flame are in-folded
> Into the crowned knot of fire
> And the fire and the rose are one.

Eliot finally sees hope of a fire that is not purgatorial. In this brief vision of paradise, spirit and matter unite. The tongues of flame which came down upon Mary and the apostles at Pentecost were a physical, sensible reality, but they were also the Holy Spirit, the purest of spiritual reality. Similarly, Heraclitus's fire is a physical entity, one of the four elements, but it is also the purely spiritual *Logos*. It is aethereal fire, simultaneously physical and psychical. Eliot is seeing heaven now, but it is not a disembodied world. He emphasizes the physical nature of the fire by using the corporeal metaphor, "tongues" of flame, and by describing them as "infolded" into a "crowned knot." Like Dante, Eliot must use physical description even when approaching the spiritual realm; but like Dante, he is also a Christian who believes in "the resurrection of the body." The Christian expects a new Jerusalem, a real city peopled by glorified bodies—neither flesh nor fleshless. The "crowned knot of fire" symbolizes that paradoxical state, for it is a substantial form made of pure energy. Eliot writes with the awareness that physics has rediscovered such an intersection of matter and energy, validating Heraclitus's concept of fire.

Initially, the fire symbolizes energy and the rose symbolizes matter. They are one because they have taken on the same pattern: the tongues of flame are folded like the petals of the flower, both becoming symbols of divine wholeness. These mandalas knot together in a sacred marriage the fundamental antinomies, an "impossible union / Of spheres of existence." The sharply defined petals and tongues are the many folded into the one crown (in the "crowned knot"), a crown being a circular form uniting many points. Energy and matter, fire and rose, can become one because we have discovered that they were one all along. Fire is also substantial; a flower is full of energy. This profoundly resonant last line is informed by the new physics, which finds that the fire and the rose are, indeed, one already in this world.

The Jungian language of mandala and sacred marriage seems appropiate at this point, and Elizabeth Drew has previously used Jungian terminology to elucidate this passage. Jung found that the circular mandala frequently enclosed a cross, which divided it into quadrants. He saw the number four turning up everywhere in myth and dream as a symbol of integration and wholeness. *Four Quartets* are four quaternios, four multiplied by itself. Eliot's mandala figure here at the end of the poem knots or in-folds the four elements, the four seasons, the four corners of the earth (represented loosely by the four locales of the poem)—knots them into a crown or a rose. Now, when the mandala is encircling a quaternio, there is a point (or sometimes a smaller circle) at the center where the dividing lines cross. A point by definition takes up no space, but it centers the quaternio and orders it, turning it into the quincunx, a symbol of unified opposites.[87] The point is an infinitesimal circle which generates the all-enclosing circle at the outer edge and around which the four elements turn as they live each other's deaths. All four touch it at all times. That point symbolizes the fifth element, the immaterial point that centers and unites the four. Each of the *Quartets* has five movements, suggesting the importance of a fifth element. In *The Waste Land,* the quintessence was absent until the fifth section, but here it is a constant presence in the four poems, uniting them in the strife that divides them. It is the holy center of the paradisal rose, the still point at the center of the turning world.

More Rumors of the Aether

The patient reader who has persevered thus far knows that the author is fascinated by the idea of the quintessence. If the reader is not by now convinced that T. S. Eliot was (through his intense study of classical literature and philosophy, and particularly through his devotion to Heraclitus) at least half as interested in the aether as his present interpreter, this section will surely seem superfluous. For I intend to consider what happened to the idea in modern times and how that might have affected Eliot's conception of the aether in *Four Quartets.*

Though thinkers as early as Democritus had denied the existence of the aether, nearly everyone found the idea of a true void inconceivable and appalling. The medieval schoolmen settled it with an axiom: Nature abhors a vacuum and so rushes in to fill it. Even Descartes, who usually receives more than his share of blame for the materialism of much scientific thinking, believed in the aether. In fact, it continued to be considered essential to a *mechanistic* description of the universe in the age of Newtonian physics. Both Isaac Newton and Christian Huygens, though they differed as to whether light was initially propagated as particles or waves, believed that light waves, like sound waves, had to have a medium to make waves in. Sound makes waves in air and cannot pass through a space in which there is a vacuum. Light can pass through such a space, but the scientists assumed that the supersubtle aether was still there functioning as the medium for the light waves. Huygens pictured the aether as being made of material particles much smaller than particles of ordinary matter, and spread evenly throughout the universe. In explaining the transmission of light he writes,

> And I do not believe that this movement can be better explained, than by supposing that that which is inside luminous bodies which are liquid, like a flame, and apparently the sun and stars, is composed of particles which float in a material which is much more subtle, and which agitates them with great rapidity, and makes them collide with particles of the aether, which surround them and which are much smaller than they.[88]

Thus, in the seventeenth century, the idea of an aether continued to be unquestioned, but it is important to note that the aether was no longer defined as a quasi-spiritual substance. It was thought to be made of tiny round atoms, like every other substance. This material conception of the aether was accepted without any challenge until A. A. Michelson began, just a year before Eliot was born, his experiments to determine the speed of light.

Michelson assumed that the aether was a subtle gas such as Huygens had described, so he also assumed there would be a kind of aether wind created as the earth traveled through space and that it would therefore make a difference whether the light he was measuring was moving in a direction perpendicular to the earth's path through the aether or along earth's path. The experiments showed no such difference. It was largely these experiments that started Einstein thinking that the speed of light was a universal constant. At the same time, they proved to him that there was no background medium in which light made its waves. The idea of aether had been experimentally disproved once and for all.

Or had it? What had certainly been disproved was the atomistic concept of aether maintained by Huygens. That, however, was really quite different from the ancient idea of a substance that was not entirely material. It was also supposed to be divine and to obey laws entirely different from those that applied to the mundane elements. Standard accounts of modern physics assume that Einstein's was the last word on the subject, but some physicists and philosophers did not consider the question closed. I wish to examine what they have said on the subject and suggest that Eliot continued to think in terms of some all-pervading universal substratum roughly equivalent to the aethereal fire of Heraclitus.

Werner Heisenberg again gives perhaps the clearest understanding of how one could continue to think of an aether after Michelson and Einstein:

> The hypothetical substance "ether," which had played such an important role in the early discussions on Maxwell's theories in the nineteenth century, had— as has been said before—been abolished by the theory of relativity. This is sometimes stated by saying that the idea of absolute space has been abandoned. But such a statement has to be accepted with great caution. It is true that one cannot point to a special frame of reference in which the substance ether is at rest and which could therefore deserve the term "absolute space." But it would be wrong to say that space has now lost all of its physical properties.[89]

In other words, the idea of a mechanical aether filling space no longer fits the evidence, but the ancient competing idea of a void may not be the answer either. The reason space should not be considered simply empty comes, ironically, from Einstein. He abolished the aether in developing his Special Theory of Relativity, but his General Theory of Relativity pictures space as being full of *something,* though not of a material. Heisenberg elsewhere elaborates, denying total vindication to the atomists:

> From our modern point of view, we could say that the empty space between the atoms in the philosophy of Democritus was not nothing; it was the carrier for geometry and kinematics, making possible the various arrangements and movements of atoms. But the possibility of empty space has always been a controversial problem in philosophy. In the theory of general relativity the answer is given that geometry is produced by matter or matter by geometry. This answer corresponds more closely to the view held by many philosophers that space is defined by the extension of matter.[90]

It is difficult to grasp Einstein's thinking in the general theory, and I do not claim to have grasped it; but it seems that Einstein replaces the "gravitational force" of Newton's theory with non-Euclidean curved lines formed in space around objects and connecting them with other objects. This solves one problem of Newton's, which was how to explain "action at a distance," forces acting across empty space on distant objects. Einstein's mathematics does not picture one object acting at a distance on another but rather geometric relations between the two. In some sense, then, this theory pictures space as being filled with abstract forms, geometry. And yet, as Heisenberg says, these forms are not wholly immaterial but are in some manner reciprocally produced by and productive of matter.

When Eliot heard explanations like this, he must have connected them instantly with Heraclitus. Einstein's space is filled with formal *relations* between objects; Heraclitus's space is filled with fire, which is identified with the aether and also with the *Logos*. The latter is a formal principle. It patterns the elements as it changes them. In both views, invisible patterns proceed from and also direct the changes in material substances.

Bertrand Russell, in his book on relativity, also concludes that the new theories do not conceive of space as a vacuum. He describes the aethereal view and the atomistic view and takes the former:

> If there is to be any difference between one place and another, there must either be differences between the material in one place and that in another, or places where there is material and others where there is none. The former of these alternatives seems the more satisfactory. We might try to say: There are electrons and protons and the other sub-atomic particles, and the rest is empty. But in the empty regions there are light-waves, so that we cannot say that there is nothing there. According to quantum theory, we cannot even say exactly where things are, but only that one place is more likely than another to find an electron in.[91]

As Russell continues, he leaves open the question of whether all the activity in the vacant spaces is in an aether:

> Some people maintain that light-waves, and particles as well, are just disturbances in the aether, others are content to say that they are just disturbances; but in any case events are occurring wherever there are likely to be light-waves or particles. . . . We may say, therefore, that there are events everywhere in space-time, but they must be of a somewhat different kind according as we are dealing with a region where there is very likely to be an electron or proton, or with the sort of region we should ordinarily call empty.[92]

Clearly, the issue is not closed for him, and he is even inclined to use the old word "aether" so long as it refers to the kinds of events or disturbances described by the new theories. An important part of his analysis is based on the uncertainty principle, the realization that one can never know for certain that a particular point in space is void. Given this, can we say that there is a void anywhere? Also, Russell sees the light waves themselves taking the place of the aether they were formerly thought to move in. As we have seen, light has the essential quality assigned to aether in ancient physics: it is both matter and energy.

Sir Arthur Eddington, whose solar eclipse expedition gave Einstein's general theory one extremely important piece of solid empirical confirmation, also does not abandon the idea of an aether. He sees that what was disproved by Michelson was the mechanistic conception of the aether as a rarefied substance made of tiny atoms. The aether, he says, is some sort of background, not a participant in physical actions:

> There is accordingly no need to transfer to this vague background of aether the properties of a material ocean. . . . Permanent identity of particles is a property of matter, which Lord Kelvin sought to explain in his vortex-ring hypothesis. This abandoned hypothesis at least teaches us that permanence should not be regarded as axiomatic, but may be the result of elaborate constitution. There need not be anything corresponding to permanent identity in the constituent portions of the aether; we cannot lay our finger at one spot and say "this piece of aether was a few seconds ago over there."[93]

Clearly, this explanation, like Russell's, rests on the principle of uncertainty and the probability mathematics of the wave theory. Eddington also implies that the aether may be some sort of substance not made of particles, or whose particles, at least, do not have permanent identity but may go in and out of three-dimensional reality.

This notion that there may be another kind of matter that transcends the ordinary laws has been taken up again recently by a number of scientists, among them, Lawrence M. Krauss in a book called *The Fifth Essence: The Search for Dark Matter in the Universe*. As his subtitle indicates, Krauss suggests that the quintessence is actually the "dark matter" that now seems to be present throughout the universe (as evidenced by strong gravitational effects in "empty" space) but does not reflect light. Krauss argues that the dark matter may be a substratum of what are now called "virtual particles," which sometimes pop over into three-dimensional space. Krauss writes, "Because of these ideas, we now view the vacuum as anything but empty. Rather, the vacuum can be thought of as a vast storehouse of virtual particles waiting to appear."[94] He traces this idea to Paul Dirac, who suggested in 1930 that we could imagine the vacuum as being full of negative electrons. Eddington's discussion also comes close to suggesting such a model.

Thus, we see that Eddington, Russell, Dirac, and others asserted that matter should no longer be thought of as permanent bits of stuff located in particular places at particular times. They began to speak of "events" rather than particles and forces, employing a term that emphasizes the quasi-material nature of what is being described. Events are neither matter nor energy. Eddington points out the likeness between this way of describing the world and the notion of aether:

> In the relativity theory of nature the most elementary concept is the *point-event*. . . . The aggregate of all the point-events is called the *world*. . . . What we have here called the *world* might perhaps have been legitimately called the *aether;* at least it is the universal substratum of things which the relativity theory gives us in place of the aether.[95]

Just as Russell does, he suggests that the void is full of these events and that the totality of them is the quasi-material substratum beneath the world of appearance.

Sir James Jeans notes the demise of the aether and does not continue to use the word, but he too speaks of a universal substratum:

> If, then, we wish to picture the happenings of nature as still governed by causal laws, we must suppose that there is a substratum, lying beyond the phenomena and so also beyond our access, in which the happenings in the phenomenal world are somehow determined.[96]

This statement comes from his 1943 book *Physics and Philosophy,* but he was enunciating similar views as early as 1930 when he published *The Mysterious Universe.* There, an entire chapter is devoted to the topic "Relativity and the Ether." Jeans details the process by which the mechanistic notion of the aether was rejected but then points out the inability to locate particles definitively: "With a stream of water, we can say that a certain particle of water is now here, now there; with energy it is not so."[97] Like other people analyzing the new situation, he evidently takes this to mean that we cannot say there is a void in the old sense of the word (that is, the sense employed by the atomists). He suggests that "it seems appropriate to discard the word 'ether' in favour of the term 'continuum.'"[98] The point is presumably that the nonlinear geometry of the space-time continuum simply prevents us from thinking of a three-dimensional void in a particular spot. Jeans and others also seem to think of the new mathematics as describing a universal substratum which is neither material nor immaterial. Such thinking would have reminded Eliot of the Heraclitean *Logos.*

Clearly, the idea of the aether did not die at the turn of the century. As in other areas, the new theories forced thinkers back in the direction of Greek philosophy and the original definition of the word. Eliot read some of these books and must have assented instantly to this direction, though I have not come across any explicit comment of his on the subject. The discussion earlier in this chapter of Heraclitean aether may now be placed in a new context, which reinforces the connections. Helen Gardner is not overstating the case when she says that the quintessence is "the subject of the whole poem." The poem continually returns to the intersection between that substratum and the world of appearances.

"The vacant interstellar spaces," which were filled with aether in the old cosmology, are still filled—with Einstein's geometry or light waves or space-time events. There is "neither plenitude nor vacancy" in a universe of vast spaces filled with such immaterial phenomena. The darkness and immensity of space is overwhelming to the modern mind, which conceives it as a deadly vacuum; yet the best modern minds suggest that the dark vacuum may be the substratum and matrix for all that exists in the sensory world. So Eliot bids his soul be still and accept the darkness, which shall then be known as the still point between plenitude and vacancy, and ultimately as "the darkness of God." The one possible reference to the quintessence comes in the description of the mind "under ether," which is "conscious but conscious of nothing." That yielding of the mind to vacancy may be deadly or it may be contemplative. The contemplative mind discovers God in the darkness. This discovery is more than analogous to the physicist's discovery that the interstellar spaces are not really vacant. In Eliot's thinking, the psychic and physical spaces are finally filled with the same divine presence. The poor souls stuck between stations in the underground with nothing to think about may be praying, as Lyndall Gordon tells us Eliot did. They may then be meditating on the nothingness, the stillness "between two waves of the sea," which is like the nothing between quantum waves, not really a void. Thus, the "empty silence" is also "the heart of light" out of which water fills the empty pool—matter arising momentarily from the substratum.

As in *The Waste Land,* the "winter lightning" is here a momentary manifestation of the aethereal fire, the thunderbolt that "steers all" according to Heraclitus. The image of "Thunder rolled by the rolling stars" connects the thunder with the eternal realm of the stars and also suggests what is in the vacant interstellar spaces, the divine thunderbolt. The lightning is a perfect symbol for the momentary "events" of quantum theory, which are material epiphanies from the substratum.

The empty stillness between stars or electrons is suddenly seen as being full of Aristotelian *potentia.* The places in between are precisely where the impossible union of spheres of existence is actual, a union that is possible in the paradoxical domain of the aether. It is in this way that Eliot makes the fifth element the subject of the poem without naming it.

SACRAMENTAL PHYSICS

The "aethereal rumours" of *The Waste Land* are half heard in *Four Quartets* in the hidden voices of the waterfall and the voices of children. They revive another "broken Coriolanus," the "broken king" of *Little Gidding,* who is King Charles—and T. S. Eliot, and all of us. The prime reference is to the King of Kings, who rose from the dead. We must not forget that the poem is finally a Christian meditation. How does the conjunction of classical and modern physics fit with the religious theme? The answer is fairly obvious: if the old aether or the new mathematical substratum is the point of intersection between the opposites, Christ is He who lives precisely and entirely at that point. If we meditate on this connection, we will find that Eliot is suggesting throughout the poem a physics that makes his brief allusions to the Incarnation feel natural, even expected, normal. That mystery becomes a striking instance of the ordinary mystery of existence.

I have spoken repeatedly ("Shall I say it again?") of the place where "the impossible union / Of spheres of existence is actual." The explicit reference of this phrase is to the Incarnation, which comes to mind in "the moment in and out of time" when one senses "The wild thyme unseen, or the winter lightning / Or the waterfall, or music heard so deeply / That it is not heard at all" (the music of the spheres rolling in their perfect circles through the aether). All these quasi-sensible beauties

> are only hints and guesses,
> Hints followed by guesses; and the rest
> Is prayer, observance, discipline, thought and action.
> The hint half guessed, the gift half understood, is Incarnation.
> Here the impossible union
> Of spheres of existence is actual,
> Here the past and future
> Are conquered, and reconciled. . . .
>
> (*DS*, V)

The moments in and out of time when these hints come to us are, he says, rare for everyone but the saints, yet they do come to ordinary people, and they are inspired by nature—wild thyme, lightning, waterfall. The physical world of the elements has something within it that strikes a chord in the deepest reaches of our psyche. This is not Romantic nature worship, though, but rather a recognition that the elements are, like us, creatures made by the Creator. As in Saint Francis's "Canticle of the Creatures," sun and wind and earth and water are our brothers and sisters. In *Four Quartets,* these moments when the elements speak to us of the Creator are painfully rare, but they also seem to be always ready to happen, to be happening always just on the edge of our awareness:

> Sudden in a shaft of sunlight
> Even while the dust moves
> There rises the hidden laughter
> Of children in the foliage
> Quick now, here, now, always. . . .
>
> (*BN*, V)

They are a virtual reality parallel to our ordinary reality. The view of the physical world this study has been exploring supports this feeling that God is immanent in the physical world. In every atom and in every beam of light and even in the vacant spaces, there is a continual conjunction of time and eternity, matter and spirit. The moments when we somehow sense this actuality are hints and guesses pointing to the "gift half understood."

The section of *The Dry Salvages* preceding this Incarnation passage is appropriately devoted to Mary and focuses on the Annunciation. It begins,

> Lady, whose shrine stands on the promontory,
> Pray for all those who are in ships, those
> Whose business has to do with fish, and
> Those concerned with every lawful traffic
> And those who conduct them.
>
> (*DS*, IV)

The location is one of the many harbor churches in the world dedicated to "Our Lady of Good Help" (or it may be "Our Lady of Good Voyage" in Gloucester). She becomes here the patroness of all those who go about mundane tasks to earn their daily bread. Their "traffic" is the uninspiring material world of commerce Eliot the bank clerk knew so well, yet it is simultaneously the adventurous traffic of the preceding section ("fare forward, voyagers"), where Krishna tells Arjuna that he must take his place in the events of the illusory physical world. Mary is first among those who accept the suffering of mundane labor, whose prime instance is the labor of childbirth.

The phrase "Pray for all those who are in ships" recalls the words of the *Ave Maria:* "Pray for us now and at the hour of our death." Reference to this prayer gives another meaning to the rose garden, for the name of the rosary comes from the word *rosarium,* rose garden.[99] The rosary is a circlet of roses whose beginning is also its end. Mary is further identified with gardens in being called the *hortus conclusus,* the enclosed garden.

In this passage, however, Mary is identified not with earth but with the other primal element which acts as a matrix for life, while it also receives the dead. The sea symbolizes matter—formless, dark, unfathomable, and deadly. Fishermen, therefore, represent particularly well all those who work with the world of matter to keep their families alive. "Humility is endless," though, so this humble work, like Mary's humble acceptance of her role in the divine drama, brings spiritual fulfillment. After all, "those / Whose business has to do with fish" are like the fishermen of Galilee who became the first disciples of the fish, *ICHTHYS* (the Greek acronym for "Jesus Christ, God and Savior") and became fishers of men. In the depths of matter and mundane action is the spiritual essence.

Mary, the mother of God, is identified in profound ways with the material world. The poet asks her to

> Repeat a prayer also on behalf of
> Women who have seen their sons or husbands
> Setting forth, and not returning:
> Figlia del tuo figlio,
> Queen of Heaven.

(DS, IV)

Mary is invoked here as a protectress, but she is also identified with the sea itself. In the litany, Mary is called *stella maris,* Star of the Sea. Mother is *mater,* and hence associated with matter. It is in the sea of amniotic waters that the child floats before birth. The mother of sailors relives the pangs of childbirth as she releases her sons to the greater sea, where they may be once more, and finally, engulfed. Mary, who was told as she presented her infant son in the temple that a sword would pierce her heart, experienced this double suffering to the highest degree possible, knowing her son divine. Again, her mundane suffering is found to be inherently holy: the patron of matter is "Queen of Heaven." Eliot quotes the opening line of the final canto in the *Paradiso,* in which Dante addresses Mary as *Vergine madre* and *figlia del tuo figlio.* As daughter of her son, she transcends time and causality—but in an entirely earthly, physical way.

Finally, the poet implores her to pray for all the dead who have been dissolved again into the material world from which they arose:

> Also pray for those who were in ships, and
> Ended their voyage on the sand, in the sea's lips
> Or in the dark throat which will not reject them
> Or wherever cannot reach them the sound of the sea bell's
> Perpetual angelus.

This is, of course, a reprise of the "death by water," in which the body is drowned and dissolved in one element. Here, however, the resurrection of the body is implicit in the "sea bell's / Perpetual angelus." We have heard that "The tolling bell / Measures time not our time, rung by the unhurried / Ground swell . . . the ground swell that is and was from the beginning" (*DS,* I). This phrase should make us half hear one of Eliot's favorite texts: in the beginning "darkness was upon the face of the deep" but then "the Spirit of God moved upon the face of the waters" (Gen. 1:2). The darkness is "the darkness of God," and so the "bone's prayer to Death its God" modulates into "the hardly, barely prayable / Prayer of the one Annunciation" (*DS*, II). That prayer is the "Perpetual angelus" of the passage we have been exploring. Like the sea bell rung by the tides, the Angelus marks the passing of time, for it is traditionally prayed regularly at morning, noon, and night within the liturgy of the hours, the daily cyclical prayer of the Church, which continually consecrates the temporal world. The Angelus is the prayer of the Annunciation: "The angel of the Lord declared unto Mary, and she conceived of the Holy Spirit. Behold the handmaid of the Lord; be it done unto me according to your word. And the Word was made flesh and dwelt among us." Mary conceives of the Holy Spirit much as the dark waters of Genesis did. The Spirit, or the *Logos,* repeats this pattern of creative action time and time again. The pattern is built into created matter from the beginning and is thus present in every moment. In this sense, the sea bell and the Angelus are "perpetual," marking the continual intersection of time and eternity. Mary lived in a dramatic and complete way at this intersection.

Eliot transposes into Christian terms the epigraph "The way up is the way down." The way down into created matter is the way up of salvation. The Word becomes flesh in Genesis and again in the Incarnation, and this descent enables the way up of resurrection and ascension. The drowned sailors go down into the depths of matter, and God is already there; for matter has been sanctified by the original creation and again by Mary's *fiat,* her willingness to receive the Word into her body.

The physics of Heraclitus corresponds with the Christian revelation because both reject dualism; both say that the mutable physical world is essentially good. For Heraclitus, the world of change is held in a divine pattern by the aether-fire, the *Logos.* This conception obviously resonates with the Christian idea of the *Logos* through whom the world was made and who entered that world at a particular moment in time. Modern physics no longer finds such thinking entirely strange, for it has found that ordinary matter partakes of a similar mystery. This discovery, in turn, infuses Eliot's writing with a sense that the Incarnation is not so much a setting aside of the laws of nature as a manifestation of nature's deeper laws. Nature herself, the Mother of the dark material world, is daughter of her son, full of grace.

Closely related to the mystery of the Incarnation in *Four Quartets* is the mystery of the sacraments. Christianity does not finally consider the physical world to be pure illusion, as attested by the original goodness of creation, God's providential action in biblical history, the Incarnation, physical miracles of the Gospel accounts, Christ's resurrection, and the insistence in the Apostles' Creed on the "resurrection of the body." Catholic sacramental theology develops from this insistence on the unity of body and soul, and it makes use of Aristotle's argument that form and matter are not separable.[100] Hence the efficacy of a sacrament is said to derive from the act itself, *ex opere operato*. Anglican Catholics can at times be even more insistent on the physical actuality of the sacraments than Roman Catholics, and Eliot was this type of Anglican.

When he describes drowning, then, we may be sure that the sacrament of baptism is not far from our poet's mind. The water of baptism is called a "sacramental," and this term implies that its efficacy does not result from an arbitrary, culturally determined symbolism, which God randomly chooses to use in conferring spiritual graces. The significance is inherent in the substance itself—form and matter are one. The water of baptism, even when immersion is not total, "is what it always was," the fatal flood. Eliot knew the dangers of the sea first hand. He tells somewhere the story of his being caught by a storm off the Massachusetts coast and having to spend the night on an island. All his drowned sailors are undergoing the real transformation of baptism "into something rich and strange"— Christians.

Similarly, when Eliot speaks of marriage, the "commodious sacrament of matrimonie," it is not for him a social convention to which the sacrament somehow adds spiritual meaning. The spiritual meaning was built into the very physical being of human persons, who were created male and female and told to leave their parents and become one flesh. In this sacrament, one could say that the bodies of the husband and wife are the sacramental substance. It is interesting to note that in Catholic teaching the man and woman are themselves technically the ministers of this sacrament. There is no marriage until it is consummated by the physical union, and a marriage that has not been consummated is invalid. There is no dualism of body and spirit in this sacramental idea of marriage.

It is, however, the prime sacrament of the Church, the Eucharist, which receives the greatest attention in *Four Quartets*. There had been a glancing allusion to it already in the preconversion *Waste Land,* in the passage describing the disciples on the road to Emmaus, for it was there that they recognized the master "in the breaking of the bread." In *East Coker,* Eliot calls to mind the primitive analogues of the communion rite as he describes it:

> The dripping blood our only drink,
> The bloody flesh our only food:
> In spite of which we like to think
> That we are sound, substantial flesh and blood—
> Again, in spite of that, we call this Friday good.
>
> (*EC,* IV)

Most reformed denominations drew away from the doctrine of transubstantiation, partly because of the cannibalistic implications, which Eliot here emphasizes. The reformers became acutely aware that the Church's rituals had often developed out of pagan rituals and continued to carry with them primitive magical thinking, which did not distinguish between physical and spiritual worlds. Eliot accepted this Catholic primitivism as a good thing (at least potentially). We saw earlier that this was a major issue for him when he was reading Frazer and preparing to write *The Waste Land,* and we saw that he went in the direction of proclaiming a positive continuity between our mind and the primitive mind. For him, the sacrament cannot be merely an arbitrary, contingent metaphor, any more than our bodies can be only discardable vehicles for our souls.

The Reformation more or less coincided with the scientific revolution and the Cartesian split between mind and body. Eliot, of course, came to see all of this as a highly problematic development. From his point of view, the reformers had cut themselves off from the body and from the directly physical significance of the sacraments, resulting in a religious dissociation of sensibility. So in these lines he takes what he will call in the next poem "The backward half-look / Over the shoulder, towards the primitive terror" (*DS,* II). Looking directly into the "moment of agony" he sees there, he declares that "in spite of that, we call this Friday good." Salvation came through a physical act of atonement and a physical death, not through a spiritual infusion of grace. Here Eliot consciously echoes the words of that prime undissociated sensibility, John Donne, whose "Good Friday 1613. Riding Westward" meditates on the physical suffering of the one who created the physical world. For Eliot, the idea of a sacrament is, like an idea of Donne's, "as immediate as the odour of a rose." In the sacraments, physical and spiritual realities are indistinguishable. The Eucharistic service in the Mass is a bloodless yet physical reenactment of the Good Friday sacrifice.

In these lines, Eliot looks at the mysterious conjunction in the Eucharist from both sides. Pure spirit comes to us in the sacrament in a grossly physical form, and this is hard to understand. Equally incredible, though, is the obverse realization that our bodies are not purely material. In spite of the sacrament, "we like to think / That we are sound, substantial flesh and blood." As the Word can become flesh without altering His spiritual nature, so our flesh can become spirit but still be our very bodies. The Eucharist challenges us to believe in the resurrection of the body. Eliot describes the dead in *Little Gidding:*

> See, now they vanish,
> The faces and the places, with the self which, as it could, loved them,
> To become renewed, transfigured, in another pattern.
>
> (*LG,* III)

"Transfigured" here plays upon "faces" (French *figures*) and upon "figures" as "patterns." This answers Gerontion, whose dead are dissolved into atoms. These Christian dead take part in the Transfiguration on Mount Tabor, in which Jesus was still himself but revealed in his energetic, glorified body, too bright to look upon.

Again, both Heraclitean and contemporary physics are compatible with the sacramental idea. Bits of matter do not have permanent identity but can be destroyed and reformed as other sorts of particles (or, in older terms, as other elements). That is possible because matter is also fundamentally energy (or fire) and can be reduced to the energetic substratum to reemerge as something different. This process is analogous to the putrefaction and sublimation of the alchemical work, too. Such a theory of physics finds transubstantiation credible, if still mysterious.

As the Eucharist unites spirit and matter, it also unites all people who partake of it, and Eliot alludes to this communion:

> Here or there does not matter
> We must be still and still moving
> Into another intensity
> For a further union, a deeper communion. . . .
>
> (*EC*, V; 1974 ed.)

Again, we find language that corresponds to the principle of indeterminacy: "Here or there does not matter." Possibly Eliot is playing on "matter," for in a world of atomistic matter, here and there matter completely. In the quantum world location ceases to have importance because it cannot be determined. When the physicists discuss the implications of the theory, their language can begin to sound theological. Jeans, for instance, rhapsodizes,

> Photons are no longer independent individuals, but members of a single organization or whole—a beam of light—in which their separate individualities are merged, not merely in the superficial sense in which an individual is lost in the crowd, but rather as a raindrop is lost in the sea. . . . As it is with light and electricity, so it may be with life; the phenomena may be individuals carrying on separate existences in space and time, while in the deeper reality beyond space and time we may all be members of one body.[101]

Here, a scientist finds himself adopting the mystical analogy of the raindrop in the sea, and as he speaks of phenomena as "members of one body," he approaches the Christian ideas of Communion and the Mystical Body of Christ. Jeans is speaking of simple physical phenomena. If such a mystical union occurs in an immaterial substratum for elementary particles, the Communion of Saints need not be conceived of as a supernatural union of disembodied souls. It may be thought of as already forming (or eternally formed) in another dimension of the natural world—a dimension that is higher but not unnatural. This "deeper reality beyond space and time" is just what Eliot had begun to think about in 1905, when he wrote, "If space and time, as sages say, / Are things that cannot be. . . ." *Four Quartets* is a profound fulfillment of the promise in that little poem.

The Communion of Saints appears to the poet as the "familiar compound ghost" of *Little Gidding,* which I discussed earlier in relation to the uncertainty principle. The ghost is "both one and many," like the particles Jeans describes as "members of one body." This communion exists "Between two worlds become much like each other," united by Heraclitus's *Logos,* which is, as the epigraph declares, "common to all." The Eucharistic Communion, similarly, unites people without abolishing strife or erasing their separate identities. The members of the mystical body remain completely individual even as they are completely united. They are the separate tongues of flame "in-folded / Into the crowned knot of fire" in the heavenly rose.

In this great poem, Eliot has succeeded in uniting all the tongues of flame that had spoken to him through the years. He achieves what all great poets must, a single vision of the world which does not leave out any important element. Such a vision became possible for him through his lifelong meditation on the point of connection between the physical and spiritual worlds.

Notes

Chapter 1: Abstract Materialism and Incarnational Symbolism

1. Eliot, *Harvard Advocate* 83, no. 7 (3 June 1907): 96. *Poems Written in Early Youth* (New York: Farrar, 1967), 10.

2. Henri Bergson, *Duration and Simultaneity,* trans. Leon Jacobson (Indianapolis: Bobbs-Merrill, 1965), 63. First French edition, 1922.

3. Quoted by T. S. Eliot, *Knowledge and Experience in the Philosophy of F. H. Bradley* (New York: Farrar, 1964), 110.

4. Sanford Schwartz, *The Matrix of Modernism: Pound, Eliot, and Early Twentieth-Century Thought* (Princeton: Princeton University Press, 1985), 12. This Panglossian positivism, though it seems naive to many scientists today, has nevertheless been surprisingly resilient. It has been further popularized recently by Carl Sagan, who declares in the introduction to *Broca's Brain* that this is the only really interesting time in history because fifty years ago we knew nothing but superstitions and fifty years hence we will know everything. See Sagan, *Broca's Brain* (New York: Random House, 1974), xv.

5. Eliot, *Inventions of the March Hare: Poems 1909–1917,* ed. Christopher Ricks (New York: Harcourt, 1996), 71.

6. See also Manju Jain, *T. S. Eliot and American Philosophy: The Harvard Years* (Cambridge: Cambridge University Press, 1992), 203: "Eliot's hostility to Bergsonism, idealism, and scientific materialism is evident in the image of the universe as a geometric net, which the scientists have laid out on paper." This hostility is almost exclusively directed toward scientific materialism—certainly not toward Bergson, whom Eliot admired during this period, and who would have approved of the sentiments expressed here.

7. See Cyril Bailey, *The Greek Atomists and Epicurus* (New York: Russell, 1964), 435–37.

8. Whitehead, *Science and the Modern World* (1925; reprint, New York: New American Library, 1948), 18.

9. Eliot, unpublished review of *Science and the Modern World* and *Religion in the Making,* by A. N. Whitehead. Galley proofs are in the Cornell University Library.

10. Eliot, "William James on Immortality," *New Statesman* 9, no. 231 (8 September 1917): 547.

11. Whitehead, *Science,* 96.

12. Bergson, *Creative Evolution* (1907), trans. Arthur Mitchell (New York: Holt, 1911), 349.

13. Hyatt Howe Waggoner, *The Heel of Elohim: Science and Values in Modern American Poetry* (Norman: University of Oklahoma Press, 1950). Thomas H. Jackson, "Positivism and Modern Poetics: Yeats, Mallarmé, and William Carlos

Williams," *ELH* 46 (1979): 509–40. See also Jewel Spears Brooker and Joseph Bentley, *Reading "The Waste Land": Modernism and the Limits of Interpretation* (Amherst, Mass.: University of Massachusetts Press, 1990), 30: "In fact, most of the techniques in the twentieth-century revolution in the arts stem from a conscious rejection of materialism (the notion that reality has to do with matter) and a conscious adoption of idealism (the notion that reality has to do with mind)."

14. Michael Webster, "E. E. Cummings Public and Private: Science as Threat and Authority," (paper presented at the American Literature Association Conference, Baltimore, Md., May 1995).

15. Waggoner, *Heel of Elohim*, 74.

16. See Herbert Howarth, *Notes on Some Figures Behind T. S. Eliot* (Boston: Houghton Mifflin, 1964), 67–69.

17. William Blissett, "T. S. Eliot and Heraclitus" (Unpublished MS). I was pleased to find that many of Professor Blissett's conclusions in this magisterial essay are compatible with my own.

18. Eliot, "Eeldrop and Appleplex," in *The Little Review Anthology,* ed. Margaret Anderson (New York: Horizon Press, 1953), 103.

19. Evelyn Underhill, *Mysticism* (1911; reprint, New York: Noonday, 1955), 4.

20. Waggoner, *Heel of Elohim*, 72.

21. Whitehead, *Science*, 18–19.

22. F. H. Bradley, *Appearance and Reality* (1893; reprint, Oxford: Oxford University Press, 1962), 15.

23. Ibid., 14.

24. Joseph Needham, "Religion and the Scientific Mind," *Criterion* 10 (1931): 239–40. Note that the "round hard balls" here are the atoms. The mechanistic theory needed atomism, for matter could be perfectly reduced to Newtonian mathematics only if it were made of discreet, countable units. The discovery of the quantum physicists that this was not the case was a death blow to mechanistic theories. Atomism is discussed in chapter 3.

25. Eliot, "Francis Herbert Bradley" (1927), *SE,* 403.

26. Eliot, "William Blake" (1920), *SE,* 279.

27. Eliot, London Letter, *Dial* 71, no. 4 (October 1921), reprinted in *A Dial Miscellany,* ed. William Wasserstrom (Syracuse, New York: Syracuse University Press, 1963), 49.

28. Eliot, introduction to *The Art of Poetry,* by Paul Valéry, trans. Denise Folliot (London: Routledge, 1958), xx. Eliot does not approve entirely of Valéry's emphasis here. He goes on to say, "Sometimes, I think, Valéry allowed himself to be carried away too far by his metaphors of the clinic and the laboratory . . ." (xxi).

29. Herbert J. Muller, *Science and Criticism: The Humanistic Tradition in Contemporary Thought* (1943; reprint, New York: George Braziller, 1956), 118 and passim.

30. Russell Kirk, *Eliot and His Age: T. S. Eliot's Moral Imagination in the Twentieth Century* (New York: Random House, 1971), 288.

31. Gail McDonald, *Learning to Be Modern: Pound, Eliot, and the American University* (Oxford: Oxford University Press, 1993), 75–78.

32. Ibid., 77. See also David Ward, *T. S. Eliot Between Two Worlds* (London: Routledge, 1973), who says Eliot is using an irrelevant scientific analogy here merely to establish a certain unemotional antiromantic tone (53).

33. McDonald, *Learning to be Modern,* 87.

34. Mark Jeffreys, "The Rhetoric of Authority in T. S. Eliot's *Athenaeum* Reviews," *South Atlantic Review* 57, no. 4 (1992): 97.

35. Eliot, "Modern Tendencies in Poetry," *Shama'a* 1, no. 1 (April 1920): 12. Quoted by James Longenbach, *Modernist Poetics of History: Pound, Eliot, and the Sense of the Past* (Princeton: Princeton University Press, 1987), 209.

36. Eliot, "The *Pensées* of Pascal" (1931), *SE,* 356.

37. Eliot, "The Perfect Critic," *SW,* 13.

38. Jeffreys, "Rhetoric of Authority," 97–98.

39. Richard Shusterman, *T. S. Eliot and the Philosophy of Criticism* (New York: Columbia University Press, 1988), 64–65.

40. Eliot, "Style and Thought," *Nation* 22, no. 25 (23 March 1918): 770.

41. Eliot, "Why Mr Russell Is a Christian," *Criterion* 6 (1927): 177–79.

42. Eliot, introduction to *Leisure: The Basis of Culture,* by Josef Pieper (1952; reprint, New York: New American Library, 1963), 12.

43. Eliot, "Lancelot Andrewes" (1926), *SE,* 305. James Longenbach points to another field of study which had been deeply affected by scientific thinking, history. He argues that Pound and Eliot rejected the positivistic assumptions of nineteenth-century "scientific" historiography, assumptions operative in the works of Spengler and Toynbee. See Longenbach's *Modernist Poetics of History,* 6.

44. Eliot, "Modern Education and the Classics" (1932), *SE,* 457.

45. Eliot, "Literature, Science, and Dogma," *Dial* 82, no. 3 (March 1927), reprinted in *A Dial Miscellany,* ed. William Wasserstrom, 306–7.

46. Ibid., 306.

47. Ibid., 307.

48. Ibid., 309.

49. Eliot, "Poetry and Propaganda," *The Bookman* 70 (1930): 596.

50. Eliot, "In Memoriam," *SE,* 293.

51. Eliot, "A Romantic Patrician," *Athenaeum,* no. 4644 (2 May 1919): 266.

52. Eliot, *The Varieties of Metaphysical Poetry,* ed. Ronald Schuchard (New York: Harcourt, 1993), 226. This text, along with Ronald Schuchard's excellent introduction and notes, is extremely helpful to anyone seeking to understand Eliot's thought at this period. I cite it parenthetically hereafter as *VMP.*

53. Descartes, quoted by Eliot, *VMP,* 81. Schuchard gives the translation from *The Philosophical Works of Descartes:* " . . . although I examine all things with care, I nevertheless do not find that from this distinct idea of corporeal nature, which I have in my imagination, I can derive any argument from which there will necessarily be deduced the existence of the body."

54. Jeffreys, "Rhetoric of Authority," 105.

55. William Skaff, *The Philosophy of T. S. Eliot: From Skepticism to a Surrealist Poetic, 1909–1927* (Philadelphia: University of Pennsylvania Press, 1986), 30.

56. Jewel Spears Brooker and Joseph Bentley, *Reading "The Waste Land,"* 18. As the present book was in the final stages of revision, Brooker published an essay on Eliot and Descartes: "Civilization and Its Discontents: Eliot, Descartes, and the Mind of Europe," *The Modern Schoolman* 73, no. 1 (November 1995): 59–70. I am pleased to find that Brooker reaches there many of the same conclusions I do here.

57. Schwartz, *Matrix of Modernism,* 177n.

58. Eliot, "Three Reformers," review of *Three Reformers: Luther, Descartes, Rousseau,* by Jacques Maritain *Times Literary Supplement,* no. 1397 (8 November 1928): 818.

59. Ibid., 818. Eliot says the section on Descartes is the best part of the book, indicating perhaps his own interest as much as Maritain's. He also points out that Maritain grew up a Protestant and was a disciple of Bergson before converting to Roman Catholicism—an intellectual and spiritual path similar to that of Eliot, who wrote this just after his own conversion to Anglo-Catholicism.

60. Eric Sigg, *The American T. S. Eliot: A Study of the Early Writings* (Cambridge: Cambridge University Press, 1989), 65.

61. Eliot, "John Bramhall" (1927), *SE*, 313.

62. Eliot, "Thoughts after Lambeth" (1931), *SE*, 327.

63. Eliot, "Religion and Science: A Phantom Dilemma," *The Listener* (23 March 1932): 428–29. For further discussion, see chapter 5.

64. Eliot, *A Sermon: Preached in Magdalene College Chapel* (Cambridge, Mass.: Cambridge University Press, 1948). See also Jain, *The Harvard Years*, 14.

65. Sigg, *American T. S. Eliot*, 6.

66. Quotations of the Bible are from the King James Version.

67. Stanley L. Jaki, *Cosmos and Creator* (Edinburgh: Scottish Academic Press, 1980).

68. All of this is, of course, too theoretical to give a feeling of the mind of the Hebrews, who simply did not make the intellectual divisions prompting this discussion.

69. John Burnet, *Early Greek Philosophy*, 4th ed. (London: Adam and Charles Black, 1930), 11. The first edition was published in 1892.

70. Eliot, Houghton Library MS Am 1691 (129), "Notes on Philosophy," [Cambridge, ca. 1907].

71. Burnet, *Philosophy*, 49.

72. Houghton Library MS Am 1691.14 (9). The library's catalog lists this as notes on Philosophy 12, which is what is written on the spine. Inside the cover, however, Eliot has written "Philosophy 10 / T. S. Eliot / 16 Ash Street."

73. Houghton Library MS Am 1691.14 (9).

74. Burnet, *Philosophy*, 74–5.

75. Eliot, Houghton Library MS Am 1691.14 (9).

76. Fr. 27. Burnet, *Philosophy*, 120. The sense of earth as source and end of all things is pervasive in the opening section of *East Coker*.

77. Eliot, Houghton Library MS Am 1691.14 (9).

78. Ibid.

79. Burnet, *Philosophy*, 145.

80. Werner Heisenberg, *Physics and Philosophy: The Revolution in Modern Science* (New York: Harper, 1958), 63–64.

81. Heraclitus, Fr. 22 (Burnet's numbering and translation). Burnet, *Philosophy*, 135. Diels, Fr. 90.

82. Burnet, *Philosophy*, 146–47.

83. Eliot, Houghton Library MS Am 1691.14 (9).

84. Burnet, *Philosophy*, 166. Eliot, Houghton Library MS Am 1691 (129).

85. G. T. W. Patrick, *Heraclitus of Ephesus* (1889; reprint, Chicago: Argonaut, 1969), 115. Eliot's notes on Patrick's introduction are in the Houghton Library collection, MS Am 1691 (129).

86. Patrick, *Heraclitus*, 61.

87. Heraclitus, Fr. 63, Patrick edition.

88. Burnet, *Philosophy*, 269.

89. Patrick, *Heraclitus*, 61–62.

90. Herbert Howarth, *Notes on Some Figures behind T. S. Eliot* (Boston: Houghton Mifflin, 1964), 68.

91. Patrick, *Heraclitus,* 77.

92. Ibid., 72.

93. Shusterman, *Philosophy of Criticism,* 4.

94. William Charron, "T. S. Eliot: Aristotelian Arbiter of Bradleyan Antinomies," *The Modern Schoolman* 73, no. 1 (1995): 91–92.

95. Eliot, "The Relationship between Politics and Metaphysics," Houghton MS Am 1691 (25). See Jain, *The Harvard Years,* 50.

96. William Pratt, "Eliot at Oxford: From Philosopher to Poet to Critic," *Soundings* 78 (1995): 334.

97. Eliot, Houghton Library MS Am 1691.14 (9).

98. Eliot, Houghton Library MS Am 1691.14 (28).

99. Eliot, "The Development of Leibniz' Monadism," *The Monist* 26 (October 1916), reprinted in *Knowledge and Experience in the Philosophy of F. H. Bradley* (New York: Farrar, 1964), 188.

100. Ibid., 187.

101. Eliot, "Dante" (1929), *SE,* 234.

102. Eliot, Houghton Library MS Am 1691.14 (29).

103. Eliot, Houghton Library MS Am 1691.14 (16), [Notes on Aristotle].

104. Eliot, "The Development of Leibniz' Monadism," 195.

105. Eliot, "Sir John Davies" (1926), *OPP,* 133.

106. Thomas Aquinas, *Summa theologica* I:381, quoted by Eliot, *VMP,* 113.

107. Eliot, Houghton Library MS Am 1691.14 (17), [Notes on Aristotle].

108. Skaff, *Philosophy of T. S. Eliot,* 24.

109. Paul Douglass, *Bergson, Eliot, and American Literature* (Lexington: Univ. Press of Kentucky, 1986), 9.

110. Eliot, Houghton Library MS Am 1691.14 (17).

111. Eliot, Houghton Library MS Am 1691 (130). The small mistake in this passage is a rarity in Eliot's notes on the lectures, which are beautifully clear.

112. Douglass, *American Literature,* 56.

113. Eliot, Houghton Library MS Am 1691 (132).

114. Douglass, *American Literature,* 59.

115. Ibid., 61.

116. Skaff, *Philosophy of T. S. Eliot,* 35.

117. Leszek Kolakowski, *Bergson* (Oxford: Oxford University Press, 1985), viii. See also Douglass, *American Literature,* 24–26.

118. Douglass, *American Literature,* 63.

119. Shusterman, *Philosophy of Criticism,* 43.

120. F. H. Bradley, *Essays on Truth and Reality* (Oxford: Clarendon, 1914), 159–60. Quoted by Piers Gray, *T. S. Eliot's Intellectual and Poetic Development, 1909–1922* (Sussex: Harvester Press, 1982), 152.

121. Skaff, *Philosophy of T. S. Eliot,* 15.

122. Cf. Ann Bolgan, *What the Thunder Really Said: A Retrospective Essay on the Making of "The Waste Land"* (Montreal: McGill-Queen's University Press, 1973), 105–8.

123. Eliot, "The Development of Leibniz' Monadism," 188.

124. Bolgan, *What the Thunder Really Said,* 110.

125. See Brooker and Bentley, *Reading "The Waste Land,"* 39; Bolgan, *What the Thunder Really Said,* 129–30; Skaff, *Philosophy of T. S. Eliot,* 13.

126. Brooker and Bentley, *Reading "The Waste Land,"* 39.

127. Bolgan, *What the Thunder Really Said,* 134.

128. Douglass, *American Literature,* 52.

129. Skaff, *Philosophy of T. S. Eliot,* 33.

130. Ibid., 31.

131. Eliot, "A Prediction in Regard to Three English Authors," *Vanity Fair* 21, no. 6 (February 1924): 29.

132. Brooker and Bentley, *Reading "The Waste Land,"* 43.

133. See Skaff, *Philosophy of T. S. Eliot,* 61, 66.

134. Houghton Library MS Am 1691 (129).

135. Skaff, *Philosophy of T. S. Eliot,* 36–37.

136. Shusterman, *Philosophy of Criticism,* 16.

137. Gray, *Intellectual and Poetic Development,* 165.

138. Brooker and Bentley, *Reading "The Waste Land,"* 125–26.

139. Eliot to J. H. Woods, 2 March 1915, *The Letters of T. S. Eliot,* ed. Valerie Eliot, vol. 1 (New York: Harcourt, 1988), 89–90.

140. Houghton Library MS Am 1691.14 (17).

141. Eliot, "Francis Herbert Bradley" (1927), *SE,* 404.

142. Douglass, *American Literature,* 78.

143. Shusterman identifies Eliot with Gadamer (3), and also, albeit in a qualified way, with Richard Rorty's anti-essentialism (205). Brooker and Bentley suggest that "Readers who know such figures as Lévi-Strauss, Derrida, and Gadamer, however, will be able to see that Eliot in his philosophical work arrived at theories before 1916 that have much in common with contemporary insights" (6). Beehler, in *T. S. Eliot, Wallace Stevens, and the Discourses of Difference* (Baton Rouge: Louisiana State University Press, 1987), finds Eliot's passage about C. S. Peirce in his dissertation compatible with Derrida's reading of Peirce (22–23). Kearns sees a connection between Derrida and Eliot via their common interest in Buddhism. See her "T. S. Eliot, Buddhism, and the Point of No Return," in *The Placing of T. S. Eliot,* ed. Jewel Spears Brooker (Columbia, Mo.: University of Missouri Press, 1991), 135. See also Gregory S. Jay, *T. S. Eliot and the Poetics of Literary History* (Baton Rouge: Louisiana State University Press, 1983), 4, 101, and passim. These are but a few examples of the tendency to find common ground between Eliot and the antifoundationalists.

144. Jain, *The Harvard Years,* 151.

145. Robert Crawford, *The Savage and the City in the Works of T. S. Eliot* (Oxford: Oxford University Press, 1987), Ch. 3 and passim.

146. Paul Ricoeur, *Interpretation Theory: Discourse and the Surplus of Meaning* (Fort Worth: Texas Christian University Press, 1976), 61.

147. Arthur Symons, *The Symbolist Movement in Literature,* rev. ed. (New York: Dutton, 1919), 2–3.

148. Ibid., 3.

149. Ibid., 1.

150. Quoted by Symons, ibid., 2.

151. Ibid., 5. Sigg notes this religious tendency in Symons (144).

152. Ibid., 70.

153. Ibid., 72.

154. Ronald Bush, *T. S. Eliot: A Study in Character and Style* (New York: Oxford University Press, 1983), 123.

155. Ibid., 177.

156. Michael Beehler, *T. S. Eliot, Wallace Stevens, and the Discourses of Difference* (Baton Rouge: Louisiana State University Press, 1987), 22–23.

157. Hartshorne and Weiss, eds., *Collected Papers*, I, 171. Qtd. by Beehler, *Discourses of Difference*, 22.

158. Beehler, *Discourses of Difference*, 23.

159. Ibid., 31.

160. Mircea Eliade, *The Sacred and the Profane: The Nature of Religion*, trans. Willard R. Trask (New York: Harper, 1961), 93–94.

161. Ricoeur, *Interpretation Theory*, 61.

162. Eliot, *Christianity and Culture: The Idea of a Christian Society and Notes toward the Definition of Culture* (New York: Harcourt, 1940), 48.

163. Eliot, Houghton Library MS Am 1691 (129).

164. Symons, *Symbolist Movement*, xx, 89.

165. Ibid., 17.

166. Underhill, *Mysticism*, 208.

167. Eliot, Preface to *Transit of Venus* by Harry Crosby (Paris: Black Sun Press, 1931), viii.

168. Sigg, *American T. S. Eliot*, 73.

169. Eliot, Preface to *Transit of Venus*, ix.

170. Brooker and Bentley, *Reading "The Waste Land,"* 94.

171. Symons, *Symbolist Movement*, 81.

172. Grover Smith, *The Waste Land* (London: Allen and Unwin, 1983), 37–38.

173. Bornstein, *Transformations of Romanticism in Yeats, Eliot, and Stevens* (Chicago: University of Chicago Press, 1976), 120–23.

174. Coleridge, *Biographia Literaria*, ed. George Watson (London: Dent, 1965), 174. Quoted by Eliot, *SE*, 256–57; also, *UPUC*, 71.

175. Coleridge, from *The Statesman's Manual*, in *Criticism: The Major Texts*, ed. Walter Jackson Bate (San Diego: Harcourt, 1970), 386.

176. Coleridge, *Lay Sermons*, ed. R. J. White (Princeton: Princeton University Press, 1972), 30. Cf. Longenbach, *Modernist Poetics*, 200.

177. Eliot, "Swinburne as Poet," *SE*, 327.

178. Eliot, *Letters*, vol. 1, 86–87.

179. Bolgan, *What the Thunder Really Said*, 116. Schwartz (166) points out that Husserl also spoke of an *objektive Korrelat*.

180. Skaff, *Philosophy of T. S. Eliot*, 160.

181. Symons, *Symbolist Movement*, 75.

182. McDonald, *Learning to Be Modern*, 168.

183. Edward Finegan and Niko Besnier, *Language: Its Structure and Use* (New York: Harcourt, 1989), 3.

184. Grover Smith takes up this argument briefly in his book *The Waste Land,* where he states that the problem with structuralism is the assumption that "every literary text must reduce itself to language." The writer, Smith maintains, knows that he has only words but labors to escape this limitation: "I mean that the vision of the artist, though expressible only through his medium, transcends it both in contemplation of the artistic act and in the objective achievement" (154). Just so, and symbolism is the most powerful means a poet has of transcending the linguistic medium.

185. Skaff, *Philosophy of T. S. Eliot*, 169, 202–3.

186. Ibid., 202.

187. Eliot, introduction to *Leisure: The Basis of Culture*, 11.

188. Skaff, *Philosophy of T. S. Eliot*, 7, 38. It is a bit difficult to imagine what a nonliteral belief in dogmas such as the Incarnation and the Real Presence might mean.

189. Jay, *Poetics of Literary History,* 155.

190. Ronald Schuchard, "Eliot and Ignatius: Discovery and Abandonment in Donne," *The Modern Schoolman* 73, no. 1 (1995): 13.

191. Eliot, "Donne in Our Time," in *A Garland for John Donne,* ed. Theodore Spencer (Cambridge: Harvard University Press, 1931), 8. In this essay, Eliot goes so far as to identify Donne with Descartes, because though Donne feels his ideas, he does not concern himself with their truth, as a medieval thinker would (11–12).

192. *VMP,* 58. Cf. Dominic Manganiello, *T. S. Eliot and Dante* (London: Macmillan, 1989), 15.

CHAPTER 2: POLIS AND COSMOS IN *PRUFROCK AND OTHER OBSERVATIONS*

1. Eliot, "Baudelaire" (1930), *SE,* 340.

2. George Bornstein, *Transformations of Romanticism in Yeats, Eliot, and Stevens* (Chicago: University of Chicago Press, 1976), Ch. 3.

3. C. S. Lewis, "A Confession," in *Poems,* ed. Walter Hooper (London: Geoffrey Bless, 1964), 1.

4. Hugh Kenner, *The Invisible Poet: T. S. Eliot* (1959; reprint, New York: Citadel Press, 1964), 4.

5. Marion Montgomery, *T. S. Eliot: An Essay on the American Magus* (Athens, Ga.: University of Georgia Press, 1969), 91.

6. Alfred North Whitehead, *Science and the Modern World* (1925; reprint, New York: New American Library, 1948), 87.

7. H. Rushton Fairclough, trans. *Virgil,* rev. ed. (Cambridge: Harvard University Press, 1935). The following two passages from Virgil are also from this edition and give Fairclough's translation.

8. Elizabeth Drew seems to have in mind the contrast between ancient and modern ethers when she comments that these lines make us think "of the ether which is not the breath of spirit, but the deadener of consciousness and volition." See her *T. S. Eliot: The Design of His Poetry* (New York: Scribners, 1949), 33.

9. Piers Gray, *T. S. Eliot's Intellectual and Poetic Development, 1909–1922* (Sussex: Harvester Press, 1982), 56.

10. Eliot, Houghton MS Am 1691 (129), "Notes on Philosophy."

11. This observation was suggested to me by Ethan Lewis.

12. Robert Crawford, *The Savage and the City in the Works of T. S. Eliot* (Oxford: Oxford University Press, 1987), 9.

13. Eliot, *Christianity and Culture: The Idea of a Christian Society and Notes Toward the Definition of Culture* (New York: Harcourt, 1940), 48.

14. Crawford, *Savage and the City,* 67.

15. See B. C. Southam, *A Student's Guide to the Selected Poems of T. S. Eliot* (London: Faber and Faber, 1968), 35.

16. Bornstein, *Transformations,* 134.

17. Kenner, *Invisible Poet,* 12.

18. Back in 1952, Conrad Aiken identified the model for the "Portrait" as a lady who entertained Harvard undergraduates at teas: "our dear deplorable friend, Miss X, the *precieuse ridicule* to end all preciosity, serving tea so exquisitely among her bric-a-brac" (quoted by Southam, *Student's Guide,* 36). In face of this evidence (not to mention the evidence of the poem itself), it is remarkable that so many critics have imagined an amorous entanglement here.

19. This pun on the poet's name has been noted previously by Crawford, *Savage and the City*, 77.

20. Eliot, "Matthew Arnold" (1933), *UPUC*, 111. See also Eliot, *OPP*, 142.

21. Charles-Louis Philippe, *Bubu de Montparnasse*, trans. Laurence Vail (Paris, 1932). Quoted by Grover Smith, *T. S. Eliot's Poetry and Plays: A Study in Sources and Meaning* (Chicago: University of Chicago Press, 1956), 20.

22. Eric Sigg, *The American T. S. Eliot: A Study of the Early Writings* (Cambridge: Cambridge University Press, 1989), 39.

23. Eloise Knapp Hay, *T. S. Eliot's Negative Way* (Cambridge: Harvard University Press, 1982), 2. Cf. Lyndall Gordon, *Eliot's Early Years* (New York: Oxford University Press, 1977), 34–35, 62.

24. Mircea Eliade, *The Sacred and the Profane: The Nature of Religion*, trans. Willard R. Trask (New York: Harper, 1959), 93–94. Manju Jain, in *T. S. Eliot and American Philosophy: The Harvard Years* (Cambridge: Cambridge University Press, 1992), interprets this passage similarly, seeing it as a critique of Bergsonian progressivism: "The cosmos is not shown as revolving progressively forward, animated by a vital impulse and creating new forms of life. It revolves ceaselessly, devoid of meaning and depleted of vitality" (56–57). This is a fine description of the passage, though the brunt of Eliot's attack probably falls on ordinary scientific progressivism rather than on Bergson's vitalism.

25. Smith, *Eliot's Poetry and Plays*, 21.

26. Ibid., 22.

27. Sigg, *American T. S. Eliot*, 60.

28. Eliot, "A Sceptical Patrician," *Athenaeum*, no. 4647 (23 May 1919): 361–62.

29. Smith, *Eliot's Poetry and Plays*, 30.

30. William Blissett, "T. S. Eliot and Heraclitus" (unpublished paper).

Chapter 3: Physics and Metaphysics in *Poems* of 1920

1. Northrop Frye, *T. S. Eliot* (Edinburgh: Oliver and Boyd, 1963), passim.

2. John Davies, *Orchestra, or A Poem on Dancing*, in *Silver Poets of the Sixteenth Century*, ed. Gerald Bullett (London: Dent, 1947), 323.

3. Jonathan Swift, *A Tale of a Tub* (London: Dent, 1909), 106–7.

4. Paul Elmer More, *Hellenistic Philosophies* (1923; reprint, New York: Greenwood Press, 1969), 54–55.

5. Lyndall Gordon, *Eliot's Early Years* (Oxford: Oxford University Press, 1977), 39.

6. Eliot, *Inventions of the March Hare: Poems 1909–1917*, ed. Christopher Ricks (New York: Harcourt, 1996), 71.

7. John Crowe Ransom, "Gerontion," in *T. S. Eliot: The Man and His Work*, ed. Allen Tate (New York: Dell, 1966), 135.

8. Sanford Schwartz, *The Matrix of Modernism: Pound, Eliot, and Early Twentieth-Century Thought* (Princeton: Princeton University Press, 1985), 32.

9. Edward Fitzgerald, Letter to Frederick Tennyson, quoted by Grover Smith, *T. S. Eliot's Poetry and Plays: A Study in Sources and Meaning* (Chicago: University of Chicago Press, 1956), 63. See also the extended treatment of this allusion in Vinnie-Marie D'Ambrosio's *Eliot Possessed: T. S. Eliot and FitzGerald's "Rubáiyát"* (New York: New York University Press, 1989), esp. 162–63.

10. John Henry Newman, quoted by Gordon, *Eliot's Early Years*, 103.

11. Bradley, quoted by Eliot, "Francis Herbert Bradley," in *Selected Essays* (New York: Harcourt, 1950), 397. Hugh Kenner points out that Eliot also quoted this passage in a review in *The New Statesman* the year before this volume was published. See *The Invisible Poet: T. S. Eliot* (1959; reprint, New York: Citadel Press, 1964), 92.

12. Hyatt Howe Waggoner, *The Heel of Elohim: Science and Values in Modern American Poetry* (Norman: University of Oklahoma Press, 1950), 67.

13. Harmon M. Chapman, "Realism and Phenomenology," in *The Return to Reason: Essays in Realistic Philosophy,* ed. John Wild (Chicago: Regnery, 1953), 9.

14. Houghton MS Am 1691.14 (32). Quoted by Manju Jain, *T. S. Eliot and American Philosophy: The Harvard Years* (Cambridge: Cambridge University Press, 1992), 86.

15. Eliot, *Knowledge and Experience in the Philosophy of F. H. Bradley* (New York: Farrar, 1964), 19.

16. Eliot's isolation of the verb *fought* at the end of this passage creates a syntax that mimes the disintegration of atoms.

17. Eric Sigg, *The American T. S. Eliot: A Study of the Early Poems* (Cambridge: Cambridge University Press, 1989), 176.

18. Ransom, "Gerontion," 142. Cf. David Spurr, *Conflicts in Consciousness: T. S. Eliot's Poetry and Criticism* (Urbana: University of Illinois Press, 1984), 15. Spurr notices a "random profusion" in this line and in the poem generally.

19. Henry Adams, *The Education of Henry Adams* (1918; reprint, New York: Modern Library, 1931), 451. Quoted by Smith, *Eliot's Poetry and Plays,* 62.

20. Adams, *Education,* 457–58.

21. James Longenbach, *Modernist Poetics of History: Pound, Eliot, and the Sense of the Past* (Princeton: Princeton University Press, 1987), 196.

22. Henry Adams, "A Letter to American Teachers of History" (1910), quoted by Longenbach, *Modernist Poetics,* 197.

23. Graham Greene, *The Power and the Glory* (New York: Penguin, 1962), 24–25.

24. Eliot, "A Sceptical Patrician," *Athenaeum,* no. 4647 (23 May 1919): 361. Sigg makes this connection (179).

25. Eliot, "A Sceptical Patrician," 362.

26. Adams, *Education,* 268.

27. Robert Crawford, *The Savage and the City in the Works of T. S. Eliot* (Oxford: Oxford University Press, 1987), 122–23.

28. Kenner, *Invisible Poet,* 130. Russell Kirk read this passage the same way, and it became the inspiration for his gothic tale *Lord of the Hollow Dark.*

29. Eliot, "A Sceptical Patrician," 361. Cf. Gordon, *Eliot's Early Years,* 101. As Peter Ackroyd points out, Eliot did not believe he had been raised as a Christian, since his family's Unitarian creed rejected the doctrine of the Incarnation. See Ackroyd's *T. S. Eliot: A Life* (New York: Simon and Schuster, 1984), 17.

30. Lancelot Andrewes, *Sermons,* ed. G. M. Story (Oxford: Clarendon, 1967), 85.

31. Jewel Spears Brooker has noted the importance of this "depraved ceremony" in her book *Mastery and Escape: T. S. Eliot and the Dialectic of Modernism* (Amherst: University of Massachusetts Press, 1994), 100. See also Audrey F. Cahill, *T. S. Eliot and the Human Predicament* (Pietermaritzburg: University of Natal Press, 1967), 33.

32. Andrewes, *Sermons,* 97.

33. Underhill, *Mysticism* (1911; reprint, New York: Noonday, 1955), 35–36.

34. Gordon, *Eliot's Early Years,* 101.

35. See, for example, Ransom, *"Gerontion,"* 47.

36. Several critics have pointed out that Gerontion's lack of ghosts derives from a lack of religious belief. See Wolf Mankowitz, "Notes on 'Gerontion,'" in *T. S. Eliot: A Study of His Writings by Several Hands,* ed. B. Rajan (New York: Haskell House, 1964), 132; Philip R. Headings, *T. S. Eliot* (New York: Twayne, 1964), 6; Marion Montgomery, *T. S. Eliot: An Essay on the American Magus* (Athens: University of Georgia Press, 1970), 77.

37. Eliot, Houghton Library MS Am 1691.16 (9).

38. George Bornstein, *Transformations of Romanticism in Yeats, Eliot, and Stevens* (Chicago: University of Chicago Press, 1976), 139.

39. A. R. Orage, "Henry James and the Ghostly," *The Little Review Anthology,* ed. Margaret Anderson (New York: Horizon, 1953), 231. It is quite likely that Eliot would have read this essay, since Eliot himself published several poems and essays in *The Little Review* in 1917 and 1918, including a memorial to Henry James. In the statement I have quoted from Orage, he misquotes Prospero's "We are such stuff / As dreams are made on," substituting "of" for "on." As David Huisman pointed out to me, Eliot makes the same substitution in the epigraph to this poem. The Duke in *Measure for Measure* proclaims that "Thou hast nor youth nor age, / But as it were an after-dinner sleep, / Dreaming on both," but in his epigraph Eliot puts "Dreaming of both." Is it possible that Eliot (who does not often misquote) makes this substitution because of having recently read Orage's essay?

40. Adams, *Education,* 460.

41. Santayana, *Three Philosophical Poets.* Quoted by Gray, *T. S. Eliot's Intellectual and Poetic Development, 1909–1922* (Sussex: Harvester Press, 1982), 218–19. The positive foil to the atomist is provided by the Christian soul going through death in Cardinal Newman's poem *The Dream of Gerontius* (New York: Longmans, 1904). Newman's old man goes through the experience Eliot's awaits, falling into the void of death. He feels, at the approach of death, "As though I was no more a substance now, . . . but must needs decay / And drop from out the universal frame / Into that shapeless, scopeless, blank abyss, / That utter nothingness, of which I came . . ." (26). The difference between this abyss and Gerontion's is that this one is the infernal depths created by sin, not the dissolution of the body. When Gerontius passes away, he finds that his body does fall from him, but he lives on in spirit. He eventually asks to be taken into the purgatorial abyss: "Take me away, and in the lowest deep / There let me be, / And there in hope the lone night-watches keep, / Told out for me" (63). The empty abyss he feared before death is welcomed as the place of purification, and the poem ends with a solemn song of contrition and hope sung by the souls in purgatory (64–65).

42. Perhaps Eliot is also thinking of atomism in "Animula" when he writes of "Boudin, blown to pieces." This is in contrast to mention of the "viaticum" two lines earlier—the final reception of Communion being the way-bread which makes death a union and integration rather than a division and disintegration.

43. Underhill, *Mysticism,* 9.

44. For a reading similar at several points, see Sigg, *American T. S. Eliot,* 165. Ronald Bush, on the other hand, interprets the echoes of a romantic past as Burbank's illusions about himself, which seems possible, too. See Ronald Bush,

T. S. Eliot: A Study in Character and Style (New York: Oxford University Press, 1983), 26. See also Longenbach, *Modernist Poetics,* 184–85.

45. Crawford, *Savage and the City,* 113, 115. Crawford also notes a fascinating connection between Burbank and one Luther Burbank, a celebrated hybridizer of plants and proponent of eugenics. Crawford suggests that the phrase "Chicago Semite Viennese" describes a hybridized person.

46. Waggoner, *Heel of Elohim,* 79. More recently, Lois Cuddy has also noted the Darwinian overtone of this passage, in her essay "Making a Space in Time: T. S. Eliot, Evolution, and the *Four Quartets,*" in *T. S. Eliot at the Turn of the Century,* ed. Marianne Thormählen (Lund, Sweden: Lund University Press, 1994), 81. Cuddy's analysis of evolutionary theory in Eliot's thinking goes in quite a different direction from mine, emphasizing a positive influence. She says, for example, that "Through the principles of Evolution, then, Eliot was able to understand and define his own space in time" (78). No doubt Eliot did adopt an evolutionary terminology, as all of us have, but at the same time, he rejected the notion of chance variation and natural selection as the sole mechanism of evolutionary development.

47. Waggoner, *Heel of Elohim,* 78.

48. Charles Darwin, *On the Origin of Species* (1859; facsimile edition, Cambridge: Harvard University Press, 1964), 186.

49. Darwin, *Origin of Species,* 187–88.

50. Eliot, "Eeldrop and Appleplex," *The Little Review Anthology,* ed. Margaret Anderson (New York: Horizon Press, 1953), 105.

51. Crawford, *Savage and the City,* 67.

52. Eliot, Houghton MS Am 1691 (132), "On Bergson."

53. Henri Bergson, *Creative Evolution,* trans. Arthur Mitchell (New York: Holt, 1911), 64. I am grateful to Loretta Wasserman for directing me to Bergson's discussion of the eye.

54. Ibid., 64.

55. This example of the eye has been given by several critics of the theory of natural selection as the mechanism of evolution. The biologist and philosopher Ludwig von Bertalanffy (known as the father of general systems theory) talks about the eye in much the way Bergson did and proposes an alternate "organismic" approach, which focuses on the concept of "emergent" characteristics in organic systems (also quite similar to Bergson's emphasis on organization). See Mark Davidson, *Uncommon Sense: The Life and Thought of Ludwig von Bertalanffy* (Los Angeles: Tarcher, 1983), 90. More recently, this and a host of other arguments against the doctrine of natural selection as the primary mechanism of evolution have been raised persuasively by Robert Wesson in *Beyond Natural Selection* (Cambridge: MIT Press, 1991), 59–63. See also Phillip E. Johnson, *Darwin on Trial* (Washington: Regnery, 1991), 34–35. The irreducible complexity of biochemical systems in even the simplest organisms has been pointed out by Michael Behe in *Darwin's Black Box: The Biochemical Challenge to Evolution* (New York: The Free Press, 1996).

56. See above, ch. 2. The connection between Heraclitus's statement about wet souls and Eliot's image of "damp souls" has been made by William Blissett in "T. S. Eliot and Heraclitus" (unpublished paper).

57. Sigg, *American T. S. Eliot,* 141.

58. Adams, *Education,* 230.

59. See Wesson, *Beyond Natural Selection,* 38–53.

60. Adams, *Education,* 399–400.

61. Crawford, *Savage and the City,* 66.

62. Cf. Waggoner, *Heel of Elohim,* 68–69. Schwartz (30n.) writes that Bergson "incorporated the theory of biological evolution into a cosmology that reaffirmed the spiritual aspirations of humankind." Like atomism, the Darwinian notion of evolution through gradual change also has an ancestry in ancient materialism. Lucretius asserts that *nihil per saltum facit natura,* nature does nothing by leaps. Critics of the gradualist tenet in the theory of natural selection continue to point out that nature does seem to have made leaps in the course of evolution. If the "missing links" were (as they must have been) well adapted, there should be more of them still thriving today. The theory of "punctuated equilibrium" tries to take account of the apparent leaps in evolutionary history.

63. Paul Elmer More, *The Essential Paul Elmer More,* ed. Byron C. Lambert (New Rochelle, New York: Arlington House, 1972), 58.

64. Eliot, "Paul Elmer More," *Princeton Alumni Weekly,* 37, no. 17 (5 February 1937): 374. Actually, Eliot had reviewed More's *Aristocracy and Justice* for the *New Statesman* in 1916, so he knew More's thinking earlier than this statement suggests. David Huisman documents Eliot's early knowledge of More's work in his essay "Title and Subject in *The Sacred Wood*," *Essays in Criticism* 39 (1989): 228-29.

65. Bergson, *Creative Evolution,* 363–68. Spencer was also assailed in a review published in *The Criterion.* See William Harrison, review of *Charles Darwin: The Fragmentary Man,* by Geoffrey West, *The Criterion* 17 (1938): 785. Harrison writes, "Even the phrase 'survival of the fittest,' as we are prone to forget, was not his [Darwin's], but Spencer's; and Herbert Spencer, as the ardent disciple, moralized beyond the master's intentions."

66. See, for example, Sigg, *American T. S. Eliot,* 159–60; Crawford, *Savage and the City,* 104–10.

67. Bornstein, *Transformations,* 142.

68. Jain, *The Harvard Years,* 18, 63.

69. Sigg, *American T. S. Eliot,* 151.

70. Gail McDonald, *Learning to be Modern: Pound, Eliot, and the American University* (Oxford: Oxford University Press, 1993), 33.

71. Ralph Waldo Emerson, "Self-Reliance," *The Collected Works of Ralph Waldo Emerson,* ed. Joseph Slater et al., vol. 2 (Cambridge: Harvard University Press, 1979), 50. See Crawford, *Savage and the City,* 104–8.

72. Sigg, *American T. S. Eliot,* 83.

73. More, *The Essential Paul Elmer More,* 37.

74. Rudolf Otto, *The Idea of the Holy,* trans. John W. Harvey (1923; reprint, New York: Oxford University Press, 1958), 12–30.

75. G. T. W. Patrick, *Heraclitus of Ephesus* (1889; reprint, Chicago: Argonaut, 1969), 82.

76. Kenner, *Invisible Poet,* 91.

77. Ibid., 92.

78. Paul Elmer More, *The Catholic Faith* (Princeton: Princeton University Press, 1931), 110.

CHAPTER 4: ELEMENTS AND SACRAMENTS IN *THE WASTE LAND*

1. B. C. Southam, *A Student's Guide to the Selected Poems of T. S. Eliot* (London: Faber and Faber, 1968), 65.

2. Eliot, London Letter, *Dial* 71, no. 4 (October 1921), reprinted in *A Dial Miscellany*, ed. William Wasserstrom (Syracuse, New York: Syracuse University Press, 1963), 48.

3. Eliot, "A Prediction Concerning Three English Authors," *Vanity Fair* 21, no. 6 (February 1924): 29.

4. Robert Crawford, *The Savage and the City in the Works of T. S. Eliot* (Oxford: Oxford University Press, 1987), 167.

5. Sir James George Frazer, *The Golden Bough*, vol. 11 (London: Macmillan, 1911), 309. See Jewel Spears Brooker and Joseph Bentley, *Reading "The Waste Land": Modernism and the Limits of Interpretation* (Amherst: University of Massachusetts Press, 1990): "Frazer put his faith in science and celebrated what he called the evolution from magic to religion to science" (49).

6. See Manju Jain, *T. S. Eliot and American Philosophy: The Harvard Years* (Cambridge: Cambridge University Press, 1992), 119.

7. G. K. Chesterton, *The Everlasting Man* (1925; reprint, New York: Doubleday, 1955), 107–8.

8. Piers Gray, *T. S. Eliot's Intellectual and Poetic Development, 1909–1922* (Sussex: Harvester Press, 1982), 115. Crawford, *Savage and the City,* 91–94.

9. Eliot, "The Ballet," *Criterion* 3 (1925): 441. I hesitate to confuse the issue by introducing terminology from a writer Eliot never seems to have liked, but Jung's concept of the unconscious and conscious mind fits Eliot's thinking here very well. Like Eliot, Jung was strongly influenced by Lévy-Bruhl.

10. Eliot, [Essay on the Interpretation of Primitive Ritual], MS, King's College Library. Quoted by Gray, *Intellectual and Poetic Development,* 129.

11. Quoted by Gray, *Intellectual and Poetic Development,* 130.

12. Frazer, *The Golden Bough,* vol. 4, 266–67.

13. Paul Elmer More, *The Catholic Faith* (Princeton: Princeton University Press, 1931), 1–2.

14. Jessie L. Weston, *From Ritual to Romance* (1920; reprint, New York: Doubleday, 1957), 167.

15. Ibid., 142.

16. Ibid., 203–4. Cf. John Vickery, *The Literary Impact of "The Golden Bough"* (Princeton: Princeton University Press, 1973): " . . . far from being destroyed, Christianity actually gained by being linked with Adonis and the other dying gods. . . . The gain for Christianity is found to consist in the revelation of its having a longer and wider tradition than heretofore known, one as old as man himself" (243–44). In other words, the links between pagan and Christian beliefs highlighted a universal element in Christianity. See also Jain, *The Harvard Years,* 131.

17. Evelyn Underhill, *Mysticism* (1911; reprint, New York: Noonday, 1955), 254.

18. Eliot, *"Tarr,"* *Egoist* 5, no. 8 (September 1918): 106.

19. Eliot, "War Paint and Feathers," *Athenaeum,* no. 4668 (17 October 1919): 1036.

20. Eliot, "Ulysses, Order, and Myth," *Dial* 75, no. 5 (November 1923): 483.

21. Crawford, *Savage and the City,* 137.

22. Ronald Bush, *T. S. Eliot: A Study in Character and Style* (New York: Oxford University Press, 1983), 71–72.

23. Underhill, *Mysticism,* 148.

24. Underhill, *Mysticism,* 146.

25. Elisabeth Schneider, *T. S. Eliot: The Pattern in the Carpet* (Berkeley and Los Angeles: University of California Press, 1975), 62n.

26. Northrop Frye, *T. S. Eliot* (Edinburgh: Oliver and Boyd, 1963), 66.

27. Marshall McLuhan, introduction to *Empedocles,* by Helle Lambridis (Alabama: University of Alabama Press, 1976), viii.

28. It should be noted that Eliot was planning on four sections as late as January of 1922. He wrote to Scofield Thayer on 20 January 1922, "I shall shortly have ready a poem of about four hundred and fifty lines, in four parts. . . ." See *The Letters of T. S. Eliot,* ed. Valerie Eliot, vol. 1 (New York: Harcourt, 1988), 502. In spite of this comment, the drafts of the poem show that "What the Thunder Said" was a separate section from the beginning.

29. Frye, *T. S. Eliot,* 66.

30. G. S. Kirk and J. E. Raven, *The Presocratic Philosophers* (Cambridge: Cambridge University Press, 1957), 10.

31. Eliot, *SE,* 59. Frank Justus Miller's translation: "Go on through the lofty spaces of high heaven and bear witness, where thou ridest, that there are no gods." Seneca, *Medea,* 1026–27, in *Seneca's Tragedies,* 2 vols., trans. Frank Justus Miller (Cambridge, Mass.: Harvard University Press, 1917). Note that *aethere* is simply translated as "heaven."

32. W. K. C. Guthrie, *The Greeks and Their Gods* (Boston: Beacon, 1950), 207.

33. See, for example, B. A. G. Fuller, *A History of Philosophy,* vol. 1 (New York: Holt, 1938; rev. ed., 1955), 182–85. The author of this standard history of philosophy was an assistant to George Herbert Palmer, the same man who taught the Harvard course in ancient philosophy that Eliot attended as a sophomore. See Herbert Howarth, *Notes on Some Figures Behind T. S. Eliot* (Boston: Houghton Mifflin, 1964), 68. Fuller is also mentioned by Jean Verdenal in a letter to Eliot. Speaking of people at the *pension* where he and Eliot had lived in Paris, Verdenal writes of "votre philosophe Fuller," your philosopher Fuller. *Letters,* vol. 1, 30.

34. Werner Jaeger, *Paideia: The Ideals of Greek Culture,* vol. 1, trans. Gilbert Highet (Oxford: Oxford University Press, 1943), 139.

35. Weston, *From Ritual to Romance,* 165.

36. Ezra Pound, "Phanopoiea," in *The Little Review Anthology,* ed. Margaret Anderson (New York: Horizon, 1953), 232.

37. Underhill, *Mysticism,* 154–55. Underhill is referring to modern physics. Newton and other modern physicists continued to posit the aether as a medium for the transmission of light.

38. Fragment 64. Fragment 25 in John Burnet's *Early Greek Philosophy* 4th ed. (London: Adam and Charles Black, 1930). Burnet's translation.

39. Kirk and Raven, *Presocratic Philosophers,* 200.

40. Fr. 80; Kirk and Raven, *Presocratic Philosophers,* 195.

41. Weston, *From Ritual to Romance,* 47.

42. Quoted by Weston, *From Ritual to Romance,* 13.

43. Richard Wagner, *Tristan and Isolde,* trans. Stewart Robb (New York: Dutton, 1965), 112–13.

44. See Robb, introduction to *Tristan and Isolde,* xii–xiii: " . . . even in *Tristan and Isolde* he cannot help adding a touch of mysticism to the bleak concept of death as 'prime oblivion.' . . . In this philosophy [that of Shopenhauer and Wagner] some have seen a resemblance to the Nirvana of Buddhism."

45. Bush, *Character and Style,* 107.

46. Quoted by Christopher Ricks, *T. S. Eliot and Prejudice* (London: Faber, 1988), 172.

47. Ibid., 173–74.

48. Southam, *A Student's Guide*, 75. Walter Pater, *The Renaissance*, in *Selected Works*, ed. Richard Aldington (London: Heinemann, 1948), 266.

49. Mircea Eliade, *The Myth of the Eternal Return*, trans. Willard Trask (New York: Pantheon, 1954), 92.

50. Eliot, *Criterion* 13 (1934): 452. Quoted by Joseph Ciari, *T. S. Eliot: Poet and Dramatist* (New York: Barnes and Noble, 1972), 22. Ciari misquotes Eliot's phrase "branch of lilac" as "bunch of lilac."

51. Weston, *From Ritual to Romance*, 53.

52. David Jones, *In Parenthesis* (1937; reprint, New York: Chilmark Press, 1961), 182.

53. Kenner, *The Invisible Poet: T. S. Eliot* (1959; reprint, New York: Citadel Press, 1964), 161–62.

54. Grover Smith, *The Waste Land* (London: Allen and Unwin, 1983), 40. If the one who hails Stetson is not a ghost, he may feel himself to be a ghost because of his avoidance of life, or he may be, like Dante in the *Inferno,* taken for a ghost by the dead whom he is visiting.

55. James Longenbach, *Modernist Poetics of History: Pound, Eliot, and the Sense of the Past* (Princeton: Princeton University Press, 1987), 23, 217.

56. T. S. Eliot, *The Waste Land: A Facsimile and Transcript of the Original Drafts, Including the Annotations of Ezra Pound,* ed. Valerie Eliot (London: Faber, 1971), 17.

57. Kenner, *Invisible Poet,* 153–4.

58. Horace, *The Art of Poetry,* in *Satires, Epistles and Ars Poetica,* trans. H. Rushton Fairclough (Cambridge: Harvard University Press, 1926), 453.

59. Smith points out that Rossetti translated the word *ampulla* in this passage as "cage." Smith, *The Waste Land,* xiii.

60. James Karman, "Quest and Questioning in a Waste Land," *Parabola* 12, no. 3 (Fall 1988): 82.

61. Guthrie, *Greeks and Their Gods,* 207–8.

62. Facsimile Edition, 13n. Translation from Temple Classics edition of the *Inferno.*

63. Quoted by Underhill, *Mysticism,* 357.

64. Kenner, *Invisible Poet,* 156.

65. Juan Leon, "'Meeting Mr. Eugenides': T. S. Eliot and Eugenic Anxiety," *Yeats Eliot Review* 9, no. 4 (Summer/Fall 1988): 170.

66. Ibid., 171.

67. Ibid., 172.

68. Kenner, *Invisible Poet,* 157.

69. Weston, *From Ritual to Romance,* 84–85.

70. *Sappho,* trans. Mary Bernard (Berkeley: University of California Press, 1958), poem 16.

71. *Purgatorio* VIII, 1–3. Ciardi translation.

72. Helen Gardner, *The Art of T. S. Eliot* (New York: Dutton, 1950), 94n.

73. Leon, "Eliot and Eugenic Anxiety," 173.

74. St. Augustine, *Confessions,* vol. 1, trans. William Watts, Loeb Classical Library (Cambridge: Harvard University Press, 1912), 99, 95. The Loeb edition seems to have a proofreading error in the first line of Book III. It has "a whole frying-pan full abominable loves": I have silently introduced the missing "of."

75. Ibid., 111.

76. Eliot read these statements of the mystics concerning fire in Underhill's *Mysticism*. See pp. 189, 193, 203.

77. Herbert Howarth, *Notes on Some Figures Behind T. S. Eliot* (Boston: Houghton Mifflin, 1964), 241.

78. Helen Luke, *Woman: Earth and Spirit; The Feminine in Symbol and Myth* (New York: Crossroad, 1990), 42.

79. Weston, *From Ritual to Romance*, 80.

80. Francis Macdonald Cornford, *The Origin of Attic Comedy* (1914; reprint, New York: Doubleday, 1961).

81. It will be obvious that my interpretation is at odds with a common reading that finds no regeneration in this section of the poem. The latter view is to be found, for example, in Brooker and Bentley's book *Reading "The Waste Land,"* 162.

82. Heraclitus, Fr. 72, Patrick edition. Patrick, 120n.

83. C. G. Jung, *Memories, Dreams, Reflections*, ed. Aniela Jaffé, trans. Richard and Clara Winston (New York: Pantheon, 1961), 369.

84. If Eliot's extensive reading in Renaissance works brought to his attention Sir Thomas Browne's book *The Garden of Cyrus*, he would have found a rich symbolism associated with the numbers four and five. Browne claims that many ancient gardens were arranged in the pattern called the quincunx, which is a square with a fifth point in the center. The central point stabilizes and unites the four corners. Browne suggests that the Garden of Eden might have been in such a pattern, with the Tree of Life at the center. Similarly, the fifth section of *The Waste Land* becomes a center that unites the other four, an aethereal matrix for the four earthly elements. See Thomas Browne, *The Garden of Cyrus*, vol. 3 of *The Works of Thomas Browne*, ed. Charles Sayle (Edinburgh: Grant, 1912). If Eliot did not read this work, he would certainly have encountered similar ideas elsewhere, for this is fairly standard numerological doctrine from Plato on.

85. Crawford, *Savage and the City*, 142.

86. T. E. Hulme, *Speculations: Essays on Humanism and the Philosophy of Art* (London: Routledge, 1924), 131.

87. Marion Montgomery, *T. S. Eliot: An Essay on the American Magus* (Athens: University of Georgia Press, 1969), 4.

88. Meister Eckhart, quoted by Underhill, *Mysticism*, 206.

89. Ibid., 260.

90. Eloi Leclerc, *The Canticle of Creatures: Symbols of Union*, trans. Matthew J. O'Connell (Chicago: Franciscan Herald Press, 1977), 222.

91. See Weston, *From Ritual to Romance*, 47.

92. Underhill, *Mysticism*, 258.

93. A. D. Moody, "T. S. Eliot: The American Strain," in *The Placing of T. S. Eliot*, ed. Jewel Spears Brooker (Columbia, Mo.: University of Missouri Press, 1991), 83.

94. Harold Hannyngton Child, *TLS*, 26 Oct. 1922, quoted in *Letters*, vol. 1, 595n.

95. Longenbach, *Modernist Poetics*, 226. *SE*, 357–58.

96. Bush, *Character and Style*, 73.

97. St. John of the Cross and Richard Rolle, quoted by Underhill, *Mysticism*, 354.

98. See the "Smaragdine Table," in *Pharmacopeia Londinensis*, ed. W. Salmon (London, 1696), 258; also Laurinda S. Dixon, *Alchemical Imagery in*

Bosch's "Garden of Delights" (Ann Arbor: UMI Research Press, 1981), 29 and Fig. 64.

99. Facsimile edition, 111.

100. Facsimile edition, 112.

101. Calvin Bedient, *He Do the Police in Different Voices: "The Waste Land" and Its Protagonist* (Chicago: University of Chicago Press, 1986), 177. Bedient's book seems to me one of the finest things written to date on *The Waste Land.*

102. Underhill, *Mysticism,* 449.

103. Frye, *T. S. Eliot,* 66; Smith, *The Waste Land,* 2. See also Crawford, *Savage and the City,* 131: "'The Waste Land' is not a Christian poem."

104. Facsimile edition, 100.

105. Crawford, *Savage and the City,* 129, 148.

106. Ibid., 148.

107. Eliot, *Christianity and Culture: The Idea of a Christian Society and Notes Toward the Definition of Culture* (New York: Harcourt, 1940), 48. Quoted above (chapter 1).

108. Sir Thomas Malory, *Works,* ed. Eugene Vinaver, 2d ed. (Oxford: Oxford University Press, 1970), 536.

109. Ibid., 558.

110. Ibid., 531.

111. George Bornstein, *Transformations of Romanticism in Yeats, Eliot, and Stevens* (Chicago: University of Chicago Press, 1976), 145.

112. Edwin Arlington Robinson, *Merlin,* in *Modern Arthurian Literature,* ed. Alan Lupack (New York: Garland, 1992), 369. I wish to thank the students in my 1995 Arthurian literature seminar, who helped me note these and several other Arthurian connections in *The Waste Land.*

113. Kenner, *Invisible Poet,* 174. The figure of a cock stands on many church steeples, symbolizing the call to repentance and renewal.

114. Bedient, *Different Voices,* 193n.

115. See Anne C. Bolgan, *What the Thunder Really Said: A Retrospective Essay on the Making of "The Waste Land"* (Montreal: McGill-Queen's University Press, 1973), 180: " . . . Eliot's reference to *Appearance and Reality* merely provides the reader with a convenient index both to the nature of the malady and the direction of its cure."

116. Bedient, *Different Voices,* 199.

117. There are other resonances in this line. As Robert Franciosi says, "Both the sound and sense of 'aetherial' certainly evoke Shakespeare's airy spirit from *The Tempest.*" See "The Poetic Space of *The Waste Land,*" *American Poetry* 2, no. 2 (Winter 1985): 27. This observation is compatible with the present analysis, as is Bolgan's association of the aethereal rumors with the Bradleyan Absolute (153).

118. Josef Pieper, *Leisure: The Basis of Culture* (1952; reprint, New York: New American Library, 1963), 87.

119. E. P. Bollier, "A Broken Coriolanus: A Note on T. S. Eliot's *Coriolan,*" *Southern Review* 3 (1967): 629.

120. I am reminded of the Easter vigil, in which all the elements come into play. The priest dips the base of the burning Paschal candle into the font of water, then breathes on the water in a reenactment of Genesis. At this ritual conjunction of the material elements, the water becomes the holy water of baptism, potent to transform a soul. Such a transformation takes place under the stormy conjunction of elements at the Chapel Perilous.

121. Montgomery, *American Magus*, 9.

122. Weston, *From Ritual to Romance*, 184–85.

123. Longenbach, *Modernist Poetics*, 234–35.

124. Gardner, *The Art of T. S. Eliot*, 126.

125. Milton Miller, "What the Thunder Meant," *ELH* 36 (1969): 452.

126. Bornstein, *Transformations*, 146.

127. G. T. W. Patrick, introduction to *Heraclitus of Ephesus*, (1889; reprint, Chicago: Argonaut, 1969), 65.

128. Though drawing on different sources, Longenbach comes to a similar conclusion: "The emphasis on fragmentation is made possible by Eliot's belief that truth is wholeness; the very idea of a fragment implies the idea of a unified whole of which it is a part" (201). Longenbach sees this idea of a wholeness formed from fragments as deriving from Bradley's concept of a system that can combine relativistic elements. Bradley's "system" has the unifying and ordering role of Heraclitus's *Logos*.

129. I. A. Richards, *Science and Poetry* (1926; reprint, New York: Haskell House, 1974), 64n. For further discussion, see above, chapter 1.

130. Eliot, "Literature, Science, and Dogma" (1927), in *A "Dial" Miscellany*, ed. William Wasserstrom (Syracuse, N.Y.: Syracuse University Press, 1963), 309.

CHAPTER 5: UNITED BY STRIFE: ANCIENT AND MODERN
PHYSICS IN *FOUR QUARTETS*

1. Grover Smith, *T. S. Eliot's Poetry and Plays: A Study in Sources and Meaning* (Chicago: University of Chicago Press, 1956), 254.

2. Helen Gardner, *The Composition of "Four Quartets"* (London: Faber, 1978), 18. Lyndall Gordon calls the elemental structure "superficial" in *Eliot's New Life* (New York: Farrar, 1988), 114. M. L. Rosenthal calls it "pointless" in "Psychological Pressure in *Four Quartets*," in *T. S. Eliot: Essays from the "Southern Review*," ed. James Olney (Oxford: Oxford University Press, 1988), 180. My analysis does not support these views.

3. Quoted by Gardner, *Composition*, 18n.

4. Ronald Bush, *T. S. Eliot: A Study in Character and Style* (New York: Oxford University Press, 1983), 220.

5. Helen Gardner, *The Art of T. S. Eliot* (New York: Dutton, 1950), 44–45.

6. Russell Kirk, *Eliot and His Age: T. S. Eliot's Moral Imagination in the Twentieth Century* (New York: Random House, 1971), 295, 300, 306; Thomas R. Rees, *The Technique of T. S. Eliot* (The Hague: Mouton, 1974), 308–9; Marshall McLuhan, introduction to *Empedocles*, by Helle Lambridis (Alabama: University of Alabama Press, 1976), x.

7. Edmund Wilson, *Axel's Castle* (New York: Scribner's, 1931), 76.

8. Gardner, *The Art of T. S. Eliot*, 45.

9. Abbot Justin McCann, ed., *The Cloud of Unknowing* (London: Burns and Oates, 1924), 8.

10. Sir John Davies, *Orchestra, Or a Poem on Dancing*, in *Silver Poets of the Sixteenth Century*, ed. Gerald Bullett (London: Dent, 1947), 337.

11. Heraclitus, Fr. 2, trans. G. S. Kirk and J. E. Raven, *The Presocratic Philosophers* (Cambridge: Cambridge University Press, 1957), 188.

12. Fr. 41; ibid., 204.

13. Fr. 10; ibid., 191.

14. Fr. 60; ibid., 189.

15. Smith, *Eliot's Poetry and Plays,* 256.

16. Ibid., 288.

17. Fr. 24; trans. John Burnet, quoted by B. A. G. Fuller, *A History of Philosophy,* vol. 1 (New York: Holt, 1938; rev. ed., 1955), 53.

18. This hierarchy is also described by Sir Thomas Elyot. See *The Boke Named the Governour* (1531; London: Dent, 1907), 3.

19. Eliot, "The Development of Leibniz' Monadism," *The Monist* 26 (October 1916), reprinted in *Knowledge and Experience in the Philosophy of F. H. Bradley* (New York: Farrar, 1964), 187.

20. Fr. 88; Kirk and Raven, *The Presocratic Philosophers,* 189.

21. Eliot uses the phrase "round square" in his paper for Royce's seminar. See Manju Jain, *T. S. Eliot and American Philosophy: The Harvard Years* (Cambridge: Cambridge University Press, 1992), 143. The paper is "Suggestions Toward a Theory of Objects," Houghton MS Am 1691 (22). See also Nancy Duvall Hargrove, *Landscape as Symbol in the Poetry of T. S. Eliot* (Jackson, Miss.: University Press of Mississippi, 1978), 140.

22. Sir Thomas Browne, *The Garden of Cyrus,* vol. 3 of *The Works of Thomas Browne,* ed. Charles Sayle (Edinburgh: Grant, 1912), 201–2.

23. This reading is at odds with that of Steve Ellis, who finds that this passage "has little of that affirmatory response to the cycle of fertility and rejuvenation described by Bakhtin." See Steve Ellis, *The English Eliot: Design, Language and Landscape in "Four Quartets"* (London: Routledge, 1991), 96. Eliot's Heraclitean assumption is that, because it is a cycle, the rejuvenation is inevitable, is already there in the decay.

24. See Richard D. McKirahan, Jr., *Philosophy Before Socrates* (Indianapolis: Hackett, 1994), 122. This possible connection was brought to my attention by a student of mine, Mandy Yoes.

25. Cf. Cynthia Olson Ho, "Savage Gods and Salvaged Time: Eliot's *Dry Salvages,*" *Yeats Eliot Review* 12, no. 1 (Summer 1993): 18–19.

26. Quoted by Gardner, *Composition,* 49. My comments here on the river passage were written in 1993, just after the worst flood on record swept away many of the levees and forced the temporary closing of some bridges across the mighty river.

27. Eliot, "Religion and Science: A Phantom Dilemma," *The Listener* (23 March 1932): 429.

28. William Harrison, review of *Charles Darwin: The Fragmentary Man,* by Geoffrey West, *Criterion* 17 (1938): 785.

29. Geoffrey West, quoted by Harrison, ibid., 786–87. Another review in *The Criterion* addresses the issue of evolutionary theory. John MacMurray, in the course of reviewing Arthur Eddington's *The Nature of the Physical World,* asserts that the new physics calls into question the materialism and determinism assumed by popular ideas of evolution: ". . . the conception of scientific law has had to undergo such a transformation that it no longer carries the implications of popular determinism. The rigid all-pervasive necessitation of the older laws, which supported the fatalistic sentiment of evolutionary materialism, and made science the ally of the tendency to degrade or deny the spontaneity of the human soul, is declared to be the result of a hidden tautology, and so a matter of words." See John MacMurray, review of *The Nature of the Physical World,* by A. S. Eddington, *Criterion* 8 (1929): 707–8.

30. Lois Cuddy notes likenesses between *Four Quartets* and John Boodin's

Cosmic Evolution (1925). See "Making a Space in Time: T. S. Eliot, Evolution, and the *Four Quartets*," in *T. S. Eliot at the Turn of the Century,* ed. Marianne Thormählen (Lund, Sweden: Lund University Press, 1994), 77–90. To my mind, Boodin's rhapsodies sound too pantheistic for Eliot to accept.

31. Fr. 91, Plato, *Cratylus:* "Heraclitus somewhere says that all things are in process and nothing stays still, and likening existing things to the stream of a river he says that you would not step twice into the same river" (Kirk and Raven, *The Presocratic Philosophers*, 197).

32. Paul Ricoeur, *Interpretation Theory: Discourse and the Surplus of Meaning* (Fort Worth: Texas Christian University Press, 1976), 62.

33. David Jones, *In Parenthesis* (New York: Chilmark Press, 1961), 154, 156. This poem was first published in 1937 by Faber.

34. Julian of Norwich, *Showings,* trans. Edmund Colledge and James Walsh (New York: Paulist Press, 1978), 210–11.

35. Ibid., 232–33.

36. In an essay on "The Heraclitean Element in Eliot's 'Four Quartets,'" Merrel Clubb sums up the interrelated ideas succinctly: "The one unchanging reality which unites the substrate and the process is the Logos, the law which is common to all things (Frag. 2), directs all things (Frag. 1), and persists through all change. This governing law Heraclitus calls the one wisdom (Frag. 41) and identifies with fire (Frag. 64)." See Merrel D. Clubb, Jr., "The Heraclitean Element in Eliot's 'Four Quartets,'" *Philological Quarterly* 40 (January 1961): 22.

37. Bush, *Character and Style*, 162–64. Eliot wrote an introduction to Knight's book *The Wheel of Fire: Interpretations of Shakespearean Tragedy* (1930; New York: Meridian, 1957). For the identification of Sonnet 86 as a source, see Smith, *Eliot's Poetry and Plays*, 290. There is, of course, a play on the word "familiar," which is a type of ghost.

38. Gregory Jay claims that "Eliot's attempt to identify the Heraclitean logos of his epiphanic moments and poetic gatherings with the Logos of Christianity does not work." See *T. S. Eliot and the Poetics of Literary History* (Baton Rouge: Louisiana State University Press, 1983), 206. Jay receives his understanding of Heraclitus from Heidegger. Eliot did not.

39. Quoted by Gardner, *Composition*, 197.

40. Kirk and Raven, *The Presocratic Philosophers*, 191.

41. Quoted by Gardner, *Composition*, 18.

42. Lyndall Gordon, *Eliot's New Life*, 131.

43. Ellis, *The English Eliot*, 105.

44. Ibid., 126.

45. Alan J. Friedman and Carol C. Donley, *Einstein as Myth and Muse* (Cambridge: Cambridge University Press, 1985), 80.

46. Steven Foster, "Relativity and *The Waste Land:* A Postulate," *Texas Studies in Literature and Language* 7 (1965): 78–82.

47. Charles Mauron, "On Reading Einstein," trans. T. S. Eliot, *Criterion* 10 (1930): 30–31. Another related piece published in *The Criterion* is Montgomery Belgion's review of Einstein's *The World As I See It*, *Criterion* 14 (1935): 707–14. Belgion writes, "To judge by this present book, outside his own domain he is an affable and extremely pleasant man, but not a very interesting man" (711).

48. Mauron, "On Reading Einstein," 31.

49. Friedman and Donley, *Myth and Muse*, 81.

50. Ellis, *The English Eliot*, 87–90.

51. Michael Beehler, intent on making Eliot out to be a proto-

deconstructionist, also makes the error of equating Einstein's relativity with philosophical relativism. See his *T. S. Eliot, Wallace Stevens, and the Discourses of Difference* (Baton Rouge: Louisiana State University Press, 1987), 11.

52. Bertrand Russell, *The ABC of Relativity* (1925; rev. ed., London: Allen and Unwin, 1958), 133.

53. Henri Bergson, *Duration and Simultaneity*, trans. Leon Jacobson (1922; English edition, Indianapolis: Bobbs-Merrill, 1965), 113. For a summary of Bergson's argument, see the translator's introduction in the English edition.

54. Russell, *ABC of Relativity*, 42.

55. Sir Arthur Eddington, *Space, Time, and Gravitation: An Outline of the General Relativity Theory* (1920; reprint, New York: Harper, 1959), 51.

56. Ole Bay-Petersen, "T. S. Eliot and Einstein: The Fourth Dimension in the *Four Quartets*," *English Studies* 66 (1985): 153.

57. Sir James Jeans, *Physics and Philosophy* (1943; reprint, Ann Arbor: University of Michigan Press, 1958), 119.

58. Russell, *ABC of Relativity*, 136.

59. Werner Heisenberg, *Physics and Philosophy: The Revolution in Modern Science* (New York: Harper, 1958), 63–64.

60. Marion Montgomery, "Eliot and the Particle Physicist: The Merging of Two Cultures," *Southern Review* 10 (1974): 587.

61. Heisenberg, *Revolution in Modern Science*, 160.

62. Ibid., 41.

63. Eddington, *Space, Time, and Gravitation*, 197.

64. Russell, *ABC of Relativity*, 127.

65. Ibid., 134.

66. Jeans, *Physics and Philosophy*, 192.

67. Ibid., 193. See also John MacMurray, review of *The Nature of the Physical World*, by A. S. Eddington, *Criterion* 8 (1929): 706–9. MacMurray, agreeing with Eddington, writes that the new physics divorces science from materialism: "So long as atoms and electrons could be conceived on the analogy of billiard-balls and marbles the world-stuff, however thinly scattered about in space, was still essentially substance. The complete failure of this analogy in the face of the facts about radiation means that whatever may be the ultimate character of matter, it is certainly not *material* in any ordinary sense of the term" (707).

68. Ibid., 204.

69. Eliot, Houghton MS Am 1691 (129).

70. Heisenberg, *Revolution in Modern Science*, 41. See full quotation earlier in the chapter.

71. Ibid., 70–71.

72. Ibid., 71.

73. See Jeans, *Physics and Philosophy*, 109.

74. Ibid., 103.

75. Friedman and Donley, *Myth and Muse*, 124.

76. Of course, instead of finding mystery in the new model, one might find subjectivism and relativism. Dominic Manganiello writes that "For quantum physicists the disruption of the notion of God's order occurred in 1927 with the formulation of Werner Heisenberg's uncertainty principle. According to this theory, the behavior of individual atoms depended on chance, and their classical quantities could not be measured accurately." See Dominic Manganiello, "Literature, Science, and Dogma: T. S. Eliot and I. A. Richards on Dante," *Christianity and Literature* 43 (1993): 63. Manganiello is concerned here with the reception

of this principle by I. A. Richards, who did understand it this way, but Heisenberg would reject this interpretation. The inability to measure and the dependence on probability do not necessarily mean that the movement of atoms is according to chance.

77. Heisenberg, *Revolution in Modern Science*, 52.

78. Jeans, *Physics and Philosophy*, 143. See also Herbert Read's review of Whitehead's *Science and the Modern World*, *Criterion* 4 (1926): 581–86. Read says Descartes' divorce of subjective mind and objective matter resulted in a separation of science and philiosophy. "But," he adds, "within the present epoch certain complexities have developed which completely shatter the old orthodox assumptions. These complexities are, briefly, the theory of relativity, which destroys the presumption of a definite present instant at which all matter is simultaneously real, and the quantum theory, which even more drastically, destroys the presumption of continuity in space."

79. Sir James Jeans, *The Mysterious Universe* (New York: Macmillan, 1930).

80. Eliot, "Religion and Science," 429.

81. Ibid., 429.

82. Manganiello, in "Literature, Science, and Dogma" (66), notes the relevance of modern physics to this passage.

83. Heisenberg, *Revolution in Modern Science*, 181.

84. Ibid., 81.

85. Ibid., 179.

86. Ibid., 174.

87. Sir Thomas Browne says that the rose was originally thought to have five leaves. See Browne, *The Garden of Cyrus*, 175–76.

88. Quoted by Lawrence M. Krauss, *The Fifth Essence: The Search for Dark Matter in the Universe* (New York: Basic Books, 1989), 18.

89. Heisenberg, *Revolution in Modern Science*, 120.

90. Ibid., 66.

91. Russell, *ABC of Relativity*, 117.

92. Ibid., 117.

93. Eddington, *Space, Time, and Gravitation*, 40.

94. Lawrence M. Krauss, *The Fifth Essence*, 38.

95. Eddington, *Space, Time and Gravitation*, 186–87.

96. Jeans, *Physics and Philosophy*, 140.

97. Jeans, *The Mysterious Universe*, 116.

98. Ibid., 117.

99. See Eithne Wilkins, *The Rose-Garden Game: The Symbolic Background to the European Prayer-Beads* (London: Gollancz, 1969), 105.

100. This theological sense of the term *sacramental* is not the one Robert Adams is using when he declares that "The one thing [the *Quartets*] do not convey is a sacramental view of the world, a rich dwelling in the holy joy of ordinary things." See his "Precipitating Eliot" in *Eliot in His Time: Essays on the Occasion of the Fiftieth Anniversary of "The Waste Land"*, ed. A. Walton Litz (Princeton: Princeton University Press, 1973), 150. This definition of *sacramental* sounds like one devised by William Carlos Williams. Using the term in the theological sense, John Timmerman suggests that Eliot's aesthetic beliefs might be called "sacramental." See *T. S. Eliot's Ariel Poems: The Poetics of Recovery* (Lewisburg, Pa.: Bucknell University Press, 1994), 54.

101. Jeans, *Physics and Philosophy*, 204.

Bibliography

All quotations of Eliot's poetry are, unless otherwise noted, from *The Complete Poetry and Plays.* New York: Harcourt, 1962.

ABBREVIATIONS

BN	*Burnt Norton*
EC	*East Coker*
DS	*Dry Salvages*
LG	*Little Gidding*
K&E	*Knowledge and Experience in the Philosophy of F. H. Bradley.* New York: Farrar, 1964.
OPP	*On Poetry and Poets.* London: Faber, 1957.
SE	*Selected Essays.* New York: Harcourt, 1950.
SW	*The Sacred Wood: Essays on Poetry and Criticism.* London: Methuen, 1920.
VMP	*Varieties of Metaphysical Poetry.* Edited by Ronald Schuchard. New York: Harcourt, 1993.
UPUC	*The Use of Poetry and the Use of Criticism: Studies in the Relation of Criticism to Poetry in England.* Cambridge: Harvard University Press, 1933.

ELIOT MANUSCRIPTS

In the Berg Collection, New York Public Library:
"He Said, This Universe is Very Plain"

In the Cornell University Library:
Review of *Science and the Modern World* and *Religion in the Making,* by Alfred North Whitehead. Galley proofs.

In the Houghton Library, Harvard University, bMS Am 1691:

(25)	[Relation between politics and metaphysics]
(129)	Notes on philosophy [Cambridge, ca. 1907]
(130)	Notes on lectures of Henri Bergson [Paris, 1910–11]
(132)	A paper on Bergson [Paris, 1910–11]

In the Houghton Library, Harvard University, bMS Am 1691.14:

(8)	Physiology of organs of skin
(9)	[Notes on] Philosophy 12
(11)	[Notes on logic]
(12)	[Notes on Eastern philosophy]
(13)	[Notes on logic]
(15)	[Notes on logic]
(16)	[Notes on Aristotle]
(17)	[Notes on Aristotle]
(18)	[Causality]
(19)	[On change]
(21)	[On objects]
(22)	Suggestions toward a theory of objects
(23)	[On objects]
(24)	[On objects]
(25)	[Object and point of view]
(26)	[On definition]
(27)	[The validity of artificial distinction]
(28)	[On matter]
(29)	[Matter and form]
(30)	[Aristotle: definition of metaphysics]
(42)	"If Time and Space, as sages say,"

PUBLISHED WORKS BY T. S. ELIOT

Introduction to *All Hallows Eve,* by Charles Williams. 1945. Reprint, New York: Pellegrini and Cudahy, 1948. ix–xviii.

"An American Critic." Review of *Aristocracy and Justice,* by Paul Elmer More. *New Statesman* 7 (24 June 1916): 284.

Introduction to *The Art of Poetry,* by Paul Valéry. Translated by Denise Folliot. New York: Random House, 1958.

"The Ballet." *Criterion* 3 (1925): 441–43.

Christianity and Culture: The Idea of a Christian Society and Notes Toward the Definition of Culture. New York: Harcourt, 1949.

The Criterion. Edited by T. S. Eliot. Collected edition, 18 vols. London: Faber, 1967.

"The Development of Leibniz' Monadism." *The Monist* 26 (October 1916). Reprint in *Knowledge and Experience in the Philosophy of F. H. Bradley.* New York: Farrar, 1964. 177–97.

"Donne in Our Time." In *A Garland for John Donne.* Edited by Theodore Spencer. 1931. Reprint, Gloucester, Mass.: Peter Smith, 1958. 3–19.

"Eeldrop and Appleplex." *Little Review* (1917). Reprint in *The Little Review Anthology.* Edited by Margaret Anderson. New York: Horizon Press, 1953. 102–9.

"The Education of Taste." Review of *English Literature During the Last Half-Century,* by J. W. Cunliffe. *Athenaeum* 4652 (27 June 1919): 520–21.

"Humanist, Artist, and Scientist." *Athenaeum* 4667 (10 October 1919): 1014–15.

"In Memory." *Little Review* (1918). Reprint in *The Little Review Anthology.* Edited by Margaret Anderson. New York: Horizon Press, 1953. 232.

Inventions of the March Hare: Poems 1909–1917. Edited by Christopher Ricks. New York: Harcourt, 1996.

"Leibniz' Monads and Bradley's Finite Centers." *The Monist* 26 (October 1916). Reprint in *Knowledge and Experience in the Philosophy of F. H. Bradley.* New York: Farrar, 1964. 198–207.

Introduction to *Leisure: The Basis of Culture,* by Josef Pieper. 1952. Reprint, New York: New American Library, 1963. 11–16.

The Letters of T. S. Eliot. Vol. 1 (1898–1922). Edited by Valerie Eliot. New York: Harcourt, 1988.

"Literature, Science, and Dogma." Review of *Science and Poetry,* by I. A. Richards. *Dial* 82 (1927). Reprint in *A Dial Miscellany.* Edited by William Wasserstrom. Syracuse, N.Y.: Syracuse University Press, 1963. 305–9.

"London Letter." *Dial* 71 (1921). Reprint in *A Dial Miscellany.* Edited by William Wasserstrom. Syracuse, N.Y.: Syracuse University Press, 1963. 47–50.

Review of *Mens Creatrix,* by William Temple. *International Journal of Ethics* 27, no. 4 (July 1917): 542–43.

"Modern Tendencies in Poetry." *Shama'a* (Urur, Adjar, India) 1, no. 1 (April 1920): 9–18.

Poems Written in Early Youth. London: Faber, 1967.

"Poetry and Propaganda." *The Bookman* 70 (1930): 595–602.

"A Prediction in Regard to Three English Authors." *Vanity Fair* 21, no. 6 (February 1924): 29, 98.

"Religion and Science: A Phantom Dilemma." *The Listener,* 23 March 1932: 428–29.

"A Sceptical Patrician." Review of *The Education of Henry Adams,* by Henry Adams. *Athenaeum* 4647 (23 May 1919): 361–62.

"Song" ["If space and time, as sages say"]. *Harvard Advocate* 78, no. 7 (3 June 1907): 96.

"Style and Thought." *The Nation* 22, no. 25 (23 March 1918): 768–70.

"A Sub-Pagan Society?" *The New English Weekly* 16, no. 9 (14 December 1939): 125–26.

"The Supernatural." *The New English Weekly* 8, no. 5 (14 November 1935): 99.

"*Tarr.*" *Egoist* 5, no. 8 (September 1918): 105–6.

Review of *Theism and Humanism,* by A. J. Balfour. *International Journal of Ethics* 26 (1916): 284–89.

"Three Reformers." Review of *Three Reformers: Luther, Descartes, Rousseau,* by Jacques Maritain. *TLS,* no. 1397 (8 November 1928): 818.

To Criticize the Critic and Other Writings. 1965. Reprint, Lincoln, Nebr.: University of Nebraska Press, 1991.

Preface to *Transit of Venus,* by Harry Crosby. Paris: Black Sun Press, 1931.

"Ulysses, Order, and Myth." *Dial* 75, no. 5 (November 1923): 480–83.

"War Paint and Feathers." *Athenaeum,* no. 4668 (17 October 1919): 1036.

The Waste Land: A Facsimile and Transcript of the Original Drafts, Including the Annotations of Ezra Pound. Edited by Valerie Eliot. London: Faber, 1971.

Introduction to *The Wheel of Fire: Interpretations of Shakespearean Tragedy,* by G. Wilson Knight. 1930. Rev. ed. New York: Meridian, 1957. xiii–xx.

"Why Mr Russell Is a Christian." *Criterion* 6 (1927): 177–79.

"William James on Immortality." *New Statesman* 9, no. 231 (8 September 1917): 547.

WORKS BY OTHER AUTHORS

Ackroyd, Peter. *T. S. Eliot: A Life.* New York: Simon and Schuster, 1984.

Adams, Henry. *The Education of Henry Adams.* New York: Modern Library, 1931.

Adams, Robert. "Precipitating Eliot." In *Eliot in His Time: Essays on the Occasion of the Fiftieth Anniversary of "The Waste Land."* Edited by A. Walton Litz. Princeton: Princeton University Press, 1973. 129–53.

Allen, Reginald E., ed. *Greek Philosophy: Thales to Aristotle.* Rev. ed. New York: Macmillan, 1985.

Asals, Heather. "The Voices of Silence and Underwater Experience." In *Poetics of the Elements in the Human Condition: The Sea.* Edited by Anna-Teresa Tymieniecka. Annalecta Husserliana, 19. Dordrecht: Reidel, 1985.

Augustine, Saint. *Confessions.* 2 vols. Translated by William Watts. Cambridge: Harvard University Press, 1912.

Bailey, Cyril. *The Greek Atomists and Epicurus.* New York: Russell, 1964.

Barfield, Owen. *Saving the Appearances: A Study in Idolatry.* New York: Harcourt, n.d.

Baudelaire, Charles. *Les Fleurs du Mal.* Paris: Bordas, 1966.

Bay-Peterson, Ole. "T. S. Eliot and Einstein: The Fourth Dimension in the *Four Quartets.*" *English Studies* 66 (1985): 143–55.

Bedient, Calvin. *He Do the Police in Different Voices: "The Waste Land" and Its Protagonist.* Chicago: University of Chicago Press, 1986.

Beehler, Michael. *T. S. Eliot, Wallace Stevens, and the Discourses of Difference.* Baton Rouge: Louisiana State University Press, 1987.

Behe, Michael. *Darwin's Black Box: The Biochemical Challenge to Evolution.* New York: The Free Press, 1996.

Belgion, Montgomery. Review of *New Pathways in Science,* by Arthur Eddington, and *The World As I See It,* by Albert Einstein. *Criterion* 14 (1935): 707–14.

Bergson, Henri. *Creative Evolution.* Translated by Arthur Mitchell. New York: Holt, 1911. First French edition, 1907.

———. *Duration and Simultaneity.* Translated by Leon Jacobson. Indianapolis: Bobbs-Merrill, 1965.

Bible. King James Version. Camden, N.J.: Thomas Nelson, 1972.

Blissett, William. "The Argument of T. S. Eliot's *Four Quartets.*" *University of Toronto Quarterly* 15 (January 1946): 115–26.

———. "T. S. Eliot and Heraclitus." Unpublished paper.

———. "Wagner in *The Waste Land.*" In *The Practical Vision: Essays in Honour of Flora Roy.* Edited by Jane Campbell and James Doyle. Waterloo: Wilfrid Laurier University Press, 1978.

Bolgan, Anne C. *What the Thunder Really Said: A Retrospective Essay on the*

Making of "The Waste Land." Montreal: McGill-Queen's University Press, 1973.

Bollier, E. P. "A Broken Coriolanus: A Note on T. S. Eliot's *Coriolan.*" *Southern Review* 3 (1967): 625–33.

Bornstein, George. *Transformations of Romanticism in Yeats, Eliot, and Stevens.* Chicago: University of Chicago Press, 1976.

Bradley, F. H. *Appearance and Reality: A Metaphysical Essay.* 1893. Reprint, Oxford: Oxford University Press, 1962.

Brooker, Jewel Spears. "Civilization and Its Discontents: Eliot, Descartes, and the Mind of Europe." *Modern Schoolman* 73, no. 1 (November 1995): 59–70.

———. *Mastery and Escape: T. S. Eliot and the Dialectic of Modernism.* Amherst: University of Massachusetts Press, 1994.

———. "The Structure of Eliot's 'Gerontion': An Analysis Based on Bradley's Doctrine of the Systematic Nature of Truth." *ELH* 46, no. 2 (1979): 314–40.

Brooker, Jewel Spears and Joseph Bentley. *Reading "The Waste Land": Modernism and the Limits of Interpretation.* Amherst: University of Massachusetts Press, 1990.

Brooks, Cleanth. *The Hidden God: Studies in Hemingway, Faulkner, Yeats, Eliot, and Warren.* New Haven: Yale University Press, 1963.

Browne, Thomas. *The Garden of Cyrus, Or the Quincuncial, Lozenge, Or Net-Work Plantations of the Ancients, Artificially, Naturally, Mystically Considered.* Vol. 3, *The Works of Thomas Browne.* Edited by Charles Sayle. Edinburgh: Grant, 1912.

Burnet, John. *Early Greek Philosophy.* 1892. 4th ed. London: Adam and Charles Black, 1930.

Bush, Douglas. *Science and English Poetry: A Historical Sketch, 1590–1950.* New York: Oxford University Press, 1950.

Bush, Ronald. *T. S. Eliot: A Study in Character and Style.* New York: Oxford University Press, 1983.

Chapman, Harmon M. "Realism and Phenomenology." In *The Return to Reason: Essays in Realistic Philosophy,* edited by John Wild, 3–35. Chicago: Regnery, 1953.

Child, Harold Hannyngton. Review of *The Waste Land,* by T. S. Eliot. *TLS,* 26 October 1922.

Chinitz, David. "T. S. Eliot and the Cultural Divide." *PMLA* 110, no. 2 (1995): 236–47.

The Cloud of Unknowing. Edited by Abbot Justin McCann. London: Burns and Oates, 1924.

Clubb, Merrel D., Jr. "The Heraclitean Element in Eliot's 'Four Quartets.'" *Philological Quarterly* 40 (January 1961): 19–33.

Cornford, Francis Macdonald. *The Origin of Attic Comedy.* 1914. Reprint, New York: Anchor Books, 1961.

Crawford, Robert. *The Savage and the City in the Works of T. S. Eliot.* Oxford: Oxford University Press, 1987.

Dakin, Arthur Hazard. *Paul Elmer More.* Princeton: Princeton University Press, 1960.

D'Ambrosio, Vinnie-Marie. *Eliot Possessed: T. S. Eliot and FitzGerald's "Rubáiyát."* New York: New York University Press, 1989.

Darwin, Charles. *On the Origin of Species.* 1859. Facsimile edition, Cambridge: Harvard University Press, 1964.

Davidson, Mark. *Uncommon Sense: The Life and Thought of Ludwig von Bertalanffy.* Los Angeles: Tarcher, 1983.

Davies, Hugh Sykes. Review of *The Mysterious Universe,* by Sir James Jeans. *Criterion* 10 (1931): 514–16.

Davies, John. *Nosce Teipsum.* In *Silver Poets of the Sixteenth Century.* Edited by Gerald Bullett. London: Dent, 1947.

———. *Orchestra, or A Poem on Dancing.* In *Silver Poets of the Sixteenth Century.* Edited by Gerald Bullett. London: Dent, 1947.

Diels, H. *Herakleitos von Ephesos.* Berlin, 1901.

Diels, H., and W. Kranz. *Die Fragmente der Vorsokratiker.* 8th ed. Berlin, 1956.

Dillingham, Thomas F. "Origen and Sweeney: The Problem of Christianity for T. S. Eliot." *Christianity and Literature* 30, no. 4 (Summer 1981): 37–51.

Dixon, Laurinda S. *Alchemical Imagery in Bosch's "Garden of Delights."* Ann Arbor: UMI Research Press, 1981.

Donoghue, Denis. "On 'Gerontion.'" *The Southern Review* 21 (1985): 934–46.

———. *The Ordinary Universe: Soundings in Modern Literature.* New York: Macmillan, 1968.

Douglass, Paul. *Bergson, Eliot, and American Literature.* Lexington: University Press of Kentucky, 1986.

Drew, Elizabeth. *T. S. Eliot: The Design of His Poetry.* New York: Scribners, 1949.

Eddington, Arthur Stanley. *Science and the Unseen World.* London: Allen and Unwin, 1929.

———. *Space, Time, and Gravitation: An Outline of the General Relativity Theory.* 1920. Reprint, New York: Harper, 1959.

Einstein, Albert, and Leopold Infeld. *The Evolution of Physics: From Early Concepts to Relativity and Quanta.* New York: Simon and Schuster, 1938.

Eliade, Mircea. *The Myth of the Eternal Return.* Translated by Willard Trask. New York: Pantheon, 1954.

———. *The Sacred and the Profane: The Nature of Religion.* Translated by Willard R. Trask. New York: Harper, 1961.

Ellis, Steve. *The English Eliot: Design, Language and Landscape in "Four Quartets."* London: Routledge, 1991.

Elyot, Thomas. *The Boke Named the Governour.* 1531. Reprint, London: Dent, 1907.

Emerson, Ralph Waldo. "Self-Reliance." In *The Collected Works of Ralph Waldo Emerson.* Edited by Joseph Slater et al. Vol. 2. Cambridge: Harvard University Press, 1979. 27–51.

Fernandez, Ramon. "The Experience of Newman." *Criterion* 3 (1924): 84–102.

Finegan, Edward, and Niko Besnier. *Language: Its Structure and Use.* San Diego: Harcourt, 1989.

Foster, Steven. "Relativity and *The Waste Land:* A Postulate." *Texas Studies in Literature and Language* 7 (1965): 77–95.

Franciosi, Robert. "The Poetic Space of *The Waste Land.*" *American Poetry* 2, no. 2 (Winter 1985): 17–29.

Frazer, James George. *The Golden Bough*. 12 vols. London: Macmillan, 1911.

Friedman, Alan J., and Carol C. Donley. *Einstein as Myth and Muse*. Cambridge: Cambridge University Press, 1985.

Frye, Northrop. *T. S. Eliot*. Edinburgh: Oliver and Boyd, 1963.

Fuller, B. A. G. *A History of Philosophy*. Vol. 1. 1938. Rev. ed. New York: Holt, 1955.

Gallup, Donald. *T. S. Eliot: A Bibliography*. Rev. ed. New York: Harcourt, 1969.

Gamov, George. *Thirty Years That Shook Physics: The Story of Quantum Theory*. 1966. Reprint, New York: Dover, 1985.

Gardner, Helen. *The Art of T. S. Eliot*. New York: Dutton, 1950.

———. *The Composition of "Four Quartets."* London: Faber, 1978.

Gish, Nancy K. *Time in the Poetry of T. S. Eliot: A Study in Structure and Theme*. Totowa, N.J.: Barnes and Noble, 1981.

Gordon, Lyndall. *Eliot's Early Years*. New York: Oxford, 1977.

———. *Eliot's New Life*. New York: Farrar, 1988.

Gray, Piers. *T. S. Eliot's Intellectual and Poetic Development, 1909–1922*. Sussex: Harvester Press, 1982.

Guthrie, W. K. C. *The Greeks and Their Gods*. Boston: Beacon Press, 1950.

Hargrove, Nancy Duvall. *Landscape as Symbol in the Poetry of T. S. Eliot*. Jackson, Miss.: University Press of Mississippi, 1978.

Harrison, William. Review of *Charles Darwin: The Fragmentary Man*, by Geoffrey West. *Criterion* 17 (1938): 784–87.

Hay, Eloise Knapp. *T. S. Eliot's Negative Way*. Cambridge: Harvard University Press, 1982.

Headings, Philip R. *T. S. Eliot*. New York: Twayne, 1964.

Heisenberg, Werner. *Physics and Philosophy: The Revolution in Modern Science*. New York: Harper, 1958.

Heraclitus. *Heraclitus of Ephesus*. Translated by G. T. W. Patrick. 1889. Reprint, Chicago: Argonaut, 1969.

Ho, Cynthia Olson. "Savage Gods and Salvaged Time: Eliot's Dry Salvages." *Yeats Eliot Review* 12, no. 1 (Summer 1993): 16–23.

Horace. *Satires, Epistles and Ars Poetica*. Translated by H. Rushton Fairclough. Cambridge: Harvard University Press, 1926.

Howarth, Herbert. *Notes on Some Figures Behind T. S. Eliot*. Boston: Houghton Mifflin, 1964.

Huisman, David. "Title and Subject in *The Sacred Wood*." *Essays in Criticism*, 39 (1989): 217–33.

Hulme, T. E. *Speculations: Essays on Humanism and the Philosophy of Art*. London: Routledge, 1924.

Ishak, Fayek M. *The Mystical Philosophy of T. S. Eliot*. New Haven: College and University Press, 1970.

Jackson, Thomas H. "Positivism and Modern Poetics: Yeats, Mallarmé, and William Carlos Williams." *ELH* 46, no. 3 (1979): 509–40.

Jaeger, Werner. *Paideia: The Ideals of Greek Culture*. 3 vols. Translated by Gilbert Highet. New York: Oxford University Press, 1943.

Jain, Manju. *T. S. Eliot and American Philosophy: The Harvard Years*. Cambridge: Cambridge University Press, 1992.

Jaki, Stanley L. *Cosmos and Creator.* Edinburgh: Scottish Academic Press, 1980.

Jay, Gregory S. *T. S. Eliot and the Poetics of Literary History.* Baton Rouge: Louisiana State University Press, 1983.

Jeans, James. *The Mysterious Universe.* New York: Macmillan, 1930.

————. *Physics and Philosophy.* 1943. Reprint, Ann Arbor: University of Michigan Press, 1958.

Jeffreys, Mark. "The Rhetoric of Authority in T. S. Eliot's *Athenaeum* Reviews." *South Atlantic Review* 57, no. 4 (1992): 93–108.

Johnson, Phillip E. *Darwin on Trial.* Washington: Regnery, 1991.

Jones, David. *In Parenthesis.* 1937. Reprint, New York: Chilmark Press, 1961.

Julian of Norwich. *Showings.* Translated by Edmund Elledge and James Walsh. New York: Paulist Press, 1978.

Jung, Carl. *The Collected Works of C. G. Jung.* Edited by Sir Herbert Read, et al. Translated by R. F. C. Hull. Bollingen Series 20. 19 vols. Princeton: Princeton University Press, 1954–1968.

————. *Memories, Dreams, Reflections.* Edited by Aniela Jaffé. Translated by Richard and Clara Winston. Rev. ed. New York: Vintage, 1965.

Karman, James. "Quest and Questioning in a Waste Land." *Parabola* 12, no. 3 (Fall 1988): 78–83.

Kenner, Hugh. *The Invisible Poet: T. S. Eliot.* 1959. Reprint, New York: Citadel Press, 1964.

Kirk, G. S. *Heraclitus: The Cosmic Fragments.* Cambridge: Cambridge University Press, 1954.

Kirk, G. S., and J. E. Raven. *The Presocratic Philosophers.* Cambridge: Cambridge University Press, 1957.

Kirk, Russell. *Eliot and His Age: T. S. Eliot's Moral Imagination in the Twentieth Century.* New York: Random House, 1971.

Kojecky, Roger. *T. S. Eliot's Social Criticism.* London: Faber, 1971.

Kolakowski, Leszek. *Bergson.* Oxford: Oxford University Press, 1985.

Krauss, Lawrence M. *The Fifth Essence: The Search for Dark Matter in the Universe.* New York: Basic Books, 1989.

Leclerc, Eloi. *The Canticle of Creatures: Symbols of Union.* Translated by Matthew J. O'Connell. Chicago: Franciscan Herald Press, 1977.

Leon, Juan. "'Meeting Mr. Eugenides': T. S. Eliot and Eugenic Anxiety." *Yeats Eliot Review* 9, no. 4 (Summer/Fall 1988): 169–77.

Lewis, C. S. *The Discarded Image.* 1964. Reprint, London: Cambridge University Press, 1978.

————. *Poems.* Edited by Walter Hooper. London: Geoffrey Bless, 1964.

Litz, A. Walton, ed. *Eliot in His Time: Essays on the Occasion of the Fiftieth Anniversary of "The Waste Land."* Princeton: Princeton University Press, 1973.

Longenbach, James. *Modernist Poetics of History: Pound, Eliot, and the Sense of the Past.* Princeton: Princeton University Press, 1987.

Luke, Helen. *Woman: Earth and Spirit; the Feminine in Symbol and Myth.* New York: Crossroad, 1990.

McDonald, Gail. *Learning to Be Modern: Pound, Eliot, and the American University.* Oxford: Oxford University Press, 1993.

McLuhan, Marshall. Introduction to *Empedocles,* by Helle Lambridis. Alabama: University of Alabama Press, 1976.

MacMurray, John. Review of *The Nature of the Physical World,* by A. S. Eddington. *Criterion* 8 (1929): 706–9.

Manganiello, Dominic. "Literature, Science, and Dogma: T. S. Eliot and I. A. Richards on Dante." *Christianity and Literature* 43 (1993): 59–73.

———. *T. S. Eliot and Dante.* London: Macmillan, 1989.

Mankowitz, Wolf. "Notes on 'Gerontion.'" In *T. S. Eliot: A Study of His Writings by Several Hands.* Edited by B. Rajan. New York: Haskell House, 1964. 129–38.

Margolis, John D. *T. S. Eliot's Intellectual Development: 1922–1939.* Chicago: University of Chicago Press, 1972.

Marlowe, Christopher. *The Plays of Christopher Marlowe.* London: Dent, 1909.

Martin, Jay, ed. *A Collection of Critical Essays on "The Waste Land."* Englewood Cliffs, N.J.: Prentice-Hall, 1968.

Martin, Stoddard. *Wagner to "The Waste Land": A Study of the Relationship of Wagner to English Literature.* Totowa, N.J.: Barnes and Noble, 1982.

Matthews, T. S. *Great Tom: Notes Towards the Definition of T. S. Eliot.* New York: Harper, 1974.

Matthiessen, F. O. *The Achievement of T. S. Eliot: An Essay on the Nature of Poetry.* 1935. Rev. ed. Oxford: Oxford University Press, 1947.

Mauron, Charles. "On Reading Einstein." Translated by T. S. Eliot. *Criterion* 10 (1930): 23–31.

Mellor, D. P. *The Evolution of the Atomic Theory.* New York: Elsevier, 1971.

Menand, Louis. *Discovering Modernism: T. S. Eliot and His Context.* New York: Oxford University Press, 1987.

Miller, Milton. "What the Thunder Meant." *ELH* 36 (1969): 440–54.

Montgomery, Marion. "Eliot and the Particle Physicist: The Merging of Two Cultures." *Southern Review* 10 (1974): 583–89.

———. *The Reflective Journey toward Order: Essays on Dante, Wordsworth, Eliot, and Others.* Athens, Ga.: University of Georgia Press, 1973.

———. *T. S. Eliot: An Essay on the American Magus.* Athens, Ga.: University of Georgia Press, 1969.

More, Paul Elmer. *The Catholic Faith.* Princeton: Princeton University Press, 1931.

———. *The Essential Paul Elmer More.* Edited by Byron C. Lambert. New Rochelle, N.Y.: Arlington House, 1972.

———. *Hellenistic Philosophies.* 1923. Reprint, New York: Greenwood Press, 1969.

———. *Platonism.* 1917. 3rd ed. Princeton: Princeton University Press, 1931.

———. *The Religion of Plato.* Princeton: Princeton University Press, 1921.

Muller, Herbert J. *Science and Criticism: The Humanistic Tradition in Contemporary Thought.* 1943. Reprint, New York: George Braziller, 1956.

Needham, Joseph. "Religion and the Scientific Mind." *Criterion* 10 (1931): 233–63.

Newman, John Henry. *The Dream of Gerontius.* New York: Longmans, 1904.

Orage, A. R. "Henry James and the Ghostly." *Little Review* (1918). Reprint in *The Little Review Anthology.* Edited by Margaret Anderson. New York: Horizon, 1953. 230–32.

Otto, Rudolf. *The Idea of the Holy.* Trans. John W. Harvey. New York: Oxford, 1958.

Patrick, G. T. W. Introduction to *Heraclitus of Ephesus.* 1889. Reprint, Chicago: Argonaut, 1969.

Perl, Jeffrey M. *Skepticism and Modern Enmity: Before and After Eliot.* Baltimore: Johns Hopkins University Press, 1989.

Pieper, Josef. *Leisure: The Basis of Culture.* 1952. Reprint, New York: New American Library, 1963. Introduction by T. S. Eliot.

Plato. *The Collected Dialogues of Plato.* Edited by Edith Hamilton and Huntington Cairns. New York: Pantheon, 1961.

Pound, Ezra. "Phanopoiea." *Little Review* (1918). Reprint in *The Little Review Anthology.* Edited by Margaret Anderson. New York: Horizon, 1953. 232.

Pratt, William. "Eliot at Oxford: From Philosopher to Poet to Critic." *Soundings* 78 (1995): 321–37.

Ransom, John Crowe. "Gerontion." In *T. S. Eliot: The Man and His Work.* Edited by Allen Tate. New York: Dell, 1966. 133–58.

Read, Herbert. Review of *Science and the Modern World,* by Alfred North Whitehead. *Criterion* 4 (1926): 581–86.

Rees, Thomas. *The Technique of T. S. Eliot.* The Hague: Mouton, 1974.

Richards, I. A. *Science and Poetry.* 1926. Reprint, New York: Haskell House, 1974.

Ricks, Christopher. *T. S. Eliot and Prejudice.* London: Faber, 1988.

Ricoeur, Paul. *Interpretation Theory: Discourse and the Surplus of Meaning.* Fort Worth: Texas Christian University Press, 1976.

Rosenthal, M. L. "Psychological Pressure in *Four Quartets.*" In *T. S. Eliot: Essays from the "Southern Review."* Edited by James Olney. Oxford: Oxford University Press, 1988. 179–90.

Russell, Bertrand. *The ABC of Relativity.* 1925. Rev. ed. London: Allen and Unwin, 1958.

Sagan, Carl. *Broca's Brain.* New York: Random House, 1974.

Sambursky, S. *The Physical World of the Greeks.* Translated by Merton Dagut. New York: Collier, 1962.

Schneider, Elisabeth. *T. S. Eliot: The Pattern in the Carpet.* Berkeley: University of California Press, 1975.

Schwartz, Joseph. "T. S. Eliot's Idea of the Christian Poet." *Renascence* 43 (1991): 215–27.

Schwartz, Sanford. *The Matrix of Modernism: Pound, Eliot, and Early Twentieth-Century Thought.* Princeton: Princeton University Press, 1985.

Sencourt, Robert. *T. S. Eliot: A Memoir.* Edited by Donald Adamson. New York: Dodd, Mead, 1971.

Shaw, George Bernard. *Back to Methuselah.* 1921. Reprint, New York: Penguin, 1977.

Shusterman, Richard. *T. S. Eliot and the Philosophy of Criticism.* New York: Columbia University Press, 1988.

Sigg, Eric. *The American T. S. Eliot: A Study of the Early Writings.* Cambridge: Cambridge University Press, 1989.

Skaff, William. *The Philosophy of T. S. Eliot: From Skepticism to a Surrealist Poetic, 1909–1927*. Philadelphia: University of Pennsylvania Press, 1986.

Smith, Grover, ed. *Josiah Royce's Seminar, 1913–1914, As Recorded in the Notebooks of Harry T. Costello*. New Brunswick, N.J.: Rutgers University Press, 1963.

———. *T. S. Eliot's Poetry and Plays: A Study in Sources and Meaning*. Chicago: University of Chicago Press, 1956.

———. *The Waste Land*. London: Allen and Unwin, 1983.

Southam, B. C. *A Guide to the Selected Poems of T. S. Eliot*. New York: Harcourt, 1968.

Spurr, David. *Conflicts in Consciousness: T. S. Eliot's Poetry and Criticism*. Urbana, Ill.: University of Illinois Press, 1984.

Swift, Jonathan. *A Tale of a Tub*. London: Dent, 1909.

Symons, Arthur. *The Symbolist Movement in Literature*. 1899. Rev. ed. New York: Dutton, 1919.

Tate, Allen, ed. *T. S. Eliot: The Man and His Work*. New York: Dell, 1966.

Timmerman, John H. *T. S. Eliot's Ariel Poems: The Poetics of Recovery*. Lewisburg, Pa.: Bucknell University Press, 1994.

Tymieniecka, Anna-Teresa, ed. *Poetics of the Elements in the Human Condition: The Sea*. Analecta Husserliana, 19. Dordrecht: Reidel, 1985.

Underhill, Evelyn. *Mysticism*. 1911. Reprint, New York: Noonday, 1955.

Unger, Leonard. *T. S. Eliot: Moments and Patterns*. Minneapolis, Minn.: University of Minnesota Press, 1956.

Van Laue, Max. *History of Physics*. New York: Academic Press, 1950.

Vickery, John B. *The Literary Impact of "The Golden Bough."* Princeton: Princeton University Press, 1973.

Waggoner, Hyatt Howe. *The Heel of Elohim: Science and Values in Modern American Poetry*. Norman: University of Oklahoma Press, 1950.

Wagner, Richard. *Tristan and Isolde*. Translated by Stewart Robb. New York: Dutton, 1965.

Waite, A. E. *The Pictorial Key to the Tarot*. London, 1911.

Ward, David. *T. S. Eliot between Two Worlds*. London: Routledge, 1973.

Wasserstrom, William, ed. *A "Dial" Miscellany*. Syracuse, N.Y.: Syracuse University Press, 1963.

Wesson, Robert. *Beyond Natural Selection*. Cambridge: MIT Press, 1993.

Weston, Jessie. *From Ritual to Romance*. 1920. Reprint, New York: Doubleday, 1957.

Whitehead, Alfred North. *Science and the Modern World*. 1925. Reprint, New York: New American Library, 1948.

Wilkins, Eithne. *The Rose-Garden Game: The Symbolic Background to the European Prayer-Beads*. London: Gollancz, 1969.

Williams, Charles. "The Index of the Body." *Dublin Review* (1942). Reprint in *Charles Williams: Selected Writings*. Edited by Anne Ridler. London: Oxford University Press, 1961. 112–21.

Williamson, George. *A Reader's Guide to T. S. Eliot.* New York: Noonday Press, 1953.

Wilson, Edmund. *Axel's Castle.* New York: Scribner's, 1931.

Yeats, William Butler. "Rosa Alchemica." *The Savoy* (April 1896). Reprint in *The Savoy: Nineties Experiment.* Edited by Stanley Weintraub. University Park: Pennsylvania State University Press, 1966. 70–84.

Index